INTERVENTION IN CIVIL WARS

This book investigates the extent to which traditional international law regulating foreign interventions in internal conflicts has been affected by the human rights paradigm. Since the adoption of the Charter of the United Nations, foreign armed interventions in internal conflicts have turned into a common practice. At first sight, it might seem that state practice has developed in a chaotic fashion; however, on closer examination, specific patterns emerge. The book charts these patterns by examining the traditional doctrines of intervention and testing them against state practice.

The book has two aims. Firstly, it seeks to clarify the current legal framework regulating interventions in internal conflicts. Secondly, it plots the emergence of new trends and investigates whether they are becoming part of positive international law. By taking this dual focus, it offers the first truly comprehensive examination of foreign interventions in internal conflicts.

Volume 80 in the series Studies in International Law

Studies in International Law

Recent titles in this series

Allocating International Responsibility Between Member States and International Organisations

Nikolaos Voulgaris

Predictability and Flexibility in the Law of Maritime Delimitation, 2nd edition

Yoshifumi Tanaka

Feminist Engagement with International Criminal Law: Norm Transfer, Complementarity, Rape and Consent

Eithne Dowds

Asylum Control and Access to Protection: Admission, Readmission and Human Rights

Mariagiulia Giuffré

Intertemporal Linguistics in International Law: Beyond Contemporaneous and Evolutionary Treaty Interpretation

Julian Wyatt

The Responsibility to Protect and the Failures of the United Nations Security Council

P M Butchard

The Role of Multilateral Environmental Agreements: A Reconciliatory Approach to Environmental Protection in Armed Conflict

Britta Sjostedt

Prosecutorial Discretion at the International Criminal Court

Anni Pues

Judicial Deference in International Adjudication: A Comparative Analysis

Johannes Hendrik Fahner

Human Rights Commitments of Islamic States: Sharia, Treaties and Consensus

Paul McDonough

For a complete list of titles in this series, see www.bloomsburyprofessional.com/uk/series/studies-in-international-law

Intervention in Civil Wars

Effectiveness, Legitimacy, and Human Rights

Chiara Redaelli

• HART •
OXFORD • LONDON • NEW YORK • NEW DELHI • SYDNEY

HART PUBLISHING

Bloomsbury Publishing Plc

Kemp House, Chawley Park, Cumnor Hill, Oxford, OX2 9PH, UK

1385 Broadway, New York, NY 10018, USA

29 Earlsfort Terrace, Dublin 2, Ireland

HART PUBLISHING, the Hart/Stag logo, BLOOMSBURY and the Diana logo are trademarks of Bloomsbury Publishing Plc

First published in Great Britain 2021

A catalogue record for this book is available from the British Library.

Library of Congress Cataloging-in-Publication data

Names: Redaelli, Chiara, author.

Title: Intervention in civil wars : effectiveness, legitimacy, and human rights / Chiara Redaelli.

Description: Oxford, UK ; New York, NY : Hart Publishing, an imprint of Bloomsbury Publishing, 2021. | Series: Studies in international law ; volume 80 | Includes bibliographical references and index.

Identifiers: LCCN 2020051792 (print) | LCCN 2020051793 (ebook) | ISBN 9781509940547 (hardback) | ISBN 9781509947058 (paperback) | ISBN 9781509940561 (epdf) | ISBN 9781509940554 (Epub)

Subjects: LCSH: Intervention (International law). | Civil War. | Humanitarian law. | Human rights.

Classification: LCC KZ6368 .R44 2021 (print) | LCC KZ6368 (ebook) | DDC 341.6/8—dc23

LC record available at https://lccn.loc.gov/2020051792

LC ebook record available at https://lccn.loc.gov/2020051793

ISBN: HB: 978-1-50994-054-7
ePDF: 978-1-50994-056-1
ePub: 978-1-50994-055-4

Typeset by Compuscript Ltd, Shannon

To find out more about our authors and books visit www.hartpublishing.co.uk. Here you will find extracts, author information, details of forthcoming events and the option to sign up for our newsletters.

To Carlo

Acknowledgements

WRITING THIS BOOK would not have been possible without the guidance and support of many people who accompanied me on this journey. My gratitude goes, first and foremost, to Andrew Clapham, my PhD supervisor. Not only has he endlessly encouraged, helped, and supported me, but he has also been an enormous inspiration to me over many years. During my studies in Geneva, I have been lucky to benefit from the constant encouragement and help provided by Andrea Bianchi. I am extremely grateful for his insightful comments, which have been a constant source of challenge and improvement. My heartfelt thanks also go to Anthony Cullen for the interest he has always shown in my research. He has been exceptionally generous in giving me his time and feedback, and I am greatly indebted to him from both an academic and a personal point of view. In addition, I owe an enormous debt of gratitude to Michael Strauss, who has shown great interest in my work and whose countless comments, suggestions, and edits on this study helped improve the final manuscript. Michael has been extraordinary also from a human point of view, filling countless discussions with goodwill, encouragement, and optimism.

Abstract

THE OBJECTIVE OF the present study is to pinpoint the effect of human rights on foreign interventions in internal conflicts. Specifically, its aims are twofold. First, it seeks to clarify the current legal framework regulating interventions in internal conflicts. Second, it endeavours to detect the emergence of new trends and to investigate whether they are becoming part of positive international law. Part I focuses on the evolution of the relationship between concepts that crucially form the basis of our discussion: intervention, sovereignty, and human rights. By guiding the reader through an historical survey, this part follows the development of these key concepts and analyses their meaning and significance under the current legal framework. Having set out the basis of our discussion, Part II examines interventions in favour of governments. Specifically, it investigates the traditional doctrines of intervention that were developed by the scholarship since the adoption of the UN Charter and tests them against state practice. Ultimately, this part identifies new trends that emerged over the last decades and assesses whether they have entered into positive international law. Lastly, Part III is devoted to analysing interventions in favour of opposition groups. Notably, it examines the legitimacy of rebels under international law, the use of force by and against rebels recognised as legitimate, and the status of intervention in favour of such groups. This study concludes that human rights are emerging as a parameter of legitimacy and that this in turn has crucial consequences on the legal framework regulating foreign interventions in internal conflicts.

Contents

PART II

INTERVENTIONS IN FAVOUR OF GOVERNMENTS

PART III
INTERVENTIONS IN FAVOUR OF REBELS

Abbreviations

ACHR	American Convention on Human Rights
AFDL	Alliance des Forces Démocratiques pour la Libération du Congo-Zaire
AFISMA	African-led International Support Mission in Mali
ANSA	Armed Non-State Actor
API	Protocol Additional to the Geneva Conventions of 12 August 1949, and relating to the Protection of Victims of International Armed Conflicts (Protocol I)
APII	Protocol Additional to the Geneva Conventions of 12 August 1949, and relating to the Protection of Victims of Non- International Armed Conflicts (Protocol II)
AU	African Union
CFLN	Comité Français de la Libération Nationale
CSCE	Conference on Security and Cooperation in Europe
DRC	Democratic Republic of Congo
ECHR	European Convention on Human Rights
ECOWAS	Economic Community for West African States
EU	European Union
FNLA	Frente Nacional de Libertação de Angola
FRELIMO	Frente de Libertação de Moçambique
GC	Geneva Convention
GCC	Gulf Cooperation Council
IAC	International Armed Conflict
ICC	International Criminal Court
ICCPR	International Covenant for Civil and Political Rights
ICESCR	International Covenant for Economic, Social and Cultural Rights

ICL	International Criminal Law
IDI	Institut de Droit International
ICISS	International Commission on Intervention and State Sovereignty
ICJ	International Court of Justice
ICRC	International Committee of the Red Cross
ICTR	International Criminal Tribunal for Rwanda
ICTY	International Criminal Tribunal for the Former Yugoslavia
IHL	International Humanitarian Law
IHRL	International Human Rights Law
ILC	International Law Commission
ICG	International Crisis Group
ISIS	Islamic State in Iraq and Syria
KLA	Kosovo Liberation Army
MNLA	Mouvement National de Liberation de l'Azawad
MPLA	Movimento Popular de Libertação de Angola
NATO	North Atlantic Treaty Organization
NGO	Non-Governmental Organization
NIAC	Non-International Armed Conflict
NLM	National Liberation Movement
NTC	National Transitional Council
NSGT	Non-Self-Governing Territory
OAS	Organization of American States
OAU	Organization of African Unity
OECS	Organization of Eastern Caribbean States
OSCE	Organization for Security and Co-operation in Europe
PAIGC	Partido Africano da Independência da Guiné e Cabo Verde
PKK	Partiya Karkerên Kurdistanê
R2P	Responsibility to Protect

SNC	Syrian National Council
SOC	Syrian Opposition Coalition
SWAPO	South West Africa People's Organization
UK	United Kingdom
UN	United Nations
UNGA	United Nations General Assembly
UNHCR	United Nations Commission on Human Rights
UNITA	União Nacional para a Independência Total de Angola
UNSC	United Nations Security Council
US	United States of America
VCLT	Vienna Convention on the Law of Treaties
VRS	Republika Srpska Army

Table of Cases

Arbitral Awards

International Court of Justice

International Criminal Court

International Criminal Tribunal for the Former Yugoslavia (ICTY)

International Criminal Tribunal for Rwanda

Permanent Court of Arbitration

Permanent Court of International Justice

National Courts

Table of Treaties and National Legislation

Treaties of the United Nations

Other International Instruments

Regional Treaties

Bilateral and Multilateral Treaties

Domestic Legislation

Table of Documents and Resolutions

United Nations

General Assembly Resolutions

A/RES/12/1236	14 December 1957	*Peaceful and neighbourly relations among State-s*
A/RES/1514(XV)	14 December 1960	*Declaration on Granting Independence to Colonial Countries and Peoples*
A/RES/1541(XV)	14 December 1960	*Principles Which Should Guide Members in Determining Whether or nor an Obligation Exists to Transmit the Information Called for under Article 73E of the Charter*
A/RES/2105(XX)	20 December 1965	*Implementation of the Declaration on the Granting of Independence to Colonial Countries and Peoples*
A/RES/2131 (XX)	21 December 1965	*Declaration on the Inadmissibility of Intervention in the Domestic Affairs of States and the Protection of Their Independence and Sovereignty*
A/RES/2132(XX)	30 November 1966	*Strict Observance of the Prohibition of the Threat or Use of Force in International Relations, and of the Right of Peoples to Self-Determination*
A/RES/2189(XXI)	13 December 1966	*Implementation of the Declaration on the Granting of Independence to Colonial People*
A/RES/2248(S–V)	19 May 1967	*Question of South West Africa*

A/RES/2426(XXIII)	18 December 1968	*Implementation of the Declaration on the Granting of Independence to Colonial Countries and Peoples by the Specialized Agencies and the International Institutions Associated with the United Nations*
A/RES/2383(XXIII)	7 November 1969	*Question of Southern Rhodesia*
A/RES/2508(XXIV)	21 November 1969	*Question of Southern Rhodesia*
A/RES/2625(XXV)	24 October 1970	*Declaration on x of International Law concerning Friendly Relations and Cooperation among States in accordance with the Charter of the United Nations*
A/RES/2649(XXV)	30 November 1970	*The Importance of the Universal Realization of the Right of Peoples to Self-determination and of the Speedy Granting of Independence to Colonial Countries and Peoples for the Effective Guarantee and Observance of Human Rights*
A/RES/2704(XXV)	14 December 1970	*Implementation of the Declaration on the Granting of Independence to Colonial People*
A/RES/2708(XXV)	14 December 1970	*Implementation of the Declaration on the Granting of Independence to Colonial Countries and Peoples*
A/RES/2787(XXVI)	6 December 1971	*The Importance of the Universal Realization of the Right of Peoples to Self-determination and of the Speedy Granting of Independence to Colonial Countries and Peoples for the Effective Guarantee and Observance of Human Rights*
A/RES/2795(XXVI)	10 December 1971	*Question of the Territories under Portuguese Administration*

A/RES/2796(XXVI)	10 December 1971	*Question of Southern Rhodesia*
A/RES/2945(XXVII)	1 December 1972	*Question of Southern Rhodesia*
A/RES/2955(XXVII)	12 December 1972	*The Importance of the Universal Realization of the Right of Peoples to Self-determination and of the Speedy Granting of Independence to Colonial Countries and Peoples for the Effective Guarantee and Observance of Human Rights*
A/RES/3070(XXVIII)	30 November 1973	*The Importance of the Universal Realization of the Right of Peoples to Self-determination and of the Speedy Granting of Independence to Colonial Countries and Peoples for the Effective Guarantee and Observance of Human Rights*
A/RES/3246(XXIX)	29 November 1974	*The Importance of the Universal Realization of the Right of Peoples to Self-determination and of the Speedy Granting of Independence to Colonial Countries and Peoples for the Effective Guarantee and Observance of Human Rights*
A/RES/3314	14 December 1974	*Definition of Aggression*
A/RES/3382(XXX)	10 November 1975	*The Importance of the Universal Realization of the Right of Peoples to Self-determination and of the Speedy Granting of Independence to Colonial Countries and Peoples for the Effective Guarantee and Observance of Human Rights*

A/RES/ 36(103) (1981)	9 December 1981	*Declaration on the Inadmissibility of Intervention in the Domestic Affairs of States and the Protection of their Independence and Sovereignty*
A/RES/42/22	18 November 1987	*Declaration on the Enhancement of the Effectiveness of the Principle of Refraining from the Threat or Use of Force in International Relations*
A/RES/46/7	11 October 1991	*The situation of democracy and human rights in Haiti*
A/RES/55/96	4 December 2000	*Promoting and Consolidating Democracy*
A/RES/56/83	12 December 2001	*Responsibility of States for internationally wrongful acts*
A/RES/60/1	24 October 2005	*2005 World Summit Outcome*
A/RES/63/301	1 July 2009	*Situation in Honduras: democracy breakdown*
A/RES/65/237	23 December 2010	*Credentials of representatives to the sixty-fifth session of the General Assembly*
A/RES/67/234B	2 April 2013	*The Arms Trade Treaty*
A/RES/67/262	4 June 2013	*The situation in the Syrian Arab Republic*

Security Council Resolutions

S/RES/232 (1966)	16 December 1966
S/RES/794 (1992)	3 December 1992
S/RES/876 (1993)	19 October 1993
S/RES/929 (1994)	22 June 1994
S/RES/940 (1994)	31 July 1994
S/RES/1125 (1997)	6 August 1997
S/RES/1160 (1998)	31 March 1998

S/RES/1264 (1999)	15 September 1999
S/RES/1311 (2000)	28 July 2000
S/RES/1464 (2003)	4 February 2003
S/RES/1653 (2006)	27 January 2006
S/RES/1674 (2006)	28 April 2006
S/RES/1894 (2009)	11 November 2009
S/RES/1962 (2010)	20 December 2010
S/RES/1970 (2011)	26 February 2011
S/RES/1973 (2011)	17 March 2011
S/RES/1975 (2011)	30 March 2011
S/RES/1996 (2011)	8 July 2011
S/RES/2014 (2011)	21 October 2011
S/RES/2016 (2011)	27 October 2011
S/RES/2040 (2012)	12 March 2012
S/RES/2085 (2012)	20 December 2012
S/RES/2093 (2013)	6 March 2013
S/RES/2095 (2013)	14 March 2013
S/RES/2100 (2013)	25 April 2013
S/RES/2109 (2013)	11 July 2013
S/RES/2121 (2013)	10 October 2013
S/RES/2127 (2013)	5 December 2013
S/RES/2134 (2014)	28 January 2014
S/RES/2139 (2014)	22 February 2014
S/RES/2149 (2014)	10 April 2014
S/RES/2150 (2014)	16 April 2014
S/RES/2155 (2014)	27 May 2014
S/RES/2171 (2014)	21 August 2014
S/RES/2187 (2014)	25 November 2014
S/RES/2216 (2015)	14 April 2015
S/RES/2337 (2017)	19 January 2017

Reports of the Secretary General

A/54/2000	27 March 2000	*We the Peoples: The Role of the United Nations in the 21st century*
A/59/2005	21 March 2005	*In Larger Freedom: Towards Development, Security and Human Rights for All*
A/61/636- S/2006/980	14 December 2006	*Uniting Our Strengths: Enhancing United Nations Support for the Rule of Law*

Human Rights Council

Report of the International Commission of Inquiry to investigate all alleged violations of international human rights law in the Libyan Arab Jamahiriya, 1 June 2011, A/HRC/17/44.

Situation of human rights in the Syrian Arab Republic, 22-23 August 2011, A/HRC/RES/S-17/1.

Report of the Independent International Commission of Inquiry on the Syrian Arab Republic, 23 November 2011, A/HRC/S-17/2/Add.1.

The Human Rights Situation in the Syrian Arab Republic, 2 December 2011, A/HRC/RES/S–18/1.

Report of the International Commission of Inquiry on Libya, 8 March 2012, A/HRC/19/68.

Report of the Independent International Commission of Inquiry on the Syrian Arab Republic, 5 February 2013, A/HRC/22/59.

Human Rights Committee

'General Comment No. 12: Article 1 (Right to Self-determination), The Right to Self-determination of Peoples,' 13 March 1984, HRI/GEN/1/Rev.9 (Vol. I).

'General Comment 25: Article 25 (Participation in Public Affairs and the Right to Vote), The Right to Participate in Public Affairs, Voting Rights and the Right of Equal Access to Public Service,' 12 July 1996, CCPR/C/21/Rev.1/Add.7.

International Law Commission

J. Crawford, *Second Report on State Responsibility*, 30 April 1999, A/CN.4/498/Add.2.

Draft Articles on Responsibility of States for Internationally Wrongful Acts, with commentaries, *Yearbook of the International Law Commission*, 2001.

Other United Nations Documents

Basic Principles on the Use of Force and Firearms by Law Enforcement Officials, Adopted by the Eighth United Nations Congress on the Prevention of Crime and the Treatment of Offenders, Havana, Cuba, 1990.

OHCHR, Vienna Declaration and Programme of Action, World Conference on Human Rights, 25 June 1993.

UNCHR, *Promotion of the Right to Democracy*, 27 April 1999, E/CN.4/RES/1999/5.

A more secure world: our shared responsibility, Report of the High-level Panel on Threats, Challenges and Change, A759/565, 2 December 2004.

Security Council Report, *Protection of Civilians*, Cross-Cutting Report 2008 no. 2, 14 October 2008, New York.

UN Secretary-General Ban Ki-moon, *Guidance Note of the Secretary-General on Democracy*, 11 September 2009.

UNSC Verbatim Record, UN Doc S/PV/6498, 17 March 2011.

UNSC Verbatim Record, UN Doc S/PV/6528, §10, 4 May 2011.

UNSC Verbatim Record, UN Doc S/PV/6620, §3, 16 September 2011.

Resolution RC/Res.6 (n 4) Annex I, Art 8*bis*, The Crime of Aggression, 13th plenary meeting of the ICC Assembly of States Parties at Kampala, 11 June 2010.

Identical letters dated 11 January 2013 from the Permanent Representative of France to the UN addressed to the Secretary-General and the President of the Security Council, S/1013/17, 11 January 2013.

Letter dated 20 September 2014 from the Permanent Representative of Iraq to the United Nations addressed to the President of the Security Council, S/2014/691 (2014), 20 September 2014.

Letter dated 23 September 2014 from the Permanent Representative of the United States of America to the United Nations addressed to the Secretary-General, S/2014/695, 23 September 2014.

Identical letters dated 17 September 2015 from the Permanent Representative of the Syrian Arab Republic to the United Nations addressed to the Secretary-General and the President of the Security Council, S/2015/719, 21 September 2015.

Identical letters dated 14 October 2015 from the Permanent Representative of the Syrian Arab Republic to the United Nations addressed to the Secretary-General and the President of the Security Council (16 October 2015), A/70/429 and S/2015/789.

UNGA Third Committee, Situation of Human Rights in the Syrian Arab Republic, A/C.3/66/L.57/Rev.1.

Institut de Droit International

Droits et devoirs des Puissances étrangères, au cas de mouvement insurrectionnel, envers les gouvernements établis et reconnus qui sont aux prises avec l'insurrection, Session de Neuchâtel, 8 September 1900.

Régime des représailles en temps de paix, Session de Paris, 19 October 1934.

The Principle of Non-Intervention in Civil Wars, Session of Wiesbaden, 14 August 1975.

Present Problems of the Use of Armed Force in International Law, Session de Santiago, 27 October 2007.

Present Problems of the Use of Force in International Law: Sub-Group C – Military assistance on request, Session de Rhodes, 8 September 2011.

Present Problems of the Use of Force in International Law: Sub-group D – Authorization of the Use of Force by the United Nations, Session de Rhodes, 9 September 2011.

Other Documents

Islamic Council of Europe, Universal Islamic Declaration on Human Rights, 1981.

Santiago Commitment to Democracy and the Renewal of the Inter-American System, 4 June 1991.

OAS Doc. AG/RES. 1080 (XXI-0/91), 5 June 1991, *Representative Democracy.*

Conference on Security and Cooperation in Europe, *Document of the Moscow Meeting on the Human Dimension of the CSCE*, 30 I.L.M. 1670, 1677, 3 October 1991.

Immigration and Refugee Board of Canada, Syria: Syrian presidential election in 2000; confirmation of whether businessmen and/or other influential people in the community were pressured by security officers to collect other people's identity cards for the security officer's use in the election (June–July 2001), 24 March 2003, SYR41225.E.

Report of the Independent International Fact-Finding Mission on the Conflict in Georgia, Vol. II, 25 September 2009.

Communiqué, AU document PSC/PR/COMM(CCLXI), 23 February 2011.

African Union, Peace and Security Council, 268th meeting, Addis Ababa, 10 March 2011, PSC/PR/COMM.2(CCLXV).

Council of the League of Arab States, Resolution 7360, 12 March 2011.

Secretary-General of the Organization of the Islamic Conference, 'Ihsanoglu: Political solution to the Libyan crisis is the only way to bring lasting peace to Libya,' 7 May 2011.

Council of the European Union, Council conclusions on Libya, 3091st Foreign Affairs Council Meeting, Brussels, 23 May 2011.

'Responsibility while Protecting: Elements for the Development and Promotion of a Concept,' letter dated 9 November 2011 from the Permanent Representative of Brazil to the United Nations addressed to the Secretary-General, A/66/151–S/2011/701, 9 November 2011.

OSCE Document on Small Arms and Light Weapons, FSC.DOC/1/00/Rev.1, 20 June 2012.

Framework for Elimination of Syrian Chemical Weapons, Joint National Paper by the Russian Federation and the United States of America, EC-M-33/NAT.1, 17 September 2013.

ECOWAS, Fiftieth Ordinary Session of the ECOWAS Authority of heads of State and Government, Final Communiqué, 17 December 2016, Abuja, Federal Republic of Nigeria.

Communiqué, AU Peace and Security Council, PSC/PR/COMM. (DCXLVII), 13 January 2017.

Introduction

SINCE THE ADOPTION of the Charter of the United Nations,[1] foreign armed interventions in internal conflicts have turned into a common practice. At first sight, it might seem that state practice has developed in a chaotic fashion, thus suggesting that politics, rather than law, governs foreign interventions. For instance, in 2014 and 2015 the democratically elected presidents of Ukraine and Yemen lost control of their respective countries and sought refuge in neighbouring states. They then invited the host countries to intervene in order to regain control of their home states. Although the two cases appear identical, the Russian intervention upon the invitation of President Viktor Yanukovich met the condemnation of the international community, while the foreign military operations in Yemen were generally endorsed. The French intervention in Mali (2012) and the ECOWAS involvement in The Gambia (2017) raise analogous dilemmas: while France intervened in favour of the coup government, ECOWAS provided military assistance to the ousted President. Nevertheless, in both cases the international community supported the interventions. Finally, a number of countries have provided military and non-lethal assistance to certain opposition groups fighting in Libya and Syria, a practice which is normally deemed unlawful in positive international law.

The foregoing draws attention to key issues regarding foreign interventions in internal conflicts. Notably, it raises critical questions that will be examined in this book. Can foreign countries intervene in a non-international armed conflict upon invitation of the government? Under what conditions, if ever, is it possible to provide assistance to opposition groups? Do considerations of legitimacy change the terms of the discourse?

The significance of these questions, however, goes beyond the aforementioned cases. As a matter of fact, the international legal framework regulating foreign interventions in internal conflicts has been traditionally vague and ambiguous. The reason for this lack of clarity can be traced to the international legal order established by the UN Charter. Following the end of World War II, the primary aim of the international community was to prevent the recurrence of similarly devastating wars. It is thus understandable that the main focus of the UN Charter was to hinder international armed conflicts (IACs). Yet, as the Charter came into force, the international landscape was facing crucial changes and ensuing challenges. Notably, since the 1950s the number of non-international

[1] Charter of the United Nations, 1945 (hereinafter, UN Charter).

armed conflicts has increased dramatically, while IACs have been less and less common.[2] Furthermore, foreign interferences in NIACs have turned into common practice. In other words, the cases in which the Charter system was meant to operate have become comparatively uncommon, while new issues have emerged.

With the adoption of the UN Charter, the international community agreed to ban the threat or use of force among states in their international relations. The Charter envisages two exceptions to the ban: the right to self-defence and the authorisation of the UN Security Council (UNSC). Nevertheless, Cold War dynamics impaired the functioning of these rules and posed significant challenges. On the one hand, the use of the veto power substantially paralysed the UNSC. On the other hand, the US and the Soviet Union engaged in interventions and counter-interventions in order to support their allies and to extend their spheres of influence. The contraposition between the two blocs was reflected in legal debates on decolonisation: while the Soviet position supported the legality of military interventions in favour of national liberation movements, Western countries firmly opposed such an idea.

After the end of the Cold War, the Security Council saw a crucial increase in its activity. Nevertheless, new challenges highlighted its limits. Notably, the failure to react in a timely and effective manner to the Rwandan genocide (1994) and to prevent the massacre that took place in Srebrenica (1995) questioned the capacity of the UNSC to enhance civilian protection. These events triggered animated debates as to the possibility to forcibly intervene for humanitarian purposes, notwithstanding the lack of the authorisation by the Security Council. More recently, the use of chemical weapons by the Syrian government fuelled new debates on humanitarian interventions. Following unsuccessful attempts within the UNSC to authorise an intervention in Syria, in 2017 and 2018 the US and allied powers conducted airstrikes against the Assad government as a response to chemical weapons attacks perpetrated against the civilian population.[3]

[2] According to *The War Report 2018*: '[i]n 2018, at least 69 armed conflicts occurred on the territory of 30 states … At least a total of 51 non-international armed conflicts occurred in 2018 in the territory of 22 states: Afghanistan, the Central African Republic, Colombia, DRC, Egypt, India, Iraq, Libya, Mali, Mexico, Myanmar, Nigeria, Pakistan, the Philippines, Somalia, South Sudan, Sudan, Syria, Thailand, Turkey, Ukraine and Yemen'. A. Bellal, *The War Report: Armed Conflicts in 2018* (Geneva Academy of International Humanitarian Law and Human Rights, 2019) 19.

[3] Chemical attacks allegedly perpetrated by the Syrian government in 2017 and 2018 triggered military interventions by the US and allied forces. Notably, on 6 April 2017 the US launched military strikes on Syria: '[t]he Pentagon announced that 59 Tomahawk cruise missiles had been fired at Al Shayrat airfield in Syria. The missiles were aimed at Syrian fighter jets, hardened aircraft shelters, radar equipment, ammunition bunkers, sites for storing fuel and air defense systems', see MR Gordon, H Cooper and MD Shear, 'Dozens of U.S. Missiles Hit Air Base in Syria' (*The New York Times*, 6 April 2017), available at www.nytimes.com/2017/04/06/world/middleeast/us-said-to-weigh-military-responses-to-syrian-chemical-attack.html. More recently, on 14 April 2018 the US, UK, and France engaged in airstrikes against the Assad regime, see J Borger and P Beaumont,

In light of the foregoing, a number of scholars wondered whether the UN Charter was substantially unfit to face new challenges that emerged after World War II. Indeed, lacking clear rules regulating foreign interventions in internal conflicts, it might seem that state practice has developed in a confused way. However, specific patterns emerge on closer examination. As human rights have gained momentum, they have reframed longstanding debates on military interferences. Discussions on humanitarian interventions highlight the nexus between the ban on the use of force, the principle of non-intervention, and the human rights paradigm. However, the significance of human rights has more far-reaching implications at the level of *jus ad bellum*. Accordingly, this study seeks to pinpoint the bearing of human rights on foreign interventions in internal conflicts.

SCOPE OF THE STUDY

The objective of the present study is to investigate the extent to which traditional international law regulating foreign interventions in internal conflicts has been affected by the human rights paradigm. Specifically, its aims are twofold. First, it seeks to clarify the current legal framework regulating interventions in internal conflicts. Second, it endeavours to detect the emergence of new trends and to investigate whether they are becoming part of positive international law.

While addressing key questions on foreign interventions, this work engages in discussions on a broader spectrum of related conundrums which have gripped scholarship and practice for a long time: the juxtaposition of effectiveness and legitimacy, the relationship between sovereignty and human rights, and the question of self-determination and intervention. These dilemmas have deeper roots, which can be traced back to an era in which waging war was considered a right pertaining to sovereignty. Although the adoption of the UN Charter and the ensuing ban on the use of force contributed to reframing the discussion, they did not provide a clear answer to these issues. Accordingly, this work seeks to clarify the legal framework regulating foreign armed interventions in internal conflicts. In doing so, this analysis will dig into the values and objectives of the international legal system.

'Syria: US, UK and France launch strikes in response to chemical attack' (*The Guardian*, 14 April 2018), available at www.theguardian.com/world/2018/apr/14/syria-air-strikes-us-uk-and-france-launch-attack-on-assad-regime. While the US and France did not provide any legal arguments to justify the intervention, the UK explicitly relied on humanitarian intervention: '[t]he UK is permitted under international law, on an exceptional basis, to take measures in order to alleviate overwhelming humanitarian suffering. The legal basis for the use of force is humanitarian intervention', see Office of the Prime Minister, 'Syria action – UK government legal position' (Policy Paper, 14 April 2018), available at www.gov.uk/government/publications/syria-action-uk-government-legal-position/syria-action-uk-government-legal-position.

This study rests on the hypothesis that, although *prima facie* inconsistent, state practice displays certain patterns with regard to foreign interventions in internal conflicts and that human rights have substantially influenced these issues. In a famous passage of the *Nicaragua* case, the International Court of Justice (ICJ) maintained that:

> It is not to be expected that in the practice of States the application of the rules in question should have been perfect, in the sense that States should have refrained, with complete consistency, from the use of force or from intervention in each other's internal affairs. The Court does not consider that, for a rule to be established as customary, the corresponding practice must be in absolutely rigorous conformity with the rule. In order to deduce the existence of customary rules, the Court deems it sufficient that the conduct of States should, in general, be consistent with such rules, and that instances of States conduct inconsistent with a given rule should generally have been treated as breaches of that rule, not as indications of the recognition of a new rule. *If a State acts in a way prima facie incompatible with a recognized rule, but defends its conduct by appealing to exceptions or justifications contained within the rule itself, then whether or not the State's conduct is in fact justifiable on that basis, the significance of that attitude is to confirm rather than to weaken the rule.*[4]

Accordingly, this book will adopt the general criteria expounded by the ICJ in examining state practice. In particular, it will analyse the justifications provided by third countries and the subsequent reactions of the international community with the ultimate aim of assessing whether the traditional rules are confirmed, or whether new trends are affecting positive international law.

Before developing these arguments further, one caveat seems to be in order. Interventions in internal conflicts necessarily entail political considerations: the decision to intervene in an internal conflict is essentially political. State practice can be perceived as chaotic. Therefore, it may be easy to conclude that every intervention is guided by its own political logic and that international law substantially plays an inconsequential role. It is undeniable that political considerations ultimately affect decisions as to whether to intervene. Likewise, a state might criticise an intervention for political reasons which are not based on legal grounds. Nevertheless, this book seeks to demonstrate that patterns emerge from state practice and that it is possible to draw a picture of the legal framework regulating interventions in internal conflicts beyond political considerations.

[4] ICJ, *Military and Paramilitary Activities in and against Nicaragua, (Nicaragua v United States of America)*, Judgment (Merits), 27 June 1986 (hereinafter, *Nicaragua* case), §186, emphasis added.

OUTLINE

It is commonplace, even trite, that we have to know the past to understand the present. As Cassese noted:

> A still photograph of the current state of law would be incomprehensible – how could one understand the way the law is today if one does not study its evolution into the current state? Can we understand a human being without delving into his or her biography? Can we understand a polity without exploring his history? How, then, can we hope to understand legal parameters … if we do not trace [their] antecedents at the beginning?[5]

This study subscribes to this statement. Accordingly, Part I of this work is devoted to investigating the evolution of the relationship of concepts that crucially set the basis of our discussion: intervention, sovereignty, and human rights. As this study will show, tensions among these concepts have been central to legal debates for centuries. Since the Middle Ages, legal scholarship has engaged in discussions on the scope of the principle of non-intervention, the possibility to intervene to protect civilians and the contraposition between effectiveness and legitimacy. For instance, already in the thirteenth century Thomas Aquinas wondered about the criteria to identify the legitimate authority to wage war,[6] while Hugo Grotius supported the right to intervene to protect people from a tyrant, which we could see as humanitarian intervention *ante litteram*.[7] By guiding the reader through a historical survey, Part I will follow the development of paramount concepts and will analyse their meaning and significance under the current legal framework.

Having set the basis of our discussion, Part II will examine interventions in favour of governments, paying particular attention to interventions upon invitation. It will start analysing the traditional doctrines of intervention that were developed by the scholarship since the adoption of the UN Charter. While some authors claim that interventions in civil wars upon invitation of the government would violate the principle of non-intervention and the right

[5] A Cassese, *Self-Determination of Peoples: A Legal Reappraisal* (Cambridge University Press, 1995) 3.

[6] T Aquinas, *Summa Theologiae* (Blackfriars, 1972), Secunda Secundae, Quaestio 11,1: '[t]he first thing is the authority of the prince by whose command the war is to be waged'. See also P Piirimäe, 'The Westphalian Myth and the Idea of External Sovereignty' in H Kalmo and Q Skinner (eds), *Sovereignty in Fragments: The Past, Present and Future of a Contested Concept* (Ashgate, 2010) 67; J von Elbe, 'The Evolution of the Concept of the Just War in International Law' (1939) 33(4) *American Journal of International Law* 668.

[7] D Rodogno, *Against Massacre: Humanitarian Interventions in the Ottoman Empire, 1815–1914* (Princeton University Press, 2012) 4; S Chesterman, *Just War or Just Peace? Humanitarian Intervention and International Law* (Oxford University Press, 2001) 15.

to self-determination, others propound that governments can invite foreign forces to quell a rebellion. However, they disagree as to the criteria for identifying the authority capable to speak on behalf of the state: should it be the organ that exercises effective control over territory and population? Or should preference be given to democratically elected governments, even if ineffective? In order to answer these and related questions, the traditional doctrines will be tested against state practice. Ultimately, this part will identify new trends that emerged over the last decades and will assess whether they have entered into positive international law.

Part III will be devoted to investigating interventions in favour of opposition groups. Broadly speaking, interventions in favour of rebels are unlawful. However, since the adoption of the UN Charter there have been cases when armed non-state actors (ANSAs) have been recognised as legitimate and this triggered discussions on the possibility to intervene in their favour. Part III will start examining the legitimacy of rebels under international law. During the decolonisation period, national liberation movements were recognised as legitimate representatives of their people; over the past decade, the same definition was attributed to certain Libyan and Syrian opposition groups. Is it possible to identify common criteria, or did the recent narrative bring about a break with the past? Furthermore, this Part will focus on the consequences of the recognition of legitimacy from three angles. First, it will examine the use of force by the government against legitimate rebels. The crucial question is whether the traditional presumption that the government can forcibly react against opposition groups would be at least partially reversed. Second, this Part will seek to investigate when, if ever, legitimate rebels might enjoy a right to use force against the government. Finally, it will address the question of foreign interventions in favour of legitimate opposition groups.

This work will demonstrate that the human rights paradigm has been affecting foreign interventions in internal conflicts in pervasive and profound ways, which rest on a threefold structure. First, human rights play a decisive role in identifying the organ capable to speak on behalf of the state. If we refer back to the interventions in Ukraine, Yemen, Mali, and The Gambia, it is apparent that the main question regarding interventions upon invitation concerns the identification of the government. Albeit prima facie contradictory, these and similar cases would reveal a pattern, whereby human rights considerations guide the international community in establishing who is the de jure government. Notably, democratically elected governments, ie endorsed by free and fair elections, tend to be preferred over undemocratic ones and this preference is framed in terms of rights. Specifically, it rests on discussions on the emerging right to democratic governance and the right to self-determination of people.

Second, human rights have emerged as a decisive parameter to determine legitimacy. Recently, governments that have turned against their population and have committed gross and systematic violations of human rights and humanitarian law have been deemed illegitimate. This raises key questions as to the consequences attached to the loss of legitimacy, in particular as to whether such governments would forfeit their power to invite foreign countries to intervene in their favour.

Third, human rights considerations have grounded the recognition of opposition groups as legitimate representatives of a people: during the decolonisation period, this qualification was attributed to national liberation movements fighting in the exercise of their right to self-determination; more recently, the same terminology was addressed to certain opposition groups fighting in Libya and Syria. Therefore, in both cases this qualification was based on human rights considerations and triggered discussions on the possibility to intervene in favour of rebels. Ultimately, this study will show that human rights are emerging as parameter of legitimacy and that this in turn has crucial consequences on the legal framework regulating foreign interventions in internal conflicts.

Part I

Sovereignty, Intervention, and Human Rights: The Evolution of a Close Relationship

Remember the lessons of history. …
How many powerful men have craved to
dominate the world – and by overreaching
have lost everything they once possessed!

Xenophon

That men do not learn very much
from the lessons of history is the most
important of all the lessons of history.

Ariel Durant

SINCE THE ADOPTION of the UN Charter, interventions in internal conflicts have been extremely common: governments and rebels alike have frequently sought foreign help to defeat their enemies. However, the legal framework regulating these instances is substantially unclear, while state practice is often perceived as chaotic. This confusion derives in part from the paucity and lack of clarity of rules explicitly addressing interventions in internal conflicts: while the principle of non-intervention and the ban on the use of force are the primary sources regulating these instances, their exact content is uncertain. Furthermore, the question of the legality of interventions in internal conflicts touches upon fundamental dilemmas of international law, namely sovereignty, human rights, and intervention. In light of this, this Part seeks to define and clarify crucial concepts addressed in this study. Specifically, it will analyse pivotal issues relating to interventions in internal conflicts, thus framing our discussion.

The practice of interventions in internal conflicts did not emerge *ex abrupto* during the twentieth century: since the Middle Ages, dilemmas on the possibility to intervene to protect people from a tyrant, on the relationship between intervention and sovereignty, and on the legality of the use of force have been central in legal debates. Therefore, before engaging in discussions on the current legal framework regulating interventions in internal conflicts, it is crucial to analyse how the relationship between sovereignty, human rights, and intervention evolved over the centuries. Indeed, as noted by Hoffmann:

> To be able to talk intelligently about what looks like the extraordinary amount of intervention that occurs in the present-day international system, or about the seemingly original network of contemporary transnational relations, it is useful to be able to compare the present system with past ones. We may discover that the amount of intervention today is not at all that unusual and that the network of transnational relations is far less original than many have claimed.[1]

Bearing these considerations in mind, this part is structured as follows. Chapter one will focus on interventions in internal conflicts in the pre-Charter era. Specifically, it will invite the reader to follow the evolution of concepts which are going to have a crucial role in this study. Unlike what is commonly believed, in ancient times war was not waged without restraint. Notably, theories on just wars flourished in the Middle Ages and raised conundrums which are still relevant nowadays. Furthermore, the emergence of the principle of non-intervention triggered debates on sovereignty and its limits. Finally, in the nineteenth century, the recognition of belligerency and insurgency helped reframe the terms of the discussion. However, questions on sovereignty, intervention, and human rights did not lose their relevance.

Building on this historical analysis, chapter two will clarify the main concepts addressed in this work. First, it will define the concepts of intervention and non-international armed conflict. Despite its crucial significance in international law, the meaning and scope of the principle of non-intervention is still unclear. Similarly, determining the existence of a NIAC is not always an easy task, especially due to the lack of certain criteria to identify the lower threshold and the increase of situations when both internal and international conflicts take place simultaneously in a country. Second, chapter two will discuss the content and nature of the ban on the use of force. Furthermore, it will address longstanding debates on the threshold of control required to attribute the actions of rebels to a state that is helping them. Lastly, this Part will analyse the current state of the relationship between non-intervention, sovereignty, and human rights in light of the historical overview conducted in chapter one.

[1] S Hoffmann, 'Hedley Bull and His Contribution to International Relations' (1986) 62(2) *International Affairs* 179–95.

1

Interventions in Internal Conflicts in the Pre-Charter Era

I. THE USE OF FORCE AS CRUCIAL PREROGATIVE OF STATE SOVEREIGNTY: FROM *BELLUM JUSTUM* DOCTRINES TO THE RIGHT TO WAR

A. Just War Doctrines

i. The Origins of Bellum Justum Doctrines

THERE IS A common perception that in ancient times war was waged without restraint and with no attempts to avoid it. However, this assumption does not reflect the historical realities. Already in the first millennium BCE some nations had developed a legal framework regulating the use of force. For instance, Jewish religious thought distinguished between *mitzvah*, ie an obligatory war ordered by God to defend Israel, and *reshut*, the war which was permitted in other circumstances at the discretion of the ruler.[1] However, Walzer notes that such distinction between commanded/permitted war did 'not translate into just/unjust'.[2] Thus, restraints on the use of force seemed to stem more from 'instrumental prudence' than from moral considerations on the justness of war.[3]

It was only with the Greek and Roman cultures that the idea of justice (*dikê/justitia*) was introduced into decisions as to whether to wage war.[4] In ancient Greece people were well aware of the trauma stemming from war and its impact on society. Homer describes the struggle of the men who returned from war: people who 'have fallen victim to useless labour and dreadful diseases and hardly curable madness'.[5] Xenophon writes about ritualistic dances practised for

[1] GA Raymond, 'The Greco-Roman Roots of the Western Just War Tradition' in HM Hensel (ed), *The Prism of Just War: Asian and Western Perspectives on the Legitimate Use of Military Force* (Ashgate, 2010) 9.

[2] M Walzer, 'War and Peace in the Jewish Tradition,' in T Nardin (ed), *The Ethics of War and Peace: Religious and Secular Perspectives* (Princeton University Press, 1996) 104.

[3] See Raymond (n 1) 9–10.

[4] ibid, 10.

[5] Gorgias, *Encomium of Helen*, quoted by LA Tritle, '"Laughing for Joy": War and Peace Among the Greeks' in KA Raaflaub (ed), *War and Peace in the Ancient World* (Blackwell Publishing, 2007) 181.

their therapeutic value.[6] In Athens, the cathartic function of theatre was directed towards the same end.[7] As the Greeks experienced the horrors of war and its dramatic consequences, they also developed means to prevent armed conflicts. War was considered as a last resort: peaceful means to resolve differences should have been undertaken when feasible.[8] For instance, Homer, describing the tense period preceding the Trojan War, mentions diplomacy as crucial effort to settle conflicts before the kings turned into wars.[9] Should endeavours to peacefully settle differences fail, the use of military force had to be based on a just cause. While self-defence was the most common justification, commentators also mentioned breaking treaty obligations and breaching neutrality.[10]

Similarly, the Romans often mentioned self-defence as a basis for legitimately waging war: in the words of Cicero, 'if our lives are endangered by enemies, any and every method of protecting ourselves is morally right'.[11] However, a just cause was not sufficient: the decision to engage in an armed conflict could be adopted only by a person who had the legitimate authority.[12] According to Cicero, 'no war is just unless it is waged after a formal demand for restoration, or unless it has been formally announced and declared beforehand'.[13] *Bellum justum* was hence a defensive war conducted in response to an offence against Rome and as such in line with the will of the Gods.[14] The *fetiales* were a special priesthood whose duties entailed ensuring the justness of war. When Rome suffered a grievance, the *fetiales* were in charge of following specific rituals and procedures that could lead to waging war. First, the priests had to ask for satisfaction (*rerum repetitio*). In case the opponent did not comply with such demand within a specific time frame, the *fetiales* could proceed with a formal declaration of war, following specific rituals.[15] Thus, *bellum* was not *justum* unless it followed specific and complex procedures and had the final imprimatur of the *fetiales*.[16]

[6] Xenophon, *Anabasis* (Rizzoli, 1978) at 6.1.5-13.

[7] Tritle (n 5) 183.

[8] KA Raaflaub, 'Introduction: Searching for Peace in the Ancient World' in Raaflaub (n 5) 17.

[9] ibid, 18; KA Raaflaub, 'Politics and Interstate Relations in the World of Early Greek Poleis: Homer and Beyond' (1997) 31 *Antichthon* 2–8.

[10] For instance, during the Peloponnesian War (431–404 BC), Athenians offered to avoid war through arbitration, but Sparta rejected the bid. As a result, the Athenians claimed that 'they had justice and the Gods on their side' and that they could thus use force against the enemy. See Raaflaub (n 9). See also C Phillipson, *The International Law and Custom of Ancient Greece and Rome*, vol 2, (Macmillan, 1911) 182–92.

[11] See Raymond (n 1) 12.

[12] ibid.

[13] ibid, 13.

[14] N Rosenstein, 'War and Peace, Fear and Reconciliation at Rome,' in Raaflaub (n 5) 229.

[15] Livy, *Ab Urbe Condita* (Mondadori, 2007), Book I, § XXII, 5–14. See also Y Dinstein, *War, Aggression and Self-Defence* (Cambridge University Press, 2011) 65; J von Elbe, 'The Evolution of the Concept of the Just War in International Law' (1939) 33(4) *The American Journal of International Law* 666; Phillipson (n 10) 328.

[16] Cicero, *De Officiis* (Mondadori, 1984), Book I, §XI, at 36; Cicero, *De Re Publica* (Rizzoli, 2008), Book III, §XXIII, at 35.

ii. Just War in the Scholastic Thought

Bellum justum doctrines did not fall out of fashion with the *fetiales*: the Canonist thought embraced and developed the idea that war should be just. Inasmuch as the Roman Empire was pagan, the Church adopted a strictly pacifist approach: war was in contrast with the evangelical message and Christians could not become soldiers. However, with Constantine and his Edict (313 AD) Christians were integrated into the empire. The army was no longer synonymous with persecution and thus 'the stigma which the originally pacific spirit of the Church had attached to war gradually disappeared'.[17] As the official religion of the Empire, the Church had to change its absolute rejection of war and sought to find grounds from within the Christian doctrine in order to justify the use of force.[18] The *impasse* was overcome by reviving the Romans' *bellum justum* doctrine.[19] Notably, a war was deemed to be just if it met two criteria: legitimate authority and just cause (*justa causa belli*).[20] The evolution of these two concepts followed parallel but strictly connected lines. Both of them tended towards a gradual secularisation of just war doctrines which culminated in the affirmation of a general right to war pertaining to sovereign states.

Augustine of Hippo (354–430) was the first to theorise under what circumstances the use of force could find a place in the Christian theological system. The Christianised Roman Empire was a unitary system whose political and spiritual aspects had to be integrated; the institution of war had thus to be explained in theological terms. It is against this backdrop that the idea of war as punishment emerged: war was considered 'as means of punishment which God inflicts upon the sinful world'.[21] Thus, wars were just when they redressed a wrongful act (*injuria*) and when they were aimed at preserving the social order.[22] Only God and the ruler had the authority to decide whether the use of force was necessary: 'the natural order conducive to peace among mortals demands that the power to declare and counsel war should be in the hands of those who hold the supreme authority'.[23]

[17] von Elbe (n 15) 667; Dinstein (n 15) 60; W Ballis, *The Legal Position of War: Changes in its Practice and Theory from Plato to Vattel* (Springer, 1937) 35–41; D Beaufort, *La guerre comme instrument de secours ou de punition* (Martinus Nijhoff, 1933) 8.

[18] von Elbe (n 15) 668.

[19] HM Hensel, 'Theocentric Natural Law and Just War Doctrine' in HM Hensel (ed), *The Legitimate Use of Military Force: the Just War Tradition and the Customary Law of Armed Conflict* (Ashgate, 2008) 10.

[20] HM Hensel, 'Christian Belief and Western Just War Thought' in Hensel (n 1) 42–46.

[21] von Elbe (n 15) 668.

[22] Augustine, *De Civitate Dei Contra Paganos*, Book XIX, §VII. See also Dinstein (n 15) 60; J Bartelson 'Double Binds: Sovereignty and the Just War Tradition' in H Kalmo and Q Skinner (eds), *Sovereignty in Fragments: The Past, Present and Future of a Contested Concept* (Cambridge University Press, 2010) 89; Q Skinner, *The Foundations of Modern Political Thought*, vol 1 (Cambridge University Press, 1978) 245.

[23] Augustine, *Contra Faustus the Manichean*, quoted in Bartelson (n 22) 89–90.

Drawing upon Augustine, Gratian (ca. 1075/80–1145/47) – the founder of Canon Law and author of the *Decretum Gratiani* (*Concordia Discordantium Canonum*, ca. 1140) – delineated the conditions for waging war. The crucial challenge was to reconcile the idea that the use of force was not a sin *per se* with the so-called 'precepts of patience', ie the passages from the New Testament which invite Christians to embrace a passive rather than active approach to violence. Quoting Augustine, Gratian suggested that when Christ said to 'turn the other cheek' he was referring only to the internal intentions of the person, and not to the external actions. Consequently, war could be waged only with the right intention of the soul, namely without sentiments of revenge or moved by the desire of conquest.[24] Having clarified that war was not manifestly in contrast with Christian thought, Gratian propounded two causes that could justify the use of force: self-defence and the punishment of a wrongdoing.[25] These two justifications provided the basis for discussions on *jus ad bellum* among successive scholastics.

Thomas Aquinas (1225–74) was the most prominent scholar to develop a comprehensive doctrine of just war. Notably, he identified three criteria for a war to be just: legitimate authority (*auctoritas principis*), just cause (*justa causa*), and right intention (*intention recta*).[26] In line with the ideas put forward by Augustine and Gratian, according to Thomas Aquinas a just war is first and foremost a punitive action following a culpable act: the ultimate aim is to redress a wrong suffered, thus re-establishing peace and justice. The legitimate authority to wage war was embodied in the prince. Indeed, as the prince had the right to punish wrongdoing among his subjects, it was only logical to extend such right to waging war:

> And just as they use the sword in lawful defence against domestic disturbance when they punish criminals ... so they lawfully use the sword of war to protect the commonweal from foreign attacks.[27]

Thus, in the Canonist thought the right to wage war descended from God and rested in the prince's hands. Notably, war was deemed just when directed at protecting or re-establishing the social order and to punish any attempts to destroy it. During the Middle Ages, the majority of scholars agreed that

[24] GM Reichberg, '*Jus ad Bellum*' in L May (ed), *War: Essays in Political Philosophy* (Cambridge University Press, 2008) 13.

[25] Gratian, *Decretum*, Akademische Druck-u. Verlagsanstalt, Graz, 1959, §2, causa 23.

[26] T Aquinas, *Summa Theologiae* (Blackfriars, London, 1972), Secunda Secundae, Quaestio 40,1.

[27] ibid, Secunda Secundae, Quaestio 11,1: '[t]he first thing is the authority of the prince by whose command the war is to be waged. ... [S]ince the care of the commonwealth is entrusted to princes, to them belongs the protection of the common weal of the city, kingdom, or province subject to them. And as they lawfully defend it with the material sword against inward disturbances by punishing male-factors, so it belongs to them also to protect the commonwealth from enemies without by the sword of war'. See also P Piirimäe, 'The Westphalian Myth and the Idea of External Sovereignty' in Kalmo and Skinner (n 22) 67.

the authority to use force descends from God: the prince was granted legitimacy inasmuch as he was *minister dei*. Consequently, he was the only one to be granted a right to punish the enemy for its wrongdoing.[28] Nonetheless, in the thirteenth century French and Italian jurists started challenging this approach and expounded the idea that the prince was sovereign in his own reign, thus opposing the position of supremacy so far recognised as residing in the Church.[29] Their approach was further developed in the sixteenth century: on the one hand, Lutherans focused on challenging the temporal power of the Church; on the other hand, numerous jurists opposed to the feudal conceptions of the king started to elaborate the idea of absolute sovereignty.[30] According to the latter, only a centralised and stable power could limit internal conflicts and religious wars.[31] Consequently, several scholars believed in the necessity of having an absolute sovereign.[32]

Jean Bodin's (1529–96) *Six Books of the Commonwealth* constitutes the first comprehensive systematisation of the nature of sovereignty.[33] In his view, 'the authority of the sovereign was absolute and indefeasible'.[34] Although the primary power of the sovereign was to legislate, to produce rules that did not bind him, this power was not arbitrary: it entailed also responsibilities towards God, his subjects, and other rulers. First, the law promulgated by the sovereign was to be modelled on the law of God.[35] Second, Bodin opposed the idea of sovereignty as tyranny: the prince was responsible for his subjects. According to the French author, there is a 'mutual obligation between the subject and the sovereign, by which, in return for the faith and obedience rendered to him, the sovereign must do justice and give counsel, assistance, encouragement and protection to the subject'.[36] Third, the sovereign was accountable towards the other princes, who could have embraced arms to punish a tyrant.[37] Thus, according to Bodin, the sovereign is *legibus soluto* with regard to the rules meant to govern his own population, but this does not imply that his sovereignty is absolute: the respect of the people subject to his power was crucial and other princes could intervene in case he turned his reign into a tyranny.

[28] von Elbe (n 15) 670; Hensel (n 20) 12.

[29] L Glanville, *Sovereignty and the Responsibility to Protect: A New History* (University of Chicago Press, 2014) 31; A Osiander, 'Before Sovereignty: Society and Politics in Ancien Régime Europe' (2001) 27(05) *Review of International Studies* 144–45.

[30] Q Skinner, *The Foundations of Modern Political Thought*, vol 2 (Cambridge University Press, 1978) 351–52.

[31] ibid, 284.

[32] J. Burns, 'The Idea of Absolutism' in J Miller (ed), *Absolutism in Seventeenth-Century Europe* (Macmillan, 1990) 22.

[33] CE Merriam, *History of the Theory of Sovereignty since Rousseau* (Columbia University Press, 1900) 13; FK Abiew, *The Evolution of the Doctrine and Practice of Humanitarian Intervention* (Kluwer Law International, 1999) 27.

[34] Glanville (n 29) 34.

[35] ibid, 35; Merriam (n 33) 14.

[36] J Bodin, *Six Books of the Commonwealth* (Blackwell, 1955) §i–viii; Glanville (n 29) 35.

[37] Bodin, (n 36) §i–viii.

While Bodin's work is one of the most comprehensive attempts to systematise the nature of sovereignty, it was Hugo Grotius (1583–1654) who endeavoured to make a comprehensive systematisation of *jus ad bellum* and just war theories.[38] In line with the ideas expressed by Thomas Aquinas, he identified two just causes of war: war as punishment and war aimed at protecting oppressed people.[39] This idea of war as punishment was already present in Francisco Suárez (1548–1617), who delineated the right to war in line with the emerging ideas of absolute sovereignty.[40] As there was no higher authority than the sovereign, the right to punish rested in his hands:

> In the world as a whole, there must exist ... some power for the punishment of injuries inflicted by one state upon another; and this power is not to be found in any superior, for we assume that these states have no commonly acknowledged superior; therefore, the power in question must reside in the sovereign prince of the injured state.[41]

Drawing upon Suárez, Grotius explained that such right would not descend from God, but from the fact that all rulers have no 'commonly acknowledged superior'.[42] War as punishment was seen as necessary in a world where no entities were recognised as higher than the sovereign. However, while his predecessors admitted such right only if some basis for jurisdiction justified it, Grotius extended it to any injuries that 'excessively violate the law of nature or of nations in regard to a person whatsoever'.[43]

Second, war was just when directed to protect people from a tyrant. This was already recognised as a cause of just war among scholastic writers. The idea was first suggested by Ambrose (ca. 339–97) in *De Officiis Ministrorum*[44] and then further elaborated by Francisco de Victoria (1480–1546), who advanced the progressive idea of the *jus defendi innocents a morte iniusta*, 'the right to defend innocents from unjust death'.[45] It is against this backdrop that Grotius argued for the existence of a legal right to wage war against a sovereign who oppresses his subjects.[46] He recognised that 'it is a rule established by the laws

[38] S Chesterman, *Just War or Just Peace? Humanitarian Intervention and International Law* (Oxford University Press, 2001) 9; SJ Hemleben, *Plans for World Peace through Six Centuries* (University of Chicago Press, 1943) 42–44.

[39] Piirimäe (n 27) 67; T Rauert, 'Early Modern Perspectives on Western Just War Thought,' in Hensel (n 1) 91–93.

[40] Glanville (n 29) 45.

[41] F Suárez, *Selections from Three Works of Francisco Suárez, S.J.: De legibus, ac Deo legislatore, 1612, Defensio fidei catholicae, et apostolicae adversus anglicanae sectae errores, 1613, De triplici virtute theologica, fide, spe, et charitate, 1621* (Clarendon Press, 1944) 818.

[42] ibid.

[43] H Grotius, *De Jure belli ac Pacis* (Liberty Fund, 1646) II.i §2.

[44] Chesterman (n 38) 14.

[45] D Rodogno, *Against Massacre: Humanitarian Interventions in the Ottoman Empire, 1815–1914* (Princeton University Press, 2012) 4; Abiew (n 33) 33.

[46] Rodogno (n 45) 4; Chesterman (n 38) 15.

of nature and of social order, and a rule confirmed by all the records of history, that every sovereign is supreme judge in his own kingdom and over his own subjects, in whose disputes no foreign power can justly interfere'.[47] Nevertheless, when a sovereign 'abandons all the laws of nations'[48] and causes grievances to the people under his jurisdiction, then he loses 'the rights of independent sovereign'.[49] As a consequence, foreign countries could intervene in order to protect the oppressed population. Nonetheless, the same right is not granted to the victims. According to Grotius, 'it would be fraught with the greatest dangers if subjects were allowed to redress grievances by force of arms'.[50] The reason, he continues, is that individuals 'cannot transfer their natural allegiance from their own sovereign to another'.[51] However, the same limitation does not apply to foreign powers, which are not tied by the same bond with the sovereign and can thus intervene on behalf of the oppressed.

The recognition of what we could call a humanitarian intervention *ante litteram* provoked an animated discussion as to whether the right to defend oppressed people would imply also a right of the victims to defend themselves against the sovereigns. While Protestants were generally opposed to the recognition of a right to rebel against a tyrant, Catholics and Presbyterians admitted such a possibility. As aforementioned, the authority of the sovereign was believed to descend from God. Inasmuch as the prince was considered God's 'lieutenant to command the rest of mankind', his sovereign was inviolable and *legibus soluto*.[52] Nonetheless, his absolute authority was not arbitrary: albeit not bound by his own rules, the sovereign had to follow the laws of God. Therefore, the sovereign and his people were bound by a unique relationship: the ruler had to govern and protect his population according to the laws of God; in return, the subjects of his power would be obedient and faithful.[53] As a consequence, Protestants accepted the right of foreign forces to intervene in order to defend oppressed people from the abuses of a tyrant:

> Unless we wish to make sovereigns exempt from the law and bound by no statutes and no precedents, there must also of necessity be some one to remind them of their duty and hold them in restraint.[54]

On the other hand, Catholics and Presbyterians adopted a substantially different approach. As explained by Suárez, a right to intervene in favour of oppressed

[47] Grotius (n 43) II, XXV, §8.
[48] ibid.
[49] ibid.
[50] ibid.
[51] ibid.
[52] Glanville (n 29) 35.
[53] Burns (n 32) 29–30.
[54] R Tuck, 'Grotius, Hobbes and Pufendorf on Humanitarian Intervention' in S Recchia and J Welsh (eds), *Just and Unjust Military Intervention: European Thinkers from Vitoria to Mill* (Cambridge University Press, 2013) 103.

people would exist only if a correspondent, internal right to react is recognised for the victim population:

> The reason for this limitation is that a wrong done to another does not give me the right to avenge him, unless he would be justified in avenging himself and actually proposes to do so. Assuming, however, that these conditions exist, my aid to him is an act of cooperation in a good and just deed; but if [the injured party] does not entertain such a wish, no one else may intervene, since he who committed the wrong has made himself subject not to every one indiscriminately, but only to the person who has been wronged. Wherefore, the assertion made by some writers, that sovereign kings have the power of avenging injuries done in any part of the world, is entirely false, and throws into confusion all the orderly distinctions of jurisdiction; for such power was not [expressly] granted by God and its existence is not to be inferred by any process of reasoning.[55]

During the nineteenth century, the central role of state sovereignty and the emergence of its corollary, the principle of non-intervention, obfuscated any references to the legitimacy of revolts.[56] International law adopted a neutral attitude towards rebellions, neither legitimising nor banning them. At the same time, the secularisation of the just war doctrine raised a crucial question: 'could war qualify as just on both sides?'[57]

B. The Right to Wage War

i. Emergence of the Right to War as a Prerogative of Sovereignty

For the Canonists, doubts on the just causes of war could be resolved by God. However, the secularisation that started towards the end of the Middle Ages challenged this approach: if sovereigns are subject to none, who has the last word on the justness of a *causa belli*?[58] Having recognised that both parties invoke just causes to wage war and that no superior authority could decide on which side resides justness, the only way to solve the *impasse* was to acknowledge the obsolescence of *bellum justum* doctrines and to recognise a general right to war attached to sovereignty.[59] States benefited from full discretion in deciding whether to use force: they could hence 'resort to war for a good reason, a bad reason, or no reason at all'.[60] If war was a prerogative of every

[55] Suárez (n 41) 817.

[56] F Mégret, 'Le Droit International Peut-il Etre un Droit de Résistance? Dix Conditions pour un Renouveau de l'Ambition Normative Internationale' (2008) 39(1) *Revue Études Internationales* 53.

[57] Dinstein (n 15) 68.

[58] Chesterman (n 38) 12–13.

[59] JL Brierly, 'International Law and Resort to Armed Force' (1932) 4(3) *The Cambridge Law Journal* 308.

[60] HW Briggs, *The Law of Nations. Cases, Documents, and Notes* (Appleton-Century-Crofts, 1952) 976. Some authors, such as Verosta, claim that even after the obsolescence of just war

sovereign state, international law did not have to investigate the justness of causes to use force, and it started focusing instead on the identification and the consequences of war.

It is against this backdrop that the law of belligerency and neutrality developed in the nineteenth and early twentieth centuries. At the time, war was perceived as a phenomenon outside the law, comparable to a natural disaster or plague.[61] Armed conflicts were thus inevitable and international law had 'no alternative but to accept war, independently of the justice of its origin, as a relation which the parties to it may set up if they choose'.[62] The use of force was considered an unavoidable event 'beyond the reach of international law … neither legal nor illegal':[63] '[w]ar is a fact recognized, and with regard to many points regulated, but not established, by International Law'.[64] The common position among scholars at the time was thus that international law could not regulate when states could lawfully wage war (*jus ad bellum*), but only how they could use force during the conduct of hostilities (*jus in bello*).[65] This approach to war led to a 'logical impossibility'.[66] On the one hand, states are the primary subjects of international law, members of the international community. On the other hand, by granting them the right to wage war with nearly no restrictions, international law put in jeopardy the primary interest of states, namely their very existence.[67]

ii. First Endeavours to Restrict the Right to War

The freedom to wage war led states to include a prohibition on using force in nearly all bilateral treaties concluded in the nineteenth century: instead of resolving differences forcibly, the parties assumed the obligation to seek the peaceful settlement of disputes.[68] However, the treaties presented limitations both *ratione*

doctrines states had to justify why they intended to wage war. However, the majority of scholars do not agree with this position, which does not seem to be confirmed by state practice. See eg S Verosta, 'The unlawfulness of wars of aggression before 1914' in E Bello and B Ajibola (eds), *Essays in Honour of Judge Taslim Olawale Elias*, vol 1 (Martinus Nijhoff, 1992) 117–24; Dinstein (n 15) 78.

[61] C Eagleton, *International Government* (The Ronald Press Company, 1957) 455; Q Wright, 'Changes in the Conception of War' (1924) 18(4) *American Journal of International Law* 761.

[62] Dinstein (n 15) 76.

[63] JL Brierly, *The Outlook for International Law* (Clarendon Press, 1944) 22.

[64] L Oppenheim, *International Law: A Treatise*, vol 2 (Longmans, 1952) 202.

[65] Dinstein (n 15) 77.

[66] Brierly (n 63) 21.

[67] Q Wright, 'The Present Status of Neutrality' (1940) 34(3) *American Journal of International Law* 399.

[68] See eg Tegucigalpa Treaty of Friendship, Commerce and Extradition, 1978 (Honduras and Nicaragua); Washington Treaty for the Establishment of a Permanent Commission of Enquiry, 1913 (Guatemala and United States); Locarno Treaty of Mutual Guarantee, 1925 (Belgium, France, Germany, Great Britain, Italy); Teheran Treaty of Friendship and Security, 1926 (Persia and Turkey). See Dinstein (n 15) 80.

personae and *ratione temporis*. First, they were applicable only between the contracting parties, thus in no way could they have any effect in their relationships with third states. Second, they had a fixed time limit, whose expiration would free the parties from the ban on the use of force. Furthermore, the temporal scope of application was also limited by the possibility granted to each party to terminate the treaty early.[69] One of the most famous attempts to regulate the use of force between states is the so-called Bryan treaties, adopted by the US at the beginning of the twentieth century. In case of dispute between the US and the other contracting party, the quarrel was to be submitted to a Commission that had to adopt a decision within one year. Anticipating the approach adopted by the League of Nations, the rationale underpinning this procedure was to introduce a 'cooling-off period'[70] in the hope that states would not use force impulsively. The idea that with time passions would calm down and states would not resort to war as a result was proved wrong: 'passage of time, far from cooling off hot tempers, may only exacerbate incipient tensions.'[71]

The provisions limiting the use of force among two or more states were adopted in a period when peace was maintained through a delicate 'system of weights and counter-weights'[72] which was dramatically destroyed with World War I. States soon acknowledged that a fragile balance of powers, coupled with bilateral agreements limiting the use of force, was not enough to maintain peace. It is against this backdrop that states decided to create the League of Nations (1919), the first multilateral endeavour 'to promote international co-operation and to achieve international peace and security'[73] through dispute settlement and collective security mechanisms.

Article 11 of the Covenant of the League of Nations provided that '[a]ny war or threat of war … is … a matter of concern to the whole League'. In case a dispute arose between members of the League, the states concerned were bound to submit the case 'either to arbitration or to inquiry by the Council' (Article 12); after the adoption of the decision, states had to wait three months before resorting to war. Furthermore, states had the possibility to submit the dispute to the Permanent Court of International Justice for a judicial settlement (Articles 13 and 14); in this case, war was not admissible against the state that had complied with the Court's decision. Last but not least, Article 15(8) established that if a dispute concerned 'a matter which by international law is solely within the domestic jurisdiction of that party', the Council should abstain from making any recommendations. In this case, the party concerned would be free to resolve the issue as it likes, resort to war included.[74]

[69] Dinstein (n 15) 79.

[70] A Zimmern, *The League of Nations and the Rule of Law, 1918–1935* (Macmillan, 1939) 129.

[71] Dinstein (n 15) 80.

[72] Rodogno (n 45) 19. See also PW Schroeder, *The Transformation of European Politics 1763–1848* (Oxford University Press, 1994).

[73] Covenant of the League of Nations (1924), preamble.

[74] E Lieblich, *International Law and Civil Wars: Intervention and Consent* (Routledge, 2013) 109.

Although the Covenant constitutes a valuable attempt to prevent war, it did not have a general scope of application, as only a limited, albeit significant, number of states were party to the Covenant. Most importantly, it did not prohibit the use of force per se, but simply distinguished between 'legal and illegal wars'.[75] Indeed, after an attempt at peaceful dispute settlement, states could still resort to the use of force. Therefore, the Covenant represented the positivist approach whereby war was an inevitable event, a crucial prerogative of sovereign states that could not be banned but only limited through specific procedures.[76] In order to fill the gaps left by the Covenant, shortly after its adoption states concluded the Geneva Protocol on the Pacific Settlement of International Disputes (1924), whose Article 2 banned the use of force, with the only exceptions being self-defence and the authorisation of the League of Nations' Council or Assembly. However, the endeavour to ban war did not succeed, as the Protocol did not enter into force.

A few years later, the Kellogg-Briand Pact, signed in Paris on 27 August 1928,[77] proved more successful. In the treaty, the parties 'condemn recourse to war for the solution of international controversies, and renounce it, as an instrument of national policy in their relations with one another' (Article 1). Furthermore, they agreed 'that the settlement or solution of all disputes or conflicts of whatever nature or of whatever origin they may be, which may arise among them, shall never be sought except by pacific means' (Article 1).

Banning the use of force with no exceptions, the Pact represented a positive step forward if compared to the League of Nations, but it still granted states a certain leeway. Indeed, lacking a definition of war, states could overcome the ban by resorting to armed force without formally declaring war or calling it as such.[78] This led to 'unforeseen consequences of the Kellogg Pact',[79] namely the conduct of 'undeclared wars'.[80] Furthermore, the parties renounced 'war as an instrument of national policy', but they failed to define the term 'national

[75] I Brownlie, *International Law and the Use of Force by States* (Oxford University Press, 1963) 57; E Borchard, 'War, Neutrality and Non-Belligerency' (1941) 35(4) *American Journal of International Law* 618–25; Brierly (n 59) 310.

[76] The limits of the League of Nations emerged during the Spanish civil war. See below, Section IIIC.

[77] General Treaty for Renunciation of War as an Instrument of National Policy (hereinafter Kellogg-Briand Pact) 1928.

[78] PM Brown, 'Editorial Comment: Undeclared Wars' (1939) 33 *American Journal of International Law* 540; O Schachter, 'The Right of States to Use Armed Force' (1984) 82(5) *Michigan Law Review* 1624.

[79] Brown (n 78) 540.

[80] ibid. Both the Covenant of the League of Nations and the Kellogg-Briand Pact outlawed war. However, during the first half of the twentieth century it became clear that states could simply engage in hostilities without declaring war. This is one of the reasons why the Charter of the United Nations (1945) specifically bans the use of force, and not war: 'the term *force* was a more factual and wider word to embrace military action'. See Schachter (n 78) 1624.

policy', thus leaving open the possibility to wage war as international policy.[81] Kelsen endorsed this approach when he claimed that 'a war which is a reaction against a violation of international law, and that means a war waged for the maintenance of international law, is considered an instrument of international and hence not of national policy'.[82] Last but not least, the Pact did not regulate measures short of war, hence forcible acts such as retaliations were not banned. The Kellogg-Briand pact did not constitute a replacement of the League of Nations: it was rather an attempt to fill the gaps of the League's Covenant, notably the absence of a more general proscription to wage war. In any case, the concomitant application of the two treaties did not have the force to prevent the outbreak of World War II.

II. THE EMERGENCE OF THE PRINCIPLE OF NON-INTERVENTION AS FUNDAMENTAL RULE PROTECTING SOVEREIGNTY

A. Ne Pas Se Mêler: The Principle of Non-intervention in the Eighteenth Century

The principle of non-intervention made its first appearance in the international law discourse only in the mid-eighteenth century. Christian Wolff (1679–1754) is credited with being the first to explicitly affirm the principle, which was grounded in natural law:

> By nature, no nation has the right to any act which belongs to the exercise of the sovereignty of another nation. For sovereignty as it exists in a people or originally in a nation is absolute.[83]

Central in Wolff's discourse is the idea that sovereignty reaches a level of perfection when it is exercised 'independently of the will of any other'.[84] However, Wolff does not draw the principle in an absolute fashion. In the German philosopher's view, states are members of a *civitas maxima*, a supreme state where 'the nations as a whole have a right to coerce the individual nations, if they should be unwilling to perform their obligation'.[85] Consequently, on the one hand, sovereignty implies a general right of non-intervention, on the other hand, sovereignty is limited by a fictional supreme state that could coercively force nations to comply with their obligations. Wolff's ideas on the right to conduct

[81] Dinstein (n 15) 86; L Kopelmanas, 'The Problem of Aggression and the Prevention of War' (1937) 31(2) *American Journal of International Law* 246; H Wehberg and EH Zeydel, *The Outlawry of War* (Carnegie Endowment for International Peace, 1931) 76.
[82] H Kelsen, *Principles of International Law* (Rinehart & Company, 1952) 43.
[83] C Wolff, *Jus Gentium Methodo Scientifica Pertractatum* (Clarendon Press, 1934) §ii.255.
[84] ibid.
[85] ibid.

war as punishment are consistent with this approach: whenever a state suffers an injury not otherwise reparable, it has the right to use force against the state that committed the offence.[86]

Emer de Vattel (1714–67) is the author who more extensively focused on the inviolability of the internal affairs of nations. He wanted to distance himself from both Wolff's *civitas maxima* and Thomas Hobbes' (1588–1679) idea that states cannot be bound by any obligation and are immune from temporal accountability.[87] To this end, Vattel described the international community as a 'society of independent states'[88] governed by the law of nations, which he defined as sovereigns: 'free and independent states' that he considered as 'moral persons.'[89] Taking a different approach to previous discourses on natural law, present for instance in Grotius, Vattel grounded the law of nations on the will of states: he adopted a positivist approach, whereby states consent to the law which binds them.[90]

Sovereignty implies the right to be free from external interference: no country has the right to intervene in the internal affairs of other states. In the words of Vattel, 'enfin, toutes ces choses [i.e. the internal affairs of the state] n'intéressant que la Nation, aucune Puissance Etrangère n'est en droit de s'en mêler ni ne doit y intervenir'.[91] Despite the fact that Vattel clearly articulated the right of non-intervention as a corollary of state sovereignty, he also admitted the right to wage war in two circumstances.[92] Drawing upon precedent scholars, he recognised in each nation the right to use force to punish a state that committed an injury and the right to intervene in favour of oppressed populations.[93] However, in contrast with the ideas of Bodin and Grotius, he claimed that people subject to tyranny have the right to resist their sovereign: 'those monsters who, under the title of sovereigns, render themselves the scourges and horror of the human race … are savage beasts, whom every brave man justly exterminate from the face of the earth'.[94]

Vattel's thought has to be read in light of the mainstream theories of his contemporaries. For centuries, a corollary of sovereignty has been the right to wage war and scholars devoted their efforts to identify when the use of force

[86] ibid, §636.

[87] ibid, §637. See also Chesterman (n 38) 17.

[88] E de Vattel, *The Law of Nations: Principles of the Law of Nature, Applied to the Conduct and Affairs of Nations and Sovereign* (Clarendon Press, 1758) i.i.12.

[89] Glanville (n 29) 56.

[90] ibid, 57.

[91] de Vattel (n 88) vol. 1. See also R Sapienza, *La guerra civile nell'evoluzione del diritto internazionale* (Editpress, 2010) 43.

[92] According to de Vattel, waging war was one of the main prerogatives of state sovereignty. As explained by Bartelson to de Vattel, 'as long as the ruler is capable of defending the self-interest of his state in this way, his authority cannot be challenged on any legal grounds'. See Bartelson (n 22) 94. See also Rauert (n 39) 98–100.

[93] de Vattel (n 88) xiii, §169.

[94] ibid, ii.iv, §56.

was just. Thus it should not be surprising if in Vattel the tension between non-intervention and the right to wage war is strikingly present: sovereignty has to be protected from external interference; nonetheless, it also implies a right to use force. As noted by Wright, 'International Law suffer[ed] a fatal inconsistency'[95] inasmuch as it accepted the coexistence of a rule aimed at preserving the existence of the international community – the principle of non-intervention – and another which threatens to jeopardise the existence of states – the right to wage war. However, at the time scholars did not consider the discrepancy to be problematic.[96]

B. The Principle of Non-intervention in the Nineteenth Century

In the nineteenth century, the principle of non-intervention meant 'an often hybrid politico-military process, a coercive and unrequested political and/or forcible action of some kind by an outside state (or states), laying at the intersection between peace and war'.[97] It is impossible to understand the role played by this principle without analysing the international legal order in force at the time. During the nineteenth and the beginning of the twentieth centuries, the concepts of sovereignty and civilisation were strictly connected. As European states were aiming to maximise their influence in the colonies, lawyers provided the legal basis to pursue this objective by dividing the world into civilised, half-civilised, and barbarous communities.[98] Highlighting cultural differences between Europe and the rest of the world, legal scholars concluded European culture was superior to any other: it alone, based on Christianity, was deemed to be civilised and thus it 'held the legitimate authority to control those of the other two spheres'.[99] In 1894, Westlake, one of the most prominent scholars at the time, affirmed that:

> International law has to treat natives as uncivilised. It regulates, for the mutual benefit of the civilised states, the claims which they make to sovereignty over the region and leaves the treatment of the natives to the conscience of the state to which sovereignty is awarded.[100]

This distinction between civilised and uncivilised communities implied that only the first were sovereign nations. This led to two crucial consequences: first, the law of nations did not apply to non-European countries, as they were not sovereigns. Second, as the principle of non-intervention was a corollary

[95] Wright (n 67) 399.
[96] Dinstein (n 15) 79.
[97] Rodogno (n 45) 20.
[98] ibid, 48; M Koskenniemi, *The Gentle Civilizer of Nations: The Rise and Fall of International Law 1870–1960* (Cambridge University Press, 2004) 127; J Westlake, *Chapters on the Principles of International Law* (Cambridge University Press, 1894) 101.
[99] Rodogno (n 45) 48.
[100] Westlake (n 98) 143; Koskenniemi (n 98) 127.

of sovereignty, only civilised countries would be protected by this principle.[101] This position was maintained by John Stuart Mill (1806–73) in his seminal essay *A Few Words on Non-intervention*, where he explained that 'barbarians have no rights as a nation, except a right to such treatment as may, at the earliest possible period, fit them for becoming one'.[102] The British philosopher explained that the reason why the rules governing civilised nations cannot apply to barbarous entities is twofold. First, such rules demand reciprocity, 'but barbarians will not reciprocate'.[103] Second, non-civilised nations would benefit from foreign domination, as it would lead them towards a civilisation process.[104]

With regard to the international relations of European countries, Mill was very clear in excluding any form of intervention. Nevertheless, he recognised that people fighting for liberty against a tyrant presents 'conflicting moral considerations'.[105] Reflections on people taking up arms against oppression were already present in *bellum justum* doctrines, when the majority of scholars accepted the use of force in favour of an oppressed population as *justa causa belli*. During the nineteenth century, interference in a European country was not conceivable. However, intervention was admissible against uncivilised and half-civilised entities.[106] In line with the ideas of contemporary authors, Mill excluded the possibility to intervene in a civilised country in favour of opposition groups fighting against their ruler. However, he wondered whether it would be lawful to help the government in such circumstances, and concluded that:

> Assistance to the government of a country in keeping down the people, unhappily by far the most frequent case of foreign intervention, no one writing in a free country needs take the trouble of stigmatizing. A government which needs foreign support to enforce obedience from its own citizens, is one which ought not to exist; and the assistance given to it by foreigners is hardly ever anything but the sympathy of one despotism with another.[107]

[101] H. Steiger, 'From the International Law of Christianity to the International Law of the World Citizen – Reflections on the Formation of the Epochs of the History of International Law' (2001) 3(2) *Journal of the History of International Law* 187; J Hornung, 'Civilisés et Barbares' (1885) 17 *Revue de droit international et de législation comparée* 447–70; A Anghie, *Imperialism, Sovereignty and the Making of International Law* (Cambridge University Press, 2004) 59; J Pitts, 'Boundaries of Victorian International Law' in *Victorian Visions of Global Order: Empire and International Relations in Nineteenth-Century Political Thought* (Cambridge University Press, 2007) 67–70.

[102] JS Mill, 'A Few Words on Non-Intervention' (1859) 8 *Foreign Policy Perspectives* 5. See also MW Doyle, 'A Few Words on Mill, Walzer, and Nonintervention' (2010) 23(4) *Ethics & International Affairs* 349–69. According to Doyle, Mill 'is among the first to address the conundrums of modern intervention' (see ibid, 350).

[103] Mill (n 102) 4.

[104] ibid; see also Lieblich (n 74) 106.

[105] Mill (n 102) 5.

[106] Koskenniemi (n 98) 114; Rodogno (n 45) 47–50.

[107] Mill (n 102) 5.

The majority of lawyers at the time backed the idea that full sovereignty and its corollary principle of non-intervention pertain only to civilised nations and justified on this basis Western interferences in barbarous countries. Nevertheless, few authors recognised the hypocrisy behind this approach. Notably, the Swiss lawyer Joseph Hornung (1857–1931) heavily criticised the actions of European countries in the colonies, as well as the double standard of the principle of non-intervention. Indeed, if an intervention in favour of the Christian population oppressed by the Ottoman Empire was deemed to be lawful, the same should have been possible in cases of African and Asian populations brutally dominated by European countries.[108] Nonetheless, Hornung did admit that colonisation was justified, 'but only in the interests of the colonizer'.[109] Even authors who tried to denounce European states' actions in the colonies never went as far as to overcome the distinction between civilised and uncivilised countries. Nonetheless, nearly all lawyers accepted that non-European individuals enjoyed humanitarian or natural rights:[110] barbarous populations did not find themselves outside the juridical community, as it encompasses humanity as a whole.[111] As a result, they could enjoy certain human rights 'regardless of the degree of civilization of their communities',[112] but these rights did not extend to their communities.

While the discourse on natural rights was starting to emerge among scholars, the idea of intervention to protect oppressed people was revived in the works of European lawyers. Clearly not an option in European countries, interventions for humanity were welcomed by some scholars, in particular in favour of Christian minorities in the Ottoman Empire.[113] Polygamy, slavery, and the high degree of corruption were amongst the reasons why it was considered a barbarous country, thus not protected by the principle of non-intervention.[114] Bluntschli explained that a forcible intervention would have been admissible when directed to protect the individual rights of oppressed people: European countries had the responsibility to develop and ensure the respect of rights of

[108] Hornung (n 101) 449–450.

[109] Koskenniemi (n 98) 129.

[110] P Fiore, *Le droit international codifié et sa sanction juridique* (Pedone, 1890); P Fiore, 'La science du droit international: Horizons nouveaux' (1909) XVI *Revue Générale de Droit International* 469, where the author explained that natural rights are 'eux qui ont leur fondement dans la nature des êtres, tels qu'ils existent suivant l'ensemble des exigences indispensables pour que l'être puisse conserver et défendre les caractères essentiels et distinctifs qui constituent sa nature comme tel. Ces exigences ne se trouvent écrites dans aucun code, mais sont intuitives, induites et déduites par la raison humaine qui, considérant la nature des êtres tels qu'ils sont (comme un fait historique), comprend et détermine l'ensemble des conditions, qui doivent se réaliser pour que l'être maintienne sans altération sa nature comme tel'.

[111] ibid, 478.

[112] Koskenniemi (n 98) 128.

[113] HH Weathon, *Elements of International Law* (Sampson Low, Son & Co., 1866) II, I, §10. See also S Chesterman (n 38) 24.

[114] Rodogno (n 45) 41–42.

humanity. As the Ottoman Christians were an oppressed minority, they 'had successfully provoked foreign interventions several times'.[115] Some scholars opposed a right to humanitarian intervention, highlighting the high risk of abuse: '[f]oreign intervention, even when triggered by apparent humanitarian reasons, achieved only platonic objectives and was always superseded by the self-interests of the intervening states'.[116] Nonetheless, this did not prevent European countries from intervening in the name of humanity in the Ottoman Empire.[117]

In light of the foregoing, it is fairly clear that the principle of non-intervention has always been strictly connected with sovereignty. At the moment when the right to wage war was recognised as a nearly unlimited prerogative of sovereign entities, Wolff and Vattel recognised the necessity to protect the *domaine réservé* of states. However, this principle was limited on two fronts. On the one hand, the right to wage war had never been disputed. Even attempts to limit the use of force, such as the Kellogg-Briand Pact and the League of Nations, never outlawed war, but simply set procedures in order to (try to) avoid it. When such procedures failed, states were free to use force. On the other hand, the principle of non-intervention could protect only sovereign entities, namely civilised nations. As a consequence, it was never seen as an absolute prerogative, applicable worldwide. Nonetheless, it did play a role with regard to interference in civil wars, as well as during the forcible interventions portrayed by European countries in the Ottoman Empire as aimed at protecting Christian populations.

III. INTERVENTIONS IN INTERNAL CONFLICTS BEFORE THE GENERAL BAN ON THE USE OF FORCE

During the nineteenth century, the medieval distinction between *bellum publicum*, namely inter-state war, and *bellum privatum*, ie internal conflict, was still valid.[118] Sovereignty meant states' freedom to exercise their power over the people under their jurisdiction. As explained before, Wolff and Vattel recognised that a corollary of sovereignty was the principle of non-intervention in the internal affairs of the state. Internal conflicts were deemed to fall within states' *domaine réservé* and thus considered as mere internal matters. This led to two crucial consequences.

[115] ibid, 57; JC Bluntschli, *Le Droit International Codifié* (Guillaumin, 1870) § 478.
[116] Rodogno (n 45) 58; F Despagnet, *Cours de Droit international public* (Larose & Forcel, 1905).
[117] Several humanitarian interventions took place in the nineteenth century, such as the interventions in Greece (1821–33), the Ottoman Lebanon and Syria (1860–61), and Crete (1896–1900). See Rodogno (n 45); B Simms and DJB Trim (eds), *Humanitarian Intervention: A History* (Cambridge University Press, 2011) 111–226.
[118] Sapienza (n 91) 137.

First, the law governing armed conflicts did not apply to clashes between the state and insurgents. Indeed, 'la guerre civile est étrangère au droit international, qui ne s'occupe que des rapports entre Etats indépendants'.[119] Consequently, internal conflicts were regulated only by domestic law: international law was silent on the right to embrace arms against the sovereign or on the rules governing such conflicts. Second, foreign countries were bound by the principle of non-intervention, thus they had to abstain from any interference in the internal affairs of the state, insurrections included.[120] However, situations where rebels were supported by foreign countries did occur, perhaps encouraged by the fact that international rules governing internal conflict were nearly non-existent at the time.[121] The interests of third states could be compromised by a civil war. For instance, the security of foreign citizens and goods in the country facing the conflict would have been jeopardised. Furthermore, a third country could have been interested in the outcome of the conflict, hoping for the victory of the party in line with its political orientations.[122] Consequently, foreign interferences were not uncommon and contributed to the emergence of the belligerency and insurgency doctrines, which will be analysed in turn.

A. Recognition of Belligerency

In the nineteenth and early twentieth centuries, the belligerency doctrine was the prevailing rule with regard to internal conflicts. The American War of Independence against Great Britain (1776–81) was the first case when the rebels were granted a certain degree of recognition. Upon the request of Great Britain, the laws of war were applied during the conflict, while the majority of foreign countries maintained neutral relationships with the parties to it. These circumstances were a novelty, given that the laws of war and neutrality were meant to regulate international conflicts. Furthermore, France and Spain intervened in favour of the colonies, thus breaching the principle of non-intervention in the internal affairs of states, while Portugal joined in on Great Britain's side.[123]

[119] Despagnet (n 115) 536. See also P Fauchille, *Traité de droit international public* (Rousseau & Cie, 1921), who clarified that: '[i]l faut distinguer suivant que la guerre est internationale ou civile. La guerre internationale est seule soumise aux lois de la guerre'.

[120] Sapienza (n 91) 137–38.

[121] E Castrén, *Civil War* (Suomalainen Tiedeakatemia, 1966) 39.

[122] Sapienza (n 91) 138.

[123] The first legal document concerning the American war of independence was a law adopted by the British Parliament, whereby the inhabitants of the 13 colonies where defined as rebels and every commercial relationship with them was banned. According to some scholars, this law constituted an implicit declaration of war. At the outbreak of the war, Great Britain intended to apply the law of armed conflicts, which regulated only international wars at the time, a suggestion that was favourably accepted by Washington. See J Siotis, *Le Droit de la Guerre et les Conflits Armés d'un Caractère Non-international* (Librairie Générale de Droit et de Jurisprudence, 1958) 54–61.

The first explicit recognition of rebels took place during the war of independence of the Spanish colonies in America (1810–24). In 1820 Bolivar, at the head of Colombian insurgents, concluded a treaty of armistice and one regarding the regulation of warfare with Spain.[124] This is particularly significant: concluding a treaty with the rebels implies recognising them as at least partially subjects of international law. Insurgents were recognised by the US and Great Britain respectively in 1817 and 1823, and both countries applied the rules of neutrality. On the other hand, Austria and Russia, members of the Holy Alliance, immediately condemned the actions of the colonies and planned an intervention in favour of Spain, although it never took place.[125] The war of independence of the Spanish colonies is notable inasmuch as it was the first time that insurgents were granted the status of belligerents. At the time, this narrative was new and still not clearly distinguished from the recognition of new states, and the first was often considered as a premise for the latter.[126]

Subsequent state practice contributed to the establishment of the recognition of belligerency, which turned into a consolidated practice by the end of the nineteenth century. It consisted in a 'declaration, expressed or implied, that hostilities waged between two communities … are of such character and scope as to entitle the parties to be treated as belligerents engaged in a war in the sense ordinarily attached to that term by international law'.[127] The recognition could have been granted by the government fighting the opposition group, as well as by third states. Nevertheless, the criteria for determining when rebels could be granted the status of belligerents were not clear-cut. To resolve the issue, the *Institut de Droit International* adopted a Resolution clarifying the content of the customary rules developed by the practice of states. Notably, the opposition group could not be recognised as belligerents:

(1) S'il n'a pas conquis une existence territoriale distincte par la possession d'une partie déterminée du territoire national.
(2) S'il n'a pas réuni les éléments d'un gouvernement régulier exerçant en fait sur cette partie du territoire les droits apparents de la souveraineté.
(3) Si la lutte n'est pas conduite en son nom par des troupes organisées, soumises à la discipline militaire et se conformant aux lois et coutumes de la guerre.[128]

[124] Castrén (n 121) 40–41.
[125] Siotis (n 123) 70.
[126] Castrén (n 121) 41.
[127] Lieblich (n 74) 77.
[128] Institut de Droit International (IDI), *Droits et devoirs des Puissances étrangères, au cas de mouvement insurrectionnel, envers les gouvernements établis et reconnus qui sont aux prises avec l'insurrection* (hereinafter *Droits et devoirs des Puissances étrangères*), Session de Neuchâtel, 8 September 1900, Art 8. See also A Cullen, *The Concept of Non-International Armed Conflict in International Humanitarian Law* (Cambridge University Press, 2010) 19–20; VA O'Rurke, 'Recognition of Belligerency and the Spanish Civil War' (1937) 31(3) *American Journal of International Law* 401–402; RR Oglesby, *Internal War and the Search for Normative Order* (Martinus Nijhoff, 1971) 62–69.

Central to the recognition of belligerency was thus the effectiveness of the insurgents. This position was put forward for the first time by the US during the war of independence fought by Spanish colonies in Latin America: according to the US, 'belligerence was a question of fact obliging third states to maintain an attitude of neutrality when war in fact existed'.[129] This approach was utterly in contrast with the position maintained by the Holy Alliance, which affirmed that 'the rebels could not in any case be treated on an equal footing with the parent government, not even in matters concerning the conduct of hostilities'.[130]

The consequences of the recognition varied depending on the party that granted the belligerent status to rebels. In case of recognition by the government, the main consequence was the application of the law governing armed conflicts.[131] Warfare was regulated at the international level and as such its scope of application was limited to inter-state wars. The recognition thus meant an acknowledgment that the conflict had reached an intensity comparable with international conflicts.[132] Prior to recognition, only domestic law applied to the insurrection, hence rebels were considered as mere criminals. After the recognition, members of the opposition group could benefit from the law regulating warfare, which concerned not only the conduct of hostilities per se, but extended also to the status of prisoners of war. Consequently, rebels could 'no longer be punished, either during the civil war or after its conclusion, for participating in the fighting'.[133]

The recognition of belligerency was hence more advantageous for the rebels than for the government. Indeed, it had the effect of reducing the 'legal inequality' between the parties.[134] Why then would the sovereign have granted to rebels such an appealing status? First, after the recognition, the law of war would have bound both parties. Therefore, members of the state's army could have expected a better treatment from the rebels – at least in theory.[135] Furthermore, Moir noted that the government could have had other interests, in particular with regard to foreign shipping.[136] Indeed, in such cases the incumbent government was 'relieved from responsibility for acts done in the insurgent territory; its blockade of its own ports [was] respected; and it

[129] RR Oglesby (n 128) 16–17.
[130] ibid.
[131] See IDI, *Droits et devoirs des Puissances étrangères*, Art 4. In any case, the recognition by the government did not have any effect on third states; see ibid, Arts 5–6.
[132] Castrén (n 121) 152; Cullen (n 128) 16.
[133] Castrén (n 121) 156; O'Rurke (n 128) 399–400.
[134] L Moir, *The Law of Internal Armed Conflict* (Cambridge University Press, 2002) 10; Oppenheim (n 64) 66; J Stone, *Legal Controls of International Conflict: A Treatise on the Dynamics of Disputes and War Law* (Stevens & Sons, 1959) 305.
[135] Moir (n 134) 10. Castrén noted that: '[t]he struggle is a mutual matter involving reciprocity between the contending sides. It is for the lawful government to determine the exact moment for according recognition (if it be accorded), but should the insurgents be unwilling to observe the rules of war, the recognition has little value.' See Castrén (n 121) 140.
[136] Moir (n 134) 10–11.

acquired a right to exert, against neutral commerce, all the powers of a party to a maritime war'.[137] Last but not least, extensive recognition of belligerency by foreign countries could have led the incumbent government to recognise the rebels as well.[138]

Recognition of belligerency by a third state implied that it could 'consider the parties to civil war belligerents in the meaning of international law', so that opposition groups achieved 'the same status as States in an international war'.[139] Furthermore, as explained by the IDI, '[s]i la belligérance est reconnue par les Puissances tierces, cette reconnaissance produit tous les effets ordinaires de la neutralité'.[140] The law of neutrality implied that the state recognising the opposition group could not provide support to any of the parties to the conflict.[141] This circumstance would have serious consequences for the government facing a civil war. For instance, prior to recognition transfers of arms were unlawful only to rebels and permitted in favour of the government; on the contrary, after the recognition transferring arms to any parties to the conflict was unlawful.[142]

As aforementioned, internal conflicts were considered a matter pertaining to the *domaine réservé* of states. However, civil wars could have an impact on foreign countries. This might not have been the case when the conflict was conducted only on land. Nonetheless, in case the hostilities extended to the sea, they could entail significant implications for foreign countries. As explained by Wheaton:

> Where the insurgents and the parent state are maritime, and the foreign nation has extensive commercial relations and trade at the ports of both, and the foreign nation and either or both of the contending parties have considerable naval force, and the domestic contest must extend itself over the sea … the liability to political complications, and the questions of right and duty to be decided at once, usually away from home, by private citizens or naval officers, seem to require an authoritative and general decision as to the status of the three parties involved.[143]

Thus the recognition of belligerency mainly developed due to practical reasons of necessity, in order to deal with situations that, despite their internal nature, were capable of affecting third states.[144] In any case, neutrality was only an option for foreign countries: in an era where war was a crucial prerogative pertaining to sovereignty, the possibility to use force against the government,

[137] Weathon (n 113) 37.
[138] Moir (n 134) 8.
[139] Castrén (n 121) 168.
[140] IDI, *Droits et devoirs des Puissances étrangères*, Art 7.
[141] A. Möller, *International Law in Peace and War, Part II* (Levin & Munksgaard, 1935); S Sivakumaran, *The Law of Non-International Armed Conflict* (Oxford University Press, 2014) 15.
[142] O'Rurke (n 128) 409.
[143] Weathon (n 113) 35.
[144] M Bernard, *A Historical Account of the Neutrality of Great Britain during the American Civil War* (Applewood Books, 1870) 113–14.

hence supporting the rebels, was always open. As explained above, neutrality was useful for foreign countries as it granted them protection, especially in maritime situations. However, by no means was it an obligation: 'a third state could choose to exercise its war prerogative and intervene forcefully *regardless* of belligerency recognition or its absence'.[145]

Despite the fact that recognition of belligerency was fairly common during the nineteenth century, state practice was at times contradictory. The reason could be found in the highly political value of recognition. Being a discretionary power, states could decide whether to grant the status of belligerent or not depending on political and self-interest considerations.[146] Rebels could have been prematurely recognised – as was the case for Greek rebels fighting against the Ottoman Empire (1821–29)[147] – or not recognised notwithstanding the presence of all the required criteria.[148] This inconsistent attitude is easily explained by taking into consideration the implications of the recognition: in case of victory of the opposition group, a foreign state would have benefited from recognising it during the civil war. However, a conflict with the opposite result could have had irremediably compromised the relationship between the two countries.[149]

B. Recognition of Insurgency

The recognition of belligerency was useful for practical reasons: it was not only a way to express support to the rebels, but also a practice capable of clarifying the positions of the third parties to the conflict and to preserve their commerce. Nevertheless, there were cases when the intensity of the conflict or the organisation of the opposition group were not enough to justify the recognition of belligerency, or when such recognition was not desirable for other reasons. As already explained, granting the status of belligerent party to the rebels would have jeopardised the relationship with the government; furthermore, it would have affected trade, especially at sea. Nevertheless, foreign countries could have considered it useful or necessary to grant certain rights to the rebels. States thus developed the practice of the recognition of insurgency.[150]

[145] Lieblich (n 74) 80.

[146] Discussing the motives which could lead a third country to grant the status of belligerent, Weathon posited that: 'the reason which requires and can alone justify this step by the government of another country is that its own rights and interests are so far affected as to require a definition of its own relations to the parties.' See Weathon (n 113) 35.

[147] Castrén (n 121) 42.

[148] This was the case during the Polish rebellion against Russia (1830); see Sapienza (n 91) 140.

[149] Weathon (n 113) 34–37; Moir, *The Law of Internal Armed Conflict* (n 134) 8–9.

[150] Castrén, (n 121) 207; Lieblich (n 74) 82–83; RR Wilson, 'Recognition of Insurgency and Belligerency' (1937) 31 *Proceedings of the American Society of International Law at Its Annual Meeting (1921–1969)* 138.

During an internal conflict, rebels' ships did not sail under internationally recognised flags, as they did not intend to use the flag of the government they were fighting. As a result, opposition groups which were not recognised as belligerents would have been considered as pirates, ie *hostis humani generis*. However, the US deemed such a conclusion unacceptable and unjustified, as rebels lacked the *animus furandi* and were moved by political reasons.[151] Therefore, they started developing the recognition of insurgency for cases when the conflict did not meet the criteria for granting rebels the status of belligerents.[152] US Secretary of State Hamilton Fish was the first to introduce this original narrative during the Haitian civil war (1867–70).[153] However, it was only with the Cuban conflict that the practice was utilised. On 6 December 1869, US President Ulysses S Grant specified that:

> The contest has at no time assumed the conditions which amount to war in the sense of international law or which show the existence of a *de facto* political organization of the insurgents sufficient to justify a recognition of belligerency.[154]

Nevertheless, the exceptional circumstances of the conflict and considerations of humanity pushed for the application of the laws of neutrality. As these were not applicable without a recognition of belligerency, and since this was not an option because not all the criteria were met, the US decided to resort to the recognition of insurgency.[155] This decision was then acknowledged by the Supreme Court in the *Three Friends* case (1897), where the Court concluded that:

> The political department has not recognized the existence of a *de facto* belligerent power engaged in hostility in Spain, but has recognized the existence of insurrectionary warfare prevailing before, at the time and since this forfeiture is alleged to have been incurred. … We are thus judicially informed of the existence of an actual conflict of arms in peace and amity, although acknowledgment of the insurgents as belligerents by the political department has not taken place; and it can not be doubled that, this being so, the act in question [the neutrality statute] is applicable.[156]

During the years following the Cuban civil war, the US extensively resorted to the practice of recognition of insurgency, applying it mainly during the Latin American wars against Spain. Notably, during the Colombian insurrection (1885–86), the Secretary of State acknowledged the measures adopted by the opposition group in order to prevent goods from reaching Spain.[157] In the same vein, during the civil wars in Chile (1891) and Brazil (1893), Great

[151] Oglesby (n 128) 22; RR Wilson, 'Insurgency and International Maritime Law' (1907) 1(1) *American Journal of International Law* 47.
[152] Siotis (n 123) 208.
[153] ibid, 120.
[154] ibid, 91.
[155] Castrén (n 121) 209; Siotis (n 123) 91–103; JH Beale, 'The Recognition of Cuban Belligerency' (1896) 9(6) *Harvard Law Review* 406–19.
[156] US Supreme Court, *United States v The Three Friends et al* (1897) 166 US 1.
[157] Siotis (n 123) 122.

Britain and the US recognised some measures adopted by the rebels, such as blockades, despite the fact that they did not intend to recognise the status of belligerents.[158]

The recognition of insurgency consisted of the admission of the existence of a civil war of significant level, which led to the attribution of certain rights and duties to the rebels.[159] The main difference between insurgency and belligerency, as highlighted by Lauterpacht, is the vast flexibility of the first practice, inasmuch as it granted states the possibility to decide the *quantum* of consequences to be connected with it.[160] The recognition of insurgency was thus a useful instrument for foreign states, as they could recognise the existence of a conflict and have an ad hoc relationship with the rebels without necessarily applying the laws of neutrality, as the latter were an automatic consequence only in the case of a recognition of belligerency.[161] On the other hand, the rebels benefited from the recognition, as it was a sign of attention, and possibly sympathy, for their cause at the international level.[162]

C. The Spanish Civil War and the Failure of the Recognition Doctrines

As we have seen, in the nineteenth century, international law recognised three stages of armed violence within a country. Rebellion was a less intense insurrection that the government could overcome relatively easily, ie 'situations of internal disturbances and tensions, such as riots, isolated and sporadic acts of violence and other acts of a similar nature' (Article 1(2) of the Additional Protocol II).[163] This situation remained domestic in character and thus there

[158] Castrén (n 121) 210. Despite the fact that the practice was mainly developed by the US, European states used it during the Spanish Civil War. However, as we shall see, it is exactly this conflict that signalled the failure of the recognition of belligerency and insurgency.

[159] RA Falk, 'Janus Tormented: The International Law of Internal War' in JN Rosenau (ed), *International Aspects of Civil Strife* (Princeton University Press, 1964) 199.

[160] H Lauterpacht, *Recognition in International Law* (Cambridge University Press, 1947) 276–77: '[a]ny attempt to lay down the conditions of recognition of insurgency leads itself to misunderstanding. Recognition of insurgency creates a factual relation in the meaning that legal rights and duties as between insurgents and outside States exist only in so far as they are expressly conceded and agreed upon for reasons of convenience, of humanity, or of economic interest'.

[161] For Falk, the recognition of insurgency 'serves as a partial internationalization of the conflict, without bringing the State of belligerency into being. This permits third States to participate in an internal war without finding themselves at war, which would be the consequence of intervention on either side once the internal war had been identified as a State of belligerency. Interventionary participation in an insurgency may arouse protest and hostile response, but it does not involve the hazards and inconveniences that arise if a State of war is established with one or the other faction' (Falk (n 159) 200). See also Cullen (n 128) 10–13.

[162] The recognition of insurgency was mainly used by third countries. However, in theory also governments fighting against the rebels could have recurred to it. See Castrén (n 121) 215–18; Lauterpacht (n 160) 276–77.

[163] Protocol Additional to the Geneva Conventions of 12 August 1949, and relating to the Protection of Victims of Non-International Armed Conflicts (Protocol II), 8 June 1977 (hereinafter, Additional Protocol II).

was no foreign involvement in the conflict.[164] The second stage was insurgency, intended as a more substantial threat to the incumbent government. The opposition group was sufficiently organised and the scale of violence reached a higher level as compared to simple rebellions. Due to the intensity of the conflict, foreign countries could not always remain indifferent, and they could thus decide to recognise the rebels as insurgents.[165] Lastly, a conflict reached the status of belligerency when it met certain criteria, namely intensity, territorial control by rebels, organisation of the parties, and respect for the law of war.[166] One can draw a comparison between this practice and the scope of application of the Additional Protocol II to the Geneva Conventions:

> This Protocol … shall apply to all armed conflicts … which take place in the territory of a High Contracting Party between its armed forces and dissident armed forces or other organized armed groups which, under responsible command, exercise such control over a part of its territory as to enable them to carry out sustained and concerted military operations and to implement this Protocol.[167]

Common to the recognition of belligerency and insurgency was their discretionary nature: they would allow states to internationalise an otherwise internal matter and to grant an international status to opposition groups. However, the Spanish Civil War revealed their limits and highlighted their obsolescence.

On 17 July 1936, a rebellion started in the Spanish African Territories and spread to Spain, quickly turning into a civil war.[168] On 9 August 1936, the government announced that the captured insurgents would be granted prisoner of war status and declared the areas affected by the rebellion as zones of war and subject to blockade. Despite the fact that these decisions could be interpreted as recognising the status of belligerents to the insurgents, Madrid did not grant such status formally.[169] Several neighbouring countries took sides in the conflict. On the one hand, Portugal, Italy, and Germany sent troops and weapons to the Franco-Nationalists; on the other hand, France and the Soviet Union helped the incumbent government both financially and by sending fighters. Due to the worrying escalation of European countries' involvement, the French Prime Minister suggested concluding a non-intervention agreement, which

[164] Moir (n 134) 4; Falk (n 159) 197: '[r]ebellion is supposed to be invoked in response to a sporadic challenge to the legitimate government'.

[165] Lauterpacht (n 160) 270–71.

[166] See IDI (n 128); Lieblich (n 74) 79.

[167] Additional Protocol II, Art 1(1).

[168] See NJ Padelford, 'International Law and the Spanish Civil War' (1937) 31(2) *American Journal of International Law* 227: '[t]he line of demarcation between rebellion or revolution and civil war may often be drawn only with difficulty and by reference to a concrete situation. Properly speaking, civil war is present when, in addition to the prerequisites of insurrection and rebellion, hostilities between organized and disciplined forces are conducted on the basis of military science, tactics, and regulations, with the winning of specific military objectives as the immediate goal of the fighting'.

[169] ibid, 226–29.

was signed by 27 states.[170] The International Committee for the Application of the Agreement Regarding Non-intervention in Spain was then established in London.[171] Nevertheless, foreign involvement in the civil war remained significant: on 19 November 1936, Italy and Germany recognised Franco's regime as the *de jure* government; furthermore, they did not interrupt their material help to Franco's forces, notwithstanding the fact that they signed the Non-intervention Agreement.[172] On the other hand, France and the UK maintained a close relationship with the Republican government.[173]

The utility of the Non-intervention Agreement has often been questioned by scholars.[174] Upon the outbreak of an internal conflict, international law imposed on states a strict policy of non-interference; in case the situation reached a sufficient degree of intensity, third countries could have proceeded with the recognition of belligerency or insurgency. A non-intervention agreement could thus appear as unnecessary. Nonetheless, it was valuable insofar as European countries consented to a common policy whose aim was to maintain peace.[175] As noted by Falk: '[t]he Spanish Civil War marked the end of any prospect of insulating a civil war situation from the overall currents of world politics'.[176] The recognition of belligerency and insurgency thus proved obsolete, unable to provide the legal framework necessary to develop the new values emerging in the international community. The maintenance of peace was on the rise as the basis of the international system, together with the importance of giving 'the

[170] NJ Padelford, 'The International Non-Intervention Agreement and the Spanish Civil War' (1937) 31(4) *American Journal of International Law* 579.

[171] B Aguilera-Barchet, *A History of Western Public Law: Between Nation and State* (Springer, 2015) 593–96; A de Zayas, 'Spanish Civil War (1936–39)' *Max Planck Encyclopedia of Public International Law* (Oxford University Press, 2013).

[172] JW Garner, 'Recognition of Belligerency' (1938) 32(1) *American Journal of International Law* 106–13; WC Askew, 'Italian Intervention in Spain: The Agreement of March 31, 1934 with the Spanish Monarchist Parties' (1952) 24(2) *The Journal of Modern History* 181–83; BR Sullivan, 'Fascist Italy's Military Involvement in the Spanish Civil War' (1995) 59(4) *The Journal of Military History* 697–727.

[173] NJ Padelford, 'Foreign Shipping During the Spanish Civil War' (1938) 32(2) *American Journal of International Law* 264–79. See also JP Weber, *Problèmes de droit international public posés par les guerres civiles* (Imprimerie du Journal de Genève, 1940) 191: '[i]l n'en reste pas moins que, dans le cas particulier dernière guerre civile espagnole, les Nationalistes ont été reconnus implicitement comme personne juridique internationale par les Etats tiers, non par l'accord de non-intervention, mais notamment, par l'échange de communications entre le gouvernement nationaliste et le gouvernement de Londres (pour ne citer que lui) au sujet de l'exécution du plan de non-intervention, des importations en Espagne, de l'intégrité du territoire de ce pays et du Maroc espagnol, du retrait des volontaires, etc. etc., communications qui toutes constituent des rapports non-diplomatiques bilatéraux entre les gouvernements de Londres et de Bourgos'.

[174] See Siotis (n 123) 171: '[l]a non-reconnaissance n'a nullement résolu le problème de l'intervention étrangère, au contraire, elle l'a favorisée en laissant à chaque Etat le choix de sa politique'.

[175] Weber (n 173) 176.

[176] RA Falk, 'Introduction' in RA Falk and Q Wright (eds), *The International Law of Civil War* (Johns Hopkins Press, 1971) 14. See also O Corten, *La rébellion et le droit international: le principe de neutralité en tension* (Martinus Nijhoff, 2014) 100.

Spanish people the possibility of deciding its own destiny', which would soon be recognised as the right to self-determination.[177]

IV. CONCLUDING OBSERVATIONS

The brief historical overview conducted in this chapter showed that there have always been limits to states' powers and prerogatives: sovereignty has never been absolute.[178] The rights and responsibilities attached to sovereignty have never been immutable, but have evolved over the centuries, reflecting the characteristics of the international community where they were meant to operate.[179] The question of the relationship between sovereignty, intervention, and human rights did not emerge *ex abrupto* in the twentieth century. Indeed, already in the Middle Ages scholars identified specific circumstances when war was justified, namely to punish a wrongdoing committed by another state and to defend innocents from a tyrant. Interestingly, debates on the possibility to intervene to protect the population from the abuses of the sovereign recall contemporary arguments on humanitarian intervention and the responsibility to protect.

In the eighteenth century, scholars elaborated the principle of non-intervention for the first time and defined it as a corollary of sovereignty.[180] However, it was limited on two fronts. On the one hand, the nearly absolute right to wage war crippled its scope of action. On the other hand, the principle of non-intervention could protect only civilised nations, which were the sole nations to benefit from sovereign rights. As we shall see in the next chapter, with the adoption of the Charter of the United Nations, the limits to the principle of non-intervention were overcome: first, Article 2(4) of the UN Charter introduced a general ban on the use of force;[181] second, all states were considered equal,[182] thus all members of the international community could expect the respect of their sovereign rights and of the corollary principle of non-intervention.[183]

[177] *League of Nations Official Journal*, May–June 1937, 333–34.

[178] M Trachtenberg, 'Intervention in Historical Perspective,' in C Kaysen and L Reed (eds), *Emerging Norms of Justified Intervention* (American Academy of Arts and Sciences, 1993) 22.

[179] Glanville (n 29) 21.

[180] ibid, 56–8. Reus-Smit advanced an alternative conception, suggesting that the principle of non-intervention is not related to sovereignty; see C Reus-Smit, 'The concept of intervention' (2013) 39(5) *Review of International Studies* 1057–76.

[181] See ch 2.

[182] UN Charter, Art 2(1): '[t]he Organization is based on the principle of the sovereign equality of all its Members.'

[183] M Jamnejad and M Wood, 'The Principle of Non-intervention' (2009) 22(2) *Leiden Journal of International Law* 346.

2

Intervention and Use of Force in the United Nations Era

I. INTERVENTIONS IN INTERNAL CONFLICTS

A. The Principle of Non-intervention: Meaning and Typologies

THE TERM 'INTERVENTION' can refer to two different realities. On the one hand, it covers any kind of interference, regardless of legal considerations. This is a descriptive notion: any acts or omissions committed by a state and that have an influence in another country amount to intervention. From this perspective, intervention is an empirical phenomenon.[1] On the other hand, there exists a legal notion of intervention, which is the object of our analysis. One example of the first would be for instance an offer to provide good offices, which could fall within the descriptive meaning of intervention, but it does not amount to a violation of the principle of non-intervention.[2]

The principle of non-intervention is not directly acknowledged in the UN Charter. Nonetheless, it can be implicitly deduced from other provisions,[3] namely Article 2(1), which grounds the UN on 'the principle of the sovereign equality of all its Members', and Article 2(3), which establishes that '[a]ll Members shall settle their international disputes by peaceful means'.[4] According to the International Court of Justice (ICJ), the fact that 'the principle was not, as such, spelt out in the Charter' is not problematic: 'it was never intended that the Charter should embody written confirmation of every essential principle of international law in force'.[5] In any event, the principle has

[1] E Lieblich, *International Law and Civil Wars: Intervention and Consent* (Routledge, 2013) 39.

[2] P Kunig, 'Prohibition of Intervention' in *Max Planck Encyclopedia of Public International Law* (Oxford University Press, 2008) §6: '[b]etween military and the offer to provide good offices, which clearly does not lie within the non-principle, there are many acts which States perform that touch the affairs of another State but are not clear-cut interventions'.

[3] NG Onuf, 'The Principle of Non-intervention, the United Nations, and the International System' (1971) 25(2) *International Organization* 212; Kunig (n 2) §§9–10.

[4] M Kinactoğlui, 'The Principle of Non-intervention at the United Nations: The Charter Framework and the Legal Debate' (2005) *Perceptions: Journal of International Affairs* 16.

[5] ICJ, *Military and Paramilitary Activities in and against Nicaragua*, (*Nicaragua v United States of America*), Judgment (Merits), 27 June 1986 (hereinafter *Nicaragua* case), §202.

been widely acknowledged in numerous declarations of the United Nations General Assembly (UNGA)[6] and treaties,[7] and is now widely accepted as 'part and parcel of customary law'.[8] However, it is debated whether it is peremptory in nature.[9]

The principle of non-intervention has never been questioned and it is widely and constantly invoked by states. Most notably, the UNGA, in the Declaration on Friendly Relations amongst States, affirms that:

> No State or group of States has the right to intervene, directly or indirectly, for any reason whatever, in the internal or external affairs of any other State. Consequently, armed intervention and all other forms of interference or attempted threats against the personality of the State or against its political, economic and cultural elements, are in violation of international law.[10]

[6] See eg A/RES/12/1236, 14 December 1957, *Peaceful and neighbourly relations among States*, which establishes that 'non-intervention in one another's internal affairs' is one of the bases of relations among states; A/RES/2131 (XX), 21 December 1965, *Declaration on the Inadmissibility of Intervention in the Domestic Affairs of States and the Protection of Their Independence and Sovereignty*, which mentions that '[n]o State has the right to intervene, directly or indirectly, for any reason whatever, in the internal or external affairs of any other State. Consequently, armed intervention and all other forms of interference or attempted threats against the personality of the State or against its political, economic and cultural elements, are condemned'. The most important UNGA resolution on non-intervention is the *Declaration on Principles of International Law concerning Friendly Relations and Co-operation among States in accordance with the Charter of the United Nations*, A/RES/25/2625 (XXV), 24 October 1970 (hereinafter Declaration on Friendly Relations), whose third principle is 'the principle concerning the duty not to intervene in matters within the domestic jurisdiction of any State, in accordance with the Charter'. See also M Jamnejad and M Wood, 'The Principle of Non-intervention' (2009) 22(2) *Leiden Journal of International Law* 352–55; Kunig (n 2) §20.

[7] See eg UN Charter, Art 2(7): '[n]othing contained in the present Charter shall authorise the United Nations to intervene in matters which are essentially within the domestic jurisdiction of any state or shall require the Members to submit such matters to settlement under the present Charter; but this principle shall not prejudice the application of enforcement measures under Chapter Vll', and the Vienna Convention on Diplomatic Relations 1961, Art 41(1): '[w]ithout prejudice to their privileges and immunities, it is the duty of all persons enjoying such privileges and immunities to respect the laws and regulations of the receiving State. They also have a duty not to interfere in the internal affairs of that State'. The principle of non-intervention is broadly acknowledged at the regional level as well. See eg the Charter of the Organization of American States 1948, Art 3(e): '[e]very State has the right to choose, without external interference, its political, economic, and social system and to organize itself in the way best suited to it, and has the duty to abstain from intervening in the affairs of another State. Subject to the foregoing, the American States shall cooperate fully among themselves, independently of the nature of their political, economic, and social system'; the Constitutive Act of the African Union 2000, Art 4: '[t]he Union shall function in accordance with the following principles: … non-interference by any Member State in the internal affairs of another'. See also Jamnejad and Wood (n 6) 363–66.

[8] *Nicaragua* case, §202. See also Kunig (n 2) §7; Jamnejad and Wood (n 6) 351–55.

[9] In favour of the *jus cogens* nature of the principle, see eg Kunig (n 2) §7; Judge Sette-Cama, however, stated that the non-intervention principle 'would certainly qualify' as *jus cogens* (*Nicaragua* case, *Separate opinion of Judge Sette-Cama*, at 189). The contrary view is expressed, for instance, by Jamnejad and Wood (n 6) 358–59.

[10] Declaration on Friendly Relations (n 6).

However, its actual content and meaning are vague: what amounts to intervention 'is nowhere set out clearly'.[11] The ICJ, in the *Nicaragua* decision, defined the content of intervention as follows:

> A prohibited intervention must accordingly be one bearing on matters in which each State is permitted, by the principle of State sovereignty, to decide freely. One of these is the choice of a political, economic, social and cultural system, and the formulation of foreign policy. Intervention is wrongful when it uses methods of coercion in regard to such choices, which must remain free ones. The element of coercion, which defines, and indeed forms the very essence of, prohibited intervention, is particularly obvious in the case of an intervention which uses force, either in the direct form of military action, or in the indirect form of support for subversive or terrorist armed activities within another State.[12]

The definition of unlawful intervention advanced by the ICJ distinguishes two constitutive elements: the interference has to be in the domestic affairs of the state, and it has to be coercive. As for the first requirement, an intervention is unlawful if it interferes with the *domaine réservé*, namely 'the areas of State activity that are internal or domestic affairs of a State and are therefore within its domestic jurisdiction or competence'.[13] What falls within the scope of internal affairs of states is strictly related to sovereignty. However, as '[s]overeign rights are socially and historically constructed', 'it follows that there is nothing that is inherently a "domestic affair" that sovereign states have a right to decide for themselves'.[14] This was confirmed by the Permanent Court of International Justice in 1923 in its Advisory Opinion on *Nationality Decrees Issued in Tunis and Morocco*, where it specified that 'the question whether a certain matter is or is not solely within the jurisdiction of a State is an essentially relative question; it depends on the development of international relations'.[15]

Intervention within the domestic affairs of a state does not violate per se the principle of non-intervention: the interference has to be coercive.[16] Oppenheim

[11] Jamnejad and Wood (n 6) 347. See also P Klein and O Corten, *Droit d'ingérence ou obligation de réaction? Les possibilités d'action visant à assurer le respect des droits de la personne face au principe de non-intervention* (Bruylant, 1992) 9; JN Rosenau, 'Intervention as a Scientific Concept' (1969) 13(2) *Journal of Conflict Resolution* 153.

[12] *Nicaragua* case, §205.

[13] KS Ziegler, 'Domaine Réservé' in *Max Planck Encyclopedia of Public International Law* (Oxford University Press, 2013) §1.

[14] L Glanville, *Sovereignty and the Responsibility to Protect: A New History* (University of Chicago Press, 2014) 21.

[15] Permanent Court of International Justice, *Nationality Decrees Issued in Tunis and Morocco*, Advisory Opinion, 7 February 1923, at 24. See also Ziegler (n 13) §§2–3; Kunig (n 2) §3.

[16] M Wood, 'The Principle of Non-intervention in Contemporary International Law: Non-Interference in a State's Internal Affairs Used to be a Rule of International Law: Is it Still?' *Chatham House International Law discussion group meeting*, no. 26, February 2007, at 2; Kunig (n 2) §6; Jamnejad and Wood (n 6) 348; M Kohen, 'The Principle of Non-intervention 25 Years after the *Nicaragua* Judgment' (2012) 25(1) *Leiden Journal of International Law* 161; S Sivakumaran, *The Law of Non-International Armed Conflict* (Oxford University Press, 2012) 17–20.

specifies that 'the interference must be forcible or dictatorial, or otherwise coercive, in effect depriving the state intervened against of control over the matter in question. Interference pure and simple is not intervention'.[17] The requirement of coercion is central in the definition of intervention: interference upon invitation would not be unlawful even in matters which pertain to the domestic jurisdiction of a state. The crucial aspect is the intention of one state to subordinate the exercise of the sovereign rights of another country.[18] The element of coercion is apparent in the case of intervention entailing the use of force. In this circumstance, the forcible intervention would violate also the ban on the use of force. The ICJ expressed this view in the *Nicaragua* case:

> The element of coercion, which defines, and indeed forms the very essence of, prohibited intervention is particularly obvious in the case of an intervention which uses force, either in the form of military action, or in the indirect form of support for subversive or terrorist armed activities within another State.[19]

With regard to foreign interference in internal conflicts, it is debatable what amounts to a violation to the principle of non-intervention. In order to address the issue, it is necessary to distinguish between the recipient of the foreign help. Generally speaking, as we shall see in the next chapter, an intervention in favour of the government is lawful if the latter consents to the intervention. However, part of the scholarship posits that interventions upon invitation would violate the principle of non-intervention and the right to self-determination of people when conducted during a civil war, ie a high intensity non-international armed conflict.[20] Therefore, no assistance could be provided in such a case. On the other hand, other authors believe that providing help upon invitation of the government would not amount to a violation of the principle of non-intervention. Nevertheless, in this case the challenge would be to identify the government.[21]

It is generally accepted that interventions in favour of the rebels are prohibited. The most uncontroversial case is sending troops to assist them in their fight against the government. As clarified by the ICJ, this would amount to a violation of the ban on the use of force and of the principle of non-intervention.[22] What about other forms of intervention, short of the direct use of force?

[17] L Oppenheim, *Oppenheim's International Law* (Oxford University Press, 2008) 428; Jamnejad and Wood (n 6) 348.

[18] Jamnejad and Wood (n 6) 348. See Declaration on Friendly Relations: '[n]o State may use or encourage the use of economic, political or any other type of measures to coerce another State in order to obtain from it the subordination of the exercise of its sovereign rights and to secure from it advantages of any kind'.

[19] *Nicaragua* case, §205. See also Kohen (n 16) 162. It is worth noting that the objective of the intervention is irrelevant, as specified by the ICJ in *Armed Activities in the Congo (Democratic Republic of Congo v Uganda)*, Judgment (Merits), 19 December 2005 (hereinafter *Congo* case), §163.

[20] See eg C Gray, *International Law and the Use of Force* (Oxford University Press, 2008) 82.

[21] See ch 3.

[22] *Nicaragua* case, §246.

The starting point for this assessment is the *Nicaragua* case, where the Court affirmed that 'arming and training' opposition groups can amount to 'threat or use of force', as well as to unlawful intervention.[23] This view is largely supported by a number of UNGA resolutions. For instance, the Declaration on the Inadmissibility of Intervention establishes that 'no State shall organize, assist, foment … armed activities directed towards the violent overthrow of the régime of another State'.[24] Similar declarations have been reiterated in the UNGA Declaration on Friendly Relations Declaration and in the Declaration on the Inadmissibility of Intervention.[25] Accordingly, it is now generally accepted that the transfer of weapons to rebel groups violates both the ban on the use of force and the principle of non-intervention in the internal affairs of the state.[26]

Identifying which kind of non-forcible instances amount to unlawful intervention is more problematic. At what point economic measures amount to a violation of the principle of non-intervention is highly debated.[27] Several states receive and arguably rely on economic aid granted from other countries.[28] The issue arises when the helping state stops granting economic assistance, hence creating financial problems for the receiving state. Is it unlawful interference? The issue was addressed by the ICJ in the *Nicaragua* case, where the Court affirmed that:

> As already noted, Nicaragua has also asserted that the United States is responsible for an 'indirect' form of intervention in its internal affairs inasmuch as it has taken, to Nicaragua's disadvantage, certain action of an economic nature. The Court's attention has been drawn in particular to the cessation of economic aid in April 1981; the 90 per cent reduction in the sugar quota for United States imports from Nicaragua in April 1981; and the trade embargo adopted on 1 May 1985. While admitting in principle that some of these actions were not unlawful in themselves, counsel for Nicaragua argued that these measures of economic constraint add up to a systematic violation of the principle of non-intervention. … [T]he Court … is unable to regard such action on the economic plane as is here complained of as a breach of the customary law principle of non-intervention.[29]

[23] ibid, §228.

[24] Declaration on the Inadmissibility of Intervention in the Domestic Affairs of States and the Protection of their Independence and Sovereignty, A/RES/2131(1965), 21 December 1965.

[25] Declaration on the inadmissibility of intervention and interference in the internal affairs of States, A/RES/ 36(103) (1981), 9 December 1981.

[26] T Ruys, 'Of Arms, Funding and "Non-Lethal Assistance" – Issues Surrounding Third State Intervention in the Syrian Civil War' (2014) 13(1) *Chinese Journal of International Law* 31–32.

[27] DW Bowett, 'International Law and Economic Coercion' (1976) 16(2) *Vanderbilt Journal of International Law* 245–59; R Sapienza, *La guerra civile nell'evoluzione del diritto internazionale* (Editpress, 2010).

[28] D Sylvan and S Majeski, *US Foreign Policy in Perspective Clients, Enemies and Empire* (Routledge, 2009) 91.

[29] *Nicaragua* case, §§ 244–45.

Despite the fact that the Court did not develop the issue further, it seems reasonable to conclude that ceasing to provide financial aid to another country breaches the principle of non-intervention if it entails an act of coercion, ie, if the state adopts the economic measure with the specific aim of interfering in the internal affairs of the other state. Outside this circumstance, states should be free to terminate economic aid:

> The withdrawal of aid previously given … is not considered, in general, as unlawful intervention unless it amounts to extreme economic coercion. … This notion is based on the traditional idea that states are sovereign to conduct their economic policies, whether internal or external, and that as long as state action is not limited by treaties or customary international law, it is generally not prohibited.[30]

The question regarding economic assistance to the parties of an armed conflict became central in recent years, when a number of countries started providing non-lethal assistance to rebel groups fighting against the Syrian government. The aid provided to opposition forces was not limited to food and medical supplies, but extended also to 'body armour and armoured vehicles'.[31] Furthermore, in May 2013 the European Union lifted the embargo in place towards Syria in order to supply weapons to and to buy oil from Syrian opposition groups. Specifically, Article 6 of Council Decision 2013/255/CFSP provides that:

> With a view to helping the Syrian civilian population, in particular to meeting humanitarian concerns, restoring normal life, upholding basic services, reconstruction, and restoring normal economic activity or other civilian purposes … the competent authorities of a Member State may authorize the purchase, import or transport from Syria of crude oil and petroleum products.[32]

The provision is subjected to a number of conditions, notably that 'the Syrian National Coalition for Opposition and Revolutionary Forces has been consulted in advance by the Member State concerned'.[33] Do these measures amount to unlawful intervention in the internal affairs of Syria?

In principle, any kind of unarmed interference, which aims at coercively interfering in the internal affairs of another state, amounts to unlawful intervention. As noted by the ICJ, providing 'financial support, training, supply of weapons, intelligence and logistic support, constitutes a clear breach of the principle of non-intervention'.[34] On the other hand:

> There can be no doubt that the provision of strictly humanitarian aid to persons or forces in another country, whatever their political affiliations or objectives, cannot be regarded as unlawful intervention, or as in any other way contrary to international law.[35]

[30] Lieblich (n 1) 45.
[31] Ruys (n 26) 150.
[32] Council Decision 2013/255/CFSP of 31 May 2013 concerning restrictive measures against Syria.
[33] ibid. Art 6(a).
[34] ICJ, *Nicaragua* case, §242.
[35] ibid.

Ultimately, whether the provision of non-lethal assistance, financial support, or economic transactions such as the purchase of crude oil from opposition groups violate the principle of non-intervention should be decided on a case-by-case basis. Specifically, crucial to the assessment will be the existence of guarantees that such help will be used for humanitarian assistance as opposed to helping the rebels in their fight against the government.[36]

B. Defining Non-international Armed Conflicts

Determining the existence of a non-international armed conflict (NIAC) is not always an easy task, due to the lack of certain criteria to identify the lower threshold of a NIAC[37] and the increase of situations where several conflicts – both internal and international – take place in the same country or across an international border.[38] Generally speaking, the instances when an internal armed conflict exist are threefold. First, as specified in the *Tadić* case, a NIAC occurs whenever there is protracted armed violence between governmental authorities and organised armed groups.[39] Second, a NIAC is also a situation where protracted armed violence takes place between two or more armed non-state actors (ANSAs) within a state.[40] Third, intense armed violence between non-state groups across an international border can qualify as a NIAC.[41]

[36] Ruys (n 26) 50.

[37] Article 3, common to the four Geneva Conventions of 1949, establishes a number of provisions that shall be applied, as a minimum, during non-international armed conflicts. However, it does not offer a definition of this term. On the meaning of "non-international armed conflicts" in the 1949 Geneva Conventions see A Cullen, *The Concept Non-International Armed Conflicts in international Humanitarian Law* (Cambridge University Press, 2010) 25–61.

[38] L Cameron et al, 'Article 3: Conflicts not of an international character' in K Dörmann, L Lijnzaad, M Sassòli and P Spoeri (eds), *Commentary on the First Geneva Convention: Convention (I) for the Amelioration of the Condition of the Wounded and Sick in Armed Forces in the Field* (Cambridge University Press, 2016) 141–42; M Milanović, 'The Applicability of the Conventions to "Transnational" and "Mixed" Conflicts' in A Clapham, P Gaeta and M Sassòli (eds), *The 1949 Geneva Conventions: A Commentary* (Oxford University Press, 2015) 27–50; C Kreß, 'Some Reflections on the International Legal Framework Governing Transnational Armed Conflicts' (2010) 15(2) *Journal of Conflict and Security Law* 245–74.

[39] ICTY, *Prosecutor v Tadić*, Appeal Chamber, Decision on the Defence Motion for Interlocutory Appeal on Jurisdiction, case No. IT–94–1, 2 October 1995, §70 (hereinafter *Tadić Jurisdiction Decision*). Duško Tadić is a Bosnian Serb who was charged with war crimes and crimes against humanity. In order to judge whether it had jurisdiction, the Tribunal had to address the question of whether a conflict was taking place at the time. Tadić's lawyer claimed that 'there did not exist a legally cognizable armed conflict – either internal or international – at the time and place that the alleged offences were committed' (ICTY, *Tadić Jurisdiction Decision*, §8). The Appeal Chamber rejected this position and concluded that Tadić's actions took place during a NIAC. See Cullen (n 37) 120.

[40] ICTY, *Tadić Jurisdiction Decision*, §70.

[41] S Casey-Maslen, 'Armed Conflicts in 2012 and Their Impact' in *The War Report: Armed Conflict in 2012* (Oxford University Press, 2013) 9–10.

On the other hand, 'banditry, unorganized and short-lived insurrections, or terrorist activities'[42] do not amount to armed conflicts.[43]

The problem lies in determining the threshold between a situation that does not amount to a NIAC and the notion of 'protracted armed violence' referred to in the *Tadić* decision. When does an internal conflict start? The ICTY identified a test to determine whether there is a NIAC based on two cumulative criteria: 'the intensity of the conflict and the organization of the parties to the conflict'.[44] As for the first requirement, Cullen clarifies that:

> The level of armed violence required for the application of common Article 3 must be high enough to exclude isolated or sporadic acts of violence, but low enough to include situations of internal conflict where hostilities are not necessarily carried out on a continuous basis.[45]

The ICTY addressed the issue in the *Milošević Rule 98bis Decision*, where it assessed the intensity of the violence by focusing on the escalation and the seriousness of clashes and the length of the conflict, with particular regard to the type of weaponry used.[46] However, not every case of protracted violence amounts to a NIAC: the parties 'must have a minimum degree of organization and discipline – enough to enable them to respect international humanitarian law – in order to be recognized as a party to the conflict'.[47] In assessing the level of organisation, ANSAs ought to meet certain requirements, such as 'an official joint command structure, headquarters, designated zone of operations, and the ability to procure, transport and distribute arms'.[48]

Foreign interventions in internal conflicts pose crucial challenges with regard to their classification and the applicable legal framework.[49] Specifically,

[42] ICTY, *Prosecutor v Tadić*, Trial Chamber Judgment, case No. IT–94–1, 7 May 1997, §562.

[43] H McCoubrey, 'The Qualification Framework of International Humanitarian Law: Too Rigid to Accommodate Contemporary Conflicts?' (2011) 34(1) *Suffolk Transnational Law Review* 156–57; GD Solis, *The Law of Armed Conflict: International Humanitarian Law in War* (Cambridge University Press, 2010) 153.

[44] ICTR, *Prosecutor v Rutaganda*, Trial Chamber Judgment, ICTR Case No. ICTR–96–3, 6 December 1999, §93. See also International Committee of the Red Cross (ICRC), 'How is the Term "Armed Conflict" Defined in International Humanitarian Law?' (Geneva, 2008) 3.

[45] Cullen (n 37) 128.

[46] ICTY, *Prosecutor v Miloševič*, Trial Chamber Decision on Motion for Judgment of Acquittal (hereinafter *Miloševič Rule 98bis Decision*), Case No. IT–02–54–T, 16 June 2004, §§28–31.

[47] ICRC, 'Armed Conflicts Linked to the Disintegration of State Structures: Preparatory Document drafted by the International Committee of the Red Cross for the First Periodical Meeting on International Humanitarian Law' (Geneva, 19–23 January 1998).

[48] *Milošević Rule 98bis Decision*, §23. In order to judge whether Milošević violated the laws and customs of war in Kosovo, the ICTY had to determine whether a NIAC was taking place in the relevant area at that time. Thus, it considered whether the Kosovo Liberation Army (KLA) was sufficiently organised. The Trial Chamber concluded affirmatively (*Milošević Rule 98bis Decision*, §§171–172). See Cullen (n 37) 124–26; L Moir, *The Law of Internal Armed Conflict* (Cambridge University Press, 2002) 36–38.

[49] What about indirect interventions? If a foreign country helps the rebels, the NIAC turns into an IAC if the state exercises control over the opposition group. The problem lies in determining the degree of control required. The issue will be analysed below in this chapter.

the question is whether an intervention by a third country would turn a non-international armed conflict into an international one, thus triggering the application of International Humanitarian Law (IHL) regulating international armed conflicts (IACs). While these situations used to be called 'internationalized internal armed conflicts', the term was abandoned in recent years because it was considered 'misleading in that it suggests that only the law of international armed conflict applies'.[50] Accordingly, they are now commonly referred to as 'transnational internal armed conflicts'.[51] Nevertheless, it should be noted that this is not a legal category, and it is intended as a merely descriptive term referring to NIACs that present an international element.[52]

According to part of the scholarship, transnational armed conflicts are IACs: if a foreign country intervenes in favour of an opposition group, or against an opposition group without the consent of the government, the entire situation would be classified as an international armed conflict.[53] The International Committee of the Red Cross (ICRC) proposed this approach in 1971, in its *Report on the Protection of Victims of Non-international Armed Conflicts*, submitted to the first Conference of Government Experts for the Reaffirmation and Development of International Law.[54] However, this position raises crucial issues. Indeed, it has been pointed out 'that it would tend to make these conflicts worse, as the non-governmental groups would try to attract third States in order to benefit from application of the law of international armed conflict'.[55]

[50] See T Ferraro, 'The ICRC's Legal Position on the Notion of Armed Conflict Involving Foreign Intervention and on Determining the IHL Applicable to This Type of Conflict' (2015) 97(900) *International Review of the Red Cross* 1251–52.

[51] See eg C. Kreß, 'Some Reflections on the International Legal Framework Governing Transnational Armed Conflicts' (2010) 15(2) *Journal of Conflict and Security Law* 245–74.

[52] D Carron, 'Transnational armed conflicts: An argument for a single classification of non-international armed conflicts' (2016) 7(1) *Journal of International Humanitarian Legal Studies* 11; M Milanovic and V Hadzi-vidanovic, 'A Taxonomy of Armed Conflict' in N White and C Henderson (eds), *Research Handbook on International Conflict and Security Law: jus ad bellum, jus in bello and jus post bellum* (Edward Elgar, 2012) 303–304; Sivakumaran (n 16) 228–29. A different question concerns whether the support provided by a foreign country to an opposition group turns the NIAC into an IAC. Ultimately, the issue concerns the degree of control required to consider the non-state actor as a *de facto* organ of the state. See below in this chapter.

[53] See eg ME O'Connell, 'Saving Lives through a Definition of International Armed Conflict' (2010) 40 *Proceedings of the Bruges Colloquium, Armed Conflicts and Parties to Armed Conflicts under IHL: Confronting Legal Categories to Contemporary Realities* 23–24; I Detter, *The Law of War* (Cambridge University Press, 2000) 47; E David, *Principes de droit des conflits armées* (Bruylant, 1994) 175; G Aldrich, 'The Laws of War on Land' (2000) 94(1) *American Journal of International Law* 62–63.

[54] ICRC, *Protection of Victims of Non-International Armed Conflicts*, at 17; HP Gasser, 'International Armed Conflicts: Case Studies of Afghanistan, Kampuchea, and Lebanon' (1983) 33(1) *American University Law Review* 146.

[55] S Vité, 'Typology of Armed Conflicts in International Humanitarian Law: Legal Concepts and Actual Situations' (2009) 91(873) *International Review of the Red Cross* 86–87; ICRC, *Report on the Work of the Conference of Government Experts on the Reaffirmation and Development of International Humanitarian Law Applicable in Armed Conflicts* (Geneva, August 1971) 50.

Furthermore, Article 2 common to the Geneva Conventions[56] clearly establishes that an armed conflict is international only when there are two or more states opposing each other.[57]

Other authors posit that, when a foreign country intervenes in an internal conflict against an opposition group, hostilities between the intervening state and the rebels amount to a NIAC, regardless of the consent of the host state, provided that the intensity of violence and the organisation of the non-state actor meet the threshold.[58] Scholars in favour of this approach highlight that under IHL 'the categorization of a conflict must depend on the identity of the parties'. Accordingly, in case of armed confrontations between a state and a non-state actor in the territory of another country, the situation should be classified as a NIAC. Propounding that these conflicts would amount to IACs 'does not take into account the basis of the dichotomy between iacs and niacs [sic] and leads to the application of an inappropriate law to this situation'.[59]

Lastly, the majoritarian view distinguishes the nature of the armed conflicts depending on the consent of the state. The starting point is the so-called fragmented approach, which 'consists of determining applicable IHL by examining each bilateral relationship between belligerents separately in light of the facts on the ground'.[60] The fragmented application of IHL has been validated by the ICJ in the *Nicaragua* case, where the Court identified the existence of two parallel armed conflicts: on the one hand, a NIAC between Nicaragua and the opposition groups; on the other hand, an IAC between Nicaragua and the US.[61] This approach has also been endorsed by the ICTY[62] and the ICC,[63] it is confirmed by state practice,[64] and it finds vast support in the literature.[65]

[56] Article 2, common to the Geneva Convention (I) for the Amelioration of the Condition of the Wounded and Sick in Armed Forces in the Field; Geneva Convention (II) for the Amelioration of the Condition of Wounded, Sick and Shipwrecked Members of Armed Forces at Sea; Geneva Convention (III) relative to the Treatment of Prisoners of War; Geneva Convention (IV) relative to the Protection of Civilian Persons in Time of War.

[57] K Mačák, *Internationalized Armed Conflicts in International Law* (Oxford University Press, 2018) 34; ICRC, 'How is the Term "Armed Conflict" Defined in International Humanitarian Law?', Opinion Paper (March 2008) 5.

[58] Carron (n 52) 13–14; N Lubell, *Extraterritorial Use of Force against Non-State Actors* (Oxford University Press, 2010) 95–99.

[59] Carron (n 52) 15.

[60] Ferraro (n 50) 1241.

[61] *Nicaragua* case, §219; S Vité, 'Typology of Armed Conflicts in International Humanitarian Law: Legal Concepts and Actual Situations' (2009) 91(873) *International Review of the Red Cross* 86.

[62] ICTY, *Tadić Jurisdiction Decision*, §77: 'the conflicts in the former Yugoslavia have both internal and international aspects'.

[63] International Criminal Court (ICC), *The Prosecutor v Thomas Lubanga Dyilo*, Decision on the confirmation of charges, Pre-Trial Chamber I, 07 February 2007, ICC-01/04-01/06-803-tEN, §209.

[64] For an analysis of state practice, see eg Mačák (n 57) 35.

[65] See eg M Sassòli, 'The Legal Qualification of the Conflict in the Former Yugoslavia: Double Standards or New Horizons for International Humanitarian Law?' in S Yee and T Wang (eds), *International Law in the Post-Cold War World: Essays in Memory of Li Haopei* (Routledge, 2001) 307–33; L Condorelli, 'Les attentats du 11 septembre et leurs suites: Où va le droit international?' (2001) 105(4) *Revue générale de droit international public* 829–48; Gasser (n 54).

Drawing upon the fragmented approach, the majority of the scholarship propounds that, if a foreign country intervenes in a NIAC against rebel forces, the armed confrontation between the intervening state and the opposition group is going to be considered a NIAC. However, should the intervention take place without the consent of the territorial state, there is also going to be an IAC between the latter and the intervening country, 'regardless of the concrete target of the violence'.[66] This position is endorsed by the ICRC:

> [T]he existence of consent would clearly rule out the classification of the intervention as an international armed conflict, provided the intervention stays within the limits posited by the consenting State and that the consent is not withdrawn. ... Should the third State's intervention be carried out without the consent of the territorial State, it would amount to an international armed conflict between the intervening State and the territorial State.[67]

One example could clarify this view. On 25 June 2014, Iraq sent a letter to the United Nations Security Council (UNSC), where it asked for international 'support in order to defeat' the Islamic State of Iraq and Syria (ISIS).[68] On 7 August 2014, the US began airstrikes against ISIS in Iraq and soon thereafter operation *Inherent Resolve* was launched: a multinational military campaign aimed at defeating ISIS in Iraq.[69] In September 2014, a US-led coalition extended the strikes against ISIS on Syrian territory.[70] While the military operation in Iraq took place with the consent of the government, Assad did not consent to the use of force by the US-led coalition on Syrian soil. Accordingly, the US-led intervention against the ISIS in Syria would lead to the existence of two parallel armed conflicts: a NIAC between the foreign forces and ISIS and an IAC between the

[66] Carron (n 52) 12.

[67] JM Henckaerts and others, 'Article 2: Application of the Convention' in K Dörmann, L Lijnzaad, M Sassòli and P Spoerri (eds), *Commentary on the First Geneva Convention: Convention (I) for the Amelioration of the Condition of the Wounded and Sick in Armed Forces in the Field* (International Committee of the Red Cross, 2016) §§260–61.

[68] Letter dated 25 June 2014 from the Permanent Representative of Iraq to the United Nations addressed to the Secretary-General, UN Doc. S/2014/440 (2014).

[69] V Koutroulis, 'The Fight against the Islamic State and *Jus in Bello*' (2016) 29 *Leiden Journal of International Law* 830.

[70] At first the intervention was conducted by the US, Bahrain, Jordan, Qatar, Saudi Arabia, and the United Arab Emirates. Albeit initially reluctant, Australia, Canada, France, and the UK, among others, eventually joined the US-led coalition intervening in Syria. O Corten, 'Military Operations against "Islamic State" (ISIL or Dae'sh)–2014' in T Ruys, O Corten and A Hofer (eds), *The Use of Force in International Law: A Case-based Approach* (Oxford University Press, 2018) 875–76; O Flasch, 'The Legality of the Air Strikes against ISIL in Syria: New Insights on the Extraterritorial Use of Force against Non-State Actors (2016) 3 *Journal on the Use of Force and International Law* 38; Koutroulis (n 69) 835.

foreign countries and Syria in light of the fact that the Syrian government has opposed the intervention.[71] As clarified by Mačák:

> This is because the key condition for the existence of an IAC, ie, the resort to force between states, does not require that both states must actually use force; instead, it is sufficient that one state uses force against another state.[72]

II. THE BAN ON THE USE OF FORCE

A. The Content of the Prohibition

The Covenant of the League of Nations and the Kellogg-Briand Pact are turning points in the regulation of the use of force in international relations.[73] Notably, with the Paris Act 'international law progressed from *jus ad bellum* to *jus contra bellum*'.[74] The aim of the Kellogg-Briand Pact was to go beyond the procedural restrictions to wage war established in the Covenant of the League of Nations by outlawing the recourse to war 'as an instrument of national policy'.[75] This approach presented two major flaws. First, the term 'war' was not defined in the Pact, thus leaving to the parties the discretionary power to define measures short of war.[76] Second, the 'national policy' clause implied that war as an instrument of international policy was allowed.[77] Despite the fact that the two treaties proved insufficient to prevent new conflicts, as demonstrated by the

[71] See identical letters dated 17 September 2015 from the Permanent Representative of the Syrian Arab Republic to the United Nations addressed to the Secretary-General and the President of the Security Council, UN Doc. S/2015/719 (2015): 'the United Kingdom, Australia and France are currently taking military measures against the Syrian Arab Republic. … Syria has not made any request to that effect'. For an analysis of the conflict see 'International Armed Conflicts in Syria' in Rule of Law in Armed Conflicts (RULAC), Geneva Academy of International Humanitarian Law and Human Rights, available at www.rulac.org/browse/conflicts/international-armed-conflict-in-syria.

[72] Mačák (n 57) 38–39.

[73] Y Dinstein, *War, Aggression and Self-Defence* (Cambridge University Press, 2011) 85.

[74] ibid, 85; ME Howard, *Restraints on War: Studies in the Limitation of Armed Conflict* (Oxford University Press, 1979) 11.

[75] Kellogg-Briand Pact, Art 1. See SC Neff, *War and the Law of Nations: A General History* (Cambridge University Press, 2005) 293.

[76] CHM Waldock, *The Regulation of the Use of Force by Individual States in International Law* (Hague Academy of International Law, 1952) 471–74.

[77] Dinstein (n 73) 86; H Kelsen, *Principles of International Law* (Rinehart & Company, 1952) 43: 'a war which is a reaction against a violation of international law, and that means a war waged for the maintenance of international law, is considered an instrument of international and hence not of national policy'.

outbreak of World War II,[78] they do not represent a complete failure: they were the first attempts to codify values shared by the international community, such as the peaceful settlement of disputes. Furthermore, they helped states realise that outlawing wars was not enough: it was necessary to create international institutions and a developed legal framework aimed at promoting peace and justice.[79]

One of the main purposes of the UN Charter was to amend the limits and flaws of the Covenant of the League of Nations and the Kellogg-Briand Pact. It is well-known that Article 2(4) of the UN Charter bans the threat or use of force:

> All Members shall refrain in their international relations from the threat or use of force against the territorial integrity or political independence of any state, or in any other manner inconsistent with the Purposes of the United Nations.

This article has been defined as 'the cornerstone of the United Nations Charter'.[80] While it introduces important novelties with respect to the previous attempts to limit wars, it also raises several questions of interpretation.[81] One of the main innovations concerns the fact that Article 2(4) outlaws 'the use of force' instead of 'war'.[82] The Covenant of the League of Nations and the Paris Pact clearly showed that states could easily overcome the prohibition by avoiding declaring war;[83] the term 'force' was thus intentionally used to cover measures short of war.[84] Nevertheless, the notion of *force* is not devoid of ambiguities.[85] Notably, Article 2(4) does not qualify force as *armed*. This led to passionate debates as to the scope of the ban: does it extend to other coercive measures, such as economic, political, and psychological ones?[86] While part of the international community, in particular developing countries, pushed to include coercive economic measures in the prohibition, Western countries firmly rejected this approach. The latter interpretation has become the majority

[78] R Lesaffer, 'Too Much History: From War as Sanction to the Sanctioning of War' in M Weller (ed), *The Oxford Handbook of the Use of Force in International Law* (Oxford University Press, 2015) 53. However, the Paris Pact was not completely ignored. For example, the US invoked it with regard to China and Russia in 1929, as well as in relation to the hostilities between China and Japan in 1931. See J Crawford, *Brownlie's Principles of Public International Law* (Oxford University Press, 2012) 745.

[79] A Cassese, *Voci Contro la Barbarie: La Battaglia per i Diritti Umani Attraverso i Suoi Protagonisti* (Feltrinelli, 2008) 39.

[80] *Congo* case, §148.

[81] Crawford (n 78) 747; O Schachter, 'The Right of States to Use Armed Force' (1984) 82(5) *Michigan Law Review* 1624.

[82] ibid.

[83] ibid.

[84] Dinstein (n 73) 88; D Akande, 'International Law and the Classification of Conflicts' in E Wilmshurst (ed), *International Law and the Classification of Conflicts* (Oxford University Press, 2012) 34.

[85] Schachter (n 81) 1624.

[86] RD Kearney and RE Dalton, 'The Treaty on Treaties' (1970) 64(3) *American Journal of International Law* 534.

view: it is now overwhelmingly accepted that the norm prohibits only the use of armed force.[87]

More recently, there have been lively debates as to whether cyber operations could qualify as force prohibited by Article 2(4) of the UN Charter. While the vast majority of cyber operations would not amount to use of force, they could potentially fall within the scope of Article 2(4) of the UN Charter. Indeed, it is now generally accepted that 'a use of force under international law does not depend on conventional weapons being used' because, 'instead of the *means*, the *effect* of the State's action is widely considered to be at the heart of the matter'.[88] This position finds support in the *Nuclear Weapons* advisory opinion, where the ICJ posited that Article 2(4) and Article 51 of the UN Charter 'apply to any use of force, regardless of the weapons employed'.[89] Accordingly, an emerging view propounds that cyber operations may constitute a use of force when their 'scale and effects are comparable to non-cyber operations rising to the level of a use of force'.[90]

The scope of application of Article 2(4) of the UN Charter is generally interpreted as covering only international force. In other words, the use of force by the government against insurgents and vice versa is not covered by this provision: only when opposition groups succeed in establishing a new de facto regime do they fall within the scope of Article 2(4).[91] Similarly, the use of force by the government against individuals under its jurisdiction would not violate this provision.[92] As we shall see, this view was challenged during the decolonisation period. In the 1960s, the majority of the international community

[87] The restrictive interpretation of the term 'force' is further confirmed by the *travaux préparatoires* of the UN Charter: during the San Francisco Conference, Brazil suggested extending the prohibition to include economic measures. However, the proposal was rejected. See O Dörr, 'Prohibition of the Use of Force' in *Max Planck Encyclopedia of Public International Law* (Oxford University Press, 2015) §§11–12. In favour of a restrictive interpretation of Article 2(4) of the UN Charter, see eg N Ronzitti, *Diritto dei Conflitti Armati* (Giappichelli, 2011) 29; BVA Röling, 'The Ban of the Use of Force and the U.N. Charter' in A Cassese (ed), *The Current Legal Regulation of the Use of Force* (Martinus Nijhoff, 1986) 3; O Corten, *The Law against War: The Prohibition on the Use of Force in Contemporary International Law* (Hart Publishing, 2010) 66; T Ruys, 'The Meaning of "Force" and the Boundaries of the *Jus Ad Bellum* – Are "Minimal" Uses of Force Excluded from UN Charter Article 2(4)?' (2014) 108(2) *American Journal of International Law* 163.

[88] C Kreß, 'On the Principle of Non-Use of Force in Current International Law' (*Just Security*, 2019), available at www.justsecurity.org/66372/on-the-principle-of-non-use-of-force-in-current-international-law/.

[89] ICJ, *Legality of the Threat or Use of Nuclear Weapons*, Advisory Opinion, 8 July 1986, §39. See also MN Schmitt, 'The Use of Cyber Force and International Law' in Weller (ed) (n 78) 1122.

[90] International Group of Experts, *Tallinn Manual 2.0 on the International Law Applicable to Cyber Operations* (Cambridge University Press, 2017) Rule 11 and at 330–48.

[91] The ICJ confirmed this approach in its Advisory Opinion *Accordance with International Law of the Unilateral Declaration of Independence in Respect of Kosovo*, whereby it specified that 'the scope of the principle of territorial integrity is confined to the sphere of relations between States' (*Accordance with International Law of the Unilateral Declaration of Independence in Respect of Kosovo*, Advisory Opinion, 22 July 2010, §80). See also C Kreß, 'The International Court of Justice and the 'Principle of Non-Use of Force' in Weller (ed) (n 78) 572.

[92] Dörr (n 87) §21; Kreß (n 91) 572.

and of the scholarship propounded that every state has a duty to refrain from taking action aimed at depriving peoples of their right to self-determination.[93] Some authors asserted that banning the use of force by the colonial power would descend from Article 2(4) of the UN Charter. However, this remained a minority view, while the dominant position was that such prohibition amounts to an autonomous ad hoc rule that emerged through custom.[94]

Although the scope of application of Article 2(4) is limited to armed force amongst states, the notion of *international military force* should be interpreted broadly.[95] Part of the scholarship maintains that the ban only covers force directed against the territorial integrity or political independence of states;[96] nonetheless, the final phrase of Article 2(4) seems to suggest otherwise. By extending the prohibition to using force 'in any other manner inconsistent with the purposes of the United Nations', the drafters wanted to avoid loopholes, stating 'in the broadest terms an absolute all-inclusive prohibition'.[97] This interpretation is supported by the object and purpose of the Article:[98] as explained above, one of the main aims of the UN Charter is to redress the shortcomings of the Kellogg-Briand Pact 'to save succeeding generations from the scourge of war'.[99]

Nevertheless, the exact meaning of *force* remains unclear. The attention of the scholarship has focused on the existence of various degrees of gravity that would amount to a violation of the ban on the use of force. The controversy is further nurtured by the fact that the UN Charter refers to, but does not define, the terms 'armed force' (Article 2(4)), 'armed attack' (Article 51), and 'act of aggression' (Article 39).[100] The debate developed on two fronts. On the one hand, the question concerns the existence of a *de minimis* clause, namely whether small-scale instances of force are excluded from the scope of Article 2(4) of the UN Charter. On the other hand, authors have been investigating the meaning and consequences of instances that do fall within the scope of the Article, such as frontier incidents, armed attacks, and aggressions.[101]

[93] A Cassese, *Self-Determination of Peoples: A Legal Reappraisal* (Cambridge University Press, 1995) 194–97; N Ronzitti, 'Resort to Force in Wars of National Liberation' in A Cassese (ed), *Current Problems of International Law* (Giuffrè, 1975) 320.

[94] See ch 7.

[95] Dörr (n 87) §13.

[96] AA D'Amato, *International Law: Process and Prospect* (Transnational Publishers, 1987) 57–87.

[97] *Documents of the United Nations Conference on International Organization* (San Francisco, California, 25 April to 26 June 1945) 335. See also Ruys (n 87) 164; TM Franck, *Recourse to Force: State Action against Threats and Armed Attacks* (Cambridge University Press, 2004) 12.

[98] Vienna Convention on the Law of Treaties 1969, Art 18 (hereinafter VCLT).

[99] Preamble of the UN Charter. See also Ruys (n 87) 164.

[100] Gray (n 20) 183.

[101] As we shall see, the term 'frontier incident' was first used by the ICJ in the *Nicaragua* case, §195. See also Gray (n 20) 178–83.

The first question is thus whether there exists a *de minimis* clause: a 'gravity threshold'[102] below which certain forcible acts do not trigger Article 2(4) of the UN Charter. Part of the scholarship maintains that all armed actions fall within the ban on the use of force, no matter 'how brief, limited or transitory' they are.[103] Therefore, it is not necessary to have actual armed confrontations between the two states: even small-scale or localised incursions 'that would have warranted deliberate recourse to lethal force'[104] amount to use of force in the sense of Article 2(4).[105] Nonetheless, proponents of this approach admit that small-scale forcible acts and targeted killings do not violate the ban on the use of force when they constitute mere law enforcement operations: 'forcible action against civilian aircrafts, merchant vessels, or private individuals within the state's own territory … is presumed to remain beyond the scope of UN Charter Article 2(4)'.[106]

In recent years, scholars have increasingly recognised the existence of a *de minimis* threshold, below which forcible actions do not amount to a violation of the ban on the use of force.[107] Corten explains that two criteria should be taken into consideration when analysing forcible actions. First, the operation needs to be sufficiently grave. Second, the intent of the state should play a role in the interpretation of Article 2(4): only actions directed at 'forcing the will of another state'[108] would fall within the scope of the provision. In any case, excluding the application of the ban on the use of force does not imply that other norms are not relevant: the actions could still amount to unlawful intervention in the internal affairs of the state or as a violation of state sovereignty.[109] The ICJ confirmed this approach in the *Corfu Channel* case.[110] On 22 October 1946, British vessels were passing through the Corfu Channel when they struck maritime mines in the territorial waters of Albania. One month later, the United Kingdom (UK) carried out a minesweeping operation in the Channel, although Albania did not consent to such action. The Court

[102] Corten (n 87) 77.

[103] R Higgins, *Problems and Process: International Law and How We Use It* (Clarendon Press, 1994) 240.

[104] Ruys (n 87) 210. See also Higgins (n 103) 240; Lieblich (n 1) 58.

[105] Ruys (n 87) 210.

[106] ibid, 209.

[107] ME O'Connell, 'The Prohibition of the Use of Force' in ND White and C Henderson (eds), *Research Handbook on International Conflict and Security Law: Jus ad Bellum, Jus in Bello and Jus post Bellum* (Edward Elgar, 2013) 89–119: 'Article 2(4) is narrower than it might appear on its face. Minimal or *de minimis* uses of force are likely to fall below the threshold of the Article 2(4) prohibition.'

[108] Corten (n 87) 76–77: '[w]hat matters, besides an abstract evaluation of the gravity of events, is to determine whether there is an intention on the part of a State to use force against another State. Such an intention appears to be an essential characteristic of the use of force under the Charter, and is a second criterion that is really inseparable from that of gravity'.

[109] ibid, 83.

[110] ICJ, *Corfu Channel (United Kingdom v Albania)*, Judgment (Merits), 9 April 1949 (hereinafter *Corfu Channel* case).

was called on to decide, inter alia, whether the activities carried out by the UK violated the sovereignty of Albania. Interestingly, the ICJ did not mention Article 2(4); instead, it stated that:

> The Court can only regard the alleged right of intervention as the manifestation of a policy of force, such as has, in the past, given rise to most serious abuses and such as cannot, whatever be the present defects in international organization, find a place in international law. Intervention is perhaps still less admissible in the particular form it would take here; for, from the nature of things, it would be reserved for the most powerful States, and might easily lead to perverting the administration of international justice itself. ... Between independent States, respect for territorial sovereignty is an essential foundation of international relations ... the Court must declare that the action of the British Navy constituted a violation of Albanian sovereignty.[111]

The ICJ suggested that the actions by the UK were not sufficiently grave to fall within the scope of Article 2(4),[112] thus alluding to the existence of a *de minimis* threshold. Recently, the Independent International Fact-Finding Mission on the Conflict in Georgia adopted a similar approach: its Report specifies that only 'physical force which surpasses a minimum threshold of intensity' is covered by the ban on the use of force. Moreover, it specified that '[o]nly very small incidents lie below this threshold, for instance the targeted killing of single individuals, forcible abductions of individual persons, or the interception of a single aircraft'.[113]

The term *use of force* raises questions not only with regard to its lower threshold, but also with respect to the acts that do fall within the scope of Article 2(4). The confusion stems from the recourse to a variety of terms in treaties and judgments. For instance, Article 1(1) of the UN Charter refers to 'threats to peace', 'acts of aggression' and 'other breaches of the peace'; Article 2(4) bans 'the threat or use of force'; Article 51 limits the right to self-defence as a reaction to 'armed attacks'; while Article 1(1) mentions 'the suppression of acts of aggression' amongst the purposes of the United Nations.[114] More recently, following the adoption of the Kampala Amendments to the Rome Statute,[115] the definition

[111] ibid, 35. For an in-depth analysis, see O'Connell (n 107) 102–104.

[112] *Corfu Channel* case, at 36.

[113] Report of the Independent International Fact-Finding Mission on the Conflict in Georgia, (Vol II, 25 September 2009) 242. On 2 December 2008, a Decision of the Council of the European Union established an Independent International Fact-Finding Mission on the Conflict in Georgia (IIFFMCG). See also R Kolb, *Ius contra Bellum: Le Droit International relatif au Maintien de la Paix* (Bruylant, 2009) 247.

[114] The term 'aggression' is also mentioned in Arts 39 and 53 of the UN Charter. See J Klabbers, 'Intervention, Armed Intervention, Armed Attack, Threat to Peace, Act of Aggression, and Threat or Use of Force: What's the Difference?' in Weller (ed) (n 78) 491.

[115] Resolution RC/Res.6 (n 4) Annex I, Art 8*bis*, The Crime of Aggression, 13th plenary meeting of the ICC Assembly of States Parties at Kampala, 11 June 2010 (hereinafter the Kampala Amendments).

of the crime of aggression has been added to the Statute of the International Criminal Court (ICC). Specifically, Article 8*bis*(1) defines the crime of aggression as:

> [T]he planning, preparation, initiation or execution, by a person in a position effectively to exercise control over or to direct the political or military action of a State, of an act of aggression which, by its character, gravity and scale, constitutes a manifest violation of the Charter of the United Nations.

Furthermore, Article 8*bis*(2) defines an act of aggression as:

> [T]he use of armed force by a State against the sovereignty, territorial integrity or political independence of another State, or in any other manner inconsistent with the Charter of the United Nations. Any of the following acts, regardless of a declaration of war, shall, in accordance with United Nations General Assembly resolution 3314 (XXIX) of 14 December 1974, qualify as an act of aggression.

On the other hand, the ICJ introduced some elements of uncertainty. Notably, in the *Nicaragua* case the Court distinguished 'the most grave forms of the use of force (those constituting an armed attack) from the other less grave forms'.[116] Moreover, it differentiated between actions that amount to armed attack and those that can be considered as a 'mere frontier incident'.[117] According to the Court, the difference between the two is based on 'scale and effects' of the forcible action.[118] Therefore, while the ICJ posited that there exists a gap between Article 2(4) and Article 51 and that 'a State may employ some illegal force against another without thereby unleashing a full-blown armed attack', it failed to define these terms. This 'linguistic diversity'[119] generated a lively debate on their meaning and their legal consequences.

Part of the scholarship has criticised the distinction between Article 2(4) and Article 51 *tout court*.[120] According to these authors, Article 51 does not specify that an armed attack should be especially grave in order to trigger the right to self-defence.[121] Furthermore, by way of custom, this right imposes

[116] *Nicaragua* case, §191. The distinction was reaffirmed in the *Oil Platforms* (*Islamic Republic of Iran v United States of America*), Judgment (Merits), 6 November 2003 (hereinafter *Oil Platforms* case), §§51, 62.

[117] *Nicaragua* case, §195.

[118] ibid.

[119] Klabbers (n 114) 491.

[120] JL Hargrove, 'The *Nicaragua* Judgment and the Future of the Law of Force and Self–Defense' (1987) 81(1) *American Journal of International Law* 135–43; Higgins (n 103) 251; I Brownlie, 'The Use of Force in Self-Defence' (1961) 37 *British Year Book of International Law* 245; WM Reisman, 'Allocating Competences to Use Coercion in the Post-Cold War World: Practices, Conditions, and Prospects' in LF Damrosch and DJ Scheffer (eds), *Law and Force in the New International Order* (Westview Press 1991) 39–40; JL Kunz, 'Individual and Collective Self-Defense in Article 51 of the Charter of the United Nations' (1947) 41(4) *American Journal of International Law* 878; GM Badr, 'The Exculpatory Effect of Self-Defense in State Responsibility' (1980) 10(1) *Georgia Journal of International and Comparative Law* 1.

[121] Hargrove (n 120) 139.

on states the duty to react in a proportionate manner and only when necessary. Therefore, it would seem preposterous to distinguish between 'armed attack' and 'use of force': states could resort to self-defence against nearly any use of force; the proportionality and necessity requirements suffice to ensure that the right is not abused.[122] Several authors have adopted a more nuanced approach. They agree with the ICJ that less grave forms of use of force do not amount to armed attack, and they thus focus their analysis on the gravity threshold that would trigger the application of Article 51.[123] For instance, Dinstein maintains that:

> Logically and pragmatically, the gap between Article 2(4) ('use of force') and Article 51 ('armed attack') ought to be no more than a hiatus, inasmuch as 'there is very little effective protection against States violating the prohibition of the use of force, as long as they do not resort to an armed attack'.[124]

Stahn recognises that 'the threshold that *Nicaragua* established is not in itself unreasonable or unrealistic'[125] and excludes 'isolated and sporadic acts of violence' from the notion of armed attack.[126] Similarly, d'Aspremont recognises that '[t]he conservatism of the court has probably not been useless. It seems that in practice States still believe that self-defense can only be used as long as the original attack is of sufficient gravity'.[127]

The discussion on the hiatus between Article 2(4) and Article 51 raises a further question regarding the measures available to the victim state. Authors who affirm that every form of use of force amounts to an armed attack conclude that the victim state can always react in self-defence. However, should a gap between the two articles exist, does international law allow counter-measures against less grave forms of the use of force? Article 50(a) of the International Law Commission (ILC) Draft Articles on State Responsibility seems to exclude this possibility, whereby it affirms that 'countermeasures shall not affect the obligation to refrain from the threat or use of force as embodied in

[122] ibid, 143.

[123] See eg Dinstein (n 73) 207–10; C Stahn, 'Terrorist Acts as "Armed Attack": The Right to Self-Defense, Art 51 (1/2) of the UN Charter, and International Terrorism' (2003) 27(2) *The Fletcher Forum of World Affairs* 45–46; Gray (n 20) 180–81; T Ruys, *'Armed Attack' and Article 51 of the UN Charter: Evolutions in Customary Law and Practice* (Cambridge University Press, 2010) 145–49.

[124] Dinstein (n 73) 208. See also G Nolte and A Randelzhofer, 'Action with Respect to Threats to the Peace, Breaches of the Peace, and Acts of Aggression, Article 51' in B Simma, DE Khan, G Nolte, A Paulus and N Wessendorf (eds), *The Charter of the United Nations: A Commentary*, vol II (Oxford University Press, 2012) 1397–1428.

[125] Stahn (n 123) 46.

[126] ibid.

[127] J d'Aspremont, 'Mapping the Concepts Behind the Contemporary Liberalization of the Use of Force in International Law' (2010) 31(4) *University of Pennsylvania Journal of International Law* 1119.

the Charter of the United Nations'.[128] However, the ICJ in the *Nicaragua* case alluded to such an eventuality:

> While an armed attack would give rise to an entitlement to collective self-defence, a use of force of a lesser degree of gravity cannot … produce any entitlement to take collective counter-measures involving the use of force. The acts of which Nicaragua is accused … could only have justified proportionate counter-measures on the part of the State which had been the victim of these acts.[129]

The Court refrained from clarifying whether counter-measures against less grave uses of force would also encompass armed action; however, it seems that it did strongly support this possibility.[130] Judge Simma regretted the lack of clarity: in his Separate Opinion in the *Oil Platforms* case he expressed the view that 'by such proportionate countermeasures the Court cannot have understood mere pacific reprisals'.[131] He thus suggested distinguishing:

> [B]etween (full-scale) self-defence within the meaning of Article 51 against an 'armed attack' within the meaning of the same Charter provision on the one hand and, on the other, the case of hostile action, for instance against individual ships, below the level of Article 51, justifying proportionate defensive measures on the part of the victim, equally short of the quality and quantity of action in self-defence expressly reserved in the United Nations Charter.[132]

The Institut de Droit International (IDI) expressed a similar view in its Santiago Resolution on Present Problems of the Use of Armed Force in International Law:

> An armed attack triggering the right of self-defense must be of a certain degree of gravity. Acts involving the use of force of lesser intensity may give rise to counter-measures in conformity with international law. In case of an attack of lesser intensity the target State may also take strictly necessary police measures to repel the attack.[133]

[128] International Law Commission (ILC), Draft articles on Responsibility of States for Internationally Wrongful Acts, with commentaries (2001) *Yearbook of the International Law Commission*, vol II, Part Two (hereinafter ILC Draft Articles on State Responsibility). The Draft Articles were annexed to General Assembly Resolution 56/83, *Responsibility of States for internationally wrongful acts*, A/RES/56/83, 12 December 2001. See also d'Aspremont (n 127) 1111: '[i]t is well known that Article 50 of the Articles on State Responsibility prohibits military counter-measures, that is, reactions of injured States that could involve a violation of the prohibition on the use of force. By carefully carving the substantive limits of the types of counter-measures that may be utilized by injured States, the International Law Commission aimed to reflect the classical limits of the prohibition on the use of force'.

[129] *Nicaragua* case, §249.

[130] ibid, §210; JL Hargrove (n 120) 138.

[131] ICJ, *Oil Platforms* case, Separate Opinion of Judge Simma (hereinafter *Oil Platforms* Simma Separate Opinion) §12.

[132] ibid, §12. The debate amongst scholars is still ongoing; see eg Dinstein (n 73) 209, 254; Ruys (n 123) 142; Kreß (n 91) 592; Hargrove (n 120) 141–42; Gray (n 20) 178.

[133] Institut de Droit International, *Present Problems of the Use of Armed Force in International Law*, Session de Santiago (27 October 2007). See also d'Aspremont (n 127) 1114.

'The interrelationship of aggression, frontier incident, and armed attack'[134] has proved equally problematic. The distinction between minor uses of force and more grave ones was addressed during the drafting of the 1974 Definition of Aggression.[135] Some delegates suggested the introduction of a *de minimis* clause in order to avoid the condemnation by the Security Council of less serious acts.[136] However, this proposal was heavily criticised by some authors: '[t]here are frontier incidents and frontier incidents. Some are trivial, some may be extremely grave'.[137] The debate led to the adoption of Article 2 of the Definition of Aggression, which reads as follows:

> The First use of armed force by a State in contravention of the Charter shall constitute prima facie evidence of an act of aggression although the Security Council may, in conformity with the Charter, conclude that a determination that an act of aggression has been committed would not be justified in the light of other relevant circumstances, including the fact that the acts concerned or their consequences are not of sufficient gravity.

Although the provision does not expressly mention frontier incidents, it clarifies that less grave uses of force do not amount to aggression.[138] In any event, as correctly noted by Higgins, admitting that frontier incidents would not fall within the scope of 'aggression' does not mean that these instances are lawful: indeed, they could constitute a breach of peace and trigger the powers of the United Nations Security Council (UNSC) under Chapter VII of the UN Charter.[139]

More controversial is the distinction between 'aggression' and 'armed attack'. A comparison of the French and the English versions of Article 51 of the UN Charter, both equally authentic, reflects the conundrum: while the English version limits the right to self-defence against 'armed attacks', the French one refers to 'aggression armée'.[140] The ICJ contributed to the confusion by using the Definition of Aggression to clarify the notion of armed attack with regard to indirect aggression.[141] From the negotiations on Resolution 3314, it emerges that at the time the difference between the two terms was still unclear. On the one hand, some delegates maintained that 'aggression' and

[134] Gray (n 20) 182–83.

[135] A/RES/3314, 14 December 1974, *Definition of Aggression* (hereinafter, Definition of Aggression).

[136] BB Ferencz, *Defining International Aggression: The Search for World Peace: A Documentary History and Analysis* (Oceana Publications, 1975) 367; Gray (n 20) 182.

[137] GG Fitzmaurice, 'The Definition of Aggression' (1952) 1(1) *The International and Comparative Law Quarterly* 139.

[138] Gray (n 20) 182.

[139] R Higgins, *The Development of International Law through the Political Organs of the United Nations* (Oxford University Press, 1963) 181; Gray (n 20) 182.

[140] Ruys (n 123) 127.

[141] *Nicaragua* case, §195.

'armed attack' are synonymous.[142] On the other hand, the majority agreed that there is a 'cascading relationship' between 'use of force' (Article 2(4)), 'aggression' (Article 39), and 'armed attack' (Article 51).[143] According to this view, any armed attack would also be an aggression, thus any limitation of the scope of aggression would apply to the notion of armed attack too, but the opposite would not be true.[144]

The notion of armed attack raises crucial issues also with regard to the author of the attack. Notably, since the terrorist attacks on the US on 11 September 2001, a number of states have claimed that armed attacks conducted by armed non-state actors (ANSAs) could trigger the right to self-defence under Article 51 of the UN Charter.[145] The traditional understanding of 'armed attack' posits that it is not 'an incident created by irresponsible groups or individuals, but rather an attack by one State upon another'.[146] Nevertheless, in the past there have been instances where states have suggested that an armed attack triggering the right to self-defence could also be committed by a non-state actor. For instance, in 1956 Israel intervened in Egypt as a reaction to attacks committed by *Fedayeen* based in the Sinai Peninsula, and justified the intervention by invoking the right to self-defence.[147] More recently, the question has emerged with regard to the intervention of the US-led coalition against the Islamic State in Syria.[148] Part of the scholarship supports this interpretation;[149] however, the majority view is in favour of a more strict interpretation of Article 51. Indeed, while the two UNSC resolutions adopted in the aftermath of 9/11 reaffirmed the right to self-defence and condemned the terrorist attacks, following resolutions addressing terrorism have avoided

[142] See eg A/AC.134/SR.67–78, 12 (Ecuador) and A/AC.134/SR.52–66, 90 (Cyprus). See Ruys (n 123) 134.

[143] ibid.

[144] ibid.

[145] See eg S/RES/1368 (2001), 12 September 2001; S/RES/1373 (2001), 28 September 2001. See also ICJ, *Legal Consequences of the Construction of a Wall in the Occupied Palestinian Territory*, Advisory Opinion, 9 July 2004 (hereinafter, *Wall* case), Separate Opinion of Judge Kooijmans, §35; Declaration of Judge Buergenthal, §6.

[146] United States of America, U.S. Senate, Report of the Committee on Foreign Relations on the North Atlantic Treaty, Executive Report no. 8, 13 (6 June 1949), quoted in I Brownlie, *International Law and the Use of Force by States* (Oxford University Press, 1963) 278. See also T Ruys and L Ferro, 'Divergent Views on the Content and Relevance of the Jus Ad Bellum in Europe and the United States? The Case of the U.S.-Led Military Coalition Against "Islamic State"' in C Giorgetti and G Verdirame (eds), *Concepts on International Law in Europe and the United States* (Cambridge University Press, 2016) 8.

[147] Ruys and Ferro (n 146) 8.

[148] Corten (n 70).

[149] See eg D. Bethlehem, 'Self-Defense against an Imminent or Actual Armed Attack by Nonstate Actors' (2012) 106(4) *American Journal of International Law* 770–77; E. Wilmshurst, 'Principles of International Law on the Use of Force by States in Self-Defence' (Chatam House, 1 October 2005), available at www.chathamhouse.org/publications/papers/view/108106.

mentioning self-defence.[150] Furthermore, even if the International Court of Justice (ICJ) has been ambiguous on the matter in a number of cases,[151] in the *Wall* Advisory Opinion it explicitly excluded the right to self-defence in the case of armed attacks committed by non-state actors.[152]

B. The Nature of the Prohibition

The vast majority of scholars agree that the ban on the use of force has attained the status of customary law.[153] The ICJ endorsed this conclusion in the *Nicaragua* case, where it decided that 'the United States of America … has acted, against the Republic of Nicaragua, in breach of its obligation under customary international law not to use force against another state'.[154] Similarly, in the *Wall* opinion, the Court reiterated that 'the principles as to the use of force incorporated in the Charter reflect customary international law' and that 'the same is true of its corollary entailing the illegality of territorial acquisition resulting from the threat or use of force'.[155]

In order to investigate 'the substance of the customary rules relating to the use of force in international relations',[156] the Court focused first of all on the existence of a general *opinio juris*.[157] To this end the ICJ relied, inter alia, on the Declaration on Friendly Relations, which was adopted by consensus in 1970.[158] Its first principle reproduces the exact wording of Article 2(4), with one difference: instead of binding '[a]ll members', it applies to '[e]very State'. Dinstein notes that '[t]his was done deliberately, on the ground that all States are now subject to the same rule'.[159]

It is well known that *opinio juris* alone is not sufficient to conclude that a rule is deemed to be customary: 'evidence of general practice' is equally decisive.[160] Nonetheless, in the *Nicaragua* case, the Court's analysis omitted

[150] See eg UN Doc, S/RES/1438 (2002), 14 October 2002; UN Doc. S/RES/1440 (2002), 24 October 2002; UN Doc. S/RES/1450 (2002), 13 December 2002; UN Doc. S/RES/1456 (2003), 20 January 2003; UN Doc. S/RES/1465 (2003), 13 February 2003; UN Doc. S/RES/1516 (2003), 20 November 2003; UN Doc. S/RES/1530 (2004), 11 March 2004; UN Doc. S/RES/1611 (2005), 7 July 2005. See also *Wall* case, §139.

[151] *Nicaragua* case, §§154–160; *Congo* case, §§146–47.

[152] *Wall* case, §139.

[153] O Dörr and A Randelzhofer, 'Purposes and Principles, Article 2(4)' in B Simma, DE Khan, G Nolte, A Paulus and N Wessendorf (eds), *The Charter of the United Nations: A Commentary*, vol I (Oxford University Press, 2012) 200–34.

[154] *Nicaragua* case, §292(4).

[155] *Wall* case, §87.

[156] *Nicaragua* case, §187.

[157] ibid, §188.

[158] Dinstein (n 73) 96.

[159] ibid; R Rosenstock, 'The Declaration of Principles of International Law Concerning Friendly Relations: A Survey' (1971) 65(5) *American Journal of International Law* 717.

[160] Statute of the International Court of Justice 1945, Art 38(1)(b) (hereinafter ICJ Statute).

reviewing the relevant State practice,[161] a circumstance vastly criticised by the scholarship.[162] The ICJ admitted that breaches of the ban on the use of force are not uncommon in practice. Nonetheless, it added that it is not reasonable to expect that states would perfectly obey such a prohibition:

> The Court does not consider that, for a rule to be established as customary, the corresponding practice must be in absolutely rigorous conformity with the rule. In order to deduce the existence of customary rules, the Court deems it sufficient that the conduct of States should, in general, be consistent with such rules, and that instances of State conduct inconsistent with a given rule should generally have been treated as breaches of that rule, not as indications of the recognition of a new rule. If a State acts in a way *prima facie* incompatible with a recognized rule, but defends its conduct by appealing to exceptions or justifications contained within the rule itself, then whether or not the State's conduct is in fact justifiable on that basis, the significance of that attitude is to confirm rather than to weaken the rule.[163]

The widespread violations of the ban on the use of force led part of the scholarship to declare the death of the prohibition.[164] Franck famously affirmed that 'the high-minded resolve of Article 2(4) mocks us from its grave'.[165] In a similar vein, Arend contended that states 'no longer truly accept this provision as law',[166] while Glennon claimed that 'the rule has fallen into desuetude and is no longer obligatory'.[167] These observations rest upon the premise that, when a rule is repeatedly violated by a considerable number of states over a significant timeframe, it would be preposterous to maintain that states feel compelled to oblige such a provision.[168]

[161] Dörr and Randelzhofer (n 153) 230; Dinstein (n 73) 96.

[162] See eg TM Franck, 'Some Observations on the ICJ's Procedural and Substantive Innovations' (1987) 81(1) *American Journal of International Law* 119: '[t]he customary norms cited by the Court are adhered to, at best, only by some states, on some instances, and have been ignored, alas, with impunity in at least two hundred instances of military conflict since the end of World War II'.

[163] *Nicaragua* case, §186.

[164] See eg TM Franck, 'Who Killed Article 2(4)? or: Changing Norms Governing the Use of Force by States' (1970) 64(5) *American Journal of International Law* 809–37; TM Franck, 'What Happens Now? The United Nations after Iraq' (2003) 97(3) *American Journal of International Law* 607–20; J Combacau, 'The Exception of Self-Defense in United Nations Practice' in Cassese (ed) (n 87); RA Falk, *Revitalizing International Law* (Iowa State University Press, 1989); AC Arend, *Legal Rules and International Society* (Oxford University Press, 1999); MJ Glennon, 'How international rules die' (2005) 93(3) *Georgetown Law Journal* 939–91; MJ Glennon, 'The Limitations of Traditional Rules and Institutions Relating to the Use of Force' in Weller (ed) (n 15) 79–96; d'Aspremont (n 127). It is beyond the scope of this work to investigate 'whether compliance with international legal rules is obligatory; if so, why; and whether international law plays the causative role in shaping international relations that international lawyers have long believed that it does'; Glennon, above, 939. However, the question is relevant for our discussion. Indeed, this dissertation investigates to what extent human rights are modifying the instances of lawful intervention in internal conflicts. Thus, the customary nature of the ban on the use of force and whether its violations would be capable of changing it are relevant questions.

[165] Franck (n 164) 809.

[166] Arend (n 164) 76.

[167] Glennon (n 164) 960.

[168] ibid.

On the other hand, the majority of authors believe that the ban on the use of force is not a dead letter.[169] First, while violations of Article 2(4) are tangible and manifest, it is nearly impossible to assess the extent to which states voluntarily and knowingly avoid using force.[170] Second, '[a] breach of international law, as such, cannot generate an evolution of the rule prohibiting the use of force'.[171] In order to claim otherwise, it would be necessary to prove that a new customary rule allowing the free use of force has emerged. To this end, the sole state practice would not be enough: 'the disappearance of a customary norm and its replacement by a new norm require again widespread acceptance in the international community'.[172] Nevertheless, no government has ever argued that Article 2(4) UN Charter is not binding.[173] As noted by the ICJ in the *Nicaragua* case, when resorting to force states have consistently invoked justifications within the framework of international law: they have never tried to claim that the free use of force is allowed.[174] Therefore, although admittedly the exact content of the ban on the use of force and of its exceptions tends to be blurred, it seems undeniable that its core is unscathed.[175]

The legal scholarship seems to be divided not only with regard to the customary nature of the ban on the use of force, but also as to whether it is *jus cogens*.[176] The debate does not have only a theoretical value: the qualification of the ban on the use of force as a peremptory rule entails significant practical consequences.[177] Notably, *jus cogens* provisions prevent the invocation

[169] See eg L Henkin, 'The Reports of the Death of Article 2(4) Are Greatly Exaggerated' (1971) 65(3) *American Journal of International Law* 544–48; Schachter (n 81); O Schachter, 'In Defense of International Rules on the Use of Force' (1986) 53(1) *University of Chicago Law Review* 113–46; D Wippman, 'The Nine Lives of Article 2(4)' (2007) 2 *Minnesota Journal of International Law* 387–406; Dinstein (n 73); J Crawford and R Nicholson, 'The Continued Relevance of Established Rules and Institutions Relating to the Use of Force' in Weller (ed) (n 78) 96–113.

[170] d'Aspremont (n 127) 1102. See also AC Arend and RJ Beck, *International Law and the Use of Force: Beyond the UN Charter Paradigm* (Routledge, 1993) 180: '[w]hile it is easy to count the times that a particular norm is violated, it is quite difficult to identify the times when a norm exerted a controlling influence, when states refrained from forcible action because of Article 2(4)'s proscription'.

[171] O Corten, 'Breaches and Evolution of Customary International Law' in E Cannizzaro and P Palchetti (eds), *Customary International Law on the Use of Force: A Methodological Approach* (Martinus Nijhoff, 2005) 142.

[172] R Bernhardt, 'Customary International Law' in *Encyclopedia of Public International Law* (North-Holland, 1992) 901; T Treves, 'Customary International Law' in *Max Planck Encyclopedia of Public International Law* (Oxford University Press, 2006) §17; *Nicaragua* case, §207.

[173] Henkin (n 169) 548; Dinstein (n 73) 97.

[174] Schachter (n 169) 131.

[175] Wippman (n 169) 391, 394–95; Crawford and Nicholson (n 169) 112–13.

[176] VCLT, Art 53: 'A peremptory norm of general international law is a norm accepted and recognized by the international community of States as a whole as a norm from which no derogation is permitted and which can be modified only by a subsequent norm of general international law having the same character.' See also Dinstein (n 73) 104–5.

[177] In any case, the theoretical value of the issue would per se be sufficient to justify such investigation. See A Bianchi, 'Engaging with Theory – Why Bother?' (*EJIL: Talk!*, 2017), available at www.ejiltalk.org/engaging-with-theory-why-bother/.

of circumstances precluding wrongfulness in case of violation,[178] void conflicting treaties,[179] terminate pre-existing conventions in contrast with such rules,[180] and require states to cooperate to recognise and bring an end to serious breaches of these rules.[181] Admitting the peremptory nature of the ban on the use of force would thus raise crucial issues: would interventions by invitation be lawful? Could states legally resort to forcible counter-measures against less grave forcible actions?

A relatively small part of the scholarship denies *tout court* the existence of peremptory rules, a position that would solve the problem of the nature of the ban on the use of force *ab initio*.[182] These authors notice that for a long time the category of *jus cogens* existed only in the legal literature and that the Vienna Convention on the Law of Treaties (VCLT) is the only venue where it entered the realm of positive law.[183] The introduction of peremptory rules in the Convention did not shed more light on this category of norms: their definition 'is circular in a very obvious way. It therefore has no meaning and must be discarded'.[184] Furthermore, they affirm that since 1969 the development and functions of *jus cogens* have been limited.[185]

While the existence of *jus cogens* rules is now overwhelmingly accepted,[186] a small number of writers deny, albeit with caution, that the ban on the use of

[178] ILC Draft Articles on State Responsibility, Art 26: 'Nothing in this chapter precludes the wrongfulness of any act of a State which is not in conformity with an obligation arising under a peremptory norm of general international law'.

[179] VCLT, Art 53: 'A treaty is void if, at the time of its conclusion, it conflicts with a peremptory norm of international law'.

[180] VCLT, Art 64: 'If a new peremptory norm of general international law emerges, any existing treaty which is in conflict with that norm becomes void and terminates'.

[181] ILC Draft Articles on State Responsibility, Art 41: '1. States shall cooperate to bring to an end through lawful means any serious breach within the meaning of article 40. 2. No State shall recognize as lawful a situation created by a serious breach within the meaning of article 40, nor render aid or assistance in maintaining that situation. 3. This article is without prejudice to the other consequences referred to in this Part and to such further consequences that a breach to which this chapter applies may entail under international law'. See also d'Aspremont (n 127) 1105.

[182] See eg D Shelton, 'Sherlock Holmes and the Mystery of *Jus Cogens*' in M den Heijer and H van der Wilt (eds), *Netherlands Yearbook of International Law 2015: Jus Cogens: Quo Vadis?* (Springer, 2015) 23 (claiming that: '[l]ike Sherlock Holmes, the idea of *jus cogens* emerged as a concept in the imagination of writers. Over time both Sherlock Holmes and *jus cogens* have generated widespread belief in their reality, but it is a reality that is subjectively shaped by each follower'); MJ Glennon, *Limits of Law, Prerogatives of Power: Interventionism after Kosovo* (Palgrave, 2001) 40–42; C Farhang, 'The Notion of Consent in Part One of the Draft Articles on State Responsibility' (2014) 27(1) *Leiden Journal of International Law* 55–73; AM Weisburd, 'The Emptiness of the Concept of *Jus Cogens*, as Illustrated by the War in Bosnia-Herzegovina' (1995) 17 *Michigan Journal of International Law* 1–52; GA Christenson, '*Jus Cogens*: Guarding Interests Fundamental to International Society' (1988) 28(3) *Virginia Journal of International Law* 585–648.

[183] Shelton (n 182) 33.

[184] Farhang (n 182) 70.

[185] Weisburd (n 182) 17; Shelton (n 182) 48.

[186] A Bianchi, 'Human Rights and the Magic of *Jus Cogens*' (2008) 19(3) *European Journal of International Law* 491–92; L Hannikainen, *Peremptory Norms (Jus Cogens) in International Law: Historical Development, Criteria, Present Status* (Lakimiesliiton Kustannus/Finnish Lawyers' Publishing Company, 1988); AL Paulus, '*Jus Cogens* in a Time of Hegemony and Fragmentation'

force falls within this category.[187] The reasons adduced to support this conclusion are twofold. First, the ban on the use of force seems a largely unclear rule: the exact content of the prohibition, as well as its limits and exceptions, is blurred and confused. Therefore, it would seem impossible to agree on 'a workable *jus cogens* norm that encompasses the ban on the use of force at all'.[188] Second, it is controversial whether the ban on the use of force is 'accepted and recognized by the international community of states as a whole'[189] as a peremptory norm.[190]

A preponderant number of authors uphold that the ban on the use of force is peremptory in nature.[191] Nonetheless, they disagree with regard to the exact content of the *jus cogens* norm. The debate stems from the fact that, while other peremptory norms are absolute, the ban on the use of force is peculiar inasmuch as it allows exceptions.[192] The ILC Draft Articles on State Responsibility recognises consent (Article 20) and counter-measures (Article 22) as circumstances precluding wrongfulness. On the other hand, Article 26 of the ILC Draft Articles specifies that '[n]othing in this chapter precludes the wrongfulness of any act of a State which is not in conformity with an obligation arising under a peremptory norm of general international law'. Therefore, in principle, state consent and counter-measures could not justify the use of force. However, nowadays it is generally accepted that interventions by invitation are lawful: in principle, a state can consent to forcible operations conducted by a foreign state within its territory.[193] Second, the aforementioned part of the scholarship claims that states could resort to armed counter-measures against less grave uses of force. To resolve the conundrum, authors have suggested three possible solutions.

(2005) 74(3) *Nordic Journal of International Law* 297–333; U Linderfalk, 'The Effect of *Jus Cogens* Norms: Whoever Opened Pandora's Box, Did You Ever Think about the Consequences?' (2007) 18(5) *European Journal of International Law* 853–55.

[187] J Green, 'Questioning the Peremptory Status of the Use of Force' (2011) 32(2) *Michigan Journal of International Law* 217: 'the position taken here is not necessarily that the prohibition is a norm that has failed to achieve peremptory status. Instead, it is argued that there are significant difficulties with such a conclusion and that, as a result, the widespread uncritical acceptance of the prohibition as a *jus cogens* norm is concerning'. See also T Gazzini, *The Changing Rules on the Use of Force in International Law* (Manchester University Press, 2006) 88–89.

[188] Green (n 187) 217, 234: 'ultimately, to provide a sufficiently detailed rule, it is necessary to articulate a norm so lengthy that it is unwieldy to the point of losing worth'.

[189] VCLT, Art 53.

[190] Green (n 187) 243–4.

[191] A de Hoogh, '*Jus Cogens* and the Use of Armed Force' in Weller (ed) (n 78) 1163; A Orakhelashvili, 'Changing *Jus Cogens* Through State Practice: The Case of the Prohibition of the Use of Force and its Exceptions' in ibid, 165.

[192] de Hoogh (n 191) 1165.

[193] See eg L Doswald-Beck, 'The Legal Validity of Military Intervention by Invitation of the Government' (1986) 56(1) *British Yearbook of International Law* 189–252; A Tanca, *Foreign Armed Intervention in Internal Conflicts* (Martinus Nijhoff, 1993); Lieblich (n 1). See also below, Part II.

Those who admit the possibility of using forcible counter-measures against less grave instances of the use of force draw a distinction between the prohibition of aggression and the ban on the use of force, and conclude that only the first would retain a peremptory nature.[194] To bolster their conclusion, they rely on the ILC Commentary to the Draft Articles on State Responsibility, which mentions the prohibition of aggression as an example of a peremptory norm.[195] However, this reasoning has been criticised for three reasons. First, when states mentioned the peremptory nature of Article 2(4) of the UN Charter, they did not distinguish between grave and less grave forms of the use of force:[196] while this distinction is crucial for the right of self-defence, it does not play a pivotal role when it comes to *jus cogens*.[197] Second, the choice to circumscribe the peremptory nature of Article 2(4) of the UN Charter to aggression has been justified on the basis that the latter has a more limited scope.[198] However, upon closer analysis this seems doubtful: the list of acts mentioned in the Definition of Aggression is quite broad.[199] Third, the Definition of Aggression itself seems to suggest that states can consent to an act that, without invitation, would amount to aggression.[200] Article 3(e) includes amongst the instances of aggression:

> The use of armed forces of one State which are within the territory of another State *with the agreement of the receiving State*, in contravention of the conditions provided for in the agreement or any extension of their presence in such territory beyond the termination of the agreement.[201]

Based on the above, the doctrine whereby only the ban on aggression would be peremptory in character does not seem to be confirmed. To resolve the conundrum, Orakhelashvili has suggested the opposite solution: instead of limiting the *jus cogens* nature to a part of Article 2(4), he affirmed that '*jus ad bellum* as a whole is peremptory'.[202] Others have adopted a more moderate approach,

[194] T Christakis, 'Unilateralisme et Multilatéralisme dans la Lutte contre la Terreur: L'exemple du Terrorisme Biologique et Chimique' in K Bannelier et al (eds), *Le Droit International Face au Terrorisme: après le 11 Septembre 2001* (Pedone, 2003) 159–78; M Roscini, 'Threats of Armed Force and Contemporary International Law' (2007) 54(2) *Netherlands International Law Review* 276; A Abass, 'Consent Precluding State Responsibility: A Critical Analysis' (2004) 53(1) *International & Comparative Law Quarterly* 225; N Ronzitti, 'Use of Force, *Jus Cogens* and State Consent' in A. Cassese (ed) (n 87) 159.

[195] ILC Draft Articles on State Responsibility, Commentary, at 85, §5. Furthermore, the Commentary specifies that 'in applying some peremptory norms the consent of a particular State may be relevant. For example, a state may validly consent to a foreign military presence on its territory for a lawful purpose' (ILC Draft Articles on State Responsibility, Commentary) 85, §6.

[196] Corten (n 87) 251.

[197] ibid, 200.

[198] de Hoogh (n 191) 1174.

[199] De Hoogh notes that: '[i]n reading this [the Definition of Aggression] one is struck by the fact that any use of armed force appears to constitute an act of aggression'. See ibid.

[200] Corten (n 87) 251–52.

[201] Emphasis added.

[202] A Orakhelashvili, *Peremptory Norms in International Law* (Oxford University Press, 2008) 51.

whereby only the use of force and its exceptions are *jus cogens*.[203] This view relies on Article 53 of the VCLT, which states that peremptory rules 'can be modified only by a subsequent norm of general international law having the same character'. Although this approach has an internal consistency, it could not be accepted. The first claim, whereby the whole *jus ad bellum* is peremptory, appears too broad: several rules related to the use of force could be derogated by states. For instance, the duty to report to the UNSC enshrined in Article 51 of the UN Charter does not seem to be peremptory in nature.[204] Furthermore, state practice does not seem to suggest that the international community as a whole considers the exceptions to the ban on the use of force as peremptory. Indeed, the exact content of these rules is still vastly debated and unclear.[205]

The last approach posits that only the ban on the use of force – not limited to aggression, not extended to include its exceptions – is peremptory in nature. This raises the issue of how to justify exceptions to Article 2(4) of the UN Charter, notably circumstances precluding wrongfulness and consent. With regard to the first exception, authors who extend the peremptory nature to the use of force as a whole (and not just to aggression) conclude that justifying the use of force on the basis of distress, necessity or countermeasures is not allowed under current international law.[206]

Reconciling forcible interventions by invitation with the peremptory nature of the ban on the use of force appears more problematic. The conundrum is further nurtured by the ILC Draft Articles on State Responsibility. On the one hand, it mentions consent amongst the circumstances precluding wrongfulness, on the other hand, its Commentary recognises that consent may validly authorise the use of force.[207] During the drafting of the Draft Articles, James Crawford suggested a different solution, namely to delete consent from the instances excluding wrongfulness.[208] In his view, consent does not operate as a secondary rule capable of excluding the unlawfulness of an otherwise wrongful act. Instead, it operates at the level of primary rules and has the effect 'that the rule,

[203] Hannikainen (n 186) 329–49; D Brown, 'Use of Force against Terrorism after September 11th: State Responsibility, Self-Defense and Other Responses' (2003) 11(1) *Cardozo Journal of International and Comparative Law* 19; N Ronzitti (n 194) 150–54; A Glassman, 'The Evolution of the Prohibition on the Use of Force and Its Conflict with Human Rights Protection: Balancing Equally Forceful *Jus Cogens* Norms' (2011) 16(2) *UCLA Journal of International Law and Foreign Affairs* 369.

[204] Green (n 187) 230–31; de Hoogh (n 191) 1172.

[205] Green (n 187) 234.

[206] Corten (n 87) 200, 217–25; de Hoogh (n 191) 1166.

[207] ILC Draft Articles on State Responsibility, Commentary, at 85, §6: 'by applying some peremptory norms the consent of a particular state may be relevant. For example, a state may validly consent to a foreign military presence on its territory for a lawful purpose'.

[208] J Crawford, *Second Report on State Responsibility*, 30 April 1999, A/CN.4/498/Add.2, §240.

whether or not it is considered as one of peremptory law, quite simply cannot have been violated'.[209] In the words of Crawford:

> Some peremptory norms contain an "intrinsic" consent element. For example, the rule relating to the non-use of force in international relations embodied in Article 2, paragraph 4, of the Charter of the United Nations does not apply in certain cases where one State has consented to the use of force on its territory by another State. But one State cannot by consent *eliminate* the rule relating to the use of force in international relations in its relations with another State. Thus it may be necessary to distinguish between a consent which applies Article 2 (4), which may be valid, and a purported consent which displaces or excludes it entirely, which, if Article 2 (4) is peremptory in character, would be invalid.[210]

Accordingly, consent would not operate as a circumstance excluding wrongfulness for the simple reason that *a priori* the forcible act would not constitute a violation of the ban on the use of force.[211] Another argument could support this position. As aforementioned, Article 2(4) of the UN Charter does not ban the use of any force, but only of a coercive one, which means 'force used without the consent of the affected state'.[212] Therefore, '[i]f consent is given freely, there is no imposition of will', thus no coercion. This would further prove that consent is an essential element of the provision enshrined in Article 2(4).[213] Thus consent would not operate as a circumstance precluding wrongfulness and it would not be in contrast with the peremptory nature of the ban on the use of force.

C. Forcible Interventions in Favour of Opposition Groups and the Question of State Attribution

The analysis conducted so far has focused on direct forms of intervention, namely the sending of national troops into the territory of a victim state. Nonetheless, state practice is not always as clear-cut. Since intervention in favour of rebel groups is generally unlawful, states tend to avoid sending their troops directly: they rather resort to irregular forces or forms of indirect intervention, such as financing, training and arming the rebels. The difficulties raised by these

[209] Corten (n 87) 252.

[210] Crawford (n 208) §240.

[211] T Christakis and K Mollard-Bannelier, '*Volenti non fit injuria*? Les effets du consentement à l'intervention militaire' (2004) 50(1) *Annuaire français de droit international* 107–108; Corten (n 87) 253; AVW Thomas and AJ Thomas Jr, *Non-intervention: The Law and Its Import in the Americas* (Southern Methodist University Press, 1956) 91.

[212] D Wippman, 'Treaty-Based Intervention: Who Can Say No?' (1995) 62(2) *University of Chicago Law Review* 622.

[213] ibid, 622; Corten (n 87) 253–54; Thomas and Thomas Jr (n 211) 91.

instances are twofold. First, it is necessary to evaluate the form of intervention in order to determine whether it amounts to armed attack or aggression, or if it entails a less grave form of use of force. Second, the relationship between the state and the armed non-state actor (ANSA) ought to be weighed to ascertain whether the actions of the irregular forces are attributable to the state.

With regard to the first issue, Article 3(g) of the Definition of Aggression includes amongst the instances of aggression:

> The sending by or on behalf of a State of armed bands, groups, irregulars or mercenaries, which carry out acts of armed force against another State of such gravity as to amount to the acts listed above, or its substantial involvement therein.

The ICJ in the *Nicaragua* case propounded that the same circumstance could amount to armed attack as well:

> The Court sees no reason to deny that, in customary law, the prohibition of armed attacks may apply to the sending by a State of armed bands to the territory of another State, if such an operation, because of its scale and effects, would have been classified as an armed attack rather than as a mere frontier incident had it been carried out by regular armed forces.[214]

However, the Court specified that 'the provision of weapons or of logistical or other support'[215] cannot amount to aggression, although it 'may be regarded as a threat or use of force, or amount to intervention in the internal or external affairs of other States'.[216] Therefore, under certain circumstances indirect intervention can amount to armed attack or aggression.

It appears more controversial to determine under which circumstances a state would be responsible for the actions of an armed opposition group, in case the intervening country is providing help and assistance: what is the degree of control required? The ICJ addressed the issue in the *Nicaragua* case, where it had to determine the US involvement in the rebels' activities. In order to decide on the matter, the Court distinguished between the two ANSAs operating in Nicaragua: the 'Unilaterally Controlled Latino Assets' (UCLAs) and the *contras*. With regard to the first opposition group, the ICJ found that its actions were imputable to the US: although US nationals did not take a direct part in the operations conducted by the UCLAs, the fact that they 'participated in the planning, direction and support' yields to the imputability of the rebels' acts to the US.[217] With regard to the *contras*, the Court concluded that 'by training, arming, equipping, financing and supplying the contra forces or otherwise encouraging, supporting and aiding military and paramilitary activities in and

[214] *Nicaragua* case, §195. For an analysis of whether an armed attack could be conducted by ANSAs which do not act as organs of a foreign state, see Lubell (n 58).
[215] *Nicaragua* case, §195.
[216] ibid. See A Clapham, 'The Concept of International Armed Conflict' in Clapham, Gaeta and Sassòli (eds) (n 38) 3–26.
[217] *Nicaragua* case, §86.

against Nicaragua', the US violated the principle of non-intervention and the ban on the use of force.[218] The ICJ then considered whether the US was responsible also for the conduct of the *contras*, which amounted to a violation of human rights and humanitarian law. The crucial point was whether the *contras* were to be considered de facto organs of the state.[219] The Court affirmed that, for ANSAs' conduct to give rise to legal responsibility of a state, 'it would in principle have to be proved that that state had *effective control* of the military or paramilitary operations in the course of which the alleged violations were committed'.[220]

In the *Tadić* case, the ICTY did not have to evaluate state responsibility. Instead, it was faced with the question of whether the conflict was internal or international.[221] To this end, it was necessary to ascertain if the Bosnian Serbs and the Republika Srpska Army (VRS) fighting in Bosnia were de facto organs of Yugoslavia. Only in the case of a positive answer would the conflict be classified as an IAC.[222] The Tribunal thus focused on the degree of control required to attribute the acts of an ANSA to a foreign state,[223] and identified two different solutions. The Tribunal limited the effective control test elaborated by the ICJ to acts performed by private individuals: in this case, the state would be responsible only if it provided specific instructions to the agent.[224] However, the ICTY suggested a different degree of control in order to make a state responsible for non-state groups' conduct:

> In order to attribute the acts of a military or paramilitary group to a State, it must be proved that the State wields *overall control* over the group, not only by equipping and financing the group, but also by coordinating or helping in the general planning of its military activity. Only then can the State be held internationally accountable for any misconduct of the group. However, it is not necessary that, in addition, the State should also issue, either to the head or to members of the group, instructions for the commission of specific acts contrary to international law.[225]

[218] ibid, §292. See A Cassese, 'The *Nicaragua* and *Tadić* Tests Revisited in Light of the ICJ Judgment on Genocide in Bosnia' (2007) 18(4) *European Journal of International Law* 652–53.

[219] *Nicaragua* case, §113.

[220] ibid, §115, emphasis added. Professor Cassese strongly criticised the effective control test identified by the ICJ: '[t]he "effective control" test may or may not be persuasive. What matters, however, is to establish whether it is based on either customary law (resulting from state practice, case law and *opinio juris*) or, absent any specific rule of customary law, on general principles on state responsibility or even general principles of international law. It is, however, a fact that the Court in *Nicaragua* set out that test without explaining or clarifying the grounds on which it was based. No reference is made by the Court either to state practice or to other authorities'. See Cassese (n 218) 653.

[221] MJ Ventura, 'Two Controversies in the *Lubanga* Trial Judgment of the International Criminal Court: The Nature of Co-perpetration's Common Plan and the Classification of the Armed Conflict' in S Casey-Maslen (ed), *The War Report 2012* (Oxford University Press, 2013) 486.

[222] A Cullen, 'The Parameters of Internal Armed Conflict in International Humanitarian Law' (2004) 1(1) *University of Miami International & Comparative Law Review* 219.

[223] ICTY, *Prosecutor v Tadić*, Appeal Chamber's Judgment, case No. IT–94–1, 15 July 1999, §97.

[224] ibid, §§132–36.

[225] ibid, §131. For a critical analysis of the judgment, see C Greenwood, 'International Humanitarian Law and the *Tadić* Case' (1996) 7(2) *European Journal of International Law* 272–73.

The evident contrast between the conclusions reached by the ICJ and the ICTY was addressed in the Commentary to the Draft Articles on State Responsibility.[226] Article 8 of the Draft Articles affirms that: '[t]he conduct of a person or group of persons shall be considered an act of a State under international law if the person or group of persons is in fact acting on the instructions of, or under the direction or control of, that State in carrying out the conduct'. The Commentary expressly specifies that the degree of control required is the one propounded in the *Nicaragua* case, thus the ANSA shall be under the effective control of a state in order to be considered its de facto state organ.[227] Finally, the ICJ addressed again the issue in the *Genocide* case (2007).[228] On that occasion, the Court embraced the effective control test, affirming that it is customary law.[229] In considering the *Tadić* decision, the Court highlighted that the overall control test would have the undesirable effect of excessively broadening state responsibility:

> Where an organ of the State gave the instructions or provided the direction pursuant to which the perpetrators of the wrongful act acted or where it exercised effective control over the action during which the wrong was committed, the 'overall control' test is unsuitable, for it stretches too far, almost to breaking point, the connection which must exist between the conduct of a State's organs and its international responsibility.[230]

The ICJ considered that the issues at stake in the *Nicaragua* and *Tadić* cases were substantially different: while the first was concerned with state responsibility, the other focused on the international or internal nature of the conflict.[231]

This circumstance is commonly defined as internationalisation of a NIAC, whereby 'state A intervenes on the territory of state B in support of non-state actor C against state B'; however, 'what is in dispute is the precise nature of the link between the intervening state and the non-state actor that suffices for internationalization'. See Milanović (n 38) 35. See also Solis (n 43) 154–55.

[226] See also KE Boon, 'Are Control Tests Fit for the Future? The Slippage Problem in Attribution Doctrines' (2014) 15(2) *Melbourne Journal of International Law* 8–12; AJJ de Hoogh, 'Articles 4 and 8 of the 2001 ILC Articles on State Responsibility, the *Tadić* Case and Attribution of Acts of Bosnian Serb Authorities to the Federal Republic of Yugoslavia' (2002) 72 *British Year Book of International Law* 281; Akande (n 84) 60.

[227] The Commentary underlines that in the *Tadić* case, the ICTY had to address a different issue: 'In the course of their [ICTY's judges] reasoning, the majority considered it necessary to disapprove the ICJ approach in the *Military and Paramilitary Activities in and against Nicaragua* case. But the legal issues and the factual situation in the *Tadić* case were different from those facing the Court in that case. The tribunal's mandate is directed to issues of individual criminal responsibility, not State responsibility, and the question in that case concerned not responsibility but the applicable rules of international humanitarian law.' See ILC Draft Articles on State Responsibility, Commentary, at 48, §5.

[228] *Application of the Convention on the Prevention and Punishment of the Crime of Genocide* (Bosnia and Herzegovina v. Serbia and Montenegro), Judgment (Merits), 26 February 2007 (hereinafter *Genocide* case). For a critical analysis of the judgment, see M Milanović, 'State Responsibility for Genocide: A Follow-up' (2007) 18(4) *European Journal of International Law* 669–94.

[229] *Genocide* case, §§398–99.

[230] ibid, §406.

[231] ibid, §§209–10.

Therefore, the contrast between the two decisions is only apparent: the two tests are equally valid because they regulate two different instances. On the one hand, the effective control test is relevant in assessing the responsibility of states for acts of non-state actors; on the other hand, the overall control test is useful in classifying the nature of armed conflicts.[232] This approach is valuable inasmuch as it avoids the problem of fragmentation of international law, of which '*Tadić* and *Nicaragua* have become synonymous'.[233] Nonetheless, part of the scholarship has pointed out that in reality it avoids facing a crucial issue, namely that the two cases were dealing with the same matter: the attribution to the state of acts of non-state actors.[234] Therefore, according to this approach, authors should not insist in trying to resolve the divergence between the two judgments. Instead, they should accept that the different conclusions of the ICJ and the ICTY are simply irreconcilable.[235]

III. NON-INTERVENTION, SOVEREIGNTY, AND HUMAN RIGHTS

A. Westphalian Sovereignty between Myth and Reality

Until the nineteenth century, the right to wage war and the principle of non-intervention had been considered corollary to sovereignty: on the one hand, using force was a right stemming from states' sovereignty; on the other hand, sovereignty was protected from external interference by the principle of non-intervention.[236] Furthermore, states were not considered as equal: during the nineteenth century, the world was divided between civilised, half-civilised, and barbarous countries, and only the first benefited from full sovereignty.[237] The UN Charter marked a crucial break from the past. First, Article 2(4) of the UN Charter banned the use of force in nearly absolute terms. Second, the

[232] Clapham (n 216) 17–19; T Meron, 'Classification of Armed Conflict in the Former Yugoslavia: *Nicaragua*'s Fallout' (1998) 92(2) *American Journal of International Law* 237; S Sivakumaran, 'Application of the Convention on the Prevention and Punishment of the Crime of Genocide (Bosnia and Herzegovina v. Yugoslavia (Serbia and Montenegro))' (2007) 56(3) *International and Comparative Law Quarterly* 702–703; L Van den hole, 'Towards a Test of the International Character of an Armed Conflict: *Nicaragua* and *Tadić*' (2005) 32(2) *Syracuse Journal of International Law and Commerce* 269; R van Alebeek, 'The Judicial Dialogue between the ICJ and the International Criminal Courts on the Question of Immunity' in LJ van den Herik and C Stahn (eds), *The Diversification and Fragmentation of International Criminal Law* (Martinus Nijhoff, 2012) 93–94; M Prost, *The Concept of Unity in Public International Law* (Hart Publishing, 2012) 194–201.

[233] Ventura (n 221) 488; M Koskenniemi and P Leino, 'Fragmentation of International Law? Postmodern Anxieties' (2002) 15(3) *Leiden Journal of International Law* 555–56.

[234] Cassese (n 218) 210–11; Ventura (n 221) 489.

[235] Ventura (n 221) 489–90.

[236] Dinstein (n 73) 79.

[237] D Rodogno, *Against Massacre: Humanitarian Interventions in the Ottoman Empire, 1815–1914* (Princeton University Press, 2012) 48. See ch 1.

Charter established that all states are equally sovereign, thus overcoming the distinction between civilised and barbarous countries.

Sovereignty is generally accepted as a legal status which pertains to states and which attributes to them rights and duties,[238] and that encompasses both an internal and an external dimension. The first notion regards the relationship between the state and the individuals under its jurisdiction. Since in normal situations the government has the authority to act on behalf of the state, a discourse on internal sovereignty focuses de facto on the relationship between governmental authority and non-state actors within the state.[239] On the other hand, external sovereignty looks at the relationship between states as members of the international community, which bear certain rights and obligations. It rests on the idea that 'sovereign states are regarded as equal, regardless of comparative size and wealth'.[240] The UN Charter embraces this approach by identifying the principle of sovereign equality as the basis of the Organization.[241]

In 1948, Leo Gross published a seminal article where he posited that the Peace of Westphalia contributed to consolidating the idea of sovereignty as the right of states to exercise 'untrammelled sovereignty over certain territories and subordinated to no earthly authority'.[242] Since then, the traditional

[238] A Peters, 'Humanity as the Alfa and Omega of Sovereignty' (2009) 20(3) *European Journal of International Law* 515. International law does not offer an authoritative definition of state sovereignty: its content is one of the most debated issues in the legal scholarship. See eg BR Roth, *Sovereign Equality and Moral Disagreement: Premises of a Pluralist International Legal Order* (Oxford University Press, 2011) 58; SD Krasner, *Sovereignty: Organized Hypocrisy* (Princeton University Press, 1999) 9–25; RH Jackson, *Quasi-States: Sovereignty, International Relations and the Third World* (Cambridge University Press, 2015) 26–31; H Kalmo, 'A Matter of Fact? The Many Faces of Sovereignty' in H Kalmo and Q Skinner (eds), *Sovereignty in Fragments: The Past, Present and Future of a Contested Concept* (Cambridge University Press, 2010) 114–15.

[239] Peters (n 238) 516; BR Roth, 'The Enduring Significance of State Sovereignty' (2004) 56 *Florida Law Review* 1023.

[240] International Commission on Intervention and State Sovereignty (ICISS), *The Responsibility to Protect* (International Development Research Centre 2001), at 12; P Piirimäe, 'The Westphalian Myth and the Idea of External Sovereignty' in Kalmo and Skinner (n 238) 65–66; K Chan, 'State Failure and the Changing Face of the *Jus ad Bellum*' (2013) 18(3) *Journal of Conflict and Security Law* 405; G Simpson, 'The Guises of Sovereignty' in C Sampford and R Thakur (eds), *Re-envisioning Sovereignty: The End of Westphalia?* (Ashgate, 2008) 54; P Sevastik, 'Some Aspects on the Effects of Human Rights Law and its Implications on International Law' in P Sevastik (ed), *Aspects of Sovereignty: Sino-Swedish Reflections* (Martinus Nijhoff, 2013) 35.

[241] See the UN Charter, Art 2(1): 'the Organization is based on the principle of the sovereign equality of all its Members.' See also Declaration on Friendly Relations: '[s]overeign equality includes the following elements: (a) States are juridically equal; (b) Each State enjoys the rights inherent in full sovereignty; (c) Each State has the duty to respect the personality of other States; (d) The territorial integrity and political independence of the State are inviolable; (e) Each State has the right freely to choose and develop its political, social, economic and cultural systems; (f) Each State has the duty to comply fully and in good faith with its international obligations and to live in peace with other States'.

[242] L Gross, 'The Peace of Westphalia, 1648–1948' (1948) 42(1) *American Journal of International Law* 20; R Grote, 'Westphalian System' in *Max Planck Encyclopedia of Public International Law* (Oxford University Press, 2006) §7.

view sees the Peace of Westphalia as the benchmark that determined the beginning of the modern international system.[243] Westphalian sovereignty came thus to be considered as granting states 'an indefeasible right to autonomous self-government, free from outside interference and intervention'.[244] As explained by Forsythe: 'prior to 1945, the relation between an individual and a state controlling "its" citizens was a matter for that state alone. The state was sovereign in an almost absolute sense, exercising supreme legal authority within its jurisdiction'.[245] States thus used sovereignty as a shield to act unhampered within their borders. Authors who embrace this view conclude that over the past few decades there has been an erosion of sovereignty, mainly caused by the emergence of human rights.[246]

Nevertheless, recently this traditional view has been questioned on two fronts.[247] First, a historical analysis of the settlement that emerged in 1648 shows that the imperial estates did not acquire the right to exercise absolute powers within their territories without external interference.[248] Second, the 'Westphalian myth'[249] has been disproved on a normative basis. The traditional view maintains that the Peace of Westphalia introduced a system where the sovereign exercises absolute powers within its borders and that no external authority could interfere with its domestic affairs. However, at the time of the

[243] SD Krasner, 'Compromising Westphalia' (1995) 20(3) *International Security* 115; N Schrijver, 'The Changing Nature of State Sovereignty' (2000) 70(1) *British Yearbook of International Law* 67–69.

[244] Glanville (n 14) 11.

[245] DP Forsythe, *Human Rights in International Relations* (Cambridge University Press, 2012) 24.

[246] WJ Aceves, 'Relative Normativity: Challenging the Sovereignty Norm Through Human Rights Litigation' (2001) 25(3) *Hastings International and Comparative Law Review* 264; L Henkin, 'Human Rights and State "Sovereignty"' (1994) 25 *Georgia Journal of International and Comparative Law* 33, L Henkin, 'That "S" Word: Sovereignty, and Globalization, and Human Rights, Et Cetera' (1999) 68 *Fordham Law Review* 3–7; MD Kielsgard, 'Evolving Human Rights Methodology: Have Incursions into State Sovereignty Gone Too Far ?' (2013) 22 *Tulane Journal of International and Comparative Law* 43–61; E Lauterpacht, 'Sovereignty – myth or reality?' (1997) 73(1) *International Affairs* 137–50.

[247] Glanville (n 14) 49; C Kreß, 'Major Post-Westphalian Shifts and Some Important Neo-Westphalian Hesitations in the State Practice on the International Law on The Use of Force' (2014) 1(1) *Journal on the Use of Force and International Law* 12; A Osiander, 'Sovereignty, International Relations, and the Westphalian Myth' (2001) 55(2) *International Organization* 268; A Osiander, 'Before Sovereignty: Society and Politics in Ancien Régime Europe' (2001) 27(5) *Review of International Studies* 119; Piirimäe (n 240) 65–70; Krasner (n 243) 115.

[248] Piirimäe (n 240) 64; Glanville (n 14) 50. It is not the ambition of this chapter to engage in the debate on the historical impact of the Peace of Westphalia. For an in-depth analysis, see eg Osiander, (n 247); S Beaulac, 'The Westphalian Legal Orthodoxy-Myth or Reality?' (2000) 2 *Journal of the History of International Law* 175; D Croxton, 'Peace of Westphalia of 1648 and the Origins of Sovereignty' (1999) 21(3) *International History Review* 588–89; B Simms, '"A False Principle in the Law of Nations": Burke, State Sovereignty, [German] Liberty, and Intervention in the Age of Westphalia' in B Simms and DJB Trim (eds), *Humanitarian Intervention: A History* (Cambridge University Press, 2011) 92.

[249] Osiander (n 247) 268.

Peace of Westphalia the mainstream doctrine propounded that states could wage war for two reasons: to punish another sovereign state and to defend oppressed people from a tyrant.[250] This seems to confirm that 'there has never been a golden age of sovereignty':[251] at the time of the Peace of Westphalia, the principle of non-intervention was not a corollary of sovereignty and states could forcibly intervene against another sovereign. Even when the principle of non-intervention was explicitly propounded for the first time, scholars still admitted the right to intervene to punish a prince or to protect oppressed people.[252]

B. Legitimacy, Effectiveness, and Sovereignty

The idea that sovereignty needs to be justified is not new. While the term 'legitimacy' assumes many variants in the literature and has been subject to different interpretations, in the present work it refers to 'the justification of the exercise of public authority, the latter being understood as equivalent to having the power' to speak on behalf of the state.[253] Accordingly, legitimacy should be distinguished from legality, which refers to 'conformity with international law'.[254]

The relationship between effectiveness, legitimacy, and sovereignty has changed dramatically over the centuries. For years, the king's authority was legitimised by God's investiture and by dynastic rights.[255] In the words of Cranston:

> The King … if King by Divine Right and ancient prescription, and nothing any living person does or says can alter or affect that reality. The King is not King because he does anything, or because he is thought to be something, but because he is something. The participation of other persons has only ever been needed for the purpose of lawfully marrying his parents and lawfully registering his birth as their son: duties wisely entrusted by tradition to the Church, source of the laws as well of the procedures of matrimony.[256]

[250] Piirimäe (n 240) 67.

[251] Krasner (n 243) 115; J Camilleri, 'Sovereignty Discourse and Practice – Past and Future' in C Sampford and R Thakur (eds), *Re-envisioning Sovereignty: The End of Westphalia?* (Ashgate, 2008) 35.

[252] See ch 1.

[253] See R Wolfrum, 'Legitimacy in International Law' in *Max Planck Encyclopedia of Public International Law* (Oxford University Press, 2011) §1.

[254] ibid, §1.

[255] M Cranston, 'From Legitimism to Legitimacy' in A Moulakis (ed), *Legitimacy/Legitimite: Proceedings of the Conference Held in Florence, June 3–4, 1982* (Walter de Gruyter, 1985) 36; WM Reisman, 'Sovereignty and Human Rights in Contemporary International Law' (2017) 84(4) *The American Journal of International Law* 867.

[256] Cranston (n 255) 142.

As sovereignty derived its legitimacy from the divine right of the ruler and was thus indifferent to de facto situations,[257] legitimacy was regarded with scepticism and diffidence.[258] Contractual theories and the American and French revolutions changed the terms of the debate: power had to be legitimised; nonetheless, the source of political authority was not God, but the will and support of the people. Internal sovereignty thus evolved from divine legitimacy to popular sovereignty: the Pope and the Holy Roman Emperor were no longer in charge of granting sovereignty, as this descended directly from popular will.[259]

Locke famously developed the idea of popular sovereignty in his seminal book *Two Treaties of Government*. In his work, he strongly refuted the idea that some individuals should naturally rule over others due to divine rights and posited that sovereignty should be grounded on the people's will.[260] In a state of nature, every individual is 'a judge in his own case with the authority to punish offences against his natural rights'.[261] As people left the state of nature, they decided to limit the use of violence and to create a 'body politic' that would provide order and security for every individual.[262] The authority and legitimacy of the sovereign is not based on divine or dynastic rights, but on a social contract concluded with the people under his jurisdiction. Therefore, the sovereign has not only the obligation to protect and ensure respect of the rights of his people, but he is also responsible should he breach the contract.[263]

Drawing upon Locke's ideas, Jean-Jacques Rousseau published *The Social Contract* in 1762. Similar to Locke, Rousseau put forward the idea that, when people left the state of nature, they created a 'body politic' through the conclusion of a social contract. For Rousseau, not only popular will, but also the 'performance of functions' would justify popular sovereignty: the goal of sovereignty should be the common good as an expression of the will of the people.[264] The exercise of sovereignty was thus deemed to depend upon the respect of popular will: should the first disregard the latter, it would risk losing its authority and ultimately its legitimacy.[265]

[257] Lieblich (n 1) 21; Peters (n 238) 518; TD Grant, *The Recognition of States: Law and Practice in Debate and Evolution* (Praeger Publishers, 1999) 8.

[258] GH Fox, 'The Right to Political Participation in International Law' (1992) 17 *Yale Journal of International Law* 547; BR Roth, *Governmental Illegitimacy in International Law* (Clarendon Press, 1999) 143.

[259] A Orford, *International Authority and the Responsibility to Protect* (Cambridge University Press, 2011) 141–50; M Koskenniemi, 'Conclusion: Vocabularies of Sovereignty – Power of a Paradox,' in Kalmo and Skinner (eds) (n 238) 223: 'sovereignty was surely born out of a desire to understand and explain power, a tool of analysis and polemics simultaneously'.

[260] Glanville (n 14) 62.

[261] ibid.

[262] Peters (n 238) 518.

[263] S Besson, 'Sovereignty' in *Max Planck Encyclopedias of International Law* (Oxford University Press, 2011) §21.

[264] Peters (n 238) 519.

[265] Besson (n 263) §24.

In the following years, popular sovereignty came to be understood as crucially bound to democracy, as exemplified by the American and French Revolutions. The American Declaration of Independence recognised that governments 'derived their just powers from the consent of the governed'.[266] Similarly, the French Declaration of the Rights of Man and Citizens stated that 'all sovereignty resides in the nation. No body nor individual can exercise any authority which does not proceed directly from the nation'.[267] Worried by the republican developments in France and America, traditional monarchies founded the Holy Alliance in an attempt to resurrect divine and dynastic legitimism:

> Any State forming part of the European Alliance which may change its form of interior government through revolutionary means, and which might thus become a menace to other states, will automatically cease to form a part of the Alliance. ... In the case of States where such changes have already taken place ... they will employ every means to bring the offenders once more within the sphere of the Alliance. Friendly negotiations will be the first means resorted to, and if this fails, coercions will be employed, should this be necessary.[268]

Notwithstanding the efforts of the Holy Alliance, claims of dynastic legitimacy were abandoned.[269] The American and French revolutions 'inaugurated the concept of the popular will as the theoretical and operational source of political authority'.[270] In Reisman's words, 'the sovereignty of the sovereign became the sovereignty of the people: popular sovereignty',[271] namely 'the view that individual citizens bestow legitimacy upon a government through their implied or actual consent to its rule'.[272]

C. Sovereignty and Human Rights: Erosion or Complementarity?

Since the establishment of the United Nations, human rights have emerged as a cornerstone of the UN system. Article 3(1) of the UN Charter mentions 'promoting and encouraging respect for human rights and for fundamental freedoms for all without distinction as to race, sex, language, or religion' as one of the purposes of the United Nations. Furthermore, the Universal Declaration of Human Rights in 1948 incorporates 'the moral code, political consensus and legal synthesis of human rights'.[273] Furthermore, several conventions on human

[266] Glanville (n 14) 64.
[267] ibid, 69.
[268] H Lauterpacht, *Recognition in International Law* (Cambridge University Press, 1947) 103; Roth (n 258) 143.
[269] Fox (n 258) 548.
[270] Reisman (n 255) 867.
[271] ibid.
[272] Fox (n 258) 550.
[273] ICISS (n 240) 14.

rights have been adopted both at international and regional levels.[274] In parallel, states started to be accountable with regard to human rights vis-à-vis the people under their jurisdiction: 'International Organizations, civil society activists and NGOs use the international human rights norms and instruments as the concrete point of reference against which to judge state conduct'.[275]

The traditional view suggests that sovereignty is limited by human rights; as a consequence, the emergence of the latter would inevitably lead to an erosion of the former.[276] Several authors have welcomed the 'withering away'[277] of sovereignty: 'the "S word" was a mistake built upon mistakes, which has barnacled an unfortunate mythology'.[278] Nonetheless, sovereignty does not only serve as states' shield, so that they can act untrammelled within their borders: sovereignty 'has also been a defence of the weak facing off with the strong. … Thus, the removal of the sovereignty barrier at this historical moment necessarily has ambiguous consequences.'[279] Furthermore, the respect of human rights does not necessarily imply a dilution of state sovereignty.[280] Instead, it has originated a

[274] See eg Universal Declaration of Human Rights 1948, Convention on the Elimination of All Forms of Racial Discrimination 1965, International Covenant on Civil and Political Rights 1966, International Covenant on Economic, Social and Cultural Rights 1966, Convention on the Elimination of All Forms of Discrimination against Women 1979, Convention against Torture and Other Cruel, Inhuman or Degrading Treatment or Punishment 1984, Convention on the Rights of the Child 1989, International Convention on the Protection of the Rights of All Migrant Workers and Members of Their Families 1990, Convention on the Rights of Persons with Disabilities 2006. At the regional level, see eg Convention for the Protection of Human Rights and Fundamental Freedoms 1950, American Convention on Human Rights 1969, African Charter of Human and Peoples' Rights 1981, Arab Charter of Human Rights 2004.

[275] ICISS (n 240) 14.

[276] C Tomuschat, 'Obligations Arising for States without or against Their Will' (1993) 241 *Collected courses of The Hague Academy of International Law* 292: '[s]overeignty is in a process of progressive erosion, inasmuch as the international community places ever more constraints on the freedom of action of States … driven by a global change in the perception of how the right balance between individual State interests and interests of mankind as a whole should be established'. See also HR Fabri, 'Human Rights and State Sovereignty: Have the Boundaries Been Significantly Redrawn?' in P Alston and E Macdonald, *Human Rights, Intervention, and the Use of Force* (Oxford University Press, 2008) 42; Sevastik (n 240) 61; Henkin, 'Human Rights and State "Sovereignty"' (n 246) 33; L Henkin, 'The Mythology of Sovereignty' in R St J Macdonald (ed), *Essays in Honour of Wang Tieya* (Martinus Nijhoff, 1994) 351–58; Henkin, 'That "S" Word: Sovereignty, and Globalization, and Human Rights, Et Cetera' (n 246) 3–7; Lauterpacht (n 246); CG Badescu, 'The Responsibility to Protect: Embracing Sovereignty and Human Rights' in N Shawki and M Cox (eds), *Negotiating Sovereignty and Human Rights: Actors and Issues in Contemporary Human Rights Politics* (Ashgate, 2009) 81.

[277] M Koskenniemi, 'The Wonderful Artificiality of States' (1994) 88 *American Society of International Law Procedures* 22–29.

[278] Henkin, 'Human Rights and State "Sovereignty"' (n 246) 31.

[279] K Bennoune, 'Sovereignty vs. Suffering? Re-Examining Sovereignty and Human Rights through the Lens of Iraq' (2002) 13(1) *European Journal of International Law* 248; J Conlon, 'Sovereignty vs. Human Rights or Sovereignty and Human Rights?' (2004) 46(1) *Race & Class* 86; C Reus-Smit, 'Human Rights and the Social Construction of Sovereignty' (2001) 27(4) *Review of International Studies* 537.

[280] See J Donnelly, 'State Sovereignty and International Human Rights' (2014) 28(2) *Ethics & International Affairs* 235: 'only if one conceives of sovereignty as an absolute right to do whatever

re-characterisation of sovereignty: 'from sovereignty as control to sovereignty as responsibility in both internal functions and external duties'.[281] The consequences of this new approach are twofold: on the one hand, state authorities are responsible for protecting the human rights of the people under their jurisdiction (internal sovereignty). On the other hand, they are responsible also towards the international community, which can call on states to respect their obligations towards their populations (external sovereignty).[282]

The centrality of human rights in the sovereignty discourse and the related responsibility to protect (R2P) doctrine have been endorsed by the UN, as well as at the regional level. The former UN Secretary General considered the prospects for human security and intervention in his Millennium Report (2000):

> If humanitarian intervention is, indeed, an unacceptable assault on sovereignty, how should we respond to a Rwanda, to a Srebrenica – to gross and systematic violations of human rights that offend every precept of our common humanity?[283]

Moreover, the High-level Expert Panel of 2004 addressed the issue of the responsibility to protect.[284] Similarly, the World Summit acknowledged that:

> Each individual State has the responsibility to protect its populations from genocide, war crimes, ethnic cleansing and crimes against humanity. This responsibility entails the prevention of such crimes, including their incitement, through appropriate and necessary means. We accept that responsibility and will act in accordance with it.[285]

The Security Council referred to the R2P principle in several resolutions,[286] where it reaffirmed the 'primary responsibility of each state to protect civilians',[287] 'as well as to respect and ensure the human rights of all individuals

one wants, do human rights compromise, challenge or erode sovereignty'. See also WM Reisman, 'Sovereignty and Human Rights in Contemporary International Law' (1990) 84(4) *American Journal of International Law* 872.

[281] ICISS (n 240) 13.

[282] ibid.

[283] *We the Peoples: The Role of the United Nations in the 21st Century*, Report of the Secretary General, A/54/2000, 27 March 2000, at 48, §§217–19. See also *In Larger Freedom: Towards Development, Security and Human Rights for All*, Report of the Secretary General, A/59/2005, 21 March 2005, §135; *Uniting our strengths: Enhancing United Nations support for the rule of law*, Report of the Secretary General, A/61/636-S/2006/980, 14 December 2006, §6.

[284] 'A more secure world: Our shared responsibility,' Report of the High-level Panel on Threats, Challenges and Change, UN Doc. A759/565, 2 December 2004, at 65–66.

[285] A/RES/60/1, 24 October 2005, *World Summit Outcome*, §138.

[286] See eg S/RES/1653 (2006), 27 January 2006; S/RES/1674 (2006), 28 April 2006; S/RES/1894 (2009), 11 November 2009; S/RES/1970 (2011), 26 February 2011; S/RES/1973 (2011), 17 March 2011; S/RES/1975 (2011), 30 March 2011; S/RES/1996 (2011), 8 July 2011; S/RES/2014 (2011), 21 October 2011; S/RES/2016 (2011), 27 October 2011; S/RES/2040 (2012), 12 March 2012; S/RES/2085 (2012), 20 December 2012; S/RES/2093 (2013), 6 March 2013; S/RES/2095 (2013), 14 March 2013; S/RES/2100 (2013), 25 April 2013; S/RES/2121 (2013), 10 October 2013; S/RES/2127 (2013), 5 December 2013; S/RES/2134 (2014), 28 January 2014; S/RES/2139 (2014), 22 February 2014; S/RES/2149 (2014), 10 April 2014; S/RES/2150 (2014), 16 April 2014; S/RES/2155 (2014), 27 May 2014; S/RES/2171 (2014), 21 August 2014; S/RES/2187 (2014), 25 November 2014.

[287] S/RES/1973 (2011) (n 286).

within their territory and subject to their jurisdiction'.[288] At the regional level, the Constitutive Act of the African Union (2000), after affirming 'the sovereign equality and interdependence amongst Member States of the Union',[289] expressly established 'the right of the Union to intervene in a Member State pursuant to a decision of the Assembly in respect of grave circumstances, namely: war crimes, genocide and crimes against humanity'.[290]

By requiring states to protect human rights of the people under their jurisdiction, R2P introduced human rights into the discourse on sovereignty. Therefore, the principle infused 'external sovereignty with elements of internal sovereignty'.[291] The close linkage between internal and external sovereignty leads one to conclude that respect of human rights would affect not only the authority of a government towards the people under its jurisdiction, but also the position of such government with respect to other states. Brought to its extreme consequences, 'an illegitimate state would be estopped from asserting a right against economic or even military intervention. In essence, only a legitimate state would be allowed to claim immunity from intervention'.[292] This conclusion could entail undesirable consequences, notably an excessive interventionism not regulated by certain and clear criteria. It seems preferable to adopt a more cautious approach towards the suspension of sovereignty triggered by serious violations of human rights.[293] Nevertheless, the linkage between external and internal sovereignty does exist and deserves to be carefully considered.

IV. CONCLUDING OBSERVATIONS

While the question of the relationship between sovereignty, intervention, and human rights was already debated during the Middle Ages,[294] albeit with different terminology, the re-characterisation of sovereignty as a responsibility to protect human rights had significant consequences for the principle of non-intervention.[295] If the latter is a corollary of the first, established to enable states to exercise their authority, it is evident that the new approach to sovereignty leads to a reconsideration of non-intervention. A vast literature has

[288] S/RES/2109 (2013), 11 July 2013.

[289] Constitutive Act of the African Union 2000, Art 4(a).

[290] Ibid, Art 4(h).

[291] Peters (n 238) 517.

[292] D Luban, 'Just War and Human Rights' (1980) 9(2) *Philosophy and Public Affairs* 169.

[293] Peters (n 238) 521.

[294] However, in the Middle Ages the discussion was not framed in terms of 'human rights', but as 'the right to protect innocents from an unjust tyrant'.

[295] D Fleck, 'National Sovereignty and International Responsibility: Legal and Policy Aspects' in M Bothe, ME O'Connell, and N Ronzitti (eds), *Redefining Sovereignty: The Use of Force after the Cold War* (Transnational Publishers, 2005) 55; C Reus-Smit, *The Moral Purpose of the State: Culture, Social Identity and Institutional Rationality in International Relations* (Princeton University Press, 1999) 159–60.

developed on the possibility to intervene for humanitarian reasons, in case a state does not comply with its international obligation to protect human rights of the people under its jurisdiction. Nevertheless, the implications of the close relationship between human rights and sovereignty go further than that, affecting all instances of intervention, such as intervention by invitation, intervention in case of people exercising their right to self-determination and intervention in favour of opposition groups. In order to ascertain how far human rights and the concept of sovereignty as responsibility influence and interact with *jus ad bellum*, an analysis of state practice is pivotal. The following chapters will be devoted to investigating these instances.

Part II

Interventions in Favour of Governments

What a great number of tyrant would be discovered if one might kill them.

Jean Bodin

Over the past decades, numerous states have invoked governmental consent to justify their military interferences: foreign interventions in internal conflicts have turned into a common practice. In some cases, interventions upon invitation did not raise criticism. For instance, during the Cold War, the UK and France provided military help to beleaguered governments in their former colonies and these interventions were overwhelmingly considered as lawful. More recently, the ECOWAS intervention in The Gambia (2017) met with general acquiescence from the international community. However, in the vast majority of cases reliance on the invitation by the government has proved unconvincing. In none of these cases was the principle that a valid consent can authorise a military intervention questioned per se. Instead, criticism focused on whether and under what conditions an intervention upon invitation could lawfully take place. The aim of the second part of this work is to assess when and under what circumstances interventions by invitation are lawful under the current legal framework.

A rebellion is essentially a situation where a group of people challenges the authority of the government by forcible means. In more complex situations, several armed non-state actors may take part in a conflict, each of them controlling a more or less substantial portion of the territory of the state. It is intuitive that these situations pose pivotal challenges to interventions upon invitation. Does the beleaguered government hold the authority to speak on behalf of the state? What if more entities claim to represent the state and each of them asks for foreign assistance? In the absence of clear-cut criteria regulating interventions upon invitation, resolving these issues requires an investigation into crucial values traditionally protected by international law and into the way they interact in practice. How can the principles of non-intervention and the right to self-determination be reconciled with the practice of interventions upon invitation in internal conflicts? What are the criteria to identify the de jure government, capable of acting on behalf of the state? What is the role played by states' responsibility to protect the human rights of the people under their jurisdiction?

In order to provide answers to these and related dilemmas, this analysis digs into the values and objectives of the international legal system. The principle of non-intervention – once regarded as a powerful stronghold to protect states' sovereignty and, at a later stage, the principle of self-determination – is now perceived in a less stringent and absolute fashion, while other values are emerging and re-shaping the international legal landscape. On the one hand, the emergence of democracy as an expression of the right to internal self-determination has brought to the fore discourses on legitimacy as a possible alternative to the effectiveness doctrine. On the other hand, since the end of World War II human rights have gained momentum and have reshaped the understanding of traditional values such as non-intervention and sovereignty. Accordingly, they have entered discourses on armed interventions. These considerations have an evident relevance for discussions on interventions upon invitation.

Before delving into this analysis, it is necessary to put forward a caveat. Although state consent is considered a valid alternative to the Security Council authorisation to use force, the scope of consent is not unlimited. Notably, while a government could ask for foreign help in order to quell an insurrection, at least under certain circumstances, it cannot authorise conduct which would be unlawful for the inviting government itself. Therefore, a state could not consent to or authorise violations of human rights within its territory, nor criminal acts such as genocide or ethnic cleansing.

In order to determine when and under what circumstances interventions in favour of governments are lawful, this part is divided into three chapters. Chapter three analyses the traditional doctrines regarding interventions by invitation. Some authors claim that interventions in civil wars are never allowed because they are contrary to the principle of non-intervention and the right to self-determination of people. Others propound that interventions upon invitation during internal conflicts are not (always) unlawful. However, they recognise that a beleaguered government may lose its capacity to speak on behalf of the state. The dilemma lies in determining the criteria to identify the legitimate government. On the one hand, part of the scholarship affirms that only a government that exercises effective control over territory and population can ask for foreign intervention (effectiveness doctrine). On the other hand, other authors maintain that only democratic governments are legitimate and can express a valid consent, even if they are ineffective (democratic entitlement doctrine).

Chapter four tests the traditional doctrines against state practice. Notably, it endeavours to answer a decisive question: when and under what circumstances are interventions upon invitation lawful under the current legal framework? First, it seeks to clarify whether the electoral mandate is in itself sufficient to identify the government, and whether the latter is capable to act on behalf of the state even if it does not exercise effective control over territory and population. Second, it focuses on undemocratic regimes overwhelmingly recognised by the international community. Lastly, it investigates the role of domestic constitutional orders in interventions upon invitation.

Lastly, chapter five examines the capacity of governments to invite foreign forces during an internal conflict, when the government has committed gross and systematic violations of human rights and humanitarian law. The events that took place in the aftermath of the Arab Spring show that a government which commits gross and systematic violations of human rights and humanitarian law loses its legitimacy as representative of its people, and that this could lead to the withdrawal of recognition as the government *tout court* (such as in the case of Libya). This chapter investigates the effects of this new practice on governmental powers, in particular with regard to interventions upon invitation. Furthermore, it will focus on the lawfulness of interventions in their favour.

3

Interventions by Invitation between Legitimacy and Effectiveness

I. INTERVENTION BY INVITATION: THE LEGAL FRAMEWORK

A. Legal Validity of Intervention by Invitation

OVER THE PAST decades, interventions in internal conflicts have turned into a common practice that has often been justified on the basis of an invitation by the government. The question of the conditions of its validity, however, is highly divisive. During the Cold War, the aim of limiting the influence of the adversary bloc permeated intervention policies: forcible interferences in favour of allied governments or directed at overthrowing opposing authorities were thus an instrument to reshape the spheres of influence of the two blocs.[1] On the one hand, the Soviet approach, embodied in the Brezhnev Doctrine, maintained that '[m]embers of the fraternal order of the Socialist camp, when faced with deviation, become the appropriate subject of assistance by other Socialist states to ensure that they not depart from the Socialist course'.[2] On the other hand, the Reagan Doctrine propounded that the US would 'stand by [its] democratic allies … to defy Soviet-supported aggression'.[3] With the collapse of the Soviet bloc and the end of the Cold War period, the Brezhnev Doctrine was abandoned, while some traces of the Reagan Doctrine can be found in certain views supporting unilateral forcible pro-democratic interventions.[4] Nevertheless, with the end of the Cold War, debates on intervention upon invitation did not wither away.[5]

[1] E Lieblich, *International Law and Civil Wars: Intervention and Consent* (Routledge, 2013) 125.

[2] WD Rogers, WM Reisman, LN Cutler and TM Franck, 'The Brezhnev Doctrine and the Reagan Doctrine: Apples and Oranges?' (1987) 81 *Proceedings of the Annual Meeting (American Society of International Law)* 562.

[3] ibid.

[4] Lieblich (n 1) 130; L Henkin, *International Law: Politics and Values* (Martinus Nijhoff, 1995) 118–19; JJ Kirkpatrick and A Gerson, 'The Reagan Doctrine, Human Rights, and International Law' in L Henkin (ed), *Right v. Might: International Law and the Use of Force* (Council on Foreign Relations Press, 1991) 19–36.

[5] O Schachter, 'The Right of States to Use Armed Force' (1984) 82(5) *Michigan Law Review* 1641; Lieblich (n 1) 125–26.

Generally speaking, nobody contests that a state can send troops to another country upon invitation of the latter.[6] Article 20 of the Draft Articles on State Responsibility confirms this position:[7]

> Valid consent by a State to the commission of a given act by another State precludes the wrongfulness of that act in relation to the former State to the extent that the act remains within the limits of that consent.[8]

Similarly, the validity of interventions upon invitation can be deduced *a contrario* from Article 3(e) of the Definition of Aggression, which mentions among the instances of aggression:

> The use of armed forces of one State which are within the territory of another State *with the agreement of the receiving State*, in contravention of the conditions provided for in the agreement or any extension of their presence in such territory beyond the termination of the agreement.[9]

The ICJ embraced this view in the *Nicaragua* case, where it clarified that:

> It is difficult to see what would remain of the principle of non-intervention in international law if intervention, *which is already allowable at the request of the government of a State*, were also to be allowed at the request of the opposition. This would permit any State to intervene at any moment in the internal affairs of another State, whether at the request of the government or at the request of its opposition. Such a situation does not in the Court's view correspond to the present state of international law.[10]

In the *Congo* case the Court focused on the circumstances of the withdrawal of consent, thus simply assuming that a government can consent to forcible interventions within its territory.[11] Albeit unquestioned in the *Congo* case, the obiter dictum of the ICJ in the *Nicaragua* case raised several questions and some criticism. Indeed, the Court did not specify the conditions of a valid consent, if a

[6] L Doswald-Beck, 'The Legal Validity of Military Intervention by Invitation of the Government' (1986) 56(1) *British Yearbook of International Law* 189. See also GH Fox, 'Intervention by Invitation' in M Weller (ed), *The Oxford Handbook of the Use of Force in International Law* (Oxford University Press, 2015) 816. States' consent not only plays a significant role in justifying military interventions, it also serves the purpose of grounding international law; see J Brunnée, 'Consent' in *Max Planck Encyclopedia of Public International Law* (Oxford University Press, 2010).

[7] Doswald-Beck (n 6) 189; G Nolte, 'Intervention by Invitation' in *Max Planck Encyclopedia of Public International Law* (Oxford University Press, 2010) §16; Fox (n 6) 821. For an analysis of the relationship between the *jus cogens* nature of the ban on the use of force and the lawfulness of military interventions upon invitation, see ch 2.

[8] Article 20 of the ILC International Law Commission (ILC), Draft articles on Responsibility of States for Internationally Wrongful Acts, with Commentaries, *Yearbook of the International Law Commission*, 2001, vol II, Part Two (hereinafter ILC Draft Articles on State Responsibility).

[9] Article 3(e) of the *Definition of Aggression*, A/RES/3314, 14 December 1974 (hereinafter, Definition of Aggression), emphasis added.

[10] ICJ, *Military and Paramilitary Activities in and against Nicaragua, (Nicaragua v United States of America)*, Judgment (Merits), 27 June 1986 (hereinafter *Nicaragua* case), §246, emphasis added.

[11] ICJ, *Armed Activities in the Congo (Democratic Republic of Congo v Uganda)*, Judgment (Merits), 19 December 2005 (hereinafter *Congo* case). See also Fox (n 6) 821.

beleaguered government can lawfully express its consent, or whether the nature of the opposition group could play a role in this assessment.[12] Notably, the dilemmas are twofold. First, when is states' consent valid under international law? Second, can states consent to a forcible intervention during an internal conflict, and, if so, which organ can validly express the invitation? These questions have gripped the scholarship for decades; the next paragraphs will analyse the answers provided by the traditional doctrines.

B. Requisites for a Valid Consent

In order to be valid, a state's consent must meet certain requisites as to who has the authority to express it, how the consent should be given, and when. The ILC explained that the consent of the state must be valid in international law, clearly established, positively expressed (ie, consent cannot be presumed), internationally attributable to the state, and anterior to the commission of the act to which it refers. Moreover, the intervention ought to take place within the limits determined by the inviting state with regard to its scope and duration.[13]

The most controversial requirement of a valid consent is that it must be expressed by an organ with the authority to act on behalf of the state. Both Article 3(e) of the Definition of Aggression and Article 20 of the Draft Articles on State Responsibility mention the consent of the state, but they do not specify the entity capable to express it. The ILC Commentary to the Draft Articles affirms that 'who has authority to consent to a departure from a particular rule may depend on the rule'.[14] Which organ has the authority to express its consent to a military intervention? It is generally uncontested that only the highest authorities of the state possess the capacity to express such consent, ie the government,[15] while local or diplomatic authorities could not validly invite a military intervention.[16] State practice shows that the validity of consent has

[12] ibid, 820.

[13] ILC Draft Articles on State Responsibility, at 73.

[14] ibid. The Commentary further explains that: '[i]t is one thing to consent to a search of embassy premises, another to the establishment of a military base on the territory of a State. Different officials or agencies may have authority in different contexts, in accordance with the arrangements made by each State and general principles of actual and ostensible authority' (ibid).

[15] G Hafner, 'Present Problems of the Use of Force in International Law, Sub-Group on Intervention by Invitation' (2011) 74 *Yearbook of Institute of International Law* 227; D Wippman, 'Change and Continuity in Legal Justifications for Military Intervention in Internal Conflict' (1996) 27(3) *Columbia Human Rights Law Review* 440; CJ Le Mon, 'Unilateral intervention in Civil War: The Effective Control Test Tested' (2003) 35 *New York University Journal of International Law and Politics* 759; O Corten, *The Law against War: The Prohibition on the Use of Force in Contemporary International Law* (Hart Publishing, 2010) 259; Lieblich (n 1) 130.

[16] Corten (n 15) 262–65; A Abass, 'Consent Precluding State Responsibility: A Critical Analysis' (2004) 53(1) *International & Comparative Law Quarterly* 115–16. This proved to be problematic during the US intervention in Grenada (1983), where the invitation came from the Governor-General and not from the government. See ch 4.

been frequently questioned in this regard. Since during internal conflicts the authority of the incumbent government is challenged by at least part of the population, it is questionable whether the government still retains the capacity to invite foreign forces to quell the revolt.[17] As we shall see, scholarship and practice have suggested different criteria in order to determine whether the author of the request was entitled to express an invitation on behalf of the state.[18]

Furthermore, the way in which the consent is expressed can influence its validity. Generally speaking, there are no specific requirements concerning the form of consent,[19] provided that it is clearly established, 'explicit and leave[s] no doubt that the State consents to such military assistance'.[20] Moreover, consent is valid only if freely given.[21] The reason is apparent: since consent is the expression of the will of the state, it should not be 'vitiated by error, fraud, corruption or coercion'.[22] This is confirmed by Article 51 of the Vienna Convention on the Law of Treaties, which specifies that:

> The expression of a State's consent to be bound by a treaty which has been procured by the coercion of its representative through acts or threats directed against him shall be without any legal effect.[23]

Similarly, the Institut de Droit International (IDI), in its resolution on *Military assistance on request*, propounds that consent has to reflect 'the free expression of will of the requesting State'.[24] The problem is that, in case of military intervention in internal conflicts, it is not unlikely that the consent is influenced

[17] See eg I Brownlie, *International Law and the Use of Force by States* (Oxford University Press, 1963) 317: 'the difficulty arises when the legal status of the government which is alleged to have given consent is a matter of doubt'. According to Thomas and Thomas, '[a] consent by a government in time of civil conflict to an intervention on the part of another state to establish and maintain the government could hardly be called the consent of the state, for the very fact of civil war would show that the identity of the legal representative of the state was in doubt'. See AVW Thomas and AJ Thomas Jr, *Non-intervention: The Law and Its Import in the Americas* (Southern Methodist University Press, 1956) 94. See also WE Hall, *A Treatise on International Law* (Clarendon Press, 1924) 347: 'the fact that it has been necessary to call in foreign help is enough to show that the issue of the conflict would without it be uncertain, and consequently that there is a doubt as to which side would ultimately establish itself as the legal representative of the state'.

[18] Hafner (n 15) 228.

[19] Nolte (n 7) §23.

[20] ILC Draft Articles on State Responsibility, at 73. See also Hafner (n 15) 221; E Lieblich, 'Intervention and Consent: Consensual Forcible Interventions in Internal Armed Conflicts as International Agreements' (2011) 29 *Boston University International Law Journal* 349–50.

[21] Corten (n 15) 269; Y Dinstein, *War, Aggression and Self-Defence* (Cambridge University Press, 2011) 121; A Orakhelashvili, 'Legal Stability and Claims of Change: The International Court's Treatment of *Jus ad Bellum* and *Jus in Bello*' (2006) 75(3) *Nordic Journal of International Law* 381.

[22] Hafner (n 15) 221; Corten (n 15) 269.

[23] Article 2(1)(a) of the Vienna Convention on the Law of Treaties defines 'treaty' as 'an international agreement concluded between States in *written form* and governed by international law, whether embodied in a single instrument or in two or more related instruments and whatever its particular designation' (emphasis added). Therefore, this provision does not apply when the consent is expressed orally.

[24] IDI, *Military assistance on request*, Art 1(b), 8 September 2011, Session of Rhodes.

by the intervening state.[25] For instance, the USSR's intervention in Hungary (1956) was widely criticised on the ground that the request came from a 'puppet government' established by a foreign intervention.[26] Similarly, it is at least doubtful whether the Soviet intervention in Afghanistan (1979) was triggered by a genuine and freely given consent.[27] Moreover, it is questionable whether the consent of the new Iraqi government to the presence of foreign troops from 2004 was freely given.[28] However, the lawfulness of that presence has been generally accepted even by states that considered the intervention as unlawful.[29]

The intervention of the US-led coalition against the Islamic State in Iraq and Syria (ISIS) has revived debates on the form of consent. On 25 June 2014 Iraq sent a letter to the United Nations Security Council (UNSC), where it asked for international 'support in order to defeat ISIS'.[30] The Iraqi government received considerable assistance: on 7 August 2014 the US began airstrikes against ISIS in Iraq and soon thereafter a number of other countries contributed to the military actions. Accordingly, operation 'Inherent Resolve' was launched: a multinational military campaign aimed at defeating ISIS in Iraq.[31] In September 2014 the US, Bahrain, Jordan, Qatar, Saudi Arabia, and the United Arab Emirates extended the strikes against ISIS on Syrian territory.[32] Albeit initially reluctant, Australia, Canada, France and the UK, among others, eventually joined the US-led coalition.[33] At first Syria did not protest against foreign intervention, thus raising the question as to whether it was tacitly consenting. However, in September 2015 it explicitly affirmed that the intervention was illegal:

> [T]he United Kingdom, Australia and France are currently taking military measures against the Syrian Arab Republic. … Syria has not made any request to that effect. … If any State invokes the excuse of counter-terrorism in order to be present on Syrian territory without the consent of the Syrian Government, whether on the country's land or in its airspace or territorial waters, its actions shall be considered a violation of Syrian sovereignty.[34]

[25] *Nicaragua* case, §205: '[i]ntervention is wrongful when it uses methods of coercion in regard to such choices [the choice of a political, economic, social and cultural system, and the formulation of foreign policy], which must remain free ones'.

[26] Q Wright, 'Intervention, 1956' (1957) 51(2) *American Journal of International Law* 275.

[27] Dinstein (n 21) 121.

[28] Lieblich (n 1) 18.

[29] Corten (n 15) 271.

[30] Letter dated 25 June 2014 from the Permanent Representative of Iraq to the United Nations addressed to the Secretary-General, UN Doc. S/2014/440 (hereinafter Letter dated 25 June 2014 from Iraq).

[31] V Koutroulis, 'The Fight against the Islamic State and Jus in Bello' (2016) 29(3) *Leiden Journal of International Law* 830.

[32] O Corten, 'Military Operations against "Islamic State" (ISIL or Dae'sh)–2014' in T Ruys, O Corten and A Hofer (eds), *The Use of Force in International Law: A Case-based Approach* (Oxford University Press, 2018) 875-76; Koutroulis (n 31) 835.

[33] O Flasch, 'The Legality of the Air Strikes against ISIL in Syria: New Insights on the Extraterritorial Use of Force against Non-state Actors' (2016) 3(1) *Journal on the Use of Force and International Law* 38.

[34] Identical letters dated 17 September 2015 from the Permanent Representative of the Syrian Arab Republic to the United Nations addressed to the Secretary-General and the President of the Security Council, UN Doc. S/2015/719.

Similarly, before engaging in drone strikes against al-Qaeda in Pakistan, 'the US reportedly sent multiple faxes to the Pakistani government, informing it of the planned strikes'.[35] As Pakistan did not respond, the US interpreted its silence as tacit consent and proceeded with the intervention. However, after the killing of Bin-Laden, Pakistan affirmed that the drone strikes took place without its 'knowledge or permission'.[36]

The ICJ has clarified in the Temple of Preah Vihear case that: '[w]here the law prescribes no particular form, parties are free to choose what form they please provided their intention clearly results from it'[37] and that 'tacit consent could be deduced from a failure to act on an occasion that calls for a reaction'.[38] In the same vein, the Permanent Court of Arbitration concluded that Russia tacitly consented to a renunciation of invoking its right to claim an interest on indemnities due to the fact that it refrained to do so during its correspondence with Turkey.[39] Accordingly, it seems possible to conclude that consent can be expressed tacitly, for instance by failing to react when a third country forcibly intervenes on the state territory.[40]

The timing of the consent is equally relevant in assessing its validity. According to the ILC Commentary to the Draft Articles on State Responsibility:

> Consent to the commission of otherwise wrongful conduct may be given by a State in advance or even at the time it is occurring. By contrast, cases of consent given after the conduct has occurred are a form of waiver or acquiescence, leading to loss of the right to invoke responsibility.[41]

The first instance is intuitive and generally unproblematic. On the other hand, *ex post* acquiescence to a forcible intervention can raise doubts with regard to the genuineness of the invitation.[42] The principle *ex iniuria jus non oritur* would suggest that consent expressed after an unlawful intervention ought to be deemed invalid.[43]

For instance, during the first Congolese conflict (1996–97), Uganda and Rwanda intervened in favour of the opposition group (*Alliance des forces démocratiques pour la libération du Congo-Zaire*, AFDL) and successfully

[35] Flasch (n 33) 42.

[36] K Brulliard, 'Military warns against U.S. Raids: Admits failures in intelligence' *Washington Post* (as reprinted in *Boston Globe*, 6 May 2011), available at www.boston.com/news/world/asia/articles/2011/05/06/pakistans_powerful_army_warns_against_us_raids/. See also AB Lorca, 'Rules for the "Global War on Terror": Implying Consent and Presuming Conditions for Intervention' (2012) 45(1) *New York University journal of international law and politics* 6.

[37] ICJ, *Temple of Preah Vihear (Cambodia v Thailand)*, Judgment (Merits), 26 May 1961, at 31.

[38] Flasch (n 33) 41.

[39] Russian Claim for Interest on Indemnities (Damages Claimed by Russia for Delay in Payment of Compensation Owed to Russians Injured During the War of 1877–1878) (Russia v Turkey) (1912) 11 UNRIAA 431, 446.

[40] E de Wet, *Military Assistance on Request and the Use of Force* (Oxford University Press, 2019) 161; SD Murphy, 'The International Legality of U.S. Military Cross-Border Operations from Afghanistan into Pakistan' (2009) 84 *International Law Studies* 109.

[41] ILC Draft Articles on State Responsibility, at 73.

[42] Hafner (n 15) 221.

[43] Corten (n 15) 270.

helped its leader, Laurent Désiré Kabila, to become the new President of the Democratic Republic of Congo (DRC).[44] Once the new government was established, it expressed its ex post consent to the military intervention.[45] Providing direct military support to opposition groups who are fighting against the incumbent government amounts to a violation of the principle of non-intervention and of the ban on the use of force.[46] When a foreign country sends its troops to help rebels, the intervention can even be considered an act of aggression.[47] Therefore, it seems fairly clear that Rwanda and Uganda committed an unlawful intervention in Zaire. However, in the *Congo* case the ICJ did not question that Kabila had validly consented to the armed presence of Uganda and Rwanda in DRC, although at the time of the intervention he was the leader of the opposition group.[48] Contemporary practice thus highlights that ex post consent to a military intervention should be treated with caution.

If the consent is valid, attributable to the state, clearly expressed and freely given, the military intervention is lawful inasmuch as it is limited to 'the parameters of that consent, in terms of geographic location and objectives'.[49] Furthermore, consent can be withdrawn at any time, without formalities.[50] This implies that, even if the consent was expressed through a formal treaty, it can be revoked orally. The rationale underpinning the lack of formal requirements rests on the special character of interventions by invitation. Wippman explains that 'agreements authorizing military intervention differ from other agreements' because they 'go directly to the heart of State independence and the other central values associated with State sovereignty'.[51] Consequently, the 'will of the state at the moment of the intervention should prevail over the will of the state at the moment' of the invitation.[52] This is a crucial point especially in light of Article 3(3) of the Definition of Aggression, which specifies that '[t]he use of armed forces of one State which are within the territory of another State with the agreement of the receiving State, in contravention of the conditions provided for in the agreement or any extension of their presence in such territory beyond the termination of the agreement' amounts to aggression.

[44] International Crisis Group (ICG), 'How Kabila Lost His Way: The Performance of Laurent Désiré Kabila's Government,' ICG Congo Report No. 3, 21 May 1999; M McNulty, 'From Intervened to Intervenor: Rwanda and Military Intervention in Zaire/DRC' in O Furley and R May (eds), *African Interventionist States* (Ashgate 2001) 173; N McQueen, 'Angola: Exporting Civil War' in Furley and May (eds) (n 44) 104–105.

[45] *Congo* case, §§45–46.

[46] *Nicaragua* case, §246.

[47] Definition of Aggression, Art 3(b).

[48] Corten (n 15) 271. See also CD Gray, *International Law and the Use of Force* (Oxford University Press, 2018) 78–80.

[49] *Congo* case, §52.

[50] ibid, §47.

[51] D Wippman, 'Pro-Democratic Intervention by Invitation' in GH Fox and BR Roth (eds), *Democratic Governance and International Law* (Cambridge University Press, 2000) 315.

[52] ibid, 312; Corten (n 15) 274.

II. NEGATIVE EQUALITY OR STRICT ABSTENTIONISM APPROACH

A. The Duty to Abstain from Intervening in Civil Wars

We have seen that military interventions upon invitation are admissible under international law, as confirmed by Article 3(e) of the Definition of Aggression, Article 20 Draft Articles on State Responsibility, and the ICJ in the *Nicaragua* and *Congo* cases.[53] Nevertheless, part of the scholarship posits that such interventions are unlawful when they take place in civil wars.[54] This position was clearly expressed by the Institut de Droit International in its Resolution on 'The Principle of Non-Intervention in Civil Wars', whose Article 2 provides that: '[t]hird States shall refrain from giving assistance to parties to a civil war which is being fought in the territory of another State'.[55] Generally, this approach is defined as 'strict abstentionism' or 'negative equality' doctrine.[56]

The reasoning supporting this view rests on theoretical and practical grounds. From a theoretical point of view, such instances would amount to violations of the principle of non-intervention and the right to self-determination of people.[57] Since people have the right to choose freely their economic, social, and political system, any interference in their choice would be prohibited.[58] On a practical level, some authors suggest that interventions upon invitation have been criticised only when they took place in civil wars, thus suggesting that interventions in situations below this threshold would be lawful. Scholars supporting the abstentionism approach admit counter-interventions as an exception to the general prohibition to intervene in a civil war: if a third state has already intervened in favour of the opposition group, the government could validly ask for an intervention in its favour.[59] Furthermore, a number of authors admit that the

[53] *Nicaragua* case, §246.

[54] Gray (n 48) 81; T Ruys, 'Of Arms, Funding and "Non-Lethal Assistance" – Issues Surrounding Third State Intervention in the Syrian Civil War' (2014) 13(1) *Chinese Journal of International Law* 42; Corten (n 15) 288–310; Doswald-Beck (n 6).

[55] The Resolution was adopted on 14 August 1975 during the Session of Wiesbaden. It replaced the resolution adopted in 1900 concerning 'Droits et devoirs des Puissances étrangères, au cas de mouvement insurrectionnel, envers les gouvernements établis et reconnus qui sont aux prises avec l'insurrection'. In 2011, the IDI adopted a Resolution on *Military assistance on request* (8 September 2011, Session of Rhodes), which complemented the 1975 resolution. Notably, the 2011 resolution admitted the possibility to intervene in situations 'below the threshold of non-international armed conflicts,' as defined by the Additional Protocol II to the Geneva Conventions, Art 1 (see Arts 2(1) and 4(1)).

[56] The term 'doctrine of negative equality' was first used in the Report of the Independent International Fact-Finding Mission on the Conflict in Georgia, Vol II, 25 September 2009, at 277 (hereinafter Report on the Conflict in Georgia), where the commission propounded that: 'a military intervention by a third state in a state torn by civil war will always remain an illegal use of force, which cannot be justified by an invitation'.

[57] For an in-depth analysis of the right to self-determination, see below, Part III.

[58] Doswald-Beck (n 6) 200; Corten (n 15) 513–14; de Wet (n 40) 77.

[59] Gray (n 48) 81; T Christakis and K Bannelier, '*Volenti non Fit Injuria*? Les Effets du Consentement à l'Intervention Militaire' (2004) 50(1) *Annuaire français de droit international* 130; see also UK Foreign Policy Document No 148, (1986) 57 *British Yearbook of International Law* 614 (hereinafter UK Foreign Policy Document).

intervention could be equally admissible when it is not directed at influencing the course of the civil war, for instance when aimed at countering terrorism.[60]

It is well-established that international law prevents states from denying the right to self-determination in case of colonial domination, alien occupation, and racist regimes through the use of force or other forcible actions directed towards the same goal.[61] This is usually referred to as external self-determination. In line with this approach, the UNGA has condemned any forms of foreign intervention directed towards helping the colonial power in these situations.[62] However, self-determination has also an internal dimension, namely peoples' right to 'freely determine their political status and freely pursue their economic, social and cultural development'.[63] The UNGA's Declaration on Friendly Relations recognises that:

> By virtue of the principle of equal rights and self-determination of peoples enshrined in the Charter of the United Nations, all peoples have the right freely to determine, without external interference, their political status and to pursue their economic, social and cultural development, and every State has the duty to respect this right in accordance with the provisions of the Charter.[64]

[60] Christakis and Bannelier (n 59); K Bannelier and T Christakis, 'Under the Security Council's Watchful Eyes: Military Intervention by Invitation in the Malian Conflict' (2013) 26(4) *Leiden Journal of International Law* 855–74.

[61] See eg A/RES/1514(XV), 14 December 1960, *Declaration on the Granting of Independence to Colonial Countries and Peoples*, §4, where the General Assembly asks for the cessation of 'all armed action and repressive measures of all kind directed against dependent peoples … in order to enable them to exercise peacefully and freely their right to complete independence'; A/RES/2160(XXI), 30 November 1966, *Strict Observance of the Prohibition of the Threat or Use of Force in International Relations, and of the Right of Peoples to Self-determination*, §1(b): '[a]ny forcible action, direct or indirect, which deprives peoples under foreign domination of their right to Self-determination and freedom or independence and of their right to determine freely their political status and pursue their economic, social and cultural development constitutes a violation of the Charter of the United Nations'; Definition of Aggression, preamble: 'the duty of States not to use armed force to deprive peoples of their right to Self-determination, freedom and independence, or to disrupt territorial integrity'. See A Cassese, *Self-Determination of Peoples: A Legal Reappraisal* (Cambridge University Press, 1995) 194.

[62] See eg resolutions on the *Question of Southern Rhodesia*: A/RES/2383(XXIII), 7 November 1969; A/RES/2508(XXIV), 21 November 1969; A/RES/2796(XXVI), 10 December 1971; A/RES/2945(XXVII), 1 December 1972; A/RES/34/192, 18 December 1972. See also the resolutions on *The Importance of the Universal Realization of the Right of Peoples to Self-determination and of the Speedy Granting of Independence to Colonial Countries and Peoples for the Effective Guarantee and Observance of Human Rights*: A/RES/2649(XXV), 30 November 1970; A/RES/2787(XXVI), 6 December 1971; A/RES/2955(XXVII), 12 December 1972; A/RES/3070(XXVIII), 30 November 1973; A/RES/3246(XXIX), 29 November 1974; A/RES/3382(XXX), 10 November 1975; A/RES/31/34, 30 November 1976; A/RES/32/14, 7 November 1977; A/RES/33/24, 29 November 1977; A/RES/33/24, 29 November 1978; A/RES/34/44, 29 November 1979; A/RES/35/35 [A-B], 14 November 1980, where the General Assembly condemned 'the establishment and the use of armed groups with the view to putting them against the national liberation movements'.

[63] Article 1(1) of the International Covenant of Civil and Political Rights (ICCPR, 1966) and International Covenant of Economic, Social and Cultural Rights (ICESCR, 1966). See also Doswald-Beck (n 6) 200.

[64] *Declaration on Principles of International Law concerning Friendly Relations and Co-operation among States in accordance with the Charter of the United Nations*, A/RES/25/2625 (XXV), 24 October 1970 (hereinafter Declaration on Friendly Relations).

The right to self-determination would thus determine not only the unlawfulness of interventions in favour of colonial domination, alien occupation, or racial domination, but also in civil wars where the population is fighting in name of its right to internal self-determination. When a government faces internal strife, its authority is questioned: an intervention in its favour would hence jeopardise the right of the people to freely determine its political status.[65] Some scholars thus conclude that a joint interpretation of the right to self-determination and the principle of non-intervention would ban forcible interferences in civil wars.[66] Their conclusion would be grounded on the practice of states, from which two trends emerge.[67]

First of all, states that intervene in internal conflicts seldom base their actions on the sole consent of the incumbent government. Indeed, they tend to adduce further reasons, such as the protection of nationals abroad[68] or the previous intervention of another country in favour of the opposition group (counter-intervention).[69] For instance, Belgium and the US justified their intervention in the Democratic Republic of Congo (1964) on the bases of the invitation of President Tshombe and as necessary to rescue Belgian and US citizens in the country.[70] Similarly, the French interventions in Chad (1978-83) took place upon the invitation of the incumbent government; however, France presented additional claims, namely protection of its nationals abroad and counter-intervention in reaction to the Libyan support to the rebels. On the other hand, Libya justified its operation as a humanitarian action.[71] Furthermore, although the intervention by the Economic Community of West African States (ECOWAS) in Liberia (1990) took place upon the request of the inviting state, the African organisation stressed the peace-keeping nature of its military intervention.[72] Consequently, a number of authors concluded that, if states do not base their interventions only on the request of the beleaguered government, it should mean that they do not believe that it is alone sufficient as legal justification of the intervention.[73]

[65] H Lauterpacht, *Recognition in International Law* (Cambridge University Press, 1947) 233; Q Wright, 'United States Intervention in the Lebanon' (1959) 53(1) *The American Journal of International Law* 121; Q Wright, *The Role of International Law in the Elimination of War* (Manchester University Press, 1961) 120–21; Brownlie (n 17) 327; D Bowett, 'The Interrelation of Theories of Intervention and Self-Defense,' in JN Moore (ed), *Law and Civil War in the Modern World* (Johns Hopkins University Press, 1974) 38; Christakis and Bannelier (n 59) 118–20; Gray (n 48) 81; Corten (n 15) 289–90; Report on the Conflict in Georgia, at 277.

[66] Gray (n 48) 81; Report on the Conflict in Georgia, at 277.

[67] Christakis and Bannelier (n 59) 128.

[68] This is, for example, the case of the US intervention in the Dominican Republic (1965) and of the French and Belgian intervention in Zaire (1978). See Christakis and Bannelier (n 59) 128; A Tanca, *Foreign Armed Intervention in Internal Conflict* (Martinus Nijhoff 1993) 170–72.

[69] See eg the French intervention in Zaire in 1983, justified on the basis of a previous intervention of Libya in favour of the rebel forces. Tanca (n 68) 180–181.

[70] Tanca (n 68) 29; Christakis and Bannelier (n 59) 128; Doswald-Beck (n 6) 217–18.

[71] Tanca (n 68) 172; Doswald-Beck (n 6) 221.

[72] Tanca (n 68) 35; Gray (n 48) 392–94.

[73] Christakis and Bannelier (n 59) 128.

Second, interventions in favour of the government were not criticised when they took place in situations below the civil war threshold. One example is the French intervention in Gabon. On 17 February 1964, 150 soldiers from the Gabonese army entered the capital and overthrew the incumbent government. The following day French troops intervened in Libreville with the consent of the ousted government and regained control of the city.[74] The military intervention did not meet criticism and was no object of discussion in the UN.[75] In the same vein, the international community did not question the UK military interventions in Tanganyika, Uganda, and Kenya against army mutinies (1964).[76]

By banning interventions in civil wars, the abstentionism approach would have the positive outcome of limiting the international use of force, thus mitigating the danger of escalation. Nevertheless, it seems to trigger more questions than it answers. First, it is unclear why presenting more than one justification for an intervention would automatically mean that the intervening country does not consider one of the justifications alone as sufficient. If this were the case, such reasoning would be true for all the justifications provided, not only for one of them. For instance, a state may intervene in a civil war and justify its action on the basis of the invitation of the beleaguered government and as a counter-intervention measure. Following the reasoning under exam, the need to base the intervention on two grounds would suggest that neither of the two justifications is in itself enough. However, the authors in favour of the abstentionism approach do not question the right to counter-intervention, although it is seldom presented as the sole justification for military interference.

Second, it is questionable why a duty to abstain should be limited to the sole case of civil wars. Leaving aside the fact that the definition of civil war has attracted lively debates,[77] it is not clear why interventions upon invitation in situations below the civil war threshold should be allowed. The rationale underpinning the abstentionism approach is that a civil war is a situation whereby a people is highly divided with regard to its future. Therefore, the government

[74] Tanca (n 68) 157.

[75] Gray (n 48) 85.

[76] ibid, 86.

[77] Gray admits that the civil war threshold is not self-evident and argues that the definition of NIAC provided by the Additional Protocol II to the Geneva Conventions could serve as guidance. Article 1(1) of Additional Protocol II refers to conflicts 'which take place in the territory of a High Contracting Party between its armed forces and dissident armed forces or other organized armed groups which, under responsible command, exercise such control over a part of its territory as to enable them to carry out sustained and concerted military operations and to implement this Protocol' (Protocol Relating to the Protection of Victims of Non-international Armed Conflicts, 8 June 1977). The Protocol's scope of application is narrower than the one provided by Common Article 3 to the Geneva Conventions. Therefore, according to Gray's interpretation, the duty to abstain would not apply during NIACs which would fall within the scope of application of Article 3. See Gray (n 48) 81; L Moir, *The Law of Internal Armed Conflict* (Cambridge University Press, 2002) 101; O Corten, *La Rébellion et le Droit International: le Principe de Neutralité en Tension* (Martinus Nijhoff, 2016) 108–14.

would no longer represent the population. However, this approach is based on an old-fashioned notion of non-international armed conflicts and can be criticised on two grounds. First, even cases below the civil war threshold can be fought in the name of self-determination. Why should third states be able to intervene in such instances? The intensity of the conflict would not change the reason why the opposition group is fighting against the government. Second, violent conflicts do not necessarily entail fights for self-determination. For instance, the conflict in Syria (2011-present) could be defined as a civil war. Nevertheless, it is unclear whether all the involved ANSAs are fighting for their right to self-determination.[78] Similar considerations could apply to the armed conflict in Colombia, which opposed the government on one side, and FARC and ENL on the other.

Lastly, state practice shows that states do not rely on the negative equality doctrine, nor do they mention it during discussions within the UNSC. Furthermore, over the past decade the reaction of the international community to interventions upon invitation of the government in situations that amount to civil wars has never criticised the right to intervene per se. Instead, criticism has focused on the modalities of the intervention, or whether the inviting party could be considered the government and thus whether it had the authority to issue the invitation. In light of these reasons, a duty to abstain in civil wars does not seem to exist under the current legal framework.[79]

B. Counter-intervention

Scholars supporting the duty to abstain from intervening in civil wars admit the right to counter-intervention, whereby the incumbent government can lawfully ask for help if a foreign country is already providing support to the opposition group. According to this approach, during an internal conflict none of the parties could consent to an external intervention. Nonetheless, if a third country intervenes in favour of the rebels, the beleaguered government loses its effectiveness due to the foreign intervention. Since the right to self-determination of people has been already violated by the foreign power helping the rebels, the government could invite another state in order to restore the balance. Thus, the rationale is the maintenance of the equilibrium between the parties.[80] Walzer explained that:

> As soon as one outside power violates the norm of ... nonintervention, the way is open for other powers to do so. ... [C]ounter-intervention in civil wars does not aim

[78] See ch 6.

[79] de Wet (n 40) 116.

[80] Tanca (n 68) 99; Schachter (n 5) 1642; D Wippman, 'Military Intervention, Regional Organizations, and Host State Consent' (1996) 7 *Duke Journal of Comparative and International Law* 220: '[t]his claimed right [of counter-intervention] is related to but independent of any authority the

> at punishing or even, necessarily, at restraining the intervening states. It aims instead at holding the circle, preserving the balance, restoring some degree of integrity to the local struggle.[81]

The Institut de Droit International endorsed the right to counter-intervention in Article 5 of its Resolution on 'The Principle of Non-Intervention in Civil Wars':

> Whenever it appears that intervention has taken place during a civil war in violation of the preceding provisions, third States may give assistance to the other party only in compliance with the Charter and any other relevant rule of international law, subject to any such measures as are prescribed, authorized or recommended by the United Nations.

The UK has expressed a similar position in a Foreign Policy Document, where it posited that:

> [A]ny form of interference or assistance is prohibited (except possibly of a humanitarian kind) when a civil war is taking place and control of the State's territory is divided between warring parties. But it is widely accepted that outside interference in favour of one party to the struggle permits counter-intervention on behalf of the other, as happened in the Spanish Civil War and, more recently, in Angola.[82]

State practice appears to confirm this argument. Indeed, intervening powers have often grounded their interference on the basis of the foreign help provided to the opposition group. Emblematic cases are the interventions of the US in Lebanon (1958),[83] Cuba in Angola (1975),[84] and Zimbabwe in

government might otherwise have to consent to foreign military intervention. It rests on the premise that aid in such circumstances is not a form of intervention requiring legitimation, but rather a means to neutralize an unlawful, prior intervention, thus returning control over the state's political future to internal actors to the extent that is possible'.

[81] M Walzer, *Just and Unjust Wars: A Moral Argument with Historical Illustrations* (Basic Books, 2006) 97.

[82] UK Foreign Policy Document (n 59) 616.

[83] In 1958, the political situation in Lebanon was tense. President Chamoun's authority was not widely recognised, due to the growing opposition against him. In May, tensions gained momentum with the assassination of an anti-Chaumon journalist. In June, President Chamoun addressed the Security Council, denouncing illegal infiltrations of arms and men from Syria. Thus, the UNSC sent an Observation Group to monitor the border between the two countries. In July, President Chamoun asked the US to intervene in order to counter the outside threat. President Eisenhower sent US marines the day after the request, and immediately notified the Security Council of the military action. During a meeting at the UNSC, the US justified the intervention on the basis of the invitation of the incumbent government and in order to protect the territorial integrity of Lebanon, menaced by an insurrection assisted by foreign forces; the military intervention was largely approved, notwithstanding criticism from the USSR. On the contrary, the General Assembly invited states to observe strict non-interference. See Wright (n 65) 119; Doswald-Beck (n 6) 217; Tanca (n 68) 153.

[84] In 1975, Angola was a Portuguese colony. Three opposition groups were fighting for its independence: the People's Movement for the Liberation of Angola (*Movimento Popular de Libertação de Angola*, MPLA), the National Front for the Liberation of Angola (*Frente Nacional de Libertação de Angola*, FNLA) and the National Union for the Total Independence of Angola (*União Nacional para a Independência Total de Angola*, UNITA). The warring parties concluded an agreement with

Mozambique (1985).[85] More recently, the intervention by Saudi-led coalition in Yemen was justified also in reference to Iranian assistance to the opposition groups.[86]

While the existence of the right to counter-intervention seems largely unquestioned, it raises a number of questions. First, interventions in favour of opposition groups are often covert and this causes challenges as to the possibility to ascertain with a certain degree of certitude whether a prior intervention took place.[87] As correctly noted by Ruys, this 'will be all the greater where the prior intervention is said to consist of covert arms supplies'.[88] Second, the modalities of the counter-intervention appear obscure. What is the degree of prior intervention necessary to trigger the right to counter-intervention? Should there be proportionality between the two foreign interventions and what would be the threshold of the proportionality test? According to Corten, an intervention 'would be confined to riposting to outside interference … without extending to the settlement of internal strife'.[89] Nevertheless, it is unclear how this could play out in concrete terms and state practice does not seem to offer a clear-cut answer to these issues.[90]

Portugal on 15 January 1975, whereby Angola was going to obtain its independence at the end of the year. In line with the agreement's provisions, power was transferred to a transitional government with representatives of the three opposition groups. However, due to the continuous battles among the armed groups, the organ was never effective. On 10 November 1975, the MPLA and the FNLA declared Angola's independence; the day after, UNITA did the same. Cuban troops intervened in favour of the MPLA, helping the faction to gain control over the territory. By April 1976, 78 countries had recognised the MPLA as the legitimate government. Cuba justified the intervention on the basis of the MPLA's request, albeit at the time the opposition group controlled only 20% of Angolan territory, and as a reaction against South African intervention. That South Africa intervened in Angola is unquestioned. Nevertheless, it is not clear whether it sent its troops on 23 October, as alleged by Cuba, or at the end of November, as affirmed by South Africa. In the first case, Cuban intervention could have been justified as a counter-intervention measure; on the contrary, the second option would turn lawful the South African intervention, as a reaction against the Cuban interference. See R Hallet, 'The South Africa Intervention in Angola (1975–1976)' (1979) 77 *African Affairs* 347–48; F Guimaraes, *The Origins of the Angolan Civil War: Foreign Intervention and Domestic Political Conflict, 1961–76* (Palgrave, 1998) 153 ff; Tanca (n 68) 168.

[85] In 1975, Mozambique obtained its independence from Portugal after 10 years of conflict between the colonial power and the Mozambique Liberation Front (*Frente de Libertação de Moçambique*, FRELIMO). FRELIMO started ruling as the sole party in the country. One year later, white Rhodesian officers helped establish the *Resistência Nacional Moçambicana* (RENAMO). When Rhodesia achieved its independence in 1980, South Africa took over its support of RENAMO. In 1984, South Africa and Mozambique signed the Nkomati Accord, a non-aggression agreement whereby each party took the obligation to impede its territory from being used to launch attacks against the other country. Despite the agreement, South Africa allegedly continued its support of RENAMO. Thus, Mozambique asked for assistance from Zimbabwe, which intervened, invoking the right to counter-intervention and whose forces remained in the country until 1993. See BBC Staff, 'Mozambique Profile: Timeline' (*BBC*, 2 November 2017), available at www.bbc.com/news/world-africa-13890720. See also Gray (n 48) 110.

[86] de Wet (n 40) 118.

[87] Gray (n 48) 92.

[88] Ruys (n 54) 47.

[89] Corten (n 15) 306.

[90] Ruys (n 54) 47.

Interestingly, states invoke the right to counter-intervention not only when the help accorded to rebels would amount to an armed attack, but also in instances below this threshold.[91] This is pivotal in order to distinguish the right to counter-intervention and the right of collective self-defence. While Article 51 of the UN Charter acknowledges 'the inherent right of individual or collective self-defense if an armed attack occurs against a Member of the United Nations', the counter-intervention principle allows states to intervene against an internal threat supported by external forces in order to keep the balance between the two warring parties. In other words, the right to counter-intervention exists even when the foreign assistance provided to the opposition group does not amount to armed attack. Although self-defence and counter-intervention are substantially different, two parallels can be drawn between them. First, in both cases consent is a necessary premise; this implies that counter-intervention is not a right or entitlement of the third state, as it has been suggested.[92] Second, collective self-defence and counter-interventions may overlap when the foreign aid to the opposition group is classified as an armed attack and when the actions of the rebels can be attributed to the intervening country.[93]

III. THE PURPOSE-BASED APPROACH

A number of scholars in favour of the negative equality approach posit that the duty to abstain from intervening in a civil war would not apply when the intervention aims at an objective other than influencing the outcome of the conflict. In other words, if the intervention is not directed in favour of one party or another, but pursues other purposes, it would not be in violation of the principle of non-intervention and the right to self-determination of people.[94] As explained by Bannelier and Christakis:

> The criterion of the purpose of the foreign military operations is thus decisive and external intervention by invitation should be deemed in principle unlawful when the objective of this intervention is to settle an exclusively internal political strife in favour of the established government which launched the invitation.[95]

Legal scholars have suggested a few instances when an intervention in a civil war upon invitation of the government would be lawful because of its purpose, which will be examined in turn.

[91] Christakis and Bannelier (n 59) 133.

[92] See eg JA Perkins, 'The Right to Counter-Intervention' (1987) 17(2) *Georgia Journal of International and Comparative Law* 171–73.

[93] O Schachter, *International Law in Theory and Practice* (Martinus Nijhoff, 1991) 159; Lieblich (n 1) 171; Wippman (n 80) 221; Christakis and Bannelier (n 59) 133.

[94] Ruys (n 54) 43.

[95] Bannelier and Christakis (n 60) 860.

A. Intervention to Rescue Nationals Abroad

First, a number of authors who support the strict abstentionism approach posit that an intervention upon invitation in a civil war is lawful when the intervening state does not provide help to any of the parties to the conflict and instead intervenes to protect or rescue its own nationals abroad. In this case, the territorial state could consent to the intervention inasmuch as it would not influence the outcome of the internal conflict. Accordingly, it is generally uncontested that:

> [T]his type of intervention by invitation is not in principle contested whether in terms of the principle of the non-use of force or that of non-intervention and the right to self-determination.[96]

The right to intervene in such circumstances has never been questioned per se.[97] For instance, Germany sent its armed forces in Mogadishu in 1978 in order to free nationals that were taken hostage; the operation took place with the consent of the Somali government and the cooperation of local authorities and forces and was not denounced as unlawful.[98] Nevertheless, these instances could be prone to abuses.[99] One example is the French intervention in Chad in 1978. At first, the military operation was justified to protect French nationals in the country. However, later France admitted that the intervention was also directed at helping the government.[100] Another controversial example is the military operation conducted by Belgium and the US in Stanleyville.[101] While the intervening states highlighted that the objective of the intervention was purely to save nationals abroad, a number of countries criticised the intervention and claimed that the real objective was to support the government in its fight against the rebels.[102]

B. Intervention to Fight against Opposition Groups Who Engage in Transborder Military Operations

Another example of intervention upon invitation whose purpose is not influencing the outcome of the civil war is the case of military operations directed against opposition groups who engage in transborder attacks. Indeed, if the territory of a state is used by an opposition group to train and launch attacks against another country, it is understandable that the victim state could ask the

[96] N Ronzitti, *Rescuing Nationals Abroad through Military Coercion and Intervention on Grounds of Humanity* (Martinus Nijhoff Publishers, 1985) 77–88.
[97] Corten (n 15) 292.
[98] Christakis and Bannelier (n 59) 125.
[99] ibid, 122.
[100] Tanca (n 68) 120, 172.
[101] ibid, 158.
[102] Christakis and Bannelier (n 59) 122; Tanca (n 68) 158.

territorial state to intervene and target the rebels.[103] Since the objective is not to help any of the parties to the civil war, the territorial state would have the right to consent to a foreign military intervention.[104]

The lawfulness of this intervention seems further acknowledged by the ICJ, which clarified that: 'every State's obligation not to allow knowingly its territory to be used for acts contrary to the rights of other States'.[105] Notably, this duty extends to the 'obligation to ensure that [a state's] territory is not used by irregular forces to attack other States'.[106] A number of conventions on terrorism reiterate the same duty, whereby they establish that state parties shall adopt 'all practicable measures to prevent preparations in their respective territories for the commission of those crimes within or outside their territories'.[107]

To fulfil its obligations, the state where opposition groups are based can conduct military operations against the rebels; however, it could also cooperate with the victim state and consent to a foreign intervention on its territory to join forces against the armed non-state actors.[108] The lawfulness of this kind of intervention upon invitation has been confirmed by the ICJ in the *Congo* case. Indeed, not only DRC agreed to the intervention by Uganda against the Ugandan opposition groups based in DRC, but the two countries also conducted joint military operations against the rebels. The ICJ never questioned the legality of such intervention upon invitation:

> It seems certain that from mid-1997 and during the first part of 1998 Uganda was being allowed to engage in military action against anti-Ugandan rebels in the eastern part of Congolese territory. Uganda claims that its troops had been invited into eastern Congo by President Kabila when he came to power in May 1997. The DRC has acknowledged that 'Ugandan troops were present on the territory of the Democratic Republic of the Congo with the con- sent of the country's lawful government'. It is clear from the materials put before the Court that in the period preceding August 1998 the DRC did not object to Uganda's military presence and activities in its eastern border area.[109]

[103] Christakis and Bannelier (n 59) 126.

[104] Corten (n 15) 291.

[105] *Corfu Channel (United Kingdom v Albania)*, Judgment (Merits), 9 April 1949 (hereinafter *Corfu Channel* case), at 22.

[106] Corten (n 15) 291. See also Declaration on Friendly Relations.

[107] See eg Art 4(a) of the Convention on the Prevention and Punishment of Crimes against Internationally Protected Persons, including Diplomatic Agents 1973; Art 4(a) of the International Convention against the Taking of Hostages 1971; Art 13 of the Convention for the Suppression of Unlawful Acts against the Safety of Maritime Navigation 1988; Art 15(a) of the International Convention for the Suppression of Terrorist Bombings 1998; Art 18 of the International Convention for the Suppression of the Financing of Terrorism 2002; Art 7 of the International Convention for the Suppression of Acts of Nuclear Terrorism 2007.

[108] Corten (n 15) 291; Christakis and Bannelier (n 59) 126–27.

[109] *Congo* case, §45.

C. Intervention to Counter Terrorism

Lastly, a number of scholars have suggested that the negative equality doctrine would not be applicable in the case of interventions in civil wars upon invitation of the government when the objective is to fight against terrorism. In support of this position, they rely on a number of instances when interventions upon invitation took place against terrorist groups and did not meet the condemnation of the international community. For instance, when France intervened in Mali in 2011, in the letter to the UNSC it specified that:

> France has responded today to a request for assistance from the Interim President of the Republic of Mali, Mr. Dioncounda Traoreé. *Mali is facing terrorist elements from the north*, which are currently threatening the territorial integrity and very existence of the State and the security of its population ... [T]he French armed forces, in response to that request and in coordination with our partners, particularly those in the region, are *supporting Malian units in combating those terrorist elements*.[110]

In line with its statement, France conducted its military operations against armed groups qualified as terrorists by the UN Security Council, namely Al-Qaeda in the Islamic Maghreb (AQIM) and Movement for Oneness and Jihad in West Africa (MUJAO),[111] while it avoided targeting the National Movement for the Liberation of Azawad (MNLA), a group that was fighting for the Tuareg community and the independence of Azawad.[112] Similarly, when Iraq asked for help to fight against the Islamic State in 2014, it highlighted the terrorist nature of that organisation:

> ISIL has ... been terrorizing citizens, carrying out mass executions, persecuting minorities and women, and destroying mosques, shrines and churches. ... We therefore call on the United Nations and the international community to recognize the serious threat our country and the international order are facing ... To that end, we need your support in order to defeat ISIL and protect our territory and people. In particular, we call on Member States to assist us by providing military training, advanced technology and the weapons required to respond to the situation, *with a view to denying terrorists staging areas and safe havens*.[113]

In the same vein, when Russia intervened in favour of the Syrian government in 2015, it stressed that the intervention was directed at countering terrorism:

> The Russian Federation has taken a number of measures in response to a request from the Government of the Syrian Arab Republic to the Government of the Russian Federation *to cooperate in* countering *terrorism and to provide military*

[110] Identical letters dated 11 January 2013 from the Permanent Representative of France to the UN addressed to the Secretary-General and the President of the Security Council, S/1013/17, emphasis added.

[111] See S/RES/ 2085 (2012), 20 December 2012.

[112] Bannelier and Christakis (n 60) 866.

[113] Letter dated 20 September 2014 from the Permanent Representative of Iraq to the United Nations addressed to the President of the Security Council, S/2014/691 (2014).

> *support for the counter-terrorism efforts of the Syrian Government and the Syrian Arab Army*… This support, which is being provided *in response to a request from the Government of the Syrian Arab Republic*, is fully consistent with international law, the Charter of the United Nations, international counter-terrorism instruments and Security Council resolutions 2170 (2014), 2178 (2014) and 2199 (2015), all of which reaffirm the unity, sovereignty and territorial integrity of the Syrian Arab Republic.[114]

While practice seems to suggest that states tend to highlight that their interventions upon invitation are directed against terrorist groups, claiming that countering terrorism is a legitimate purpose raises more questions than it answers.[115] Notably, as long as there is no internationally accepted definition of terrorism and terrorist group, the risk of abuse is extremely high. Indeed, states could easily label a group as terrorist with the purpose of asking for foreign assistance to fight against it.[116] Indeed, in Syria the government has labelled nearly all opposition groups as terrorists.[117] As correctly noted by de Wet:

> As a result, any recognition of a counter-terrorism exception to the prohibition of military intervention on the side of the government in a NIAC effectively amounts to an erosion and, therefore, de facto abolition of the general prohibition (to the extent that it indeed existed).[118]

IV. EFFECTIVENESS DOCTRINE: *DE FACTO* CONTROL AS REQUISITE TO EXPRESS A VALID CONSENT

It is generally uncontested that the government represents the state and can act on its behalf; therefore it can express a valid consent to foreign forcible interventions within its territory, at least in normal circumstances.[119] Nevertheless, internal conflicts are instances where the authority of the government is challenged by part of the population.[120] Does this impair the government's capacity to speak on behalf of the state? As Brownlie noted, the 'difficulty arises when the legal status of the government which is alleged to have given consent is a matter of doubt'.[121] Identifying the legitimate authority that can act on behalf of the

[114] Identical letters dated 14 October 2015 from the Permanent Representative of the Syrian Arab Republic to the United Nations addressed to the Secretary-General and the President of the Security Council (16 October 2015), A/70/429 and S/2015/789, emphasis added.
[115] Bannelier and Christakis (n 60) 859.
[116] ibid, 866.
[117] de Wet (n 40) 120.
[118] ibid, 121.
[119] Doswald-Beck (n 6) 190–91.
[120] Wippman (n 80) 212.
[121] Brownlie (n 17) 317.

state, and that is thus able to express a valid consent to forcible interventions, is essentially based on the norms on sovereignty and recognition.[122]

In international law, the primary objects of recognition are states and governments. As explained by Roth:

> International law acknowledges 'States' as bearers of a distinctive package of rights, obligations, powers, and immunities (i.e. 'sovereignty'), and attributes to each state a 'government' with the legal capacity (for the time being) to assert rights, incur obligations, exercise powers, and confer immunities on the state's behalf.[123]

Despite the fact that governments are vital to states' existence, the latter can endure also in absence of an authority capable to act on its behalf. The practice related to failed states demonstrates that the lack of an identifiable and functioning governmental authority does not cause their statehood to be questioned:[124] '[a] government does not define the state any more than the tail wags the dog'.[125] Since states exist regardless of whether they are represented by a functioning government, some authors posit that the international community should be indifferent to the methods by which a government reached power. In other words, once a state has been recognised as a member of the international community and has been granted legal personality, it exists regardless of internal changes of power and crises.[126] Consequently, the practice of recognition of governments should be abandoned. This approach was propounded by the Mexican Foreign Secretary Genaro Estrada in 1930:

> The Mexican Government shall issue no declaration in the sense of grants of recognition, since that nation considers that such a course is an insulting practice and one which, in addition to the fact that it offends the sovereignty of other nations, implies that judgment of some sort may be passed upon the internal affairs of those nations by other governments, inasmuch as the latter assume, in effect, an attitude of criticism when they decide, favourably or unfavourably, as to the legal qualifications of foreign regimes.[127]

[122] See eg Tanca (n 68) 48–50; Wright (n 65) 120; Doswald-Beck (n 6) 192–96; BR Roth, *Governmental Illegitimacy in International Law* (Clarendon Press, 1999) 136–52; Corten (n 15) 280–87.

[123] BR Roth, *Sovereign Equality and Moral Disagreement: Premises of a Pluralist International Legal Order* (Oxford University Press, 2011) 169.

[124] See D Thürer, 'Failing States' in *Max Planck Encyclopedia of Public International Law* (Oxford University Press, 2009) §3: '[a] State is usually considered to have failed when the power structures providing political support for law and order have collapsed, or are non-existent to the extent that the State ceases to be an effective member of the international community. This process is generally triggered and accompanied by anarchic forms of internal violence'. Chan argues that 'whilst recognition of "statehood" is preserved, the "sovereignty" of failed states have been treated as conditional on the existence and effectiveness of their government (which represents the peoples of the State)'. See also K Chan, 'State Failure and the Changing Face of the *Jus ad Bellum*' (2013) 18(3) *Journal of Conflict and Security Law* 395–426.

[125] Roth (n 122) 132.

[126] ibid, 137.

[127] ibid. See also PC Jessup, 'The Estrada Doctrine' (1931) 25(4) *The American Journal of International Law* 719–23; SD Murphy, 'Democratic Legitimacy and the Recognition of States and Governments' in Fox and Roth (eds) (n 51) 567.

The overwhelming majority of states has embraced the Estrada doctrine. Recently, the British Foreign Secretary endorsed this approach with regard to the Libyan National Transitional Council:

> In line with our assessment of the NTC as the legitimate interlocutor in Libya representing the aspirations of the Libyan people, the Government has invited the NTC to establish an office in the UK. This will enhance our existing relationship with the NTC, and better enable us to fulfil our commitment to protect civilians under threat of attack from the Qadhafi regime. … This arrangement does not affect our position on the legal status of the NTC: the British Government will continue to recognise States, not Governments.[128]

The aim of the Estrada Doctrine is to avoid any kind of judgement towards the authority in power, especially with respect to the form of government and the way in which the power was obtained.[129] However, this approach fails to acknowledge the peculiarities of non-international armed conflicts. During internal conflicts, the problem of recognition of governments stems from the need to identify the authority capable of representing the state:[130] sooner or later, states need to decide whom they consider the de jure government. This is necessary in order to appoint diplomatic representatives, as well as to identify the authority capable of expressing a valid consent to a foreign intervention. Ultimately, the debate boils down to a question of agency: what are the criteria to identify the organ that can validly speak for the state?

Traditionally, effective control over territory and population has been the main factor to determine the authority capable of acting on behalf of the state. The foundations of the effectiveness doctrine can be traced back to the seventeenth century in the writings of Grotius and Pufendorf.[131] The two scholars investigated whether a revolutionary authority was capable of sending diplomatic representatives to foreign countries and concluded that it is 'highly probable that he who actually holds the supreme sovereignty should, despite the fact that he seized it by base methods, be held for the time by the citizens as a lawful prince, so long as there is none who can lay a better claim to sovereignty'.[132] In the same vein, in the eighteenth century Vattel maintained that '[f]oreign powers are entitled to look to the sovereign in actual

[128] Foreign & Commonwealth Office, 'Announcement: Supporting the Libyan National Transitional Council', 13 May 2011.

[129] See *Nicaragua* case, §263: '[h]owever the régime in Nicaragua be defined, adherence by a State to any particular doctrine does not constitute a violation of customary international law; to hold otherwise would make nonsense of the fundamental principle of State sovereignty, on which the whole of international law rests, and the freedom of choice of the political, social, economic and cultural system of a State'.

[130] Lauterpacht (n 65) 98: 'the problem of recognition of governments arises not because of any unlawfulness of change, but because the accompanying violence and the resulting period of unsettlement demand an answer to the question whether the new government claiming to represent the state is in fact the government of the country'.

[131] ibid, 99.

[132] ibid.

position'.[133] In his view, preferring the de facto situation is the only way to respect the principle of non-intervention:

> Since foreigners have no right to interfere in domestic affairs of a State, they are not obliged to examine or to pass upon the justice or injustice of its conduct in the management of them; they may, if they think fit, presume that the sovereign in possession is the lawful one. When a Nation has driven out its sovereign, other powers … consider it thenceforth as a free and sovereign State, without taking it upon themselves to judge whether it has acted justly in throwing off the sovereignty of its former prince.[134]

Early arbitral decisions adopted a similar approach and endorsed the idea that the way in which the power is obtained is not relevant to identify the government: the only applicable criterion is effectiveness. For instance, in the *Dreyfus* case (1901) the Franco-Chilean Arbitral Tribunal had to decide whether the revolutionary government of Peru was unconstitutional due to the fact that it obtained its power though a coup and concluded that:

> According to a principle of international law … today universally admitted, the capacity of a government to represent the State in its international relations does not depend in any degree upon the legitimacy of its origin, so that … the usurper who in fact holds power with the consent express or tacit of the nation acts … validly in the name of the State.[135]

Similarly, in the *Tinoco Concessions* case the arbiter maintained that a revolutionary government ought to be considered as the authority representing the state, regardless of the means used to gain power:

> To hold that a government which establishes itself and maintains a peaceful administration, with the acquiescence of the people for a substantial period of time, does not become a de facto government unless it conforms to a previous constitution would be to hold that within the rules of international law a revolution contrary to the fundamental law of the existing government cannot establish a new government. This cannot be, and is not, true. The change by revolution upsets the rule of the authorities in power under the then existing fundamental law, and sets aside the fundamental law in so far as the change of rule makes it necessary. To speak of a revolution creating a de facto government, which conforms to the limitations of the old constitution, is to use a contradiction in terms.[136]

[133] ibid, 101.
[134] ibid.
[135] Permanent Court of Arbitration, *French Claims against Peru* (France against Peru), Arbitral Award, 11 October 1921 (F München).
[136] *Tinoco Concessions Arbitration*, (Great Britain c. Costa Rica), 18 October 1923 (sole arbitrator William R Taft) RSA, vol 1, at 28. In Costa Rica in 1917, Federico Tinoco overthrew the government of President Alfredo González. The new President retained power until 1919, when he went into exile in Europe. During his government, Tinoco promulgated a new Constitution and concluded some agreements with foreign companies. When Tinoco left the country, the new government declared all the acts of the former President null and void. This decision also affected the agreements concluded with the foreign companies. See Lauterpacht (n 65) 104.

The idea that de facto control is the criterion to identify the government thus rests on a longstanding tradition supported by arbitral decisions and is embraced by numerous scholars. Kelsen was one of the most prominent supporters of this approach. In his seminal book *General Theory of Law and State*, he propounded that 'a national legal order begins to be valid as soon as it has become – on the whole – efficacious; and it ceases to be valid as soon as it loses this efficacy'.[137] More recently, Tanca maintained that 'no other generally accepted criteria, apart from effectiveness – has emerged to assess the legitimacy of the inviting authority'.[138] Similarly, Wippman affirmed that 'international law presumes that when a government exercises effective control over the territory and the people of the state, the government … possesses the exclusive authority to express the will of the State in its international affairs'.[139] If only a government in de facto control can validly represent the state and act on its behalf, an ineffective one could not speak for the state.[140] Consequently, during an internal conflict a government could hardly ask for foreign help to quell the rebellion, since it is challenged by part of the population and does not retain full control of the state's territory.

The effectiveness doctrine raises a threshold question. Indeed, it is unclear which degree of effectiveness a government must meet in order to hold its consent power: how can one identify the moment when the government has lost its de facto control?[141] Does retaining control over half of the country suffice? Is it necessary to control the capital? Scholars in favour of the effectiveness approach have attempted to address this critique. For instance, Gray asserts that the incumbent government loses its consent power 'when a civil war is taking place and control of state's territory is divided between the warring parties'.[142] Nevertheless, the evaluation of the situation would ultimately rest on the discretional analysis of the intervening state.

Since the effectiveness doctrine is based on de facto considerations, inevitably it excludes any legal inquiry into the ways in which control was gained: as far as the government can fulfil the functions of the state, it is considered capable of acting on its behalf.[143] Consequently, 'the de facto situation is presumed to overrule the de jure one'.[144] The only exception would be the case of foreign military intervention in favour of the rebels, which would trigger the

[137] H Kelsen, *General Theory of Law and State* (Russel and Russel, 1961) 220–21; BR Roth, 'Secessions, Coups and the International Rule of Law: Assessing the Decline of the Effective Control Doctrine' (2010) 11(2) *Melbourne Journal of International Law* 431.

[138] Tanca (n 68) 48.

[139] Wippman (n 80) 211–12.

[140] Doswald-Beck (n 6) 196.

[141] Lieblich (n 1) 154.

[142] Gray (n 48) 81.

[143] Le Mon (n 15) 745.

[144] Wright (n 65) 120.

right to counter-intervention.[145] Apart from this specific circumstance, the principle *ex factis jus oritur* would be fully valid.[146] This conclusion has the merit of grounding the identification of governments on a 'reasonably objective and externally verifiable basis'.[147] Nonetheless, several authors consider it as highly controversial and irremediably in contrast with people's right to determine their own political future: '[i]nsofar as it is perceived as little more than an imprimatur for "might makes right" at the local level, this "effective control doctrine" is manifestly offensive to a rule-of-law sensitivity'.[148]

To overcome this problem, Roth suggested that the effective control test could be reconciled with the popular sovereignty norm:[149] in order to be effective, the government ought to exercise control over territory *and population*. Thus, the obedience of the bulk of the population is a crucial element of the effectiveness doctrine.[150] This position finds confirmation in past arbitral decisions. For instance, in the *Garrison* case it was acknowledged that: 'every government, properly so called, is a government de facto', ie 'a government which … commands the habitual respect and obedience of the bulk of the people'.[151] The same approach was endorsed in the *Caculla* arbitral decision: '[h]abitual obedience of the members of a political society (of the "bulk" of them) must, in fact, exist to constitute a government'.[152]

These decisions highlight the relationship between effective control over the territory and the will of the people: if the population habitually obeys an authority, the latter has de facto control, hence it should be considered the legitimate government.[153] Accordingly, a new order is deemed to be valid 'if the individuals whose behaviour the new order regulates actually behave, by and large, in conformity with the new order'.[154] This last consideration underlines the relationship between effectiveness and the right to self-determination, which is grounded on the actual will of people.[155] Since determining or calculating

[145] The right of counter-intervention implies that, if the opposition received foreign assistance and the government lost its control as a result, the latter could lawfully ask for a foreign intervention in its favour. See Tanca (n 68) 49–50.

[146] Wright (n 65) 120.

[147] Wippman (n 80) 212.

[148] Roth (n 123) 170. See also Wippman (n 80) 213; Schachter (n 5) 1641.

[149] For an analysis of the emergence of popular sovereignty see L Glanville, *Sovereignty and the Responsibility to Protect: A New History* (The University of Chicago Press, 2014) 61–99.

[150] Roth (n 122) 137; Le Mon (n 15) 746.

[151] Claims Commission established under the Convention concluded between the United States of America and Venezuela on 5 December 1885, *Case of Melville E. Day and David E. Garrison, as surviving executors of Cornelius K. Garrison v. Venezuela, decision of the Commissioner, Mr. Findlay* (1885), at 232.

[152] Quoted in Doswald-Beck (n 6) 193. See also Roth (n 122) 139.

[153] Lauterpacht (n 65) 115.

[154] Kelsen (n 137) 118; Roth (n 122) 138–139.

[155] A definition of the principle can be found in the UN General Assembly's Declaration on Friendly Relations: '[b]y virtue of the principle of equal rights and Self-determination of peoples enshrined in the Charter of the United Nations, all peoples have the right freely to determine, without external interference, their political status and to pursue their economic, social and cultural development, and every State has the duty to respect this right in accordance with the provisions of the Charter'.

the population's acceptance of the incumbent government through an empirical investigation would be impracticable, acquiescence of the population to the incumbent authority would seem the best way to ascertain its will.[156]

Of course, acquiescence does not imply approval from the population. However, even when the people decide to obey to the incumbent government out of fear or weakness, such a decision should still be respected. Thus, according to the effective control doctrine, the reasons why the population is obeying the incumbent government do not jeopardise or influence its capacity to represent the state: insofar as the population does not embrace the arms to oppose its authority, the government can act on behalf of the state.[157] This approach has been endorsed by Roth:

> Albeit paradoxical, it is far from ridiculous that popular sovereignty may amount, as a matter of practical application, to the right to be ruled by domestic thugs rather than by foreigners announcing benevolent intentions.[158]

According to Roth, the effective control doctrine could reconcile popular sovereignty and ideological pluralism.[159] The UN Charter 'envisages the relations among States having different political, economic and social systems on the basis of coexistence among their various ideologies'.[160] Effective control exercised over territory and population, together with the acquiescence of the latter, would thus support the presumption that the government reflects the will of the people.[161] However, when part of the population challenges the governmental authority, the presumption is broken and an intervention in favour of the ruler would thus be unlawful.

V. DEMOCRATIC ENTITLEMENT DOCTRINE: THE PREFERENCE FOR DEMOCRATIC GOVERNMENTS

A. Democratic Entitlement Doctrine

According to the effectiveness doctrine, general obedience by the bulk of the population would equate to an expression of the will of the people. Therefore,

[156] Roth (n 123) 204–205.

[157] This approach was endorsed by the High Court of Lesotho in the *Mokotso v King Moshoeshoe II* case: '[i]f the judge is satisfied that the new regime is firmly established and there is no opposition thereto, and that the people are acting by and large in conformity with the new legal order, signifying their acceptance thereof, for whatever reason, I do not see that the judge can hold that regime to be other than legitimate'. See *Mokotso v King Moshoeshoe II*, Lesotho High Court, 1998, in Roth (n 122) 140.

[158] Roth (n 123) 205.

[159] ibid, 171.

[160] *Nicaragua* case, §133.

[161] Roth (n 123) 171.

as far as there is no insurrection against the government, it should be presumed that the latter respects popular sovereignty. Nonetheless, the existence of an insurrection does not necessarily imply that the majority of the population opposes the government. The complexity of contemporary internal conflicts, where several non-state actors fight against the government and among themselves, often makes it nearly impossible to assess where the will of the bulk of the population lies. Equating the habitual obedience of the people with an expression of their will and a legitimisation of the incumbent government is at best controversial. According to Doswald-Beck, it reduces the popular will to 'the strongest and most influential body of nationals of the state'.[162] Fox expressed a similar concern: 'a regime that bases its legitimacy on nothing more than the fact that it holds power exercises no "sovereign" authority to object to such prescriptions'.[163]

In light of these observations, legitimism resurfaced during the twentieth century in the form of an emerging right to democratic entitlement. The doctrine stems from two observations: on the one hand, international law protects 'the people's sovereignty rather than the sovereign's sovereignty'.[164] On the other hand, effectiveness does not provide a convincing basis to reconcile power with popular sovereignty. Democracy was hence recognised as the ideal expression of popular sovereignty. The etymology of the term, which derives from the combination of the Greek words δῆμος (*demos*, people) and κράτος (*kratos*, power), suggests that democracy is associated with the role of the people in a state's governance.[165] This idea seems to find confirmation in Article 21(3) of the Universal Declaration of Human Rights, which provides that: '[t]he will of the people shall be the basis of the authority of government; this will shall be expressed in periodic and genuine elections which shall be by universal and equal suffrage and shall be held by secret vote or by equivalent free voting procedures'.[166]

The end of the Cold War and the wide ratification of human rights treaties furthered the hope to find a broader consensus on governmental legitimacy.[167] In an influential article published in 1992, Franck made the case for an emerging

[162] Doswald-Beck (n 6) 194.

[163] GH Fox, 'The Right to Political Participation in International Law' in Fox and Roth (eds) (n 51) 595.

[164] WM Reisman, 'Sovereignty and Human Rights in Contemporary International Law' (2017) 84(4) *The American Journal of International Law* 869.

[165] H Charlesworth, 'Democracy and International Law' (2014) 371 *Collected Courses of The Hague Academy of International Law* 54; TM Franck, 'Legitimacy and the Democratic Entitlement' in Fox and Roth (eds) (n 51) 25.

[166] See Reisman (n 164) 868; LE Fielding, 'Taking the Next Step in the Development of New Human Rights: The Emerging Right of Humanitarian Assistance to Restore Democracy' (1995) 5 *Duke Journal of Comparative & International Law* 332.

[167] Roth (n 122) 148. Fukuyama saw the end of the Cold War as the end of history and the uncontested victory of the liberal doctrine; see F Fukuyama, *The End of History and the Last Man* (Penguin Books, 1992).

right of democratic governance, which 'is rapidly becoming, in our time, a normative rule of the international system'.[168] The same year, Fox noted that the codification of political rights, coupled with an increasing number of monitored elections, would prove the existence of a right to political participation in international law.[169] In striking contrast with the effectiveness doctrine, it was suggested that a 'government cannot govern by force alone'.[170] Instead, its powers descend from the consent of its people:

> For a non-democratic regime to claim that participatory rights violate its national sovereignty begs the question of whether that regime has legitimate authority to make such a statement. When the will of the people is the basis of the authority of government, regimes that thwart the will of the people will lack legitimacy. The participatory rights provisions of the human rights conventions have succeeded in extending this notion of legitimacy from the domestic to the international sphere. It is still an open question as to how far this principle should be extended. But if political participation is to have any meaning as an internationally enforceable right, the community of states must be empowered to prescribe standards detailing how participation is to occur and to insist that parties to the major treaties adopt these standards as law.[171]

While we might agree on the fact that popular sovereignty has gained more than a mere hortatory status, it is questionable whether the right to democracy is now part of international law. It is revealing that the same author who initiated the debate on democratic entitlement and participatory rights advanced doubts with regard to the existence of a right to democratic governance. Twelve years after affirming the emergence of the right to political participation in international law, Fox wondered whether there is a right to democratic governance, and concluded that the answer must remain uncertain for three reasons.[172] First, there are few instances when states defined democracy as a right in clear terms.[173] Second, a right to democracy would represent a 'deep intrusion into

[168] TM Franck, 'The Emerging Right to Democratic Governance' (1992) 86(1) *The American Journal of International Law* 46. Although Frank's seminal article is often 'described as a legal avatar of post-Cold War Western triumphalism', Fox and Roth recently explained that 'it would be a mistake to regard The Emerging Right as a cover for imperialist domination. Indeed, Franck dedicated much of his career to advocating for the interests of non- Western peoples and states. Franck was acutely aware of how a Western-led advocacy of democratic norms could be both misused by its proponents and misperceived in the global South. The article reflects the pains he took to preempt these dangers'. See GH Fox and BR Roth, 'The Dual Lives of "The Emerging Right to Democratic Governance"' (2018) 112 *AJIL Unbound* 70.

[169] Fox (n 163) 541. See also J Crawford, 'Democracy and International Law' (1994) 64(1) *British Yearbook of International Law* 113–33, where he propounded that international law was witnessing a pro-democratic shift; S Marks, *The Riddle of All Constitutions: International Law, Democracy, and the Critique of Ideology* (Oxford University Press, 2003).

[170] Franck (n 168) 48.

[171] Fox (n 163) 595.

[172] GH Fox, 'Democracy, Right to, International Protection' in *Max Planck Encyclopedia of Public International Law* (Oxford University Press, 2008), §4.

[173] ibid, §§4–5.

traditional notions of domestic jurisdiction'.[174] Indeed, people should be free to choose the form of government that they prefer, and this might not be democratic. This finds confirmation in the UNGA Declaration on Friendly Relations, which acknowledges that: '[e]ach State has the right freely to choose and develop its political, social, economic and cultural systems'. Lastly, the very meaning of democracy is controversial. This observation must be parsed.

In the current international system, two competing notions of democracy coexist. The substantial approach looks at democracy and human rights as 'virtually intertwined'.[175] This view rests on the premise that political participation cannot be achieved without respecting other rights.[176] The UNGA endorsed this approach in its resolution on *Promoting and Consolidating Democracy*,[177] which called upon states to protect democracy by respecting an extended list of rights.[178] In the same vein, UN Secretary-General Ban Ki-moon specified that:

> Democracy, based on the rule of law, is ultimately a means to achieve international peace and security, economic and social progress and development, and respect for human rights – the three pillars of the United Nations mission as set forth in the Charter of the UN. Democratic principles are woven throughout the normative fabric of the United Nations. … The UN has long advocated a concept of democracy that is holistic: encompassing the procedural and the substantive; formal institutions and informal processes; majorities and minorities; men and women; governments and civil society; the political and the economic; at the national and the local levels.[179]

This approach presents a significant limit. If democracy is understood in broader terms, the list of relevant rights could be infinite:[180] any right could potentially

[174] ibid, §7.

[175] ibid, §10.

[176] Charlesworth (n 165) 109; J d'Aspremont, 'Legitimacy of Governments in the Age of Democracy' (2006) 38 *New York University Journal of International Law and Politics* 890–895; S Marks, 'What has Become of the Emerging Right to Democratic Governance?' (2011) 22(2) *European Journal of International Law* 515.

[177] A/RES/55/96, 4 December 2000, *Promoting and Consolidating Democracy*.

[178] Similarly, United Nations Commission on Human Rights (UNCHR) described the right to democracy as including: '(i) The rights to freedom of opinion and expression, of thought, conscience and religion, and of peaceful association and assembly; (ii) The right to freedom to seek, receive and impart information and ideas through any media; (iii) The rule of law, including legal protection of citizens' rights, interests and personal security, and fairness in the administration of justice and independence of the judiciary; (iv) The right of universal and equal suffrage, as well as free voting procedures and periodic and free elections; (v) The right of political participation, including equal opportunity for all citizens to become Candidates; (vi) Transparent and accountable government institutions; (vii) The right of citizens to choose their governmental system through constitutional or other democratic means; (viii) The right to equal access to public service in one's own country'. UNCHR, *Promotion of the Right to Democracy*, 27 April 1999, E/CN.4/RES/1999/5.

[179] UN Secretary-General Ban Ki-moon, 'Guidance Note of the Secretary-General on Democracy', 11 September 2009.

[180] Fox (n 163) 49.

be considered as a crucial premise for the exercise of the right to democracy.[181] Therefore, other scholars advanced a procedural approach, whereby democracy is defined in process-oriented terms.[182] Democracy would thus entail 'the right of people to be consulted and to participate in the process by which political values are reconciled and choices made'.[183] Since free and fair elections are widely considered the principal way to assess the preferences of the population with regard to the form of government, they would constitute the essential basis to guarantee the legitimacy of a government.[184]

B. Regional Organisations and the Preference for Democratic Governments

Over the past decades, the right to democracy has gained momentum and has fuelled the debate on recognition of governments. Several authors suggested that only democratic governments should be recognised as legitimate authorities, capable of speaking for the state. In line with this approach, regional organisations have recently started to adopt instruments hostile to coups. For instance, in the *Moscow Document* member states of the Organization for Security and Co-operation in Europe (OSCE) stressed that they:

> [C]ondemn unreservedly forces which seek to take power from a representative government of a participating State against the will of the people as expressed in free and fair elections and contrary to the justly established constitutional order; will support vigorously, in accordance with the Charter of the United Nations, in case of overthrow or attempted overthrow of a legitimately elected government of a participating State by undemocratic means, the legitimate organs of that State upholding human rights, democracy and the rule of law, recognizing their common commitment to countering any attempt to curb these basic values.[185]

[181] As explained by Marks, the substantive view encompasses a significant variety of approaches: '[a]ccording to some political theorists, democracy entails not just the right to participate in the selection of national government, but also the right to participate directly in the decision-making affecting one. For other theorists, democracy involves not just the process of selecting governments but also the process of connecting people with their governments through civil society. Still other theorists emphasise that democracy requires not just the right to vote and stand for election and associated civil liberties, but also the whole range of further rights that actually enable participation in public life on a footing of equality' (S Marks, 'International Law, Democracy and the End of History' in Fox and Roth (eds) (n 51) 558).

[182] Fox (n 163) 49.

[183] Franck (n 165) 25.

[184] Fox (n 163) 49–50. See also Reisman (n 164) 868–69: '[t]he results of such elections serve as evidence of popular sovereignty and become the basis for international endorsement of the elected government'. See *contra* KA Alfadhel, 'Toward an Instrumental Right to Democracy' (2018) 112 *AJIL Unbound* 84–88. Nevertheless, it has been pointed out that: '[t]he holding of free and fair elections alone, however, provides no guarantee that a democratic system will become firmly established and capable of resisting challenges by anti-democratic actors' (GH Fox and G Nolte, 'Intolerant Democracies' (2010) 1 *Democratic Governance and International Law* 389–435).

[185] Conference on Security and Cooperation in Europe (CSCE), *Document of the Moscow Meeting on the Human Dimension of the CSCE*, 30 I.L.M. 1670, 1677, 3 October 1991, §17. See Roth (n 122) 376; Wippman (n 80) 219; Fielding (n 166) 335; M Halberstam, 'The Copenhagen

Similarly, the Organization of African Unity (OAU) and later the African Union (AU) expressed their position against coups aimed at overthrowing democratic governments.[186] In the late 1990s, the OAU adopted a number of declarations which condemn military coups and unconstitutional changes of government. Notably, the Lomé Declaration provides a definition of 'situations that could be considered as situations of unconstitutional change of government':

> i) military coup d'etat against a democratically elected Government;
> ii) intervention by mercenaries to replace a democratically elected Government;
> iii) replacement of democratically elected Governments by armed dissident groups and rebel movements;
> iv) the refusal by an incumbent government to relinquish power to the winning party after free, fair and regular elections.[187]

The Constitutive Act of the African Union (2000) affirms the 'condemnation and rejection of unconstitutional changes of governments'.[188] More interestingly, the African Charter on Democracy, Elections and Governance (2007) provides that when 'there has been an unconstitutional change of government in a State Party', the Peace and Security Council shall suspend a member state from the exercise of its right to participate in the activities of the Union.[189] The Charter sets forth also a series of measures to be taken against coup regimes and those who perpetrated the unconstitutional change of government:

> 4. The perpetrators of unconstitutional change of government shall not be allowed to participate in elections held to restore the democratic order or hold any position of responsibility in political institutions of their State.
> 5. Perpetrators of unconstitutional change of government may also be tried before the competent court of the Union.
> 6. The Assembly shall impose sanctions on any Member State that is proved to have instigated or supported unconstitutional change of government in another state in conformity with Article 23 of the Constitutive Act.
> 7. The Assembly may decide to apply other forms of sanctions on perpetrators of unconstitutional change of government including punitive economic measures.
> 8. State Parties shall not harbour or give sanctuary to perpetrators of unconstitutional changes of government.[190]

Document: Intervention in Support of Democracy' (1993) 34(1) *Harvard International Law Journal* 163–75.

[186] M Roscini, 'Neighbourhood Watch? The African Great Lakes Pact and *Jus ad Bellum*' (2009) 69(3) *Heidelberg Journal of International Law* 955–58.

[187] OAU, The Declaration on the Framework for an OAU Response to Unconstitutional Changes of Government, AHG/Decl.5 (XXXVI), 10–12 July 2000, (hereinafter Lomé Declaration).

[188] Constitutive Act of the African Union, Art 4(p).

[189] African Charter on Democracy, Elections and Governance, Art 25(1).

[190] ibid.

In the same vein, the Organization of American States (OAS) expressed on several occasions its bias towards democratically elected governments overthrown by coups.[191] The OAS Charter (1948) acknowledges '[t]he solidarity of the American States and the high aims which are sought through it require the political organisation of those States on the basis of the effective exercise of representative democracy'.[192] Similar positions can be found in the Santiago Commitment to Democracy and the Renewal of the Inter-American System (1991),[193] which highlights the importance of 'strengthening representative democracy as an expression of the legitimate and free manifestation of people'.[194] Furthermore, the Resolution *Representative Democracy* (1991)[195] puts forward that:

> In the event of any occurrences giving rise to the sudden or irregular interruption of the democratic political institutional process or of the legitimate exercise of power by the democratically elected government in any of the Organization's member states, in order, within the framework of the Charter, to examine the situation, decide on and convene an ad hoc meeting of the Ministers of Foreign Affairs, or a special session of the General Assembly.

The resolution recalls that 'one of the basic purposes of the OAS is to promote and consolidate representative democracy with due respect for the principle of non-intervention'.[196] The following year, OAS adopted the Protocol of Washington, which amends Article 9 of the OAS Charter, which now provides that a 'Member of the Organization whose democratically constituted government has been overthrown by force'[197] could be suspended from a number of OAS organs, such as the General Assembly and the Meeting of Consultation.[198]

Notwithstanding the importance of the aforementioned instruments, the OAS has always been careful in counter-balancing the statements supporting democracy with the reaffirmation of the principle of non-intervention. More significant is the Inter-American Democratic Charter (2001),[199] which affirms that:

> An unconstitutional interruption of the democratic order or an unconstitutional alteration of the constitutional regime that seriously impairs the democratic order

[191] Roth (n 123) 209–11; BS Levitt, 'A Desultory Defense of Democracy: OAS Resolution 1080 and the Inter-American Democratic Charter' (2006) 48(3) *Latin American Politics and Society* 93–123; DS Boniface, 'Is There a Democratic Norm in the Americas? An Analysis of the Organization of American States' (2002) 8(3) *Global Governance* 365–81.

[192] OAS Charter, Art 5(d).

[193] Santiago Commitment to Democracy and the Renewal of the Inter-American System, 4 June 1991 (hereinafter, Santiago Commitment).

[194] Santiago Commitment, §3b. See also Roth (n 123) 210.

[195] AG/RES. 1080 (XXI-0/91), 5 June 1991, *Representative Democracy*.

[196] Santiago Commitment, Preamble.

[197] OAS, Protocol of Washington of 14 December 1992, OAS Doc OEA/Ser.A/2 Add. 3 (SEPF) (entered into force 25 September 1997) art 1 (amending art 9 of the OAS Charter (n 115)).

[198] Roth (n 122) 40.

[199] Inter-American Democratic Charter, adopted by the General Assembly at its special session held in Lima, Peru, on 11 September 2001. See Roth (n 123) 211.

> in a member state, constitutes, while it persists, an insurmountable obstacle to its government's participation in sessions of the General Assembly, the Meeting of Consultation, the Councils of the Organization, the specialized conferences, the commissions, working groups, and other bodies of the Organization.[200]

According to Franck, the regional documents protecting democracy, together with the Universal Declaration of Human Rights and the human rights conventions would represent 'a net of participatory elements'[201] and an unprecedented 'initiative to endorse and define a popular right of electoral democracy'.[202] Therefore, they would demonstrate a general preference for democratically elected governments over coup regimes. However, the undemocratic nature of some of the governments that participated in the adoption of these instruments would raise doubts as to their credibility and impact on state practice.

VI. CONCLUDING OBSERVATIONS

The foregoing chapter has attempted to present the traditional doctrines concerning intervention upon invitation. Foreign interferences raise pivotal dilemmas that ultimately concern conflicting aspects of popular sovereignty, such as the right to self-determination, the principle of non-intervention, and the role of democracy as an instrument to express popular will. The prevailing doctrines on intervention upon invitation endeavour to reconcile these aspects.

On the one hand, the abstentionism approach focuses on the legality of interventions in civil wars per se and posits that such interventions are unlawful because they violate the principle of non-intervention and the right to self-determination of people. However, this doctrine fails to answer some crucial questions: what is the meaning of 'civil war'? Why could foreign states intervene in situations below such threshold? Furthermore, as we shall see in the next chapter, the abstentionism doctrine appears substantially in contrast with state practice. On the other hand, proponents of the effective control and the democratic entitlement doctrines admit that interventions in internal conflicts could be lawful, at least under certain circumstances, and focus on the criteria to identify the organ with the legal capacity to request foreign assistance. Ultimately, this assessment is strictly intertwined with the issue of recognition of governments. For the effective control approach, a government is capable of speaking on behalf of the state if it exercises effective control over territory and population. Strikingly in contrast with this position, the democratic entitlement doctrine focuses on the legitimacy of the government and concludes that only democratic governments could express a valid consent to foreign interventions.

[200] Article 19, Inter-American Democratic Charter.
[201] Franck (n 168) 69; Fielding (n 166) 332–33.
[202] Franck (n 168) 67.

The traditional approaches to interventions upon invitation experience crucial challenges in maintaining their persuasiveness. The effective control doctrine is prone to criticism inasmuch as it endorses 'might makes right'. Furthermore, the generalisation that obedience by the bulk of the population would always imply that the government represents the will of the people does not always reflect the reality.[203] On the other hand, claiming that only democratic governments can speak on behalf of the state seems an overstatement: while the regional instruments mentioned above would suggest a general preference for democratic governments over coup regimes, the general acceptance of undemocratic governments by the international community is hardly deniable. In light of these challenges and dilemmas, the next chapter will test the traditional doctrines against state practice and will endeavour to clarify when and under what circumstances interventions upon invitation are lawful under the current legal framework.

[203] Roth (n 122) 197.

4

Intervention by Invitation and Governmental (Il)legitimacy: Rethinking the Traditional Approaches

I. GOVERNMENTAL LEGITIMACY: LEGITIMACY OF ORIGIN AND LEGITIMACY OF EXERCISE

THE EFFECTIVENESS DOCTRINE has been the standard position regarding the recognition of governments since the seventeenth century.[1] From time to time, other tests have emerged in scholarship and state practice. A first challenge to the effectiveness doctrine arose when the Holy Alliance supported divine and monastic legitimacy as a test of recognition.[2] Another endeavour aimed at affirming a legitimacy test was the Tobar Doctrine, propounded by the Minister of Foreign Affairs of Ecuador in 1907 and embodied in a treaty concluded by five Central American States. According to Tobar's approach, states:

> [S]hall not recognise any other government which may come into power in any of the five Republics as a consequence of a coup d'état, or of a revolution against the recognised Government, so long as the freely elected representatives of the people thereof have not constitutionally reorganised the country.[3]

More recently, the democratic entitlement doctrine emerged as a new test to identify the authority capable of speaking on behalf of the state. These approaches have in common the fact that they try to oppose some form of legitimism to the effectiveness doctrine. The de facto test is based on a factual situation and it is thus indifferent to the way in which power was obtained. It is against the arbitrary nature of the effectiveness school that legitimacy doctrines were developed.[4]

[1] H Lauterpacht, *Recognition in International Law* (Cambridge University Press, 1947) 98.
[2] For an analysis of the notion of legitimacy, see ch 2.
[3] The treaty enshrining the Tobar Doctrine was signed by Guatemala, El Salvador, Honduras, Nicaragua, and Costa Rica in 1907. See Lauterpacht (n 1) 129; SD Murphy, 'Democratic Legitimacy and the Recognition of States and Governments' in GH Fox and BR Roth (eds), *Democratic Governance and International Law* (Cambridge University Press, 2000) 123–54.
[4] BR Roth, *Governmental Illegitimacy in International Law* (Clarendon Press, 1999) 148.

Nonetheless, an attentive analysis of the scholarship in favour of the de facto test would suggest a more nuanced reading. The principle of effectiveness encompasses two elements: de facto control over the territory and the obedience of the bulk of the population. Focusing on the latter criterion, Lauterpacht noted that '[t]he requirement of such consent may be described, with some plausibility, as yet another manifestation of the principle of legitimacy'.[5] In the same vein, Roth posited that the general obedience of the population is not simply a de facto situation: if the authority of the ruler is accepted by the people, it means that he respects popular sovereignty.[6] The accent placed on the approval by the bulk of the population shows how ultimately even the effectiveness doctrine is not void of a more or less implicit quest for legitimacy.

These debates stem from a crucial problem: international law is fundamentally state-centric; since states can act through their governments, the latter play a pivotal role. Nevertheless, international law does not offer objective criteria to determine whom the government of a particular state is, nor to assess its legitimacy.[7] Ultimately, discourses on legitimacy boil it down to a question of which authority has a 'right to rule'.[8] In order to solve the dilemma, d'Aspremont broached the distinction between legitimacy of origin and legitimacy of exercise. In his article 'Legitimacy of Governments in the Age of Democracy', he explains that: 'the legitimacy of origin is a tool to assess the origin of the government (coup, dynasty, elections, etc), while the legitimacy of exercise permits evaluation of the way in which the government exerts its power'.[9] The legitimacy of origin holds a qualification role, namely it helps identify the government capable of acting on behalf of the state. Nonetheless, this recognition could be withdrawn due to the way in which the power is exercised. The legitimacy of exercise would thus have the function to disqualify an authority previously recognised as the legitimate representative of the state, should it violate certain rules.[10]

As we shall see, this distinction is particularly helpful to shed light on the current legal regulation of intervention upon invitation. On the one hand, it would explain cases when democratic but ineffective governments are preferred

[5] Lauterpacht (n 1) 115.

[6] Roth (n 4) 140.

[7] S Talmon, 'Recognition of Opposition Groups as the Legitimate Representative of a People' (2013) 12(2) *Chinese Journal of International Law* 233; J d'Aspremont, 'Legitimacy of Governments in the Age of Democracy' (2006) 38(4) *New York University Journal of International Law and Politics* 878; J d'Aspremont and E De Brabandere, 'The Complementary Faces of Legitimacy in International Law: The Legitimacy of Origin and the Legitimacy of Exercise' (2011) 34(2) *Fordham International Law Journal* 196–97.

[8] A Buchanan, *Human Rights, Legitimacy, and the Use of Force* (Oxford University Press, 2010) 134; D Bodansky, 'The Concept of Legitimacy in International Law' in R Wolfrum and V Röben (eds), *Legitimacy in International Law* (Springer, 2008) 311.

[9] d'Aspremont (n 7) 882.

[10] ibid, 910.

over de facto regimes. On the other hand, the practice that emerged in Libya and Syria, whereby governments that commit heinous crimes against their people are considered illegitimate, would confirm the disqualification function of the legitimacy of exercise. However, it does not explain why undemocratic regimes are still recognised by the international community and sit in international organisations.[11] Furthermore, it leaves open a crucial question: when are origin and exercise of power deemed to be legitimate?

Although the effectiveness and democratic entitlement approaches are considered irremediably in contrast, the proponents of both doctrines can rely on contemporary state practice. This circumstance can be explained by claiming that the absence of certain criteria to identify the government leaves ample leeway for states, which thus recognise a legitimate or effective government based on political considerations. However, from an in-depth analysis of state practice certain patterns emerge. This chapter seeks to address these dilemmas and to clarify the criteria to identify the government capable of inviting foreign forces during an internal conflict. First, we shall ask whether the electoral mandate is in itself sufficient to identify the government and whether the latter is capable of speaking on behalf of the state, even if an undemocratic authority exercises de facto control over the territory and population. This is particularly controversial when the newly elected government has never exercised power before being ousted. Second, the focus will be on undemocratic regimes overwhelmingly recognised by the international community. Notably, the question is how to reconcile this circumstance with the practice concerning the recognition of democratic but ineffective governments. Lastly, the role of domestic constitutional orders will be analysed.

II. DEMOCRATIC BUT INEFFECTIVE GOVERNMENTS

In 1947 Lauterpacht posited that:

> A government effectively established within national territory and, according to some, sanctioned by adequately expressed popular approval must, notwithstanding its revolutionary origin, be regarded as representing the State in question and as such entitled, in law, to recognition.[12]

Much has changed since then. Recent developments may suggest that the electoral mandate is key in identifying the government capable of representing

[11] According to d'Aspremont, the legitimacy of governments is intertwined with democracy. The legitimacy of origin would derive from free and fair elections, while the legitimacy of exercise would derive from the respect of substantial democracy. See d'Aspremont (n 7) 916. For the distinction between procedural and substantial democracy, see ch 3.

[12] Lauterpacht (n 1) 91.

the state and that a democratically elected, but ineffective, government would be preferred to an undemocratic authority exercising de facto control.[13]

Before looking at state practice, it is necessary to put forward a caveat. The question of pro-democratic intervention encompasses two instances. On the one hand, it refers to a right to overthrow undemocratic regimes to establish democracy, notwithstanding the absence of an invitation or a UNSC resolution. On the other hand, it refers to cases when a democratically elected government faces a coup and thus asks for external intervention in order to regain power. The distinction is crucial, although often overlooked. Proponents of the first approach posit that states could intervene to promote democracy, even if uninvited; the question thus concerns whether a new exception to Article 2(4) of the UN Charter has emerged. The second instance boils down to a question of intervention by invitation. It disputes the idea that effectiveness is the only criterion for identifying the organ that can express a valid consent and suggests that democratic governments should be granted this right, even when ineffective.

A. Unilateral Interventions to Establish Democracy

On the morning of 25 October 1983, 1,900 US soldiers together with 300 troops from Caribbean states landed on Grenada. The operation took place six days after a coup that overthrew President Maurice Bishop. The new Revolutionary Military Council, led by General Austin, was defeated on 31 October. The US provided three justifications for the intervention: a request from the Governor-General of Grenada, an invitation from the Organization of Eastern Caribbean States (OECS), and the protection of US nationals in Grenada.[14]

Six years later, on 20 December 1989, 24,000 US troops started the operation 'Just Cause', directed at ousting the government of Panama and at capturing its president, General Manuel Noriega. The relationship between the head of state and the US, once one of collaboration, deteriorated during the Reagan presidency due to accusations that Noriega was involved in drug trafficking. Despite several attempted coups allegedly backed by the US against the General, Noriega succeeded and remained in power. In May 1989, presidential elections saw the victory of Guillermo Endara Gallimany. However, Noriega refused to

[13] D Wippman, 'Pro-Democratic Intervention by Invitation' in GH Fox and BR Roth (eds), *Democratic Governance and International Law* (Cambridge University Press, 2000) 300; J d'Aspremont, *L'État Non Démocratique en Droit International: Etude Critique du Droit International Positif et de la Pratique Contemporaine* (Pedone, 2008).

[14] M Byers and S Chesterman, '"You, the People": Pro-democratic Intervention in International Law' in Fox and Roth (eds) (n 13) 272–73; A Tanca, *Foreign Armed Intervention in Internal Conflicts* (Martinus Nijhoff, 1993) 179; R Amer, *The United Nations and Foreign Military Interventions: A Comparative Study of the Application of the Charter*, Report No 33 (Department of Peace and Conflict Research, Uppsala University, 1992) 44–45.

step down and annulled the results. The US intervention proved successful in overthrowing the government and arresting Noriega. President Bush justified the operation on four grounds: 'to safeguard the lives of Americans, to defend democracy in Panama, to combat drug trafficking, and to protect the integrity of the Panama Canal Treaty'.[15]

The two US interventions were justified, inter alia, as being aimed at promoting democracy and fuelled the debate on the existence of a right to unilateral pro-democratic intervention. Reisman set the terms of the discussion in 1984,[16] when he advanced a reinterpretation of Article 2(4) of the UN Charter that would allow foreign countries to unilaterally depose undemocratic regimes.[17] Reisman notices that 'Article 2(4) was never an independent ethical imperative of pacifism. In the instrument in which it appears, there is full acknowledgment of the indispensability of the use of force to maintain community order'.[18] However, in case of the failure of the UN to maintain such order, international law would require individual states to act in self-help. Reisman suggests a two-step assessment. First, states should ask themselves whether 'a particular use of force enhance[s] or undermine[s] world order'.[19] Second, the focus should be on 'the enhancement of the on-going right of peoples to determine their own political destinies'.[20] Article 2(4) should always favour self-determination. Although interventions are regrettable, there are instances whereby coercive forcible interferences may serve 'to increase the probability of the free choice of peoples about their government and political structure'.[21] Nevertheless, this should not be interpreted too broadly:

> This is not to say that every externally motivated action to remove an unpopular government is now permitted, or that officer corps that feel obsolescence hard upon them can claim a new raison d'etre and start scouring the globe for opportunities for 'democratizing' interventions. … But it is to say that the suppression of popular sovereignty may be a justifying factor, not a justification per se but a conditio sine qua non. And it is to say that the word 'sovereignty' can no longer be used to shield the actual suppression of popular sovereignty from external rebuke and remedy.[22]

[15] G Bush, 'Address to the Nation Announcing United States Military Action in Panama' in *Public Papers of the Presidents of the United States: George Bush 1989*, vol II, US Government Printing Office, Washington, DC, 1990; 1722–24, §2. See also Byers and Chesterman (n 14) 274; Tanca (n 14) 183; Amer (n 14) 45–46.

[16] WM Reisman, 'Coercion and Self-Determination: Construing Charter Article 2(4)' (1984) 78(3) *American Journal of International Law* 642–45. For a critique to Reisman's position, see O Schachter, 'The Legality of Pro-Democratic Invasion' (1984) 78(3) *American Journal of International Law* 645–50.

[17] Reisman (n 16) 642.

[18] ibid.

[19] ibid, 643.

[20] ibid.

[21] ibid, 644.

[22] WM Reisman, 'Why Regime Change is (Almost Always) a Bad Idea' (2004) 98(3) *American Journal of International Law* 516–25.

Drawing upon Reisman's reasoning, D'Amato argued in favour of the intervention in Panama. The dictatorial nature of Noriega's government and the lack of a reaction from the UN would confirm the legality of the US military action: 'the U.S. forcible intervention in Panama did not violate Article 2(4) because the United States did not act against the "territorial integrity" of Panama: there was never an intent to annex part or all of Panamanian territory, and hence the intervention left the territorial integrity of Panama intact'.[23]

There are compelling reasons why the right to unilateral intervention to defend democracy does not seem to exist under international law.[24] First, the reaction of the international community was to overwhelmingly condemn the two US interventions.[25] Second, this doctrine does not seem desirable. As clearly expressed by the ICJ, it is not possible to 'contemplate the creation of a new rule opening up a right of intervention by one State against another on the ground that the latter has opted for some particular ideology or political system'.[26] Indeed, '[a]lbeit paradoxical, it is far from ridiculous that popular sovereignty may amount, as a matter of practical application, to the right to be ruled by domestic thugs rather than by foreigners announcing benevolent intentions'.[27] Furthermore, it is significant that Franck, one of the first authors to theorise the emerging right to democratic governance, has never gone as far as recognising a unilateral right to pro-democratic intervention.[28]

The US interventions in Grenada and Panama leave open the question as to whether a democratic government ousted by a coup could still be considered as capable of speaking for the state. The aforementioned interventions would not fall within the latter instance. In Grenada, the invitation was expressed by Governor General Paul Scoon. Certain doubts were raised regarding the authenticity of the request.[29] Moreover, although US Deputy Secretary of State Kenneth Dam defined him as 'the sole source of governmental legitimacy on the island in the wake of the tragic events', Scoon's capacity to act on behalf of the state did not descend from the democratic nature of the government.[30]

[23] A D'Amato, 'The Invasion of Panama Was a Lawful Response to Tyranny' (1990) 84(2) *American Journal of International Law* 520.

[24] Byers and Chesterman (n 14) 280–81.

[25] ibid, 266; CD Gray, *International Law and the Use of Force* (Cambridge University Press, 2008) 56–57; H Charlesworth, 'Democracy and International Law' (2014) 371 *Collected courses of The Hague Academy of International Law* 89–91.

[26] *Nicaragua* case, §263.

[27] BR Roth, *Sovereign Equality and Moral Disagreement: Premises of a Pluralist International Legal Order* (Oxford University Press, 2011) 205.

[28] TM Franck, 'Who Killed Article 2(4)? or: Changing Norms Governing the Use of Force by States' (1970) 64(5) *American Journal of International Law* 809–37; TM Franck, 'The Emerging Right to Democratic Governance' (1992) 86(1) *American Journal of International Law* 89.

[29] Byers and Chesterman (n 14) 271–72.

[30] In 1974 the Island of Grenada was granted independence from the British Commonwealth of Nations. Five years later, Maurice Bishop reached power through a coup and established a revolutionary government. Appointed as Governor General by Queen Elizabeth II in 1978, Paul Scoon retained his role after the coup led by Bishop. See Tanca (n 14) 179.

As for the intervention in Panama, President Endara was democratically elected. However, the US never based its intervention on an invitation from the government. Moreover, there is some evidence that Endara was not in favour of the intervention, about which he said that he 'would have been happier without it'.[31] In summary, the intervention in Grenada was aimed at restoring democracy, but it was not justified as invitation by an ousted democratic government. On the other hand, the intervention in Panama did restore the democratically elected president; however, the US did not rely on its consent to justify the intervention. What if an ousted democratically elected government were to ask for foreign intervention to restore its power?

B. Interventions in Favour of Democratically Elected Governments

States and international organisations systematically condemn coups d'état that overthrow democratic governments.[32] These situations raise an essential question as to whether the consent of an ousted democratically elected government can provide a legal basis for a military intervention to restore its power. This dilemma is particularly problematic when the coup regime exercises de facto control over the territory and population and seems likely to remain in power.[33] The most emblematic instances of foreign interventions directed at restoring ousted democratic governments are Haiti (1990 and 1994),[34] Sierra

[31] Byers and Chesterman (n 14) 276.

[32] D Wippman, 'Pro-Democratic Intervention' in M Weller (ed), *The Oxford Handbook of the Use of Force in International Law* (Oxford University Press, 2015) 799.

[33] ibid, 806.

[34] François Duvalier was the President of Haiti from 1957 until his death (1971), when his son, Jean Claude, inherited the position. However, his authority was not as stable as his father's was. On 7 February 1986 the Haitian army ousted the heir, starting a period of instability in which a series of military coups deteriorated the power of the Haitian institutions. In March 1990, another coup brought into power an interim government, led by Ertha Pascal-Trouillot. The president addressed the UN and the OAS, seeking help in order to hold elections. The two international organisations responded positively and successfully organised an election monitoring mission. Jean-Bertrand Aristide was nominated the President of Haiti, obtaining 67% of the votes. The newly elected president immediately tried to impose his authority over the army, backed by the majority of the population, but against the will of the conservative part of the country. Tensions arose and, on 29–30 September 1991, the Haitian army violently ousted Aristide. Following the coup, the UN and OAS expressed their criticism against the de facto government and affirmed that they would have continued to recognise the Aristide government as de jure authority in Haiti. In the following years, negotiations took place between the de facto regime and the government in exile with the aim of finding a solution by peaceful means. However, as these attempts failed, on 31 July 1994, upon request of the Aristide government, the Security Council adopted Resolution 940, under Chapter VII of the Charter of the United Nations. On 18 September 1994 the US intervened in the country and restored Aristide to power. See Murphy (n 3) 574; D Wippman, 'Military Intervention, Regional Organizations, and Host-State Consent' (1996) 7 *Duke Journal of Comparative & International Law* 218–19; Wippman (n 13) 301; Roth (n 4) 366–87; Reisman (n 22) 251–52.

Leone (1996),[35] Côte d'Ivoire (2010),[36] and South Sudan (2014).[37] In all these cases, the international community condemned the coups that overthrew the democratically elected governments and recognised the latter as de jure representatives of the state.[38] Furthermore, the foreign interventions took place upon

[35] In 1996, Ahmad Tejan Kabbah won the presidential elections in Sierra Leone with 60% of the votes. However, on 21 June 1997, the Armed Forces Revolutionary Council (AFRC) ousted the government. The coup needs to be read in light of the internal conflict which started in the country on 23 March 1991, when the Revolutionary United Front (RUF) attempted to overthrow Joseph Saidu Momoh's government with the help of Charles Taylor's National Patriotic Front of Liberia (NPFL). The action triggered a conflict that lasted for several years. The coup in Sierra Leone was immediately and overwhelmingly criticised by the international community. ECOWAS, which had troops already deployed in Sierra Leone with the consent of President Kabbah, firmly expressed its intention to reverse the overthrow. The Organization of African Unity harshly criticised the coup and authorised ECOWAS military intervention in order to restore President Kabbah. The reactions at the UN level were equally unanimous in condemning the coup. The Kabbah government's representative retained the seat in the General Assembly. Furthermore, the president of the Security Council 'strongly deplor[ed] this attempt to overthrow the democratically elected government and call[ed] for an immediate restoration of constitutional order' (S/PRST/1997/29, 27 May 1997). See J Levitt, 'Humanitarian Intervention by Regional Actors in Internal Conflicts: The Cases of ECOWAS in Liberia and Siearra Leone' (1998) 12(2) *Temple International and Comparative Law Journal* 333–77; K Nowrot and EW Schebacker, 'The Use of Force to Restore Democracy: International Legal Implications of the ECOWAS Intervention in Sierra Leone' (1998) 14 *American University International Law Review* 321–412; K Samuels, '*Jus Ad Bellum* and Civil Conflicts: A Case Study of the International Community's Approach to Violence in the Conflict in Sierra Leone' (2003) 8(2) *Journal of Conflict & Security Law* 315–38; Wippman (n 13) 303.

[36] In October 2000 presidential elections held in Côte d'Ivoire resulted in the disputed victory of Laurent Gbagbo. After five years, new elections should have been organised. However, they were postponed until November 2010. The International Crisis Group (ICG) reported that, in order to 'secure its hold on power, the regime has accompanied brazen manipulation of state institutions with a strategy of terror designed to brutally stifle any challenge from the coalition supporting Ouattara'. See ICG, 'Côte d'Ivoire: Is War the Only Option?' Africa Report No 171, 3 March 2011; J d'Aspremont, 'Duality of government in Côte d'Ivoire' (*EJIL: Talk!*, 2011), available at www.ejiltalk.org/duality-of-government-in-cote-divoire/; TF Bassett and S Straus, 'Defending Democracy in Côte d'Ivoire: Africa Takes a Stand' (2011) 90 *Foreign Affairs* 130; AJ Bellamy and PD Williams, 'The New Politics of Protection? Côte d'Ivoire, Libya and the Responsibility to Protect' (2011) 87(4) *International Affairs* 832.

[37] In 2010, democratic elections took place in South Sudan as part of the process leading to the independence of the country, that became reality in July 2011. The elections saw the victory of the People's Liberation Movement (SPLM). In December 2013, tensions between the President of South Sudan, Salva Kiir Mayardit, and the Vice-president, Riek Machar, led to the outbreak of armed confrontations in Juba and spread to other regions. Soon thereafter, Machar formed a rebel group to fight against the incumbent government. Accordingly, the President invited Uganda to forcibly intervene against the opposition forces; the intervention lasted until 10 October 2015, when Ugandan troops left the country as agreed with the South Sudan government. See Report of the Secretary-General on South Sudan UN Doc S/2011/678, 2 November 2011; BBC Staff, 'Ugandan army confirms it will leave South Sudan' (*BBC*, 12 October 2015), available at www.bbc.com/news/world-africa-34502524; Al Jazeera Staff, 'Uganda admits combat role in South Sudan' (*Al Jazeera*, 16 January 2014), available at www.aljazeera.com/news/2014/1/16/uganda-admits-combat-role-in-south-sudan.

[38] With regard to the Haitian case, the OAS continued to 'recognise the representatives of the Government of President Jean-Bertrand Aristide as the only legitimate representatives of the Government of Haiti to the organs, agencies and entities of the inter-american system' and resolved to 'adopt, in accordance with the Charter and international law, any additional measures that may be necessary and appropriate to ensure the immediate reinstatement of President Jean-Bertrand Aristide to the exercise of his legitimate authority' (MRE/RES. 1/19 Corr. 1, OEA/Ser.F/V.1, 3 October 1991, §§3 and 10). At the UN level, General Assembly Resolution 46/7 (1991) 'strongly condemn[ed]

invitation of the ousted governments. It is worth mentioning that in the case of Haiti the intervention was justified also on the basis of UN Security Council authorisation. In 1993, the UNSC adopted the Resolution 940, where:

> Acting under Chapter VII of the Charter of the United Nations, authorize[d] Member States to form a multinational force under unified command and control and, in this framework, *to use all necessary means to facilitate the departure from Haiti of the military leadership*, consistent with the Governors Island Agreement, *the prompt return of the legitimately elected President and the restoration of the legitimate authorities of the Government of Haiti*, and to establish and maintain a secure and stable environment that will permit implementation of the Governors Island Agreement, on the understanding that the cost of implementing this temporary operation will be borne by the participating Member States.[39]

The US intervention in favour of Aristide took place on 18 September 1994, hence after the adoption of the resolution. It could thus be argued that the legal basis for the intervention was also the UNSC authorisation under Chapter VII. Be it as it may, it is still relevant inasmuch as the Security Council expressed a clear preference in favour of Aristide and highlighted his legitimacy.

More recently, analogous circumstances took place in The Gambia. On 1 December 2016, elections were held in the country. Adama Barrow, a real estate developer, defeated the long-term President Yahya Jammeh.[40] While at first the incumbent accepted the results and expressed its desire to facilitate a peaceful transfer of power, on 9 December he denounced 'serious and unacceptable abnormalities which have reportedly transpired during the electoral process'.[41] He thus refused to recognise the elections' results. The international community overwhelmingly condemned Jammeh's actions and recognised Adama Barrow as the new president of The Gambia. The Economic Community of West African

the attempted illegal replacement of the constitutional president of Haiti, the use of violence and military coercion, and the violation of human rights in the country'. Furthermore, it defined 'as unacceptable any entity resulting from the illegal situation and demand[ed] the immediate restoration of the legitimate government' of President Aristide (A/RES/46/7, 11 October 1991, *The situation of democracy and human rights in Haiti*, §§1, 3). In the same vein, the coup in Côte d'Ivoire was condemned by the international community. At the regional level, both the AU and ECOWAS suspended Côte d'Ivoire from the bodies of the organisations and recognised Ouattara's government. The General Assembly approved the credentials of Ouattara's ambassador (A/RES/65/237, 23 December 2010, *Credentials of representatives to the sixty-fifth session of the General Assembly*), while the Security Council: '[u]rge[d] all the Ivorian parties and stakeholders to respect the will of the people and the outcome of the election in view of ECOWAS and African Union's recognition of Alassane Dramane Ouattara as President-elect of Côte d'Ivoire and representative of the freely expressed voice of the Ivorian people as proclaimed by the Independent Electoral Commission'. See S/RES/1962 (2010), 20 December 2010.

[39] S/RES/940 (1994), 31 July 1994, emphasis added.

[40] M Helal, 'Crisis in The Gambia: How Africa is Rewriting *Jus ad Bellum*' (*Opinio Juris*, 24 January 2017), available at http://opiniojuris.org/2017/01/24/crisis-in-the-gambia-how-africa-is-rewriting-jus-ad-bellum/.

[41] The Guardian Staff, 'Gambian president Yahya Jammeh rejects election result' (*The Guardian*, 10 December 2016), available at www.theguardian.com/world/2016/dec/10/gambian-president-rejects-election-results-yahya-jammeh-adama-barrow.

States adopted a communiqué in which it recognised the results of the elections, requested the endorsement of the AU and UN on the matter, and agreed to 'take all necessary measures to strictly enforce the results of the elections'.[42] Similarly, the Peace and Security Council of the African Union condemned the coup and declared that it no longer recognised Jammeh as the president.[43] Since diplomatic attempts failed, ECOWAS set an ultimatum to the incumbent: either step down on 19 January, or ECOWAS would forcibly intervene in favour of Barrow.[44] As Jammeh refused to comply, ECOWAS troops entered The Gambia.[45] The same day, Barrow was sworn into office in the Gambian embassy in Senegal and returned to his country on Saturday, 21 January. The UNSC issued Resolution 2337, where it urged:

> [A]ll Gambian parties and stakeholders to *respect the will of the people* and the outcome of the election which recognized Adama Barrow as President-elect of The Gambia and *representative of the freely expressed voice of the Gambian people* as proclaimed by the Independent Electoral Commission.[46]

The resolution raised a number of issues regarding the possibility of forcibly intervening in The Gambia. Indeed, while it does not consent to the use of force in favour of the elected president, it does not explicitly exclude this possibility either. This interpretation would be supported by the fact that the UNSC expressed 'its full support to the ECOWAS in its commitment to ensure, by political means *first*, the respect of the will of the people of The Gambia as expressed in the results of 1st December elections'.[47] Furthermore, the Council welcomed the decisions on The Gambia adopted by ECOWAS and by the AU, which contemplated the possibility of taking 'all necessary measures to strictly enforce' the elections' results.[48] On the other hand, during the discussion within the Security Council, a passage including the 'all necessary means' formula was excluded upon the request of Bolivia, Egypt, and Russia,[49] while the UK and Russia specified that Barrow could have asked for foreign intervention.[50]

[42] ECOWAS, Fiftieth Ordinary Session of the ECOWAS Authority of heads of State and Government, Final Communiqué, 17 December 2016, Abuja, Federal Republic of Nigeria. See also A Hallo de Wolf, 'Rattling Sabers to Save Democracy in the Gambia' (*EJIL: Talk!*, 2017), available at www.ejiltalk.org/rattling-sabers-to-save-democracy-in-the-gambia/.

[43] AU Peace and Security Council, Communiqué, 13 January 2017, Addis Ababa, Ethiopia, PSC/PR/COMM. (DCXLVII).

[44] Helal (n 40).

[45] ibid.

[46] S/RES/2337 (2017), 19 January 2017, *Peace consolidation in West Africa*, §1, emphasis added.

[47] ibid, §6, emphasis added; B Nussberger, 'The Post-Election Crisis in The Gambia: An Interplay of a Security Council's "Non-Authorization" and Intervention by Invitation' (*Opinio Juris*, 8 February 2017), available at opiniojuris.org/2017/02/08/the-post-election-crisis-in-the-gambia-an-interplay-of-a-security-councils-non-authorization-and-intervention-by-invitation/.

[48] ibid.

[49] R Janik, 'The Use of Force to (Re-)Establish Democracies: Lessons from The Gambia' (*EJIL: Talk!*, 2017), available at www.ejiltalk.org/the-use-of-force-to-re-establish-democracies-lessons-from-the-gambia/.

[50] ibid.

The preference for democratically elected governments, even when ineffective, finds further confirmation in the events that have unfolded in Libya since 2011. In February 2011, during the Arab Spring movement, peaceful anti-government demonstrations started in Libya. By the end of the month, the situation deteriorated to the point that it reached the threshold of a non-international armed conflict (NIAC). By June 2011, numerous countries had defined Gaddafi's government as illegitimate and had recognised the National Transitional Council (NTC), the leading authority of the opposition group, as the representative of Libyan people.[51] As the Gaddafi regime fell in August 2011,[52] the NTC formed an interim government with the aim of holding elections the following year.[53] Accordingly, on 8 June 2012 elections took place in Libya and the NTC transferred power to the newly elected General National Council (GNC).[54] However, the new government was immediately confronted with a challenging situation: violence between the Libyan armed forces and a number of non-state actors erupted in 2012 and 2013; the situation further deteriorated in mid-2014 and amounted to a NIAC.[55]

Parliament elections took place on 25 June 2014.[56] Nevertheless, a number of members of the GNC refused to step down and challenged the government with the support of the Muslim Brotherhood and the Islamist coalition 'Libya Dawn'. Consequently, 'only 188 of the 200 seats were filled' and the newly elected members of the Council of Deputies (ie, the Parliament) decided to be based in Tobruk instead of Tripoli.[57] In September 2014, al-Thinni was confirmed as Prime Minister and fled to Tobruk. To further complicate an already challenging situation, a number of jihadist groups and the Islamic State were operating in the country.[58] Accordingly, by September 2014 two factions were present in Libya: on the one hand, the so-called 'Tobruk government', which was democratically elected; on the other hand, the 'new General National Council',

[51] S Talmon, 'Recognition of the Libyan National Transitional Council Recognition of the Libyan' (2011) 15(16) *ASIL insights*.

[52] P Finn, 'The rise and fall of Libyan leader Moammar Gaddafi' (*The Washington Post*, 25 August 2011), available at www.washingtonpost.com/world/national-security/the-rise-and-fall-of-libyan-leader-moammar-gaddafi/2011/02/21/gIQA32NsdJ_story.html.

[53] A Lewis, 'Libya after Gaddafi: Who's in charge?' (*BBC*, 13 September 2011), available at www.bbc.com/news/world-africa-14901175.

[54] Report of the Secretary-General on the United Nations Support Mission in Libya, S/2012/ 675, 30 August 2012, §§ 2-9.

[55] S Arraf, 'Libya: Conflict and Instability Continue' in A Bellal (ed), *The War Report: Armed Conflicts in 2017* (Geneva Academy of International Humanitarian Law and Human Rights, 2018) 71.

[56] ibid, 72.

[57] A Bellal, 'Armed Conflict in Libya in 2014' in A Bellal (ed), *The War Report: Armed Conflict in 2014* (Oxford University Press, 2015) 196.

[58] See eg Report of the Secretary-General on the United Nations Support Mission in Libya UN Doc S/2015/624, 13 August 2015 §§29 ff. See also E de Wet, *Military Assistance on Request and the Use of Force* (Oxford University Press, 2019) 112.

based in Tripoli, which controlled the capital as well as a substantial part of north-west Libya.[59]

In February 2015, following the beheading of 21 Egyptian Christians by the Islamic State, the Tobruk government asked Egypt to intervene against the terrorist groups operating in the country. On 16 February 2016, Egyptians air forces conducted a military operation in Libya, in coordination with Libyan armed forces.[60] Egypt justified the intervention by highlighting the existence of consent from the legitimate government of Libya:

> States wishing to assist the legitimate Libyan Government in confronting terrorism and imposing security should be allowed to do so in the light of the severe difficulties *the legitimate Government* faces in that regard, with the condition that such assistance be provided in coordination with the Libyan Government and *with its approval*. Egypt has decided to respond to the requests and needs of the government of Libya and has provided military assistance.[61]

The intervention received the approval of the Arab League and the US, while only Qatar explicitly criticised the operation, claiming that 'the Egyptian aerial attacks could give an unfair advantage to one side in the Libyan conflict'.[62]

In 2015, UN-brokered negotiations took place between the Tobruk-based government and the Tripoli-based GNC, which resulted in the adoption of the Libyan Political Agreement on 17 December 2015. The agreement established the Presidential Council (PC) of the Government of National Accord, which served as head of state as well as Supreme Commander of the Libyan Army.[63] The Security Council endorsed the agreement and recognised 'the Government of National Accord as the sole legitimate government of Libya'.[64] Furthermore, the UNSC urged:

> Member States to swiftly *assist the Government of National Accord in responding to threats to Libyan security* and to actively support the new government in defeating ISIL, groups that have pledged allegiance to ISIL, Ansar Al Sharia, and all other individuals, groups, undertakings and entities associated with Al-Qaida operating in Libya, upon its request.[65]

Accordingly, in August 2016, the US engaged in sustained military operations against the Islamic State, with the consent of the Government of National Accord.[66]

[59] K Bannelier and T Christakis, 'Military Interventions Against ISIL in Iraq, Syria and Libya, and the Legal Basis of Consent' (2016) 29 *Leiden Journal of International Law* 757.

[60] S/PV.7387, 18 February 2015, *The Situation in Libya*, §5.

[61] ibid, §7, emphasis added.

[62] de Wet (n 58) 113.

[63] Arraf (n 55) 74.

[64] S/RES/2259 (2015), 23 December 2015.

[65] ibid, emphasis added.

[66] United States Department of Defence, 'US Airstrikes Support Government of National Accord in Libya' (*DoD* News, 4 August 2016); S Ackerman, C Stephen and E MacAskill, 'US Launches Airstrikes Against ISIS in Libya' (*The Guardian*, 1 August 2016), available at www.theguardian.com/world/2016/aug/01/us-airstrikes-against-isis-libya-pentagon.

The aforementioned cases show a growing discomfort towards coup regimes and the willingness to prefer democratic but ineffective governments over undemocratic authorities exercising de facto control.[67] This seems to be true even in cases when the ousted government was never able to exercise power after the elections. Furthermore, the UNSC practice would suggest that no previous authorisation is needed. Indeed, interventions in favour of elected governments were endorsed by the Security Council ex post. Besides the evidence provided by state practice, propounding that the electorate's mandate suffices to identify the authority capable of inviting foreign forces would respect the right to self-determination of people.

Part of the scholarship evidenced the limits of this approach by highlighting the exceptional nature of the interventions in Haiti, Sierra Leone, and Côte d'Ivoire, which required ad hoc solutions.[68] Commenting on these cases, Roth maintained that:

> The facts on the ground in each case were exceptional – including the landslide victory of the ousted President in a very recent, internationally-monitored election, and the notorious brutality and demonstrable unpopularity of the forces involved in the coup – leading a vast diversity of international actors, cutting across the international system's plurality of interests and values, to perceive in common a population's manifest will to restore an ousted government.[69]

However, it could be objected that interventions in internal conflicts often present exceptional circumstances, not least for the simple reason that these instances are indeed exceptional. It is nearly impossible to find two identical cases: historical background and geopolitical considerations can influence the decision of states to recognise (or not) a government, as well as the composition of the coalition that is going to intervene. Nevertheless, the aforementioned cases do show a trend: democratically elected but ineffective governments tend to be recognised even if they have never been in control of territory and population.

This circumstance led d'Aspremont to claim that 'democracy has become a prominent yardstick with which to assess the legitimacy of governments'.[70] On the one hand, state practice would prove that democratically elected governments are recognised as the legitimate representatives of states even if they are not effective. The legitimacy of origin would thus descend from free and fair elections. On the other hand, '[a] legitimately elected government can lose its legitimacy and be barred from speaking and acting on behalf of the state because its exercise of power conflicts with substantive elements of democracy'.[71]

[67] The AU has a consistent practice of non-recognition of coup regimes in favour of democratically elected governments, such as in Togo (2005), Mauritania (2005 and 2008), Guinea (2008), Madagascar (2009), and Niger (2010). See EY Omorogbe, 'A club of incumbents? The African Union and coups d'etat' (2011) 44(1) *Vanderbilt Journal of Transnational Law* 123–54.
[68] Gray (n 25) 58.
[69] Roth (n 27) 208.
[70] d'Aspremont (n 7) 888.
[71] ibid, 910.

D'Aspremont's extensive reliance on the democratic entitlement doctrine is open to some criticism. First, democracy is not 'the only acceptable type of regime'.[72] Although it has received increasing support by the international community and the scholarship, what the ICJ noted in the *Nicaragua* case is still true: 'the choice of a political, economic, social and cultural system' must remain a free one.[73] Furthermore, if we accept that free and fair elections are the only legitimate way to obtain power, it is unclear why the international community tends to also recognise governments that obtained power though undemocratic means. For instance, Bashar Assad was not democratically elected by the Syrian population, yet the international community did not question the legitimacy of his government when he took power.[74] Lastly, claiming that the exercise of power is legitimate if conducted respecting 'substantive elements of democracy' does not seem to be reflected in the practice of states.[75] Indeed, the international community tends not to question the legitimacy of states that notoriously behave in contrast with basic democratic principles. However, as we shall see, the situation dramatically changes when a government engages in gross and systematic violations of human rights and humanitarian law against the population.[76]

In summary, state practice does show the emergence of a new trend, whereby the origin of power plays a determining role in the legitimacy of governments, which in turn affects their capacity to ask for foreign intervention. The international community tends to grant recognition to democratic governments, elected through free and fair elections, even when an effective authority exercises de facto control of territory and population. This would prove that the effective control principle is not the pivotal criterion to identify the government capable of consenting to foreign interventions. However, this conclusion does not necessarily lead to an automatic lack of recognition of undemocratic governments in all circumstances. It is thus necessary to further analyse state practice regarding undemocratic regimes.

C. Democratically Elected Governments in Exile and the Interaction between Legitimacy of Origin and Legitimacy of Exercise

The previous section demonstrated that democratic governments in exile tend to be recognised by the international community, despite the fact that they do not exercise effective control over territory and population. Since the 1990s, state practice has been consistent in this regard and has shown that the legitimacy

[72] ibid, 885.
[73] *Nicaragua* case, §205.
[74] The situation changed after the conflict broke out in 2011; see ch 5.
[75] d'Aspremont (n 7) 910.
[76] See ch 5.

of origin of democratic governments – which descends from free and fair elections – would compensate for the lack of effectiveness. Consequently, the organ in exile could lawfully ask for foreign intervention in its home country in order to regain power. This section seeks to answer a related question, namely whether a democratic government in exile could lose its legitimacy due to the way in which it exercised its power: how does the disqualifying function of the legitimacy of exercise apply to democratic governments in exile? This question is central to solving the conundrum posed by the recent events that took place in Ukraine and Yemen. In both cases, a democratically elected president lost control of his country and sought refuge in a neighbouring state. He then invited the host country to intervene in order to regain control of his home state. Although the two cases appear identical, the Russian intervention upon the invitation of President Viktor Yanukovich met the condemnation of the international community, while the foreign military operations in Yemen were generally endorsed.

On 21 November 2013, President Yanukovich interrupted the negotiation of a trade agreement with the European Union, seeking closer cooperation with Russia instead.[77] The decision triggered protests, which led to the occupation of Kiev's city hall in December. In order to quell the demonstrations, on 23 January 2014 the Parliament issued restrictive anti-protest laws, while the opposition movement occupied government buildings.[78] Clashes reached a climax on 20 February, when snipers with Ukrainian uniforms fired at protesters, killing at least 88 people.[79] The day after, President Yanukovich signed a deal with the opposition leaders. Nevertheless, on 22 February protesters took control of presidential administration buildings, while the Parliament voted to remove Yanukovich and decided that elections would be held on 25 May. The president reacted promptly to Parliament's decision, defining its action as a coup. In the subsequent days an arrest warrant was issued against President Yanukovich, who found refuge in Russia. Arseniy Yatsenyuk was nominated Prime Minister. On 27 February pro-Russian gunmen occupied several buildings in Simferopol, the capital of Crimea, and unidentified gunmen appeared in key Crimean areas. On 1 March 2014 President Putin addressed the Council of the Russian Federation asking for authorisation to forcibly intervene in Crimea:

> In connection with the extraordinary situation that has developed in Ukraine and the threat to citizens of the Russian Federation, our compatriots, the personnel of the military contingent of the Russian Federation Armed Forces deployed on the territory of Ukraine (Autonomous Republic of Crimea) in accordance with international agreement; pursuant to Article 102.1 (d) of the Constitution of the Russian

[77] BBC Staff, 'Ukraine Crisis: Timeline' (*BBC*, 13 November 2014), available at www.bbc.com/news/world-middle-east-26248275.

[78] BBC Staff, 'Ukraine unrest: Protesters storm regional offices' (*BBC*, 13 November 2014), available at www.bbc.com/news/world-europe-25876807.

[79] BBC Staff (n 77).

> Federation, I hereby appeal to the Council of Federation of the Federal Assembly of the Russian Federation to use the Armed Forces of the Russian Federation on the territory of Ukraine until the social and political situation in that country is normalised.[80]

The Council immediately authorised the intervention and Russia deployed its forces in Crimea. Russia's UN envoy, Vitaly Churkin, during a Security Council meeting held on 4 March, justified Russian intervention, affirming that President Yanukovich expressly asked for help and showed a copy of the letter of invitation directed to President Putin.[81] The same day, during a press conference, the Russian President affirmed that:

> We have a direct appeal from the incumbent and, as I said, legitimate President of Ukraine, Mr Yanukovich, asking us to use the Armed Forces to protect the lives, freedom and health of the citizens of Ukraine.[82]

The parallels between the Ukrainian case and the interventions in Haiti, Sierra Leone, and The Gambia are hardly deniable. Nevertheless, Russian actions met with condemnation from the international community. Similar events took place in Yemen shortly after Putin's intervention in favour of Yanokovich. However, they led to opposite reactions.

Yemen has long been divided between two religious lines – the Sunni and the Zaidi Shia Muslim minority – and between the northern and southern parts of the country, which were united in 1990 as the Republic of Yemen.[83] In 2004, the Houthi movement started to confront the government; in the following years, it fought several rebellions against President Ali Abdallah Saleh. The Arab Spring, which started in December 2010 in Tunisia, fuelled the tensions in Yemen and weakened the position of President Saleh. Consequently, in November 2011 he agreed to hand over power to his deputy, Abdrabbuh Mansour Hadi.[84] However, the transition of power failed: Hadi proved unable to deal with the numerous challenges that afflicted the country, such as 'attacks by al-Qaeda, a separatist movement in the south, the continuing loyalty of many military officers to Mr Saleh, as well as corruption, unemployment and food insecurity'.[85]

In September 2014, Houthi forces, with the support of part of the Sunni population, entered the capital. The situation dramatically escalated: in

[80] See 'Vladimir Putin submitted appeal to the Federation Council' (1 March 2014), available at http://eng.kremlin.ru/news/6751.

[81] BBC Staff, 'Ukraine's Yanukovich asked for troops, Russia tells UN' (*BBC*, 4 March 2014), available at www.bbc.com/news/world-europe-26427848.

[82] See 'Vladimir Putin answered journalists' questions on the situation in Ukraine' (4 March 2014), available at http://eng.news.kremlin.ru/news/6763.

[83] See BBC Staff, 'Yemen Crisis: Who is Fighting Whom?' (*BBC*, 28 March 2017), available at www.bbc.com/news/world-middle-east-29319423. See also BBC Staff, 'Yemen Profile – Timeline' (*BBC*, 6 November 2019), available at www.bbc.com/news/world-middle-east-14704951.

[84] ibid.

[85] See BBC Staff, 'Yemen Crisis: Who is Fighting Whom?' (n 83).

February 2015 Houthi rebels arrested President Hadi, who managed to flee to Saudi Arabia the following month.[86] As soon as he reached the host country, he asked for military intervention from the Gulf Cooperation Council (GCC) and the UN Security Council.[87] In late March 2015, the United Arab Emirates, Bahrain, Qatar, and Kuwait engaged in airstrikes against the Houthi opposition group.[88] The intervention met with the support of the Arab League, the US, Canada, France, and the UK.[89] On the other hand, the European Union and China expressed their concern and hoped for a political solution.[90] However, they did not openly criticise the military interference. On 14 April the UNSC approved a Resolution which demanded the rebels to cease violence and which imposed an arms embargo on the Houthi faction.[91] Interestingly, the intervention was not the object of condemnation: Iran was the only state that openly criticised the foreign military involvement in the conflict.[92]

The similarities between the interventions in Ukraine and Yemen are striking, and Russia was quick in drawing the parallels and highlighting Western hypocrisy and double standards.[93] On the other hand, the US denied any similarities. Particularly revealing is a press briefing, where the US State Department's spokesperson, Marie Harf, affirmed that:

> QUESTION: … People have been asking why is it that the president, the Yemeni president, who fled from his capital, remains legitimate in your eyes.
>
> HARF: Well, I think —
>
> QUESTION: Whereas, like another president who fled. (Laughter.) […]

[86] BBC Staff, 'Yemen Crisis: Houthi Rebels Announce Takeover' (*BBC*, 6 February 2015), available at www.bbc.com/news/world-middle-east-31169773.

[87] Al Jazeera Staff, 'Yemen's Hadi Seeks UN Military Support to Deter Houthis' (*Al Jazeera*, 25 March 2015), available at www.aljazeera.com/news/middleeast/2015/03/yemen-hadi-seeks-military-support-deter-houthis-150324223355704.html.

[88] See ibid. See also Al Araibiya Staff, 'Egypt defense minister in Riyadh to discuss operation in Yemen' (*Al Araibiya*, 10 April 2015), available at http://english.alarabiya.net/en/News/middle-east/2015/04/10/Egypt-defense-minister-in-Riyadh-to-discuss-operation-in-Yemen.html; Ministry of Foreign Affairs and International Cooperation of the Kingdom of Morocco, 'Communiqué: Morocco decides to provide all forms of support to the coalition for support of legitimacy in Yemen' (26 March 2015); M Ghaza, 'Jordan "Fully Committed to Defending Yemen's legitimacy, Fighting Foreign Interference"' (*Jordan Times*, 2015), available at www.jordanembassyus.org/news/jordan-fully-committed-defending-yemen-s-legitimacy-fighting-foreign-interference; Sudan Tribune, 'Sudanese Planes Pound Houthi Targets in Yemen' (1 April 2015), available at www.sudantribune.com/spip.php?article54480.

[89] Z Vermeer, 'The *Jus ad Bellum* and the Airstrikes in Yemen: Double Standards for Decamping Presidents?' (*EJIL: Talk!*, 2015), available at www.ejiltalk.org/the-jus-ad-bellum-and-the-airstrikes-in-yemen-double-standards-for-decamping-presidents/.

[90] ibid.

[91] S/RES/2216 (2015), 14 April 2015, *Middle East (Yemen)*.

[92] P Hafezi, 'Iran Demands Immediate Halt to Military Actions in Yemen' (*Reuters*, 26 March 2015), available at www.reuters.com/article/us-yemen-security-iran-demand-idUSKBN0MM0S720150326.

[93] Vermeer (n 89).

HARF: It's completely different.

QUESTION: My question is the same. The similarities between the two cases are striking.

HARF: In that there aren't many? […]

QUESTION: There are a lot, I think, but anyways —

HARF: Okay. We can agree to disagree.[94]

In order to solve the conundrum, the possible explanations are threefold. First, we could conclude that 'it is almost impossible to establish clear principles applicable to governments in exile'.[95] Indeed, they are essentially a 'political and legal technique'[96] and 'no unequivocal objective criteria for assessment of a right to recognition exist':[97] recognition of governments is simply a political act and there is no legal duty in this regard.[98] Nevertheless, states do not recognise any entity or authority in exile and we have seen that practice shows certain patterns in this regard.[99]

Second, it could be possible to read the two cases in light of the effectiveness doctrine. Part of the scholarship posits that a government can lawfully seek foreign intervention only if it exercises effective control over territory and population. Since a government in exile does not hold effective control by definition, according to the effectiveness doctrine Yanukovich and Hadi could not ask for external help to regain power. Therefore, both interventions would be unlawful: the international community was right in condemning Russian intervention in Ukraine, but it should have had the same reaction against the airstrikes in Yemen. Nonetheless, it seems unlikely that the entire international community, with the only exception of Iran, would have endorsed the intervention in Yemen if it had been manifestly unlawful. Furthermore, we have seen that state practice has departed from the effectiveness doctrine: the legitimate government capable of speaking on behalf of the state is the democratic one, even when another authority holds effective control over territory and population.

A third possibility could be to look at the legitimacy of the two governments. Yanukovich and Hadi were both democratically elected, therefore their legitimacy of origin is not questioned. What about their legitimacy of exercise? While the Yemeni government was ousted by a rebellion and the president was held in prison before he managed to flee to Saudi Arabia, the circumstances that led to

[94] ibid.

[95] K Tiroch, 'Governments in Exile' in *Max Planck Encyclopedia of Public International Law* (Oxford University Press, 2011) §16.

[96] WM Reisman, 'Governments-in-Exile: Notes Toward a Theory of Formation and Operation' in Y Shain (ed), *Governments-in-Exile in Contemporary World Politics* (Routledge, 1991) 238.

[97] Tiroch (n 95) §16.

[98] I Brownlie, *Principles of Public International Law* (Clarendon Press, 1998) 90.

[99] S Talmon, 'Who is a Legitimate Government in Exile? Towards Normative Criteria for Governmental Legitimacy in International Law' in G Goodwin-Gill and S Talmon (eds), *The Reality of International Law. Essays in Honour of Ian Brownlie* (Oxford University Press, 1999) 500.

the overthrow of Yanukovich are substantially different. When protests started in Ukraine, the government reacted disproportionately, using snipers against unharmed protesters and killing 88 people in 48 hours.[100] The situation at the time was not an armed conflict: the opposition was not organised, and, albeit intense, armed violence did not reach the required threshold.[101] Consequently, the applicable legal framework was international human rights law and law enforcement. The latter provides that:

> In order not to constitute an arbitrary deprivation of life in violation of the right to life under customary international human rights law, a state must only use force when necessary; must only use the minimum necessary force in pursuit of a legitimate objective (including arrest whenever possible); and must only use force in proportion to the harm sought to be avoided. … In any event, intentional lethal use of force (which use of artillery clearly is) is only lawful when strictly unavoidable to protect life.[102]

It is thus fairly clear that Yanukovich's reaction to the protests constituted a significant violation of human rights and law enforcement standards. As we shall see, during the Libyan and Syrian conflicts a new narrative emerged: a government that uses excessive force against its own population is no longer considered to be the legitimate representative of the population, while this qualification is attributed to the opposition group fighting against it. Consequently, when a president loses his legitimacy due to heinous actions committed against his own people, flees the country, and another authority takes over the power (such as in Ukraine), the latter will be considered as the legitimate representative of people. From this it would follow that an illegitimate president in exile forfeits his right to ask for foreign intervention.

Against this interpretation, it could be objected that states have not focused on the use of force by Yanukovich against the Ukrainian people when they affirmed that he was no longer the legitimate authority and thus he could not invite Russia to intervene. Rather, the international community highlighted that the Ukrainian Parliament ousted Yanukovich by 328 votes to 0. Although Russia objected that the vote was unconstitutional, the majority of the international community did not consider this fact as sufficient to deny the legitimacy of the new government.[103] Nevertheless, the fact that the majority of states decided to focus on the Parliament's decision to oust Yanukovich could follow from the consideration that such vote provides a stronger legal basis. Since international

[100] BBC Staff (n 77).

[101] See ch 2.

[102] C Redaelli and S Casey-Maslen, 'Protecting civilians in populated areas during the conduct of hostilities after the Gotovina case' in S Casey-Maslen (ed), *The War Report 2013* (Oxford University Press, 2014) 468.

[103] Z Vermeer, 'Intervention with the Consent of a Deposed (but Legitimate) Government? Playing the Sierra Leone Card' (*EJIL: Talk!*, 2014), available at www.ejiltalk.org/intervention-with-the-consent-of-a-deposed-but-legitimate-government-playing-the-sierra-leone-card/.

law does not provide crystal-clear criteria to identify the government, it seems plausible that states decided to rely on the decision of the Parliament. Furthermore, being ousted by an overwhelming majority of the Parliament seems a clear sign of loss of legitimacy.

A second objection could be raised with regard to Yemen. The intervention of the Saudi-led coalition has met criticism inasmuch as the government of Yemen, as well as the coalition itself, has committed extensive human rights and international humanitarian law abuses.[104] One may thus wonder how this government can still claim to have any legitimacy of exercise. Specifically, it is necessary to distinguish between the outbreak of the internal conflict in Yemen and the following events. When the conflict started in Yemen, President Hadi was democratically elected. In the aftermath of the rebellion, he fled the country and asked Saudi Arabia to intervene in his favour. At the time, he possessed both legitimacy of origin – as he was democratically elected – and legitimacy of exercise – as at the time he had not engaged in gross and systematic violations of human rights and humanitarian law. Accordingly, if we look at the time when the intervention started, we can conclude that there is a substantial difference between the situation in Yemen and Ukraine and the legitimacy of the respective presidents. Following the Saudi-led intervention, the government has engaged in extensive human rights and international humanitarian law violations. Therefore, its legitimacy of exercise is questionable.[105]

The idea that a government in exile should be the legitimate representative of its population in order to be recognised as the de jure authority capable to speak on behalf of the state finds its roots in the pre-Charter scholarship. For instance, Cassin suggested that a government in exile could be recognised if states 'regard it as being representative of the national will'.[106] In the same vein, Sperduti posited that 'the recognition of a government in exile requires that it shows a sufficient quality by which it seems an emanation of the community for which it intends to act'.[107] Similarly, Landheer submitted that 'the government in exile remains the de jure government as long as it can be assumed that it represents the majority of the population'.[108] More recently, Talmon supported

[104] See eg Report of the detailed findings of the Group of Eminent International and Regional Experts on Yemen, Situation of human rights in Yemen, including violations and abuses since September 2014, A/HRC/42/CRP.1, 3 September 2019; OHCHR, 'Bachelet urges States with the power and influence to end starvation, killing of civilians in Yemen' (UN News), available at www.ohchr.org/EN/NewsEvents/Pages/DisplayNews.aspx?NewsID=23855&LangID=E; International Commission of Jurists, 'Bearing the Brunt of War in Yemen: International Law Violations and their Impact on the Civilian Population' (Geneva, 2018); Human Rights Watch, 'Yemen: Events of 2018', available at www.hrw.org/world-report/2019/country-chapters/yemen.

[105] The question here is whether a foreign country can provide assistance to a government that is committing such violations. The issue is addressed in ch 5.

[106] R Cassin, 'Vichy or Free France?' (1941) 20 *Foreign Affairs* 112.

[107] G Sperduti, 'Governi in Esilio e Comitati Nazionali all'Estero' (1952) 7 *La Comunità Internazionale* 407–08.

[108] B Landheer, 'The Legal Status of the Netherlands' (1943) 41(4) *Michigan Law Review* 651.

this conclusion with a substantial and detailed analysis of state practice. For instance, in 1943 the Comité Français de la Libération Nationale (CFLN) was not recognised by the US or the UK as the de jure government because there was 'no French authority which could be regarded as generally representative of the French people'.[109] Similarly, the Korean Provisional Government, established in China, was denied recognition because it could have not been 'regarded as representative of the Korean people'.[110]

Scholarship and practice would thus suggest that the representative character of a government in exile is considered dispositive for its continuing recognition. Furthermore, in recent years the respect of human rights and humanitarian law has been definitively recognised as the legitimate representative of the population. Although *de lege lata* it seems too early to claim that heinous human rights violations grant the right to recognise an alternative government,[111] we can conclude with Talmon that:

> *De lege ferenda*, if 'respect for human rights' is to have any meaning in international law an unrepresentative government which is guilty of massive human rights violations or even genocide of its own people is to forfeit its right to represent the people and thus its status of government when it [loses] effective control irrespective of whether or not it is deposed by outside intervention. ... A government, however, that violates the human rights of its people on a massive scale cannot be regarded as its representative.[112]

III. UNDEMOCRATIC REGIMES AND EFFECTIVENESS

A. Undemocratic, Effective Regimes

In the previous paragraphs we have seen that coup regimes are not automatically recognised as de jure governments, despite the fact that they exercise de facto control over territory and population: preference is given to the democratically elected authority, even when it has never been effective. This circumstance might suggest that undemocratic governments would never be recognised as representative of the state. However, state practice contradicts this assumption: representatives of numerous undemocratic regimes sit at international organisations. Furthermore, if a coup regime succeeds in affirming and retaining its power, eventually it will be recognised as the de jure authority: 'successful revolution sooner or later begets its own legality'.[113] Notably, from the analysis of

[109] Talmon (n 99) 509.
[110] ibid.
[111] ibid, 521.
[112] ibid, 512.
[113] SA de Smith, *Constitutional and Administrative Law* (Penguin Books, 1977) 66–67; Roth (n 27) 64; Wippman (n 13) 302–03; Murphy (n 3) 571–73; d'Aspremont (n 13).

state practice it emerges that undemocratic regimes tend to be recognised as de jure governments when there is no democratic alternative.

A good example is provided by the Syrian government. Bashar Assad has been the Syrian president since 2000, when he succeeded his father, who had ruled the country during the previous 30 years. Assad's presidency was endorsed by a referendum that took place on 11 July 2000, where the population was asked whether they wanted to confirm the Parliament's choice to designate Assad as the new president of the country.[114] Assad received the support of 99.7 per cent of the population. Nonetheless, whether the vote reflected the will of the population is questionable. Indeed, the Constitution establishes that the Ba'th Party (the party of Assad's family) is the sole ruling party. Furthermore, opposition was met with intimidation and imprisonment.[115]

In March 2011, pro-democratic demonstrations erupted in Deraa. The government responded with fire, killing several people who were taking part in the demonstrations. The episode triggered protests in the whole country. Syrians asked for Assad's resignation, while the president forcibly quelled the demonstrations. Violence quickly escalated and the disturbances degenerated into an internal conflict, notoriously still ongoing. As we shall see, during the conflict Assad was defined as illegitimate and not representative of the Syrian people.[116] However, the causes were not related to the way in which he gained power, but to the heinous crimes committed against the population. The focus was thus on the legitimacy of exercise, instead of the legitimacy of origin.[117]

Similar events unfolded in Libya during the Gaddafi regime. In 1969, Gaddafi successfully staged a coup d'état against the monarchical government and founded the Libyan Arab Republic.[118] At the time, his government was recognised

[114] Immigration and Refugee Board of Canada, *Syria: Syrian presidential election in 2000; confirmation of whether businessmen and/or other influential people in the community were pressured by security officers to collect other people's identity cards for the security officer's use in the election (June–July 2001)* (24 March 2003), SYR41225.E, available at www.refworld.org/docid/3f7d4e22e.html. See also J Kifner, 'Syrians Vote to Confirm Assad's Son As President' (*The New York Times*, 11 July 2000), available at www.nytimes.com/2000/07/11/world/syrians-vote-to-confirm-assad-s-son-as-president.html. A similar referendum took place in 2007, when Assad received 97.6% support. See I Black, 'Democracy Damascus style: Assad the only choice in referendum' (*The Guardian*, 28 May 2007), available at www.theguardian.com/world/2007/may/28/syria.ianblack.

[115] Immigration and Refugee Board of Canada (n 114).

[116] See ch 5.

[117] This is further confirmed by the circumstances that led to the awarding and withdrawal of the French Légion d'honneur. When Assad took office in 2001, France honoured him with its most prestigious award: the Légion d'honneur. However, in April 2018, following the chemical weapon attack against the population and the subsequent intervention of France, President Macron started the procedure to withdraw the award. See J Henley, 'France to strip Bashar al-Assad of his Légion d'honneur' (*The Guardian*, 17 April 2018), available at www.theguardian.com/world/2018/apr/17/france-to-strip-syria-leader-bashar-al-assad-legion-honneur; BBC Staff, 'Syria returns Légion d'honneur award to France' (*BBC*, 20 April 2018), available at www.bbc.com/news/world-middle-east-43833652. See also L Visser, 'Russia's Intervention in Syria' (*EJIL: Talk!*, 2015), available at www.ejiltalk.org/russias-intervention-in-syria/.

[118] BBC Staff, 'Libya profile – Timeline' (*BBC*, 19 April 2019), available at www.bbc.com/news/world-africa-13755445.

by the international community. Nevertheless, the perception of his legitimacy changed dramatically in 2011. Indeed, in light of 'widespread and systematic attacks'[119] committed by Libyan authorities against the civilian population, a considerable number of countries affirmed that Gaddafi and his government could no longer be considered as the legitimate representatives of their own people, while this definition was attributed to the opposition groups.[120]

Analogous considerations can be put forward with regard to the Chadian government. President Idriss Deby gained power in 1990 thanks to a coup d'état and won a fourth term as president in April 2011.[121] In February 2019, as rebel forces were advancing towards the capital of Chad to overthrow the government, President Deby invited France for help. Accordingly, France launched Operation Barkhane and engaged in airstrikes against the opposition group. While the democratic legitimacy of President Deby could be questioned, the intervention upon invitation was not criticised by the international community.[122]

These cases would show that the undemocratic nature of the government is not considered a sufficient reason to conclude that the head of state is incapable of speaking on behalf of the state. Specifically, these cases have a characteristic in common, namely that there was no democratic alternative at the time the governments reached power. When Assad became the president of Syria, there was no democratic alternative that could have been recognised by the international community and things changed only years later, with the outbreak of the internal conflict. Similarly, when Gaddafi gained power though a coup d'état in 1969, no democratic alternative was present at the time, and the same could be affirmed for Chadian President Deby. Indeed, there was no other authority that could have been recognised as a democratic organ capable of speaking on behalf of the state. We could thus wonder whether our conclusions would be different if this alternative existed. One recent example is the Venezuelan crisis.

In 2013, following the death of President Chavez, Nicolás Maduro won the presidential elections.[123] During his term, a political and economic crisis broke out in the country: hyperinflation, food shortages, unavailability of health assistance, violence, and poverty are only a few of the issues that have affected

[119] S/RES/1973 (2011), 17 March 2011.

[120] See ch 6. See also D Akande, 'Which Entity is the Government of Libya and Why Does It Matter?' (*EJIL: Talk!*, 2011), available at www.ejiltalk.org/which-entity-is-the-government-of-libya-and-why-does-it-matter/; J Serralvo, 'Government Recognition and International Humanitarian Law Applicability in Post-Gaddafi Libya' (2015) 18 *Yearbook of International Humanitarian Law* 3–41; S Talmon, 'The Difference between Rhetoric and Reality: Why an Illegitimate Regime May Still be a Government in the Eyes of International Law' (*EJIL: Talk!*, 2011), available at www.ejiltalk.org/the-difference-between-rhetoric-and-reality-why-an-illegitimate-regime-may-still-be-a-government-in-the-eyes-of-international-law/.

[121] BBC Staff, 'Chad profile' (*BBC*, 7 April 2016), available at www.bbc.com/news/world-africa-13164688.

[122] 'Rebel Incursion Exposes Chad's Weaknesses' *International Crisis Group*, 17 February 2019.

[123] BBC Staff, 'No Chavez heir Maduro wins Venezuela presidential election' (*BBC*, 15 April 2013), available at www.bbc.com/news/world-latin-america-22149202.

Venezuela. As a result, the population started to demonstrate in the streets of Caracas and called for Maduro's resignation.[124] On 20 May 2018, Maduro won the presidential elections for the second time; however, his opponents denounced irregularities and accused him of moving towards a dictatorship. Accordingly, the Lima Group and Canada issued a statement whereby they clarified that they did not recognise the elections' results.[125] In spite of pressure from foreign countries to step down and establish a transitional government, Maduro officially started his new term on 10 January 2019.[126] A few days later, Juan Guaidó, leader of Venezuela's opposition-controlled national assembly, swore himself in as interim president.[127]

The reaction of several states and international organisations has been unanimous in denouncing the illegitimacy of Maduro's presidency and in welcoming Guaidò as interim president of Venezuela. On 10 January 2019, the Permanent Council of the Organization of American States (OAS) issued a resolution where it affirmed that 'the May 20, 2018 electoral process in Venezuela lacked legitimacy' and that it did not 'recognize the legitimacy of Nicolas Maduro's new term'.[128] On 23 January 2019, US Secretary of State Mike Pompeo affirmed that the US 'recognizes Juan Guaidò as the new interim President of Venezuela, and strongly supports his courageous decision to assume that role pursuant to Article 233 of Venezuela's constitution and supported by the National Assembly, in restoring democracy to Venezuela'.[129] Similarly, Canada issued a statement where it rejected 'the Maduro regime's illegitimate claim to power' and recognised 'Juan Guaidó, President of the National Assembly, as the interim President of Venezuela'.[130]

The events that unfolded in Venezuela would confirm the conclusion reached previously, namely that the legitimacy of origin plays a critical role in the

[124] Al Jazeera Staff, 'Venezuela's crisis explained from the beginning' (*Al Jazeera*, 23 May 2018), available at www.aljazeera.com/indepth/features/2017/04/venezuela-happening-170412114045595.html.

[125] L Cohen and A Aponte, 'Venezuela's Maduro re-elected amid outcry over vote' (*Reuters*, 20 May 2018), available at www.reuters.com/article/us-venezuela-election/venezuelas-maduro-re-elected-amid-outcry-over-vote-idUSKCN1IL05U.

[126] T Phillips, 'Maduro starts new Venezuela term by accusing US of imperialist "world war"' (*The Guardian*, 10 January 2019), available at www.theguardian.com/world/2019/jan/10/venezuela-president-nicolas-maduro-begins-second-term.

[127] J Parkin Daniels and M Zúñiga, 'Venezuela: who is Juan Guaidó, the man who declared himself president?' (*The Guardian*, 23 January 2019), available at www.theguardian.com/world/2019/jan/15/juan-guaido-venezuelan-opposition-leader-challenging-maduros-rule.

[128] See *Resolution on the Situation in Venezuela*, OAS Permanent Council, 10 January 2019, E-001/19.

[129] R Janik, 'European Recognition Practice on Venezuela: The Devil in the Details' (*Opinio Juris*, 2019), available at opiniojuris.org/2019/02/08/european-recognition-practice-on-venezuela-the-devil-in-the-details/.

[130] Government of Canada, Statement, 'Canada recognizes the interim President of Venezuela' (23 January 2019), available at www.canada.ca/en/global-affairs/news/2019/01/canada-recognizes-the-interim-president-of-venezuela.html.

recognition of governments. Although Maduro won the presidential elections in 2018, it is at the least questionable whether they could be considered free and fair. Accordingly, a number of states did not 'recognise the legitimacy of the electoral process ... because it [did] not adhere to the international standards of a democratic, free, fair and transparent process'.[131] In the same vein, OAS considered the Venezuelan elections as illegitimate 'for not complying with international standards, for not having met the participation of all Venezuelan political actors, and for being carried out without the necessary guarantees for a free, fair, transparent and democratic process'.[132] Similar to the Syrian case, Maduro was elected through a seemingly undemocratic process. However, unlike in the Syrian cases, in Venezuela it was possible to identify an alternative that could be considered legitimate. In spite of the fact that Guaidó de facto took over as president, he is considered by the majority of the international community as a legitimate alternative that could guide the country to free and fair elections.[133] This would lead to conclude that undemocratic governments – ie governments that have reached power through coups d'état, through elections which were not free and fair, or whose leaders refused to step down after losing elections – are recognised as de jure governments unless there is no democratic alternative.

B. Undemocratic, Ineffective Governments

The aforementioned cases show that undemocratic but effective governments tend to be recognised by the international community, provided that there is no democratic alternative. What if the undemocratic government is not effective? And what if the alternative is considered equally undemocratic? One recent example is the Malian crisis.

Since May 2006, the Malian government has faced a low-intensity conflict in the north of the country against Tuareg rebel groups.[134] In February 2012,

[131] F Charner, P Newton and N Gallón, 'Opponents slam Venezuelan President Nicolas Maduro's election victory as a shame' (*CNN*, 20 May 2018), available at www.cnn.com/2018/05/20/americas/venezuela-elections/index.html. See also M Pompeo, 'An Unfair, Unfree Vote in Venezuela' (Press Statement, Government of the United States, 21 May 2018), available at www.state.gov/secretary/remarks/2018/05/282303.htm.

[132] See *Resolution on the Situation in Venezuela*, OAS, 5 June 2018, S-032/1.

[133] When Gaddafi and Assad obtained power, the international community did not question their legitimacy and overwhelmingly recognised them as the de jure government. Nevertheless, as we shall see in the next chapter, during the internal conflicts that unfolded in Libya and Syria, Gaddafi and Assad lost legitimacy due to the way in which they exercised power (legitimacy of exercise). As in the case of Venezuela, a considerable number of states identified an alternative that could have been considered legitimate and thus recognised certain rebel groups as legitimate representatives of their own people. See ch 5.

[134] S Casey-Maslen, 'Armed conflict in Mali in 2012' in S Casey-Maslen (ed), *The War Report 2012* (Oxford University Press, 2013) 118.

tensions dramatically increased, with the ANSAs launching new offensives against the Malian army. Poorly equipped, the latter was not able to handle the rebels, who had just received a considerable number of weapons and ammunitions from Libya.[135] On 22 March 2012 a coup ousted the elected president, Amadou Toumani Touré, and established a military junta. Consequently, ECOWAS and the AU imposed sanctions on the new regime.[136] On 6 April 2012 the Tuareg rebel group *Mouvement National de Liberation de l'Azawad* (MNLA) declared the independence of the Azawad region in the northern part of the country.[137] The same day, ECOWAS reached an agreement with the military junta: Dioncounda Traoré, the junta's spokesperson, was designated as interim president of Mali until new elections.[138] The Malian forces proved to be insufficiently armed and clearly unable to defeat the several non-state armed groups fighting in the country.[139] Therefore, upon the request of President Traoré, on 11 January 2013 France sent troops to Mali to fight against the opposition groups (Operation Serval). The African Union deployed its forces shortly thereafter. By 8 February the Malian and international troops had retaken the territories under rebel control.[140] In a letter to the Security Council, France justified its intervention as follows:

> France has responded today to a request for assistance from the Interim President of the Republic of Mali, Mr. Dioncounda Traoré. Mali is facing terrorist elements from the north, which are currently threatening the territorial integrity and very existence of the State and the security of its population. … French armed forces, in response to that request and in coordination with our partners, particularly those in the region, are supporting Malian units in combating those terrorist elements. The operation, which is in conformity with international law, will last as long as necessary.[141]

The French and African intervention received overwhelming approval from the international community. UN Secretary-General Ban Ki-moon 'welcomed the response of "bilateral partners" to the plea for assistance from the Government of Mali to counter the troubling push southward by armed rebels, some of

[135] ibid, 240.

[136] See the Constitutive Act of the African Union 2000 and the African Charter on Democracy, Elections and Governance 2007.

[137] The declaration of independence was not recognised by the AU, EU or the US, among others. See Casey-Maslen (n 134) 119.

[138] K Bannelier and T Christakis, 'Under the Security Council's Watchful Eyes: Military Intervention by Invitation in the Malian Conflict' (2013) 26(3) *Leiden Journal of International Law* 858.

[139] The main ANSAs fighting in the country at the time were the MNLA, Al-Qaeda in the Islamic Maghreb (AQIM), Ansar Dine and the Movement for Oneness and Jihad in West Africa (MOJWA). See Casey-Maslen (n 134) 121.

[140] ibid, 120.

[141] S/1013/17, *Identical letters dated 11th January 2013 from the Permanent Representative of France to the UN addressed to the Secretary-General and the President of the Security Council*, in T Christakis and K Bannelier, '*Volenti non Fit Injuria*? Les Effets du Consentement à l'Intervention Militaire' (2004) 50(1) *Annuaire français de droit international* 107.

which are associated with [terrorist] groups'.[142] The Security Council welcomed 'the swift action by the French forces, at the request of the transitional authorities of Mali, to stop the offensive of terrorist, extremist and armed groups towards the south of Mali'.[143] Similarly, the ECOWAS 'thank[ed] the French Government for its initiatives to support Mali',[144] while US Permanent Representative to the UN Susan Rice affirmed that:

> There was a great deal of expression of concern about the deteriorating situation, discussion also of the letter from the president of Mali that requested external support, particularly from the French. … The Security Council … can support and encourage the Malian government's sovereign request for assistance from friends and partners in the region and beyond. Clearly, it's up to those external players to decide what they wish to do, but I think there was clear-cut consensus about the gravity of the situation and the right of the Malian authorities to seek what assistance they can receive.[145]

The Malian case is strikingly in contrast with the instances previously examined. In The Gambia, the elected president was promptly and overwhelmingly recognised as legitimate, even if he had never led a government that exercised effective control over the country. Accordingly, his consent to the foreign intervention was recognised as valid. On the contrary, in Mali the request was issued by President Traoré, who had reached power through a coup d'état, and against whose junta both the AU and ECOWAS adopted sanctions. Surely, the agreement reached with ECOWAS, whereby Traoré was named interim president until new elections, served as de facto recognition of his authority and capacity to act on behalf of the state? However, the sole fact that ECOWAS concluded the agreement with the author of the coup diverges from what happened in The Gambia, Côte d'Ivoire, Sierra Leone, and Haiti. This would confirm that reaching power through a coup does not automatically jeopardise the government's capacity to stand for the state. Indeed, France invoked the consent of Traoré's government as justification to intervene and none questioned the government's capacity to express its consent to an armed intervention. How can this case be reconciled with the instances examined above, where democratically elected governments were granted recognition, notwithstanding their being overthrown by coups?

Some authors ground the French intervention on the combined action of the invitation of the government and UNSC Resolution 2085. The resolution

[142] UN News Centre Staff, 'Mali: Ban Welcomes Bilateral Assistance to Stop Southward Onslaught of Insurgents' (*UN News Centre*, 14 January 2013), available at www.un.org/apps/news/story.asp?NewsID=43920#.WP5TLFJaZE4.

[143] S/RES/2100 (2013), 25 April 2013, preamble. See also Bannelier and Christakis (n 138) 855–74.

[144] Statement of the President of the ECOWAS Commission on the situation in Mali (12 January 2013), available at https://reliefweb.int/report/mali/statement-president-ecowas-commission-situation-mali.

[145] US Department of State, 'Susan Rice, U.S. Permanent Representative to the United Nations, Remarks at a Press Gaggle Following UN Security Council Consultations on Mali, New York, NY, January 10, 2013', available at usun.state.gov/briefing/statements/202714.htm.

authorised the African-led International Support Mission in Mali (AFISMA) to take 'all necessary measures' to 'support the Malian authorities in recovering the areas in the north of its territory under the control of terrorist, extremist and armed groups and in reducing the threat posed by terrorist organizations'.[146] At the same time, it urged Member States to provide assistance to the Malian Forces 'in order to restore the authority of the State of Mali over its entire national territory, to uphold the unity and territorial integrity of Mali and to reduce the threat posed by terrorist organizations and associated groups'.[147] France never claimed that the Security Council authorised Operation Serval; however, it affirmed on several occasions that the intervention was in line with the UNSC resolution.[148] A number of scholars thus concluded that 'the Resolution would not by itself be a sufficient legal ground for the foreign intervention in the Malian conflict, just as the invitation by a government from Bamako on its own would not suffice. Only together do they provide a valid legal basis for a foreign intervention'.[149]

Another part of the scholarship explained the legality of the intervention in light of the purpose of the intervention. Unlike the instances previously examined, terrorist groups were operating in Mali, a fact that would in itself justify the intervention in favour of the government.[150] This would find confirmation in the fact that France directed its intervention against the terrorist movements but not against the MNLA, a group fighting for the Tuareg minority and that was seeking independence for Azawad.[151] Furthermore, the MNLA praised the French intervention, promised to help the foreign forces in their fight against terrorism, and asked for autonomy within Mali, instead of claiming independence.[152] This interpretation seems to find confirmation in the numerous references to the terrorist threat in the UNSC resolution and would support the conclusion that the risk of terrorist groups taking over the country would have warranted the decision to recognise Traoré's government, however undemocratic.[153] Nevertheless, admitting that an intervention would be lawful when directed against terrorist groups, irrespective of the legality of the invitation, raises a number of questions. Specifically, as long as there is no agreed definition of terrorism, claiming

[146] S/RES/2085 (2012), 25 December 2012, *The Situation in Mali*, §9(b).

[147] ibid, §7.

[148] See Statement by F Hollande, President of France, 12 January 2013, available at basedoc.diplomatie.gouv.fr/vues/Kiosque/FranceDiplomatie/kiosque.php?fichier=baen2013-01-14.html.

[149] V Hadzi-vidanovic, 'France Intervenes in Mali Invoking both SC Resolution 2085 and the Invitation of the Malian Government – Redundancy or Legal Necessity?' (*EJIL: Talk!*, 2013), available at www.ejiltalk.org/france-intervenes-in-mali-invoking-both-sc-resolution-2085-and-the-invitation-of-the-malian-government-redundancy-or-legal-necessity/; Bannelier and Christakis (n 138) 874.

[150] Bannelier and Christakis (n 138) 12.

[151] ibid, 13.

[152] ibid.

[153] For an analysis of the purpose-based approach, see ch 3.

that the presence of terrorist groups would allow a foreign intervention could easily lead to abuses.[154]

The intervention in Mali casts shadows over the democratic legitimacy approach. Indeed, not once did the international community question Traoré's capacity to act on behalf of the state. Even accepting that his authority derived from the fact that the UNSC resolution expressly recognised him as heading the de jure government, it is still controversial why the Security Council did not identify the democratically elected, but ousted, president instead. On the other hand, this case would not support the effectiveness criterion either. Indeed, Traoré's government was never in control of the whole territory or population. The Malian case could be explained in light of its peculiarity: the terrorist threat urged the UNSC, the African Union, and the international community to change their approach and to recognise Traoré's government as the de jure government, notwithstanding its lack of effectiveness.

IV. THE ROLE OF DOMESTIC CONSTITUTIONAL ORDERS IN INTERNATIONAL LAW

On 28 June 2009, in Tegucigalpa (Honduras), military forces entered the presidential palace and forced President Manuel Zelaya onto a flight to Costa Rica. Landing in San José still in his pyjamas, he was heard protesting: 'I am the President of Honduras!'[155] That year President Zelaya was organising a non-binding referendum on whether to convene a special assembly to reform the Honduran Constitution.[156] Zelaya's opponents criticised his intentions, claiming that his real aim was to extend his term. The president defended his action, affirming that the referendum 'was an opinion poll, and it never once mentioned extending presidential term limits'.[157] On 26 June 2009, the Honduran Supreme Court unanimously issued an arrest warrant against the president; two days later, the national army carried out the order, ousting Zelaya.[158]

The reaction of the international community was unanimous in condemning the coup and continuing to recognise Zelaya as head of the de jure government. The OAS suspended Honduras, applying Article 19 of the Inter-American Democratic Charter,[159] and its Assistant Secretary General Albert Ramdin

[154] Bannelier and Christakis (n 138) 866.

[155] E Malkin, 'Honduran President Is Ousted in Coup' (*The New York Times*, 28 June 2009), available at www.nytimes.com/2009/06/29/world/americas/29honduras.html.

[156] T Padgett, 'Honduras Quagmire: An Interview with Zelaya' (*Time*, 25 September 2009), available at: content.time.com/time/world/article/0,8599,1926383,00.html.

[157] ibid.

[158] M Lacey, 'Leader's Ouster Not a Coup, Says the Honduran Military' (*The New York Times*, 1 July 2009), available at www.nytimes.com/2009/07/02/world/americas/02coup.html.

[159] Article 19 of the Inter-American Democratic Charter: '[b]ased on the principles of the Charter of the OAS and subject to its norms, and in accordance with the democracy clause contained in the Declaration of Quebec City, an unconstitutional interruption of the democratic order or an unconstitutional alteration of the constitutional regime that seriously impairs the democratic order

affirmed that 'the current regime is not recognized as the legitimate government of Honduras'.[160] The General Assembly condemned 'the *coup d'état* in the Republic of Honduras that has interrupted the democratic and constitutional order and the legitimate exercise of power in Honduras, and resulted in the removal of the democratically elected President of that country' and demanded 'the immediate and unconditional restoration of the legitimate and Constitutional Government of the President of the Republic of Honduras, Mr. José Manuel Zelaya Rosales, and of the legally constituted authority in Honduras, so that he may fulfil the mandate for which he was democratically elected by the Honduran people'.[161] In the same vein, President Obama stated that: 'we believe that the coup was not legal and that President Zelaya remains the president of Honduras, the democratically elected president there'.[162]

Like in Haiti, Sierra Leone, Côte d'Ivoire, and The Gambia, the democratically elected government of Honduras was still recognised as the authority representing the state, notwithstanding the lack of effectiveness. What differentiates the first instances with the latter is how the coups took place. In the first cases, the opposition ousted the government by military coups. On the contrary, the Honduran army acted in light of a Supreme Court warrant, with the unanimous support of the Court itself and the majority of the Parliament.[163] This circumstance raises the question of the role played by constitutional issues in international law. Several commentators argued that the Supreme Court wrongly interpreted the constitution, as the coup was clearly against the Honduran charter.[164] The Court was also defined as 'one of the most corrupt institutions in Latin America'.[165] Nevertheless, it is arguable that the interpretation of the Constitution should be a matter essentially within the domestic jurisdiction of the state. Roth noted that 'it is hardly an exaggeration to say that if internal actors do not retain the last word on such a matter, the whole idea of a "matter

in a member state, constitutes, while it persists, an insurmountable obstacle to its government's participation in sessions of the General Assembly, the Meeting of Consultation, the Councils of the Organization, the specialized conferences, the commissions, working groups, and other bodies of the Organization'.

160 G Thompson, 'O.A.S. Votes to Suspend Honduras Over Coup' (*The New York Times*, 4 July 2009), available at www.nytimes.com/2009/07/05/world/americas/05honduras.html.

161 A/RES/63/301, 1 July 2009, *Situation in Honduras: democracy breakdown.*

162 Lacey (n 158).

163 BR Roth, 'Secessions, Coups and the International Rule of Law: Assessing the Decline of the Effective Control Doctrine' (2010) 11(2) *Melbourne Journal of International Law* 435.

164 BR Roth, 'The Honduran Crisis and the Turn to Constitutional Legitimism, Part I: The Place of Domestic Constitutional Orders in the International Legal Framework' (*EJIL: Talk!*, 2009), available at www.ejiltalk.org/the-honduran-crisis-and-the-turn-to-constitutional-legitimism-part-i-the-place-of-domestic-constitutional-orders-in-the-international-legal-framework/.

165 This opinion was expressed by Larry Birns, director of the Washington-based Council on Hemispheric Affairs. See CNN Staff, 'Police Clash with Demonstrators in Honduran Capital' (*CNN*, 29 June 2009), available at http://edition.cnn.com/2009/WORLD/americas/06/29/honduras.president.arrested/index.html?iref=werecommend.

essentially within the domestic jurisdiction" is now a nullity (and, many would say, a good riddance)'.[166]

The crucial role played by constitutional issues in determining the de jure government also emerged during the recent Ukrainian crisis. As explained above, on 22 February 2014 the Parliament voted to remove the democratically elected President Yanukovich, and decided that new elections would be held on 25 May.[167] In the following days, an arrest warrant was issued against the overthrown president, who fled to Russia. Yanukovich defined the Parliament's action as a coup, an act violating the Constitution of Ukraine. As a matter of fact, the Ukrainian Constitution requires at least three-quarters of its constitutional composition to vote in favour of impeachment in order to impeach the president. However, the members of the Parliament on 22 February were 328, while the total number of the members is 449. Therefore, the vote was null due to the lack of nine votes.[168]

The question of how to interpret claims of unconstitutional changes of power also emerged with regard to the events that unfolded in Lesotho. In May 1998, general elections took place in the country and saw the overwhelming victory of the Lesotho Congress of Democrats (LCD), the ruling party.[169] The elections were monitored by a number of observers from several non-governmental organisations, the European Union, the Organization of African Unity, and UN agencies, and a number of countries. While 'there was some disagreement between the different observer groups about the words "free and fair"', at the end of the elections the observers agreed that 'the election was conducted in a manner which should be considered acceptable according to international standard', albeit they did denounce some irregularities.[170] Soon thereafter, the opposition party contested the results and tensions arose in the country and led to rioting and episodes of armed violence. Fearing a coup, the LCD asked for help for state members of the Southern African Development Community (SADC). Accordingly, on 22 September 1998, South Africa, Botswana, and Zimbabwe sent troops to restore order and succeeded in quelling the revolt.[171] While the elections were prima facie free and fair, the foreign intervention took place without waiting for the local authorities to investigate the matter further.

[166] Roth (n 27) 215.

[167] BBC Staff, 'Ukrainian MPs vote to oust President Yanukovych' (*BBC*, 22 February 2014), available at www.bbc.com/news/world-europe-26304842.

[168] D Wisehart, 'The Crisis in Ukraine and the Prohibition of the Use of Force: A Legal Basis for Russia's Intervention?' (*EJIL: Talk!*, 2014), available at www.ejiltalk.org/the-crisis-in-ukraine-and-the-prohibition-of-the-use-of-force-a-legal-basis-for-russias-intervention/.

[169] BBC Staff, 'Lesotho profile – Timeline' (*BBC*, 14 May 2018), available at www.bbc.com/news/world-africa-13729501.

[170] R Southall and R Fox, 'Lesotho's General Election of 1998: Rigged or De Rigeur?' (1999) 37(4) *The Journal of Modern African Studies* 678.

[171] ibid, 670; A van der Vleuten and AR Hoffmann, 'Explaining the Enforcement of Democracy by Regional Organizations: Comparing EU, Mercosur and SADC' (2010) 48(3) *Journal of Common Market Studies* 752.

These cases seem to suggest that (un)constitutional changes do not affect the international recognition of governments. This is confirmed by what took place in The Gambia: a few days after the elections, the incumbent President Jammeh denounced grave irregularities in the ballots and referred the matter to the Supreme Court.[172] Pending the Court's decision, the Parliament decided to extend Jammeh's mandate for 90 days.[173] Moreover, it tried to change the Constitution accordingly. In its Resolution 2337, the Security Council strongly condemned 'the attempt by the Parliament on 18 January 2017 to extend President Jammeh's term for three months beyond his current mandate'.[174] These events raise difficult questions.[175] Could the Parliament modify the Constitution, or was it beyond its competence? Which standards apply? Most importantly, who should have the last world in constitutional issues: the elected representatives of the people or the international community?

Article 23(4) of the African Charter on Democracy, Elections and Governance provides that 'State Parties agree that the use of, inter alia, the following illegal means of accessing or maintaining power constitute *an unconstitutional change of government* and shall draw appropriate sanctions by the Union: ... Any refusal by an incumbent government to relinquish power to the winning party or candidate after free, fair and regular elections'.[176] Furthermore, Article 23(5) prohibits 'any amendment or revision of the constitution or legal instruments, which is an infringement on the principles of democratic change of government'. In the same vein, according to the Inter-American Democratic Charter '[i]n the event of an *unconstitutional alteration of the constitutional regime* that seriously impairs the democratic order in a member state the other member states and the organs of the OAS will take initiatives aimed at restoring democracy'.[177] Furthermore, Member States can be suspended if 'there has been an unconstitutional interruption of the democratic order' (Article 21). These instruments all refer to unconstitutional changes of government or of the constitutional regime.

[172] The Guardian Staff (n 41).

[173] BBC Staff, 'The Gambia's Yahya Jammeh's Term Extended by Parliament' (*BBC*, 18 January 2017), available at www.bbc.com/news/world-africa-38662000.

[174] S/RES/2337 (2017), 19 January 2017, *Peace consolidation in West Africa*. See also Nussberger (n 47).

[175] African Union Charter on Democracy, Elections and Governance, Art 23(4): '[s]tate Parties agree that the use of, inter alia, the following illegal means of accessing or maintaining power constitute an unconstitutional change of government and shall draw appropriate sanctions by the Union: ... Any refusal by an incumbent government to relinquish power to the winning party or candidate after free, fair and regular elections'.

[176] Emphasis added.

[177] Emphasis added. The Democratic Charter is not a treaty; nonetheless, it is generally considered as an authoritative interpretation of the OAS Charter. See D Cassel, 'Honduras: Coup d'Etat in Constitutional Clothing?' (2009) 13(9) *American Society of International Law Insight* 3.

In summary, in Ukraine, the Parliament did not meet the quorum to oust President Yanukovich, yet the latter was no longer considered the legitimate representative of the state. Conversely, in Honduras and The Gambia it is at least controversial whether the changes of government were unconstitutional. In the first case, the action was carried out on the basis of a Supreme Court order. In the second, the Gambian Supreme Court was asked to investigate whether the elections were affected by irregularities. It is undeniable that the modalities of expulsion of President Zelaya (forced on a plane in his pyjamas) and the alleged partiality of Gambian organs of the state raise legitimate doubts on the constitutionality of those changes. Nonetheless, this does not change the fact that internal state authorities were not recognised as the best candidates to interpret their own Constitution. Does this circumstance constitute an unlawful interference in internal affairs?

Matters exclusively within the domestic jurisdiction of states have shrunk over the past decades. Issues such as respect of human rights, once exclusively internal, have entered the international sphere. International and regional instruments such as the African Charter on Democracy, Elections and Governance and the Inter-American Democratic Charter would prove that democracy and adherence to the Constitution are now matters of international concern. The crucial question regards 'an existing government's capacity to render advance consent to otherwise-unlawful foreign interference in internal affairs, at the expense even of a future government that breaches the state's international legal obligations'.[178] Indeed, it is one thing to suspend a state due to an allegedly undemocratic change of government, but it is quite a different thing to recognise the ousted government as the de jure representative of the state.[179] Although none would deny the value of democracy and the importance of free and fair elections as a way to change government, as opposed to violent means, who should have the last say on constitutional matters is highly controversial. Leaving the matter exclusively to internal authorities could jeopardise democratic processes: cases of corruption and abuses are not uncommon. On the other hand, the intervention of the international community could equally raise concerns of possible improper use of its power. In any case, regional instruments and state practice seem to tend toward the second option.

V. CONCLUDING OBSERVATIONS

This chapter sought to test the traditional doctrines of intervention upon invitation against state practice. The idea that interventions in civil wars upon

[178] Roth (n 164) cit.

[179] BR Roth, 'The Honduran Crisis and the Turn to Constitutional Legitimism, Part II: The Pitfalls of Constitutional Legitimism' (*EJIL: Talk!*, 2009), available at www.ejiltalk.org/the-honduran-crisis-and-the-turn-to-constitutional-legitimism-part-ii-the-pitfalls-of-constitutional-legitimism/.

invitation of the beleaguered government are always unlawful is untenable and contrasts strikingly with state practice. Nevertheless, both the effectiveness and democratic entitlement doctrines seem to coexist in state practice. How to solve this conundrum?

Drawing upon the distinction between legitimacy of origin and legitimacy of exercise, the findings of this chapter suggest distinguishing between democratic and coup governments. In the first case, the legitimacy stems from the electoral mandate, regardless of whether the government is effective. On the other hand, undemocratic regimes would be recognised as de jure governments if there is no alternative democratic authority which could claim legitimacy. Furthermore, the undemocratic authority would need to be capable of remaining in power long enough: time would stabilise the situation. However, if the coup government is not effective, other circumstances need to be present in order to consider it as the authority capable of acting on behalf of the state. The latter would be the Malian case, whereby the terrorist threat prompted the UNSC, the African Union, and the international community to change approach and to recognise Traoré's government as the de jure government.

This conclusion warrants a word of caution. Decisions about recognising an entity as the government of a state and possibly intervening in its favour are ultimately political choices. While this chapter has attempted to provide a comprehensive systematisation of the international legal framework regulating interventions upon invitation and the related question of recognition of governments, it is undeniable that 'international law is structured to permit an area of discretion'.[180] It is within this area that different interests and political considerations play a decisive role.

[180] MJ Peterson, *Recognition of Governments: Legal Doctrine and State Practice, 1815–1995* (Palgrave MacMillan, 1997) 28.

5

Interventions in Favour of Governments Committing Gross and Systematic Violations of Human Rights and Humanitarian Law

I. PROTECTION OF INDIVIDUALS AND LEGITIMACY: FRAMING THE DISCUSSION

THE IDEA THAT the state ought to protect the people under its jurisdiction is not a new twentieth-century principle.[1] Already in the seventeenth century Grotius theorised that the prince loses 'the rights of independent sovereign' when he causes grievances to his own people.[2] During the following century, contract theorists propounded that ultimately the state exists for the benefit of its individuals. Locke described the relationship between the state and its population in terms of trust.[3] In the same vein, for Hobbes and Schmitt lawful authority is grounded on the capacity to guarantee protection to the population.[4] More recently, an analogous approach was adopted by the Swiss arbitrator Max Huber in the *Palmas* award (1929), where he stated that the obligation to protect individuals is a corollary to sovereignty.[5] The idea underlying these approaches is that states have never been completely free to act as they please within their territory.[6]

Although the roots of states' obligation to protect the people under their jurisdiction are grounded in the works of the founders of international law, it was only in the twentieth century that protection of individuals gained momentum. With the codification of human rights, this principle entered the realm of

[1] C Stahn, 'Responsibility To Protect: Political Rhetoric or Emerging Legal Norm?' (2007) 101(1) *American Journal of International Law* 111.

[2] H Grotius in R Tuck (ed), *De Jure Belli ac Pacis* (Liberty Fund, 2005) II, XXV, §8.

[3] J Locke, 'The Second Treatise on Civil Government' in T Laslet (ed), *Two Treatises on Government* (Cambridge University Press, 1988) ch. XIII, §149.

[4] A Orford, *International Authority and the Responsibility to Protect* (Cambridge University Press, 2011) 109; A Peters, 'Humanity as the Alfa and Omega of Sovereignty' (2009) 20(3) *European Journal of International Law* 525.

[5] Permanent Court of Arbitration, *Island of Palmas*, 4 April 1928 (M Huber), XI RIAA 831.

[6] Stahn (n 1) 112.

international law.[7] A good example is provided by IHL. While the Hague Conventions adopted in 1899 and 1907 do not explicitly mention the protection of civilians in armed conflicts, the Geneva Conventions (GC) identify the protection of civilians as the cornerstone of IHL.[8] Furthermore, the very language used to refer to this field of law has changed from 'the law of armed conflict' and 'the law of war' to 'international humanitarian law'.[9] The International Criminal Tribunal for the former Yugoslavia acknowledged this evolution in a well-known passage, where it stated that:

> A State-sovereignty-oriented approach has been gradually supplanted by a human-being-oriented approach. Gradually the maxim of Roman law *hominum causa omne jus constitutum est* (all law is created for the benefit of human beings) has gained a firm foothold in the international community as well.[10]

The evolution of international criminal law (ICL) and the creation of the International Criminal Court (ICC) and ad hoc tribunals such as the ICTY and the International Criminal Tribunal for Rwanda (ICTR) are further signs of the central role played by the principle of protection, inasmuch as ICL targets crimes committed against individuals.[11]

In the 1990s, the heinous violence that affected Somalia, Rwanda, and Kosovo put the principle of protection at the centre of the international debate on the duties and responsibilities of states towards their own people.[12] At the same time, the failure of the international community in halting the genocide in Rwanda and NATO's intervention in Kosovo triggered an enduring debate on the means to protect the population, in particular on the legality of unilateral humanitarian interventions. The responsibility to protect (R2P) emerged from this backdrop. As elaborated by the UN, the R2P doctrine has two dimensions. At the domestic level, each state bears the primary responsibility to protect the population under its jurisdiction. However, if the state is unwilling or unable

[7] S Breau, *The Responsibility to Protect in International Law: An Emerging Paradigm Shift* (Routledge, 2016) 92–121.

[8] See Convention (I) for the Amelioration of the Condition of the Wounded and Sick in Armed Forces in the Field 1949; Convention (II) for the Amelioration of the Condition of Wounded, Sick and Shipwrecked Members of Armed Forces at Sea 1949; Convention (III) relative to the Treatment of Prisoners of War 1949; Convention (IV) relative to the Protection of Civilian Persons in Time of War 1949.

[9] Although 'international humanitarian law' was at first used to indicate only the four 1949 Geneva Conventions, now it increasingly refers to the entire law of armed conflicts. See T Meron, 'The Humanization of Humanitarian Law' (2000) 94(2) *American Journal of International Law* 239.

[10] ICTY, *Prosecutor v Tadic, Decision on the Defence Motion for Interlocutory Appeal on Jurisdiction*, IT-94-1, 2 October 1995, §97. See also R Schütte, *Civilian Protection in Armed Conflicts: Evolution, Challenges and Implementation* (Springer, 2015) 135; B Von Tigerstrom, *Human Security and International Law: Prospects and Problems* (Hart Publishing, 2007) 67; EJ Criddle and E Fox-Decent, *Fiduciaries of Humanity: How International Law Constitutes Authority* (Oxford University Press, 2016) 207.

[11] E Lieblich, *International Law and Civil Wars: Intervention and Consent* (Routledge, 2013) 175.

[12] ibid, 176.

to fulfil its obligation, the responsibility to protect is shared with the international community.[13] While the latter aspect has raised criticisms and animated debates, the domestic dimension of R2P has never been questioned and is well-established in the current legal framework. Indeed, human rights law and IHL create a network of principles and guarantees that prevent states from taking advantage of their sovereignty to violate the rights of the people under their jurisdiction.[14]

These legal developments, which see the respect of human rights as an integral component of sovereignty, confirm that the protection of individuals has become a cornerstone of the international legal order. Although this development is unquestioned per se, it raises numerous fundamental questions,[15] in particular as to the consequences faced by governments that commit gross and systematic violations of human rights and humanitarian law against their own populations.[16] Over the past years, a number of states claimed that the Libyan and Syrian governments lost their legitimacy due to the heinous crimes committed against their own people. What does this mean in practice? Does it affect the governmental capacity to ask for foreign intervention to quell the rebellion? Are we witnessing the emergence of a new international rule? This chapter seeks to answer these and related questions.

II. ILLEGITIMATE GOVERNMENTS AND THE QUESTION OF CONSENT POWER

A. Gross and Systematic Violations of Human Rights and Humanitarian Law as a Parameter to Assess Governmental Legitimacy

In the previous chapter we have seen that the legitimacy of origin has a qualification function, inasmuch as it helps identify the government that is capable of speaking on behalf of the state. State practice shows that a democratic government, endorsed by free and fair elections, is generally recognised by the

[13] A/RES/60/1, 24 October 2005, *2005 World Summit Outcome*, §§138–39. The World Summit Outcome limits the scope of R2P to genocide, war crimes, ethnic cleansing and crimes against humanity.

[14] L Boisson de Chazournes and L Condorelli, 'De la "Responsabilité de Protéger", ou d'une Nouvelle Parure pour une Notion déjà Bien Établie Reference' (2006) 110(1) *Revue générale de droit international public* 13; Stahn (n 1) 112.

[15] TG Weiss, 'RtoP Alive and Well after Libya' (2011) 25(3) *Ethics & International Affairs* 292.

[16] The concept of 'gross and systematic violations of human rights' is not clearly defined under international law. The Vienna Declaration and Programme of Action, adopted by the World Conference on Human Rights (25 June 1993), at §30 propounds an illustrative list of human rights which may fall within the scope of the term: 'dismay and condemnation that gross and systematic violations and situations that constitute serious obstacles to the full enjoyment of all human rights continue to occur in different parts of the world. Such violations and obstacles include, as well as torture and cruel, inhuman and degrading treatment or punishment, summary and arbitrary executions, disappearances, arbitrary detentions, all forms of racism, racial discrimination and

international community even if it has never been effective, and even if a concurrent, de facto authority exercises effective control over territory and population. Nevertheless, state practice also shows that numerous undemocratic governments do not see their legitimacy questioned in the international arena. In these cases, the legitimacy would stem from the absence of a democratic alternative and obedience from the bulk of the population. However, this is not the end of the story: the way in which power is exercised could be the basis for disqualifying a government that was considered legitimate. The legitimacy of governments is intermittently tested and 'there are constant patterns as to whether and how this happens'.[17] Interventions upon invitation are surely among the cases when the question of legitimacy arises,[18] as is well-illustrated by recent state practice in Libya and Syria.

In February 2011, during the Arab Spring movement, peaceful anti-government demonstrations started in Libya. Protesters called for social reforms and for ending the 41-year-long regime of President Muammar Gaddafi.[19] The government was keen to prevent mass protests and reacted by arresting the persons involved in the organisation of such actions. However, these attempts triggered new, larger demonstrations. Libyan authorities thus adopted more violent forms of reaction and the situation quickly escalated: on 20 February mass demonstrations broke out in Tripoli, 'with scenes of both government use of significant force and protestors attacking governments buildings'.[20] By the end of February, the situation reached the threshold of intensity of a NIAC, with protestors controlling Tobruk, Benghazi, Misrata and Zuwarah.[21]

On 26 February 2011, the United Nations Security Council adopted Resolution 1970, where it condemned violence against civilians, imposed sanctions on the Gaddafi regime, and referred the situation to the ICC.[22] The same day, US President Barack Obama commented on the use of force by Gaddafi: 'when a leader's only means of staying in power is to use mass violence against his own people, he has lost the legitimacy to rule'.[23] Two days later, the UK's

apartheid, foreign occupation and alien domination, xenophobia, poverty, hunger and other denials of economic, social and cultural rights, religious intolerance, terrorism, discrimination against women and lack of the rule of law'. See LF Damrosch, 'Gross and Systematic Human Rights Violations' in *Max Planck Encyclopedia of Public International Law* (Oxford University Press, 2011) §10.

[17] J d'Aspremont, 'Regimes' Legitimacy Crises in International Law: Libya, Syria, and their Competing Representatives' in R Grote and TJ Röder (eds), *Constitutionalism, Human Rights, and Islam after the Arab Spring* (Oxford University Press, 2016) 58.

[18] J d'Aspremont, 'Legitimacy of Governments in the Age of Democracy' (2006) 38(4) *New York University Journal of International Law and Politics* 910.

[19] Human Rights Council, Report of the International Commission of Inquiry to investigate all alleged violations of international human rights law in the Libyan Arab Jamahiriya, 1 June 2011, A/HRC/17/44, §36.

[20] ibid, §38.

[21] ibid, §§38–9.

[22] S/RES/1970 (2011), 26 February 2011.

[23] The White House, Office of the Press Secretary, 'Readout of President Obama's Call with Chancellor Angela Merkel of Germany' (26 February 2011), available at obamawhitehouse.archives.gov/the-press-office/2011/02/26/readout-president-obamas-call-chancellor-angela-merkel-germany.

Prime Minister David Cameron commented: '[i]t is clear that this is an illegitimate regime that has lost the consent of its people'.[24] In March 2011, the G8 issued a statement where it claimed that: 'Gaddafi and the Libyan government have failed to fulfil their responsibility to protect the Libyan population and have lost all legitimacy. ... He must go.'[25] By June 2011, numerous countries had defined Gaddafi's government as illegitimate and had recognised the National Transitional Council (NTC), the leading authority of the opposition group, as the representative of Libyan people.[26]

Similar events took place in Syria. In March 2011, pro-democratic demonstrations erupted in Deraa. The government responded with fire, killing several people who took part in the demonstrations. The episode triggered protests in the whole country, which were quelled by state forces. The Independent International Commission of Inquiry on the Syrian Arab Republic considered that the excessive use of force and other human rights violations committed by the government amounted to crimes against humanity.[27] By July 2012, the violence had escalated and reached the threshold of a NIAC,[28] while the humanitarian situation dramatically deteriorated due to the commission of grave human rights violations, war crimes, and crimes against humanity.[29] On 3 October 2011, the Syrian opposition forces formed the Syrian National Council (SNC), an 'opposition umbrella group' that was then replaced by the Syrian Opposition Coalition (SOC), which had the aim of overthrowing President Assad.[30]

Following the widespread human rights and humanitarian law violations committed by the government, several countries declared that Assad could no longer be considered as the legitimate representative of his own people, while the SOC was increasingly seen as a credible alternative to the regime.[31] Notably, US President Obama declared that Assad's regime lost legitimacy due to a 'sustained onslaught' against the population.[32] In the same vein, in August 2011 the UK, France, and Germany declared that: '[o]ur three countries believe that President

[24] BBC Staff, 'Libya: David Cameron urges Gaddafi to "go now"' (*BBC*, 28 February 2011), available at www.bbc.com/news/av/uk-politics-12601851.

[25] BBC Staff, 'G8: Libya's Gaddafi "should go", say world leaders' (*BBC*, 27 May 2011), available at www.bbc.com/news/world-africa-13572830.

[26] S Talmon, 'Recognition of the Libyan National Transitional Council Recognition of the Libyan' (2011) 15(16) *ASIL insights*.

[27] Human Rights Council, Report of the Independent International Commission of Inquiry on the Syrian Arab Republic, 23 November 2011, A/HRC/S-17/2/Add.1.

[28] Human Rights Council, Report of the Independent International Commission of Inquiry on the Syrian Arab Republic, 5 February 2013, A/HRC/22/59, at 1.

[29] ibid, §1.

[30] S Talmon, 'Recognition of Opposition Groups as the Legitimate Representative of a People' (2013) 12(2) *Chinese Journal of International Law* 220; BBC Staff, 'Syria: The story of the conflict' (*BBC*, 11 March 2016), available at www.bbc.com/news/world-middle-east-26116868.

[31] BBC Staff, 'Syria conflict: UK recognizes opposition, says William Hague' (*BBC*, 20 November 2012), available at www.bbc.com/news/uk-politics-20406562.

[32] C McGreal and M Chulov, 'Syria: Assad must resign, says Obama' (*The Guardian*, 19 August 2011), available at www.theguardian.com/world/2011/aug/18/syria-assad-must-resign-obama.

Assad, who is resorting to brutal military force against his own people and who is responsible for the situation, has lost all legitimacy and can no longer claim to lead the country. We call on him … to step aside'.[33] The same month, during a debate at the Human Rights Council, Bulgaria affirmed that: '[d]espite outstanding efforts by many international mediators, the Syrian regime has continued with the policy of repression rather than dialogue, leading to a loss of legitimacy nationally and internationally'.[34]

Similar positions were affirmed more recently. For instance, US Presidential Press Secretary Josh Earnest declared that: 'Bashar al-Assad has lost legitimacy to lead that country; that, moving forward, it is impossible to imagine the country of Syria coming together and being led by a tyrant that has used the military might of the country to attack his own people.'[35] Analogous considerations were put forward at the UN level. In 2012, former UN Secretary General Ban Ki-moon maintained that: '[f]or many months, it has been evident that President Assad and his Government have lost all legitimacy'.[36] Similarly, while resigning from the position of special envoy for the United Nations and League of Arab States for Syria, Kofi Annan declared that: 'the current government has lost all legitimacy'.[37]

The Libyan and Syrian cases would show the emergence of a new narrative, whereby governments that commit gross and systematic violations of human rights and humanitarian law cease to be considered legitimate representatives of their own people,[38] while this qualification is attributed to the opposition groups.[39] However, the new narrative on governmental legitimacy did not lead to the formal withdrawal of recognition of Assad or Gaddafi's governments per se.[40] Rather, by considering them as illegitimate and not representative

[33] 'Joint UK, French and German Statement on Syria' (18 August 2011), available at www.gov.uk/government/news/joint-uk-french-and-german-statement-on-syria.

[34] OHCHR, 'Statement of Bulgaria at the Human Rights Council debates situation of human rights in Syrian Arab Republic in Special Session' (22 August 2011).

[35] The White House, Office of the Press Secretary, Press Briefing by Press Secretary Josh Earnest, (23 September 2016), available at obamawhitehouse.archives.gov/the-press-office/2016/09/23/press-briefing-press-secretary-josh-earnest-9232016.

[36] New York, Secretary-General's remarks to the General Assembly on the situation in Syria (7 June 2012), available at www.un.org/sg/en/content/sg/statement/2012-06-07/secretary-generals-remarks-general-assembly-situation-syria.

[37] Kofi Annan, 'My Departing Advice on How to Save Syria' (*Financial Times*, 2 August 2012), available at www.ft.com/content/b00b6ed4-dbc9-11e1-8d78-00144feab49a?mhq5j=e1.

[38] d'Aspremont (n 18) 908.

[39] For instance, UK Foreign Secretary William Hague informed the Parliament that: '[i]n line with our assessment of the NTC as the legitimate interlocutor in Libya representing the aspirations of the Libyan people, the Government has invited the NTC to establish an office in the UK. This will enhance our existing relationship with the NTC, and better enable us to fulfil our commitment to protect civilians under threat of attack from the Qadhafi regime. … This arrangement does not affect our position on the legal status of the NTC: the British Government will continue to recognise States, not Governments'. See Talmon (n 30) 237–39.

[40] The government of Gaddafi was de-recognised only in April 2011, when the National Transitional Council was recognised as the new government of Libya. On the other hand, Assad's government is still recognised by the international community, although it is largely considered illegitimate. See d'Aspremont (n 17) 60.

of their own people, it introduced a form short of withdrawal of recognition of governments.[41] Consequently, recognition appears to be an 'incremental process'.[42] First, the government is defined as the illegitimate representative of its own people; at the same time, the opposition group is granted this legitimacy. Second, states may withdraw the recognition of the incumbent government and recognise the rebels in this capacity.[43]

The analysis conducted so far would confirm the disqualifying character of the legitimacy of exercise. As aforementioned, governmental legitimacy is assessed on the basis of the way in which power is obtained (legitimacy of origin) and the way in which it is exercised (legitimacy of exercise).[44] The idea that governments overwhelmingly recognised by the international community could lose their legitimacy when they use excessive force against their own people reflects the pivotal importance of the protection of individuals in international law. If we accept that sovereign states bear an obligation to protect the people under their jurisdiction and to ensure respect of their basic human rights,[45] it seems reasonable to conclude that the violation of this paramount obligation leads to a loss of legitimacy. Against this conclusion, it might be objected that the withdrawal of recognition as the legitimate representative of the people is substantially a political evaluation. Indeed, it is not coincidental that the bulk of the states that defined Gaddafi and Assad as illegitimate share the same political view, while Russia and China did not proceed to de-recognise the Libyan or Syrian governments. However, as we shall see, the loss of legitimacy is not void of legal consequences.[46] The next section is devoted to assessing the extent of its effects in the international law sphere.

B. Loss of Legitimacy and Its Effects on Consent Power

The events that took place in the context of the Arab Spring suggest that a government which commits gross and systematic violations of human rights and humanitarian law against its own population loses its legitimacy as being representative of its people, and that this could lead to the withdrawal of recognition as the government *tout court*. In parallel, opposition groups have been granted the title of legitimate representatives, and in the case of Libya of the de jure government. While Part III of this work focuses on the incremental recognition of non-state actors, this section analyses the effects of this new practice on governmental powers, in particular with regard to interventions upon

[41] ibid, 68.
[42] Talmon (n 30) 230.
[43] ibid. See also d'Aspremont (n 17) 57.
[44] See ch 4.
[45] Peters (n 4) 524–25.
[46] d'Aspremont (n 17) 58.

invitation.[47] Does an illegitimate government forfeit the right to ask for foreign intervention?

We have seen that part of the scholarship argues in favour of a duty to abstain from intervening in civil wars based on the principle of non-intervention and the right to self-determination, and that this position does not stand the test of state practice.[48] Although the possibility to intervene in internal conflicts upon invitation has never been contested per se, this does not imply that the right to ask for foreign intervention is unlimited. Notably, over the last two decades there has been a growing hesitation by states to intervene in favour of governments that commit serious violations of human rights and humanitarian law.[49] One good example is provided by France's practice: while it has a consistent tradition of military interference in internal conflicts taking place in former colonies, it has tended not to interfere in favour of governments that forfeited their legitimacy of exercise. For instance, Jean-Bédel Bokassa's invitation to intervene in the Central African Republic (1979) and Laurent Gbagbo's request for help in Ivory Coast (2002) were dismissed by France due to widespread violations of human rights committed by their governments in order to repress the insurgencies.[50] Georg Nolte interpreted state practice in these terms:

> It would not seem the case that States have made the claim that a government was precluded from inviting foreign troops because of that government's policy of systematic human rights violations. Yet, third States avoid interventions based on the invitation of governments, which have acted in gross defiance of human rights in the recent past or at least they avoid placing reliance on the invitation of such a government.[51]

The developments in Syria seem to go in this direction, although they do not provide a conclusive answer. Since September 2014, US and Arab forces have conducted airborne military operations against Daesh in Syria.[52] In October 2015, other Western states joined the coalition, such as the UK, France, Canada, and Australia.[53] The choice of the US to rely on collective self-defence in favour of Iraq as a legal basis for its intervention is particularly interesting:[54] while the Syrian government invited the US to use force on its soil in

[47] Lieblich (n 11); C Kreß, 'Major Post-Westphalian Shifts and Some Important Neo-Westphalian Hesitations in the State Practice on the International Law on The Use of Force' (2014) 1(1) *Journal on the Use of Force and International Law* 11–54.

[48] See ch 3.

[49] Kreß (n 47) 20; RB Choquette, 'A Rebuttable Presumption Against Consensual Nondemocratic Intervention' (2015) 55(1) *Columbia Journal of Transnational Law* 138–77.

[50] d'Aspremont (n 18) 907.

[51] G Nolte, *Eingreifen auf Einladung* (Springer, 1999) 578–79, trans, quoted in Kreß (n 47) 21.

[52] E Cooper and E Schmit, 'Airstrikes by U.S. and Allies Hit ISIS Targets in Syria' (*The New York Times*, 22 September 2014), available at www.nytimes.com/2014/09/23/world/middleeast/us-and-allies-hit-isis-targets-in-syria.html?_r=0.

[53] R Van Steenberghe, 'From Passive Consent to Self-Defence after the Syrian Protest against the US-led Coalition' (*EJIL: Talk!*, 2015), available at www.ejiltalk.org/13758-2/.

[54] See Letter dated 23 September 2014 from the Permanent Representative of the United States of America to the United Nations addressed to the Secretary-General, S/2014/695, 23 September 2014.

the form of a coordinated action against ISIS (Islamic State in Iraq and Syria), then-President Obama ruled out such a possibility and refused to accept the invitation.[55] It has been noted that this decision can be explained in political terms: joining forces with the Syrian government would put the US and Assad on the same side of the conflict and it is intuitive why President Obama wanted to avoid this scenario. The question is whether the US decision could have legal implications. From a legal standpoint, accepting Assad's invitation could amount to aiding and assisting the Syrian government in the commission of serious violations of fundamental rights. Would it be possible to go as far as positing that a state loses its power to consent to foreign interventions when it commits widespread violations of human rights and humanitarian law against its own people?

The Syrian case does not seem conclusive on this point.[56] On the one hand, states that withdrew their recognition of the Syrian government as the legitimate representative of its own people, such as the US, have refused to intervene in favour of or to collaborate with Assad in order to fight ISIS. On the other hand, Russia has been maintaining friendly relations with Assad's regime, to the point that it intervened on his side. While initially the aid was limited to the provision of arms, in 2015 it turned into direct military assistance.[57] The legal basis provided by Russia to justify the intervention was the invitation of the Syrian President. The governments of France, Germany, Qatar, Saudi Arabia, Turkey, the UK and the US issued a joint declaration in which they expressed their 'deep concern with regard to the Russian military build-up in Syria'.[58] A similar declaration was issued by the North Atlantic Council.[59] Interestingly, none of these statements expressed the view that the intervention was unlawful due to the illegitimacy of Assad's regime. On the one hand, these instances

[55] A Gearan, 'U.S. Rules Out Coordinating with Assad on Airstrikes against Islamists in Syria' (*The Washington Post*, 26 August 2014), available at www.washingtonpost.com/world/national-security/us-rules-out-coordinating-with-assad-on-airstrikes-against-islamists-in-syria/2014/08/26/cda02e0e-2d2e-11e4-9b98-848790384093_story.html?utm_term=.8996c69d59fa. Although the US turned down the invitation by Assad's government and justified its intervention of invoking Article 51 of the UN Charter, initially Syrian authorities did not criticise US intervention on their territory. However, the position changed in September 2015, when the Syrian government issued two letters which specified that: '[i]f any State invokes the excuse of counter-terrorism in order to be present on Syrian territory without the consent of the Syrian Government whether on the country's land or in its airspace or territorial waters, its action shall be considered a violation of Syrian sovereignty'. See Identical letters dated 17 September 2015 from the Permanent Representative of the Syrian Arab Republic to the United Nations addressed to the Secretary-General and the President of the Security Council, S/2015/719, 21 September 2015. See also Van Steenberghe (n 53).

[56] See C Kreß, 'The Fine Line Between Collective Self-Defense and Intervention by Invitation: Reflections on the Use of Force against "IS" in Syria' (*Just Security*, 17 February 2015), available at www.justsecurity.org/20118/claus-kreb-force-isil-syria/.

[57] See eg BBC Staff, 'Syria conflict: Putin defends Russia's air strikes' (*BBC*, 12 October 2015), available at www.bbc.com/news/world-middle-east-34502286.

[58] See 'Joint declaration on recent military actions of the Russian Federation in Syria' (2 October 2015), available at www.gov.uk/government/news/joint-declaration-on-recent-military-actions-of-the-russian-federation-in-syria.

[59] See 'Statement by the North Atlantic Council on incursions into Turkey's airspace by Russian aircraft' (5 October 2015), available at www.nato.int/cps/en/natohq/news_123392.htm.

demonstrate a state's reluctance to deny consent power to a government that commits widespread violations of human rights and humanitarian law. On the other hand, at least part of the international community seems equally reluctant to explicitly affirm the existence of such rights. Nevertheless, if the practice of de-legitimisation of governments due to widespread violations of fundamental rights will affirm itself, it does not seem preposterous to imagine that the beleaguered government would forfeit its right to ask for foreign intervention.

III. LIMITATIONS TO THE POSSIBILITY TO INTERVENE IN FAVOUR OF GOVERNMENTS THAT COMMIT GROSS AND SYSTEMATIC VIOLATIONS OF HUMAN RIGHTS

As demonstrated in the previous section, in recent years a new trend has emerged, whereby governments that commit gross and systematic violations of human rights and IHL cease to be considered legitimate representatives of their own people. This circumstance has led scholars to wonder whether such governments can lawfully ask for foreign interventions. Although a positive answer may be undesirable, *de lege lata* it seems undeniable that illegitimate governments have the right to invite third countries to intervene in their favour. Nevertheless, this is not the end of the story: the current legal framework prevents states from assisting governments that commit gross and systematic violations of human rights and humanitarian law, at least under certain circumstances.

The issue has gained momentum during the Syrian conflict. It is well known that Russia and Iran have been providing weapons and other forms of military assistance to Assad. Furthermore, since September 2015 Russian military forces have been deployed in Syria to support the government more directly and concretely.[60] Russian intervention is expressly aimed at fighting ISIS and at targeting opposition groups.[61] A number of states maintain that Assad is no longer the legitimate representative of his own people, while this qualification is attributed to the opposition forces. His illegitimacy derives from the excessive and widespread use of force that the Syrian government has been exercising against the civilian population. This circumstance has raised some criticism against Russian and Iranian involvement in the conflict.[62] Furthermore, some

[60] T Eaton, 'Six Decisive Points that Changed Syria's War' (*BBC*, 15 March 2017), available at www.bbc.com/news/world-middle-east-39233357.

[61] I Rahman-Jones, 'Why Does Russia Support Syria and President Assad?' (*BBC*, 11 April 2017), available at www.bbc.co.uk/newsbeat/article/39554171/why-does-russia-support-syria-and-president-assad.

[62] For instance, the US criticised the supply of weapons by Russia to the Assad regime as follows: '[i]t is not technically, obviously, a violation of international law since there's not an arms embargo, but it's reprehensible that arms would continue to flow to a regime that is using such horrific and disproportionate force against its own people'. See Permanent Representative of the United States at the UN, Susan E Rice, quoted in S Lee Myers and D Goodman, 'Clinton Says Russian Inaction May Lead to Syrian Civil War' (*The New York Times*, 31 May 2012), available at www.nytimes.com/2012/06/01/world/middleeast/frustrated-clinton-says-russian-inaction-may-lead-to-syrian-civil-war.html?_r=0;

states adopted more concrete measures. For instance, in June 2012 the UK stopped in its territorial waters a Russian ship that was carrying weapons to Syria. After the British insurer Standard Club cancelled the ship's insurance, it returned to Russia.[63] Commenting on the episode, a spokesman of the Foreign and Commonwealth Office affirmed:

> We are aware of a ship carrying a consignment of refurbished Russian-made attack helicopters heading to Syria. We are working closely with international partners to ensure that we are doing all we can to stop the Syrian regime's ability to slaughter civilians being reinforced through assistance from other countries.[64]

A similar episode took place in Turkey, where a Russian flight carrying weapons to Syria was intercepted and sent back to Russia.[65] The crucial question is whether and under what conditions providing help and assistance to a government that commits gross and systematic violations of human rights and humanitarian law would constitute a breach of international law. This section will illustrate that the reasons why the supply of weapons and other assistance could be unlawful are twofold. First, the intervention could trigger the responsibility for aiding and assisting a state in the commission of wrongful acts. Second, the prohibition on providing assistance could derive from the duty to ensure respect of IHL.[66] These provisions will be discussed in turn.

A. Aiding and Assisting Violations of Human Rights and Humanitarian Law

Article 16 of the Draft Articles on State Responsibility sets out the distinction between lawful and prohibited forms of cooperation.[67] The norm provides that:

> A State which aids or assists another State in the commission of an internationally wrongful act by the latter is internationally responsible for doing so if:
>
> (a) that State does so with knowledge of the circumstances of the internationally wrongful act; and
> (b) the act would be internationally wrongful if committed by that State.

The responsibility for aiding and assisting is ancillary to the primary responsibility of the state that benefits from foreign help. Therefore, 'it may be assumed

see also Kreß (n 47) 30. As we shall see, this reasoning appears incorrect, inasmuch as it implies that providing weapons to a government that commits gross and systematic violations of human rights is always lawful, unless the UNSC imposes an arms embargo; see Lieblich (n 11) 153.

[63] Rahman-Jones (n 61).

[64] ibid. See also V Lanovoy, 'Complicity in an Internationally Wrongful Act' *SHARES Research Paper Series*, no. 38, 2014.

[65] ibid.

[66] The terms 'arm' and 'weapon' are used interchangeably in this chapter.

[67] At first the International Law Commission (ILC) used the term 'complicity'. However, this was criticised by ILC members as the term evokes a sense of participation in a criminal act. Therefore, the Commission adopted the more neutral notion of 'aid and assistance'. See Lanovoy (n 64) 4; A Clapham, 'On Complicity' in M Henzelin and R Roth (eds), *Le Droit pénal à l'épreuve de l'internationalisation* (Bruylant, 2001) 246.

that participation by aid entails a lesser degree of responsibility than equal participation in the wrongful act'.[68] When this provision was first discussed by the International Law Commission, it was considered 'a measure of progressive development' of international law. Nevertheless, it is now generally accepted that it has attained the status of customary law, as confirmed by the ICJ in the *Genocide* case.[69]

Aid and assistance are not defined by Article 16 nor by the ILC Commentary and are generally understood to encompass a broad variety of behaviour. Notably, with specific regard to interventions in internal conflicts, typical forms of aid and assistance may include the provision of weapons and other material aid, as well as 'logistical and technical assistance, and financial support'.[70] The scholarship is currently divided as to whether omissions could amount to *aid and assistance* and thus trigger a state's responsibility. The debate was fuelled by the *Genocide* case, where the ICJ held that: 'complicity always requires that some positive action has been taken to furnish aid or assistance to the perpetrators'.[71] While this position seems to reflect the majoritarian view among scholars,[72] it has been questioned by some authors. For instance, according to Lanovoy, 'any contribution insofar as it is clearly linked to the commission of the principal wrongful act would constitute aid or assistance. This arguably includes omissions'.[73] Similarly, Jackson affirms that:

> There is no good reason to exclude certain culpable omissions in the face of a specific duty from the ambit of responsibility for complicity. As a matter of basic usage, some

[68] B Graefrath, 'Complicity in the Law of International Responsibility' (1996) 2 *Revue belge de droit international* 380; H Moynihan, 'Aiding and Assisting: Challenges in Armed Conflict and Counterterrorism' (Chatham House Research Paper, Royal Institute of International Affairs, 2016) 7; V Lowe, 'Responsibility for the Conduct of Other States' (2002) 101 *Japanese Journal of International* 11.

[69] ICJ, *Application of the Convention on the Prevention and Punishment of the Crime of Genocide (Bosnia and Herzegovina v Serbia and Montenegro)*, Judgment (Merits), 26 February 2007, §417. See also HP Aust, *Complicity and the Law of State Responsibility* (Cambridge University Press, 2011) 97–191.

[70] Moynihan (n 68) 8. See also M Jackson, *Complicity in International Law* (Oxford University Press, 2015) 153; J Crawford, *State Responsibility: The General Part* (Cambridge University Press, 2013) 402; Aust (n 69) 239; Lowe (n 68) 5–6; Lanovoy (n 64) 9.

[71] *Genocide* case, §432.

[72] See eg Crawford (n 70) 403–05; Moynihan (n 68) 7; O Corten and P Klein, 'The Limits of Complicity as a Ground for Responsibility: Lessons Learned from the Corfu Channel Case' in K Bannelier, T Christakis and S Heathcote (eds), *The ICJ and the Evolution of International Law: The Enduring Impact of the "Corfu Channel" Case* (Routledge, 2011) 315–34. According to Corten and Klein, it is questionable whether the notion of complicity for omission is useful in practice, since it 'can always be substituted with the far more manageable concept of due diligence' (ibid, 332). Indeed, they argue, '[e]ither the notion of complicity is interpreted as requiring the establishment of a specific intention on the part of the accomplice, and it will therefore be far more convenient to turn to the concept of due diligence, which does not require such an element of intention. Or the notion of complicity is interpreted as not requiring the establishment of such a specific intention, but this notion then appears equivalent to – or could be even said to merge with – the concept of due diligence' (ibid, 331).

[73] Lanovoy (n 64) 15. See also Aust (n 70) 230; Lowe (n 68) 4.

> omissions do assist in the commission of wrongdoing. Moreover, some omissions are sufficiently wrongful as to link the omitting party to the ensuing harm.[74]

With specific regard to interventions in internal conflicts, complicity by omission could be envisaged when a state does not object to the use of its airspace, knowing that this will ultimately aid or assist the commission of internationally wrongful acts.[75] For instance, in September 2012 Iran started providing weapons and other military equipment to Syria, flying over Iraqi airspace in the process. A number of countries expressed their concern and pressed Iraq to shut down the air corridor.[76] Surely Iraq could have adopted several measures to prevent weapons from reaching Syria, such as imposing on flights from Iran toward Syria an inspection in Baghdad, or denying access to the airspace to Iranian flights altogether.[77] However, from a legal point of view it is unclear whether Iraq's omission would amount to aiding and assisting. Indeed, the responsibility for complicity – be it by action or omission – is triggered only under certain specific circumstances.

The ILC Commentary to the Draft Articles on State Responsibility identifies three cumulative conditions that trigger the responsibility for aiding and assisting an internationally wrongful act:

> First, the relevant State organ or agency providing aid or assistance must be aware of the circumstances making the conduct of the assisted State internationally wrongful; secondly, the aid or assistance must be given with a view to facilitating the commission of that act, and must actually do so; and thirdly, the completed act must be such that it would have been wrongful had it been committed by the assisting State itself.[78]

The double obligation requirement is intuitive and overwhelmingly accepted by scholars. In practice, the violation of a rule of customary law will automatically trigger also the responsibility for aid and assistance, provided that the other requirements are met. As for treaty law, the application of Article 16 would be limited to cases where both parties are bound by the provision of the convention.[79]

With regard to the nexus between the aid provided and the commission of a wrongful act, the ILC Commentary specifies that it is not necessary 'that the aid or assistance should have been essential to the performance of the internationally wrongful act; it is sufficient if it contributed significantly to that act'.[80] The aim is to set a *de minimis* threshold, below which no responsibility is created. Any help that is 'remotely or indirectly related to an internationally wrongful

[74] Jackson (n 70) 13.
[75] Lanovoy (n 64) 13.
[76] MR Gordon, 'Iran Supplying Syrian Military via Iraqi Airspace' (*The New York Times*, 4 September 2012), available at www.nytimes.com/2012/09/05/world/middleeast/iran-supplying-syrian-military-via-iraq-airspace.html.
[77] ibid.
[78] ILC Draft Articles on State Responsibility, Commentary, Article 16, at 66, §3.
[79] Moynihan (n 68) 10; Jackson (n 70) 162.
[80] ILC Draft Articles on State Responsibility, Commentary, at 66, §5.

act'[81] would thus be excluded from the scope of Article 16. On the other hand, if the involvement of the state is particularly significant, the assistance could turn into joint responsibility for the commission of the act. Lowe suggested that the relevant nexus would qualify as 'material facilitation' of the commission of the wrongful act.[82] In case of military intervention in internal conflicts, a typical example would be supplying arms that will be used to violate human rights and humanitarian law.[83]

The mental requirement is the most controversial. Article 16 requires that the state provides aid or assistance 'with the knowledge of the circumstances of the internationally wrongful act'.[84] On the other hand, the ILC Commentary specifies that 'aid or assistance must be given with a view to facilitating the commission of the wrongful act'[85] and that '[a] State is not responsible for aid or assistance under article 16 unless the relevant State organ intended, by the aid or assistance given, to facilitate the occurrence of the wrongful conduct'.[86]

The discrepancy between the mental element required by Article 16 – ie, knowledge – and the one requested by the ILC Commentary – ie, intent – has gripped the scholarship for a long time. On the one hand, some authors affirm that Article 16 should be read in light of the ILC Commentary, and thus conclude that the intent requirement is necessary to trigger the responsibility of the state for aiding and assisting another country in the commission of a wrongful act.[87] Nolte and Aust propound that the knowledge requirement is too broad: the mental element should be limited to intent in order 'not to discourage many typical forms of international cooperation which, on the whole, have more beneficial than adverse effects'.[88] Similarly, Crawford maintains that the scope of application of Article 16 should only cover cases where the aid or assistance was provided with the intent to help the recipient country to commit the wrongful act.[89]

In a recent research paper, Moynihan suggests that both intent and knowledge are necessary parts of Article 16, but explains that 'the disagreement between those who require only knowledge and those who also require intent is of little practical effect'.[90] Her reasoning starts by analysing the meaning of

[81] G Nolte and HP Aust, 'Equivocal Helpers – Complicit States, Mixed Messages and International Law' (2009) 58(1) *International and Comparative Law Quarterly* 10. See also Lowe (n 68) 5; see *contra*: S Talmon, 'A Plurality of Responsible Actors? International Responsibility for Acts of the Coalition Provisional Authority in Iraq' in P Shiner and A Williams (eds), *The Iraq War and International Law* (Hart Publishing, 2008) 185–230.
10. See also Lowe (n 68) 5.

[82] ibid.

[83] Jackson (n 70) 159; Moynihan (n 68) 9; Lowe (n 68) 5.

[84] Draft Articles on State Responsibility, Art 16(a).

[85] ILC Draft Articles on State Responsibility, Commentary, at 66, §1.

[86] ibid, §5.

[87] T Ruys, 'Of Arms, Funding and "Non-Lethal Assistance" – Issues Surrounding Third State Intervention in the Syrian Civil War' (2014) 13(1) *Chinese Journal of International Law* 22–25, 28.

[88] Nolte and Aust (n 81) 15.

[89] Crawford (n 70) 408.

[90] Moynihan (n 68) 21.

intent, which is not specified in the ILC Commentary. By using the definition of intent provided by Article 30(2) of the Statute to the International Criminal Court,[91] she concludes that 'the assisting state has the necessary intent if either its purpose in acting is to facilitate the recipient state's unlawful act, or it knows or is virtually certain that State B will act unlawfully in the ordinary course of events'.[92] The latter scenario would sensibly reduce the distance between intent and knowledge: if intent is equated to 'actual or near-certain knowledge of illegality', the intent threshold is met even when the state did not have the purpose of aiding the commission of the wrongful act.[93]

At the other end of the spectrum, numerous authors propound that the knowledge requirement is sufficient for the purpose of Article 16. This seems now to be the majoritarian position and finds confirmation in the *Genocide* case, where the ICJ affirmed that responsibility for aid or assistance at least requires knowledge.[94] This conclusion seems preferable for two reasons. First, it is in line with the general framework on state responsibility established by the Draft Articles on State Responsibility. Indeed, the ILC Commentary to Article 2 of the Draft Articles maintains that:

> A related question is whether fault constitutes a necessary element of the internationally wrongful act of a State. This is certainly not the case if by 'fault' one understands the existence, for example, of an intention to harm. In the absence of any specific requirement of a mental element in terms of the primary obligation, it is only the act of a State that matters, *independently of any intention*.[95]

Second, on a practical level it is nearly impossible to prove the specific purpose of the state in aiding and assisting another country. Therefore, knowledge should be sufficient for the purpose of Article 16. As for the actual meaning of knowledge, it has been suggested – correctly, in the author's view – that:

> [It] depends in part on the type of wrongful act in question. Some wrongful acts can occur with no intent at all (strict liability), others may require standards of due diligence, while a third category may have specific intent requirements (e.g. genocide).[96]

[91] Rome Statute to the International Criminal Court 1998, Art 30(2) reads as follows: '[a] person has intent where: (a) in relation to conduct, that person means to engage in the conduct; (b) in relation to a consequence, that person means to cause that consequence or is aware that it will occur in the ordinary course of events'.

[92] Moynihan (n 68) 20.

[93] ibid, 21–22.

[94] *Genocide* case, §421. See eg Graefrath (n 68) 375, who affirmed that: '[i]t seems highly questionable that such a narrow interpretation of intent as a decisive criterion for complicity is really useful'. Similarly, Lanovoy propounds that '[k]nowledge of the circumstances of the wrongful act thus appears to be a more objective and practical test than the requirement of intent'. See Lanovoy (n 64) 20. See also Jackson (n 70) 161; A Bellal, 'Arms Transfers and International Human Rights Law' in S Casey-Maslen (ed), *Weapons Under International Human Rights Law* (Cambridge University Press, 2014) 453.

[95] J Crawford, *The International Law Commission's Articles on State Responsibility: Introduction, Text and Commentaries* (Cambridge University Press, 2002) 84, §10.

[96] A Clapham, 'Article 6. Prohibitions' in S Casey-Maslen, A Clapham, G Giacca and S Parker (eds), *The Arms Trade Treaty: A Commentary* (Oxford University Press, 2016) 177–243, §6.86.

The mental element is less stringent for breaches of peremptory norms. Article 41 of the Draft Articles on State Responsibility provides that:

> States shall cooperate to bring to an end through lawful means any serious breach within the meaning of article 40.
>
> No State shall recognize as lawful a situation created by a serious breach within the meaning of article 40, nor render aid or assistance in maintaining that situation.
>
> This article is without prejudice to the other consequences referred to in this Part and to such further consequences that a breach to which this Chapter applies may entail under international law.

Although there are doubts as to whether the norm has attained customary status, it is surely stronger than Article 16 inasmuch as it does not require a state's knowledge or intent.[97] The reasons for this circumstance were explained by the ILC in its commentary, where it clarified that 'it is hardly conceivable that a State would not have notice of the commission of a serious breach by another State'.[98] A further difference between Article 16 and 41 is that the latter refers to aiding and assisting in maintaining the situation. Therefore, the help operates after the fact and would not be directed at the commission of the violation, but at the maintenance of the breach.[99]

B. Obligation to Ensure Respect for International Humanitarian Law

Article 1 common to the four Geneva Conventions establishes the obligation to 'respect and to ensure respect' for IHL. The same provision is reaffirmed in Article 1(1) of Additional Protocol I to the Geneva Conventions (AP I).[100] Similarly, Article 38 of the 1989 Convention on the Rights of the Child affirms that: 'States Parties undertake to respect and ensure respect for rules of international humanitarian law applicable to them in armed conflicts which are relevant to the child'.[101] In the *Nicaragua* case, the ICJ specified that this obligation 'does not derive only from the [Geneva] Conventions themselves, but from the general principles of humanitarian law to which the Conventions merely give specific expression'.[102] The ICRC Study on Customary Law confirmed this point whereby it clarified that the duty to respect and ensure respect of the law of armed conflicts has attained customary status and applies during both international and non-international armed conflicts.[103]

[97] Moynihan (n 68) 23; Ruys (n 87) 25.

[98] ILC Draft Articles on State Responsibility, Commentary, at 115, §11.

[99] Moynihan (n 68) 23.

[100] Protocol Additional to the Geneva Conventions of 12 August 1949, and relating to the Protection of Victims of International Armed Conflicts (Protocol I), 8 June 1977, Art 1.

[101] Convention on the Rights of the Child, Art 38, §1.

[102] ICJ, *Military and Paramilitary Activities in and against Nicaragua, (Nicaragua v United States of America)*, Judgment (Merits), 27 June 1986, §220.

[103] J-M Henckaerts and L Doswald-Beck, *Customary International Humanitarian Law*, vol I (Cambridge University Press, 2003) 509. See also M Brehm, 'The Arms Trade and States' Duty to

The personal scope of application of the duty to ensure respect for IHL extends to every state party to the Geneva Conventions. This was confirmed by the ICJ in the *Nicaragua* case, where the Court found that the US violated Common Article 1 of the Geneva Conventions by producing and disseminating among Nicaraguan opposition groups a military manual containing techniques contrary to IHL. The ICJ found that such action amounts to a breach of the 'obligation not to encourage persons or groups engaged in the conflict in Nicaragua to act in violation of the provisions of Article 3 common to the four 1949 Geneva Conventions'.[104] Nearly 20 years later, in the *Wall* Advisory Opinion, the ICJ affirmed that: 'all the States parties to the Geneva Convention … are under an obligation … to ensure compliance by Israel with international humanitarian law'.[105] Moreover, the Court clarified that the obligation to ensure respect for IHL applies to every state party to the Geneva Convention, 'whether or not it is a party to a specific conflict'.[106]

The most controversial aspect of the duty to ensure respect for IHL regards its material scope of application. The scholarship is currently divided. On the one hand, some authors adopt a broad interpretative approach and conclude that states have a positive duty to react to and adopt measures against violations of IHL.[107] On the other hand, scholars in favour of a restrictive approach propound that states hold a negative obligation, but 'it is doubtful that the obligation to ensure compliance with the Fourth Geneva Convention extends so far as to require any positive action on the part of individual States'.[108] The bulk of the discussion hence focuses on whether states have a duty to adopt positive steps to ensure respect of IHL. However, such a debate is not relevant to addressing the object of our investigation, namely whether foreign interventions in favour of states that engage in violations of IHL amount to breaches

Ensure Respect for Humanitarian and Human Rights Law' (2008) 12(3) *Journal of Conflict and Security Law* 372.

[104] *Nicaragua* case, §220. See also O Corten and V Koutroulis, 'The Illegality of Military Support to Rebels in the Libyan War: Aspects of *Jus contra Bellum* and *Jus in Bello*' (2013) 18(1) *Journal of Conflict and Security Law* 79.

[105] ICJ, *Legal Consequences of the Construction of a Wall in the Occupied Palestinian Territory*, Advisory Opinion, 9 July 2004, §159. See also Corten and Koutroulis (n 104) 83.

[106] ibid, §158.

[107] See eg JS Pictet, *Geneva Convention for the Amelioration of the Condition of the Wounded and Sick in Armed Forces in the Field: Commentary* (ICRC 1952) 26; L Boisson de Chazournes and L Condorelli, 'Quelques remarques à propos de l'obligation des États de "respecter et faire respecter" le droit international humanitaire " en toutes circonstances"' in C Swinarski (ed), *Études et essais sur le droit international humanitaire et sur les principes de la Croix-Rouge en l'honneur de Jean Pictet* (ICRC, 1984) 17–35; U Palwankar, 'Mesures auxquelles peuvent recourir les Etats pour remplir leur obligation de faire respecter le droit international humanitaire' (1994) 76 *International Review of the Red Cross* 11–28; M Sassòli, AA Bouvier and A Quintin, *How Does Law Protect in War?* (ICRC, 2011) 368–69.

[108] J Crawford, *Third Party Obligations with respect to Israeli Settlements in the Occupied Palestinian Territories*, Legal Opinion, 24 January 2012, §§41–5. See also F Kalshoven, 'The Undertaking to Respect and Ensure Respect in All Circumstances: From Tiny Seed to Ripening Fruit' (1999) 2 *Yearbook of International Humanitarian Law* 3–61.

of Common Article 1 of the Geneva Conventions. Here we are not concerned with the adoption of positive measures against an IHL violator; instead, the focus is on 'refraining from actively supporting such an offender'.[109] Intervening in favour of a government which engages in violations of humanitarian law falls within the duty to ensure respect for IHL, regardless of the interpretation adopted.

> Insofar as States are supposed to take positive steps to prevent breaches of LOAC (whatever the exact content of that obligation), it is only logical that they should a fortiori refrain from knowingly facilitating – whether intentionally or not – the commission of such breaches.[110]

Accordingly, it seems fairly clear that Common Article 1 of the Geneva Conventions encompasses a duty to refrain from providing assistance to a party to a conflict that violates IHL.[111] However, this does not clarify the exact scope of application of the prohibition: which acts are ruled out by the obligation to ensure respect for the law of armed conflicts? Notably, does the provision of weapons to the Syrian regime amount to a violation of Common Article 1? This and related questions will be addressed in the following section.

C. Arms Transfer

If we admit that the obligation to respect and ensure respect for IHL rules out support to parties to a conflict that violates international humanitarian law, there is no reason why this would not include the prohibition to supply weapons.[112] This conclusion seems reasonable if we consider that an increasing number of instruments prevent the transfer of arms when there is a risk that they might be used to commit serious violations of IHL and human rights. For instance, Article 6(3) of the ECOWAS Convention on Small Arms and Light Weapons, their Ammunition and Other Related Materials (2006) provides that:

> A transfer shall not be authorised if the arms are destined to be used:
>
> a) for the violation of international humanitarian law or infringement of human and peoples' rights and freedoms, or for the purpose of oppression;
>
> b) for the commission of serious violations of international humanitarian law, genocide or crimes against humanity.

[109] Corten and Koutroulis, 'The Illegality of Military Support to Rebels' (n 104) 84.

[110] Ruys (n 87) 27.

[111] ibid, 26–27.

[112] According to Art 2 of the Arms Trade Treaty, transfer of arms is defined as 'export, import, transit, trans-shipment and brokering'. On 2 April 2013, the General Assembly adopted the Arms Trade Treaty, with 154 votes in favour and negative votes only from Syria, Iran and the Democratic Republic of Korea. The treaty entered into force on 24 December 2014 and 92 states are party at the time of writing. See A/RES/67/234B, 2 April 2013, *The Arms Trade Treaty*.

In a similar vein, the OSCE Document on Small Arms and Light Weapons (2000) establishes that: '[e]ach participating State will, in considering proposed exports of small arms, take into account: (i) The respect for human rights and fundamental freedoms in the recipient country'.[113] Furthermore, Article 6(3) of the Arms Trade Treaty (ATT) reads as follow:

> A State Party shall not authorize any transfer of conventional arms covered under Article 2(1) or of items covered under Article 3 or Article 4, if it has knowledge at the time of authorization that the arms or items would be used in the commission of genocide, crimes against humanity, grave breaches of the Geneva Conventions of 1949, attacks directed against civilian objects or civilian objects protected as such, or other war crimes as defined by international agreements to which it is Party.

It is not preposterous to claim that the inclusion of this provision in the ATT could be read as the 'crystallization of a customary norm' which finds 'its basis in the duty to "ensure respect" for LOAC, and prohibiting the transfer of arms to known LOAC offenders'.[114]

The question of the legality of providing weapons to a state that engages in violations of IHL emerged recently before the UK High Court, whereby arms transfer by the UK to Saudi Arabia has been challenged. Specifically, the central question brought before the Court by the Campaign Against Arms Trade was whether the British government had an obligation to suspend and stop granting export licences to Saudi Arabia in light of serious breaches of IHL committed by the Saudi-led coalition during the armed conflict in Yemen.[115]

The relevant rules on the matter are Article 7 of the ATT and Article 2(2) of the Common Rules Governing the Control of Exports of Military Technology and Equipment.[116] Article 7(1)(b)(i) of the ATT specifies that:

> If the export is not prohibited under Article 6, each exporting State Party, prior to authorization of the export of conventional arms, … shall … assess the potential that the conventional arms or items … could be used to commit or facilitate a *serious violation of international humanitarian law*.[117]

[113] OSCE Document on Small Arms and Light Weapons, FSC.DOC/1/00/Rev.1, 20 June 2012, Section III(A)(2)(i). Although not all of the mentioned provisions are binding, it has been suggested that 'they constitute relevant State practice and *opinio juris*' and that Art 6 of the Arms Trade Treaty is the crystallisation of a customary norm which would outlaw the transfer of weapons that could be used to violate human rights and IHL. See Ruys (n 87) 28.

[114] Ruys (n 87) 29.

[115] UK High Court, *R (on the application of Campaign Against The Arms Trade) v The Secretary of State for International Trade and interveners*, 10 July 2017, [2017] EWHC 1726 (QB), §1.

[116] Common Rules Governing the Control of Exports of Military Technology and Equipment European Council Common Position 2008/944/CFSP, December 2008, (hereinafter EU Common Rules).

[117] Emphasis added.

Similarly, the second criterion of the EU Common Rules, titled 'Respect for human rights in the country of final destination as well as respect by that country of international humanitarian law', reads as follow:

> Having assessed the recipient country's attitude towards relevant principles established by instruments of inter national humanitarian law, Member States shall … deny an export licence if there is a clear risk that the military technology or equipment to be exported might be used in the *commission of serious violations of international humanitarian law*.[118]

The key issue regards the interpretation of the term 'serious violations of international humanitarian law'. According to the British interpretation, 'serious violations' would refer specifically to 'grave breaches' and 'war crimes' as defined in particular in the four Geneva Conventions, in Additional Protocol 1 to the Geneva Conventions and in Article 8 of the Rome Statute of the International Criminal Court.[119] As a matter of fact, there are a number of documents that would support the British position. Notably, the International Committee of the Red Cross (ICRC) in an explanatory note has clarified that '"[s]erious violations of international humanitarian law" are "war crimes". The two terms are today interchangeable'.[120] In the same vein, in a briefing it specifies that: '"serious violation of IHL" is another term for "war crime"'.[121]

Nevertheless, there are a number of reasons why this approach should not be embraced. Indeed, equating the term 'serious violations of IHL' to 'war crimes' would exclude from the definition violations of IHL that do not amount to an international crime, but that could be considered grave nonetheless.[122] This seems to find confirmation in the Commentary to the ATT, whereby Clapham specifies that the term 'serious violations' encompasses, but it is not limited to, the notion of war crimes. To support this claim, the author mentions that:

> In July 2012, at the United Nations Conference on the Arms Trade Treaty, the International Committee of the Red Cross (ICRC) distributed a document explaining that serious violations of international humanitarian law (IHL) cover grave breaches of the 1949 Geneva Conventions and 1977 Additional Protocol I, war crimes under Article 8 of the 1998 Rome Statute of the International Criminal Court, and other war crimes in customary IHL.[123]

[118] EU Common Rules, Art 2(2).

[119] E Robinson, 'Arms Exports to Saudi Arabia in the High Court: what is a "serious violation of international humanitarian law"?' (*EJIL: Talk!*, 2017), available at www.ejiltalk.org/arms-exports-to-saudi-arabia-in-the-high-court-what-is-a-serious-violation-of-international-humanitarian-law/.

[120] ICRC, 'What are "serious violations of international humanitarian law"? Explanatory Note', available at www.icrc.org/en/doc/assets/files/2012/att-what-are-serious-violations-of-ihl-icrc.pdf.

[121] ICRC, 'Protecting Civilians and Humanitarian Action through the Arms Trade Treaty' (2013) 4.

[122] Robinson (n 119).

[123] A Clapham, 'Article 7. Export and Export Assessment' in S Casey-Maslen, A Clapham, G Giacca and S Parker (eds), *The Arms Trade Treaty: A Commentary* (Oxford University Press, 2016) 244–85, at §7.39.

The UK High Court seems to adopt this approach when it posits that: 'the term "serious violation" is a general term in International Humanitarian Law which includes "grave breaches" and "war crimes"'. The use of the verb 'to include' would suggest that grave breaches and serious violations of IHL are not limited to war crimes and encompass other instances of breached of IHL.[124] These considerations regardless, the High Court concluded that the UK did not violate its obligations by authorising the transfer of weapons to Saudi Arabia. Nevertheless, in a landmark decision in 2019, the Court of Appeal in London ruled that granting new licences and not suspending current ones was unlawful.

The issue of arms transfer raises a further question. If we refer back to the case of the Russian ship and airplane that were prevented from reaching Syria because they were carrying weapons for the government, we could wonder whether the British and Turkish decisions to send the weapons back to Russia was in line with the obligation under examination. Sassòli affirms that, if a state 'knows that the receiving country systematically commits violations of international humanitarian law with certain weapons, the aiding state has to deny further transfers thereof, even if those weapons could also be used lawfully'.[125] The position suggested by Sassòli appears convincing and is supported by the overwhelming majority of the scholarship.[126] The rationale underpinning this view is that, if a state is aware of ongoing violations of IHL, it could fairly assume that the help provided is likely to facilitate further violations. In other words, a certain degree of predictability is required, and the risk should be foreseeable or likely.[127] Therefore, in line with this interpretation, it could be possible to conclude that the UK and Turkey complied with their duty to ensure respect for IHL.

[124] UK High Court (n 115) §16. These considerations regardless, the High Court concluded that the UK did not violate its obligations by authorising the transfer of weapons to Saudi Arabia. Nevertheless, in a landmark decision in 2019 the Court of Appeal in London ruled that granting new licences and not suspending current ones was unlawful. See Human Rights Watch, 'UK: Arms Sales to Saudis Suspended After Landmark Ruling' (2019), available at www.hrw.org/news/2019/06/20/uk-arms-sales-saudis-suspended-after-landmark-ruling.

[125] M Sassòli, 'State Responsibility for Violations of International Humanitarian Law' (2002) 84(846) *International Review of the Red Cross* 413.

[126] See eg Brehm (n 103) 28; A Boivin, 'Complicity and Beyond: International Law and the Transfer of Small Arms and Light Weapons' (2005) 87(859) *International Review of the Red Cross* 479; Corten and Koutroulis (n 105) 85; Ruys (n 87) 28.

[127] See K Dörmann and J Serralvo, 'Common Article 1 to the Geneva Conventions and the obligation to prevent international humanitarian law violations' (2014) 96(895) *International Review of the Red Cross* 730; H Gasser, 'Ensuring Respect for the Geneva Conventions and Protocols: The Role of the Third States and the United Nations' in H Fox and MA Meyer (eds), *Effecting Compliance* (British Institute of International and Comparative Law, 1993) 15–49; A Devillard, 'L'obligation de Faire Respecter le Droit International Humanitaire: L'article 1 Commun aux Conventions de Genève et à Leur Premier Protocole Additionnel, Fondement d'un Droit International Humanitaire de Cooperation?' (2007) 20(2) *Revue Québécoise de Droit International* 88.

IV. HUMANITARIAN ASSISTANCE AND THE CONSENT OF THE GOVERNMENT

A. Humanitarian Assistance: Meaning and Requisites

In the previous paragraphs we have shown that governments that commit gross and systematic violations of human rights and humanitarian law do not forfeit their consent power. Nevertheless, states that decide to intervene in their favour could incur an international responsibility for violating other international law norms. Similar to debates on consent power of illegitimate governments, the centrality of the protection of civilians in international law and its relationship with consent play a crucial role in the provision of humanitarian assistance. The failure to provide timely and effective humanitarian relief to the civilian population in need in Syria and other conflicts triggered heated discussions on the lawfulness of cross-border relief assistance. Notably, the pivotal question is whether a government has an obligation to consent to the provision of humanitarian assistance to a civilian population in need.

International law does not offer a definition of 'humanitarian assistance'.[128] Nevertheless, it is generally accepted that it encompasses 'providing goods and services essential for the survival of those being directly affected by man-made or natural disasters'.[129] More specifically, with regard to armed conflicts, humanitarian assistance comprises accessing the civilian population 'lacking the supplies essential to its survival' in order to provide emergency relief, such as food, water, and medical supplies.[130] Accordingly, humanitarian assistance should not be confused with humanitarian intervention and the responsibility to protect (R2P) doctrine. Indeed, in their current articulation R2P and humanitarian intervention are directed at preventing and halting the commission of certain heinous crimes. On the contrary, humanitarian assistance does not aim at enhancing the protection of civilians and is limited to the provision of relief aid to the population in need.[131]

[128] K Dörmann et al, *Commentary on the First Geneva Convention: Convention (I) for the Amelioration of the Condition of the Wounded and Sick in Armed Forces in the Field* (Cambridge University Press, 2016) §820: '"Assistance activities" refers to all activities, services and the delivery of goods carried out primarily in the fields of health, water, habitat (the creation of a sustainable living environment) and economic security (defined by the ICRC as "the condition of an individual, household or community that is able to cover its essential needs and unavoidable expenditures in a sustainable manner, according to its cultural standards"), which seek to ensure that persons caught up in an armed conflict can survive and live in dignity.' It is worth noting that the Geneva Conventions and the Additional Protocols tend to use the term 'relief'. In this work, 'assistance' and 'relief' are going to be used interchangeably. See also F Lattanzi, 'Humanitarian Assistance' in A Clapham, P Gaeta and M Sassòli (eds), *The 1949 Geneva Conventions: A Commentary* (Oxford University Press, 2015) 232.

[129] H Spieker, 'Humanitarian Assistance, Access in Armed Conflict and Occupation' in *Max Planck Encyclopedia of Public International Law* (Oxford University Press, 2015) §§1-2.

[130] Spieker (n 129) §§1-2; Lattanzi (n 128) 232; EC Gillard, 'The Law Regulating Cross-border Relief Operations' (2013) 95(890) *International Review of the Red Cross* 352.

[131] Dörmann et al (n 128) §784; Lattanzi (n 128) 232.

This instance raises dilemmas with regard to the principle of non-intervention in internal affairs of the state. Notably, the question is whether providing relief to the civilian population could be regarded as unlawful interference. This debate arose during the two World Wars, when humanitarian assistance was perceived to be in opposition to the principle of non-intervention.[132] In 1977, Additional Protocol I to the Geneva Conventions contributed to the discussion, where it specifies that: '[o]ffers of … relief shall not be regarded as interference in the armed conflict or as unfriendly acts'.[133] The issue was solved by the ICJ in the *Nicaragua* case: '[t]here can be no doubt that the provision of strictly humanitarian aid to persons or forces in another country, whatever their political affiliations or objectives, *cannot be regarded as unlawful intervention*, or as in any other way contrary to international law'.[134]

Conventional international humanitarian law regulating non-international armed conflicts addresses the issue of humanitarian assistance in two provisions. Article 3(2) GC specifies that '[a]n impartial humanitarian body, such as the International Committee of the Red Cross, may offer its services to the Parties to the conflict'. On the other hand, Article 18 of the Additional Protocol II (AP II) reads as follow:

1. Relief societies located in the territory of the High Contracting Party, such as Red Cross (Red Crescent, Red Lion and Sun) organizations, may offer their services for the performance of their traditional functions in relation to the victims of the armed conflict. The civilian population may, even on its own initiative, offer to collect and care for the wounded, sick and shipwrecked.[135]
2. If the civilian population is suffering undue hardship owing to a lack of the supplies essential for its survival, such as foodstuffs and medical supplies, relief actions for the civilian population which are of an exclusively humanitarian and impartial nature and which are conducted without any adverse distinction shall be undertaken subject to the consent of the High Contracting Party concerned.

Furthermore, customary rule 55 of the ICRC Study provides that: '[t]he parties to the conflict must allow and facilitate rapid and unimpeded passage of humanitarian relief for civilians in need, which is impartial in character and conducted without any adverse distinction, subject to their right of control'.

While both Article 3(2) of the GC and Article 18(1) of the AP II specify that relief organisations have a right to offer their services, the primary responsibility for meeting the needs of the population rests within the parties to the conflict. When they are unable or unwilling to comply with their obligations,

[132] Lattanzi (n 128) 245.

[133] Protocol Additional to the Geneva Conventions of 12 August 1949, and relating to the Protection of Victims of International Armed Conflicts (Protocol I), 8 June 1977, Art 70(1).

[134] *Nicaragua* case, §242, emphasis added. See also F Schwendimann, 'The Legal Framework of Humanitarian Access in Armed Conflict' (2011) 93(884) *International Review of the Red Cross* 997.

[135] Protocol Additional to the Geneva Conventions of 12 August 1949, and relating to the Protection of Victims of Non-International Armed Conflicts (Protocol II), 8 June 1977.

humanitarian organisations can offer the provision of relief, which is meant to be subsidiary and to complement the efforts of the parties to the conflict.[136] According to Article 3(2) of the GC, only an impartial humanitarian body can offer its relief services. Although no definition of 'impartial humanitarian body' is provided in the Geneva Conventions, nor in the Additional Protocols, it is generally understood that the humanitarian organisation's activities do not have to be limited to humanitarian ones.[137] On the other hand, the ICRC Commentary to Article 3 of the GC clarifies that economic actors cannot fall within the definition due to their 'profit-making profile … even when they provide free services within the framework of a particular humanitarian activity'.[138] Furthermore, the humanitarian organisation needs to be impartial, namely it has to adopt an impartial attitude 'vis-à-vis the persons affected by the armed conflict when planning and implementing the proposed humanitarian activities'.[139] In other words, relief has to be provided in a non-discriminatory way to the civilian population.[140]

B. The Requirement of Consent

The provisions regulating humanitarian assistance raise a critical conundrum: can a party to a conflict decline the offer of humanitarian relief? Article 3(2) of the GC specifies that humanitarian organisations 'may offer their services to the Parties to the conflict'. Notwithstanding the fact that it does not mention whether the consent of the party is needed, it is generally accepted that the possibility of offering services implies that the party receiving humanitarian relief has the liberty to refuse the offer.[141] This approach has been confirmed by the ICRC in its Commentary to common Article 3 of the GC:

> Despite the silence of common Article 3, it is clear from the logic underpinning international law in general, and humanitarian law in particular, that, in principle, an impartial humanitarian organization will only be able to carry out the proposed humanitarian activities if it has consent to do so.[142]

Article 18(1) of the AP II reiterates that humanitarian organisations 'may offer their services to the Parties to the conflict'. Furthermore, in the following

[136] Dörmann et al (n 128) §782; Gillard (n 130) 355; Y Sandoz et al, *Commentary on the Additional Protocols of 8 June 1977 to the Geneva Conventions of 12 August 1949* (Martinus Nijhoff, 1987) 1477; R Barber, 'Facilitating Humanitarian Assistance in International Humanitarian and Human Rights Law' (2009) 91(874) *International Review of the Red Cross* 386.
[137] Dörmann et al (n 128) §790.
[138] ibid, §793.
[139] ibid, §794.
[140] Y Dinstein, 'The Right to Humanitarian Assistance' (2000) 53(4) *Naval War College Review* 85.
[141] Lattanzi (n 128) 249; Dinstein (n 140) 84; Barber (n 136) 385.
[142] Dörmann et al (n 128) §828.

paragraph it explicitly clarifies that 'relief actions ... shall be undertaken subject to the consent of the High Contracting Parties'. This requirement was added during the final stage of the negotiations of the Additional Protocol because states were 'concerned with preserving their national sovereignty'.[143] Nevertheless, from the discussions that took place during the negotiations it emerges that consent was never meant to be absolute and that a party could not decline the offer of relief services for 'arbitrary or capricious' reasons.[144] This conclusion was confirmed by subsequent instruments that address the provision of humanitarian assistance. For instance, the Guiding Principles on Internal Displacement specifies that:

> International humanitarian organizations and other appropriate actors have the right to offer their services in support of the internally displaced. ... Consent thereto shall not be arbitrarily withheld, particularly when authorities concerned are unable or unwilling to provide the required humanitarian assistance.[145]

In the same vein, the Institute de Droit International adopted a Resolution on Humanitarian Assistance, which states that:

> Affected States are under the obligation not arbitrarily and unjustifiably to reject a bona fide offer exclusively intended to provide humanitarian assistance or to refuse access to the victims. In particular, they may not reject an offer nor refuse access if such refusal is likely to endanger the fundamental human rights of the victims or would amount to a violation of the ban on starvation of civilians as a method of warfare.[146]

Similarly, the Council of Europe Recommendation on Internally Displaced Persons reads as follow:

> Protecting internally displaced persons and their rights as well as providing humanitarian assistance to them is a primary responsibility of the state concerned;
>
> Such responsibility entails requesting aid from other states or international organisations if the state concerned is not in a position to provide protection and assistance to its internally displaced persons;
>
> This responsibility also entails not to arbitrarily refuse offers from other states or international organisations to provide such aid.[147]

[143] JP et al, *Commentary on the Additional Protocols of 8 June 1977 to the Geneva Conventions of 12 August 1949* (ICRC and Martinus Nijhoff, 1987) §4870.

[144] Germany, CDDH/II/SR.87, at 336–337. See also Gillard (n 130) 356.

[145] Guiding Principles on Internal Displacement, UN Doc E/CN/4/1998/Add.2, 11 February 1998 Principle 25.

[146] Institute de Droit International, Bruges Session 2003, *Resolution on Humanitarian Assistance* 2 September 2003, Art VIII.

[147] Council of Europe recommendation (2006)6 of the Committee of Ministers to Member States on Internally Displaced Persons, 5 April 2006, §4. See also International Law Commission Report on the work of its 63rd session (26 April–3 June and 4 July–12 August 2011), Protection of Persons in the Event of Disaster, provisionally adopted draft Art 11 – Consent of the affected State to external assistance, UN Doc. A/66/10, 2011, Chapter XI, §§264–289; UNGA Res. A/RES/46/182, 19 December 1991, Guiding Principle 3. See also Gillard (n 130) 356–57.

Accordingly, it is now generally accepted that 'consent may not be refused on arbitrary grounds'.[148] Nevertheless, what does amount to arbitrary denial of consent is highly debatable.[149] The scholarship has suggested a number of valid reasons to decline the offer of humanitarian relief. This would be the case, for instance, when a party is willing and able to meet the needs of the population, and if the organisation offering its services is not humanitarian or impartial, the party could refuse consent.[150]

Nevertheless, interpreting the criterion of 'arbitrariness' remains contentious. On the one hand, some authors read Article 18(2) of the AP II in light of the prohibition of starvation as a method of warfare (Article 14 of the AP II) and conclude that 'if the survival of the population is threatened and a humanitarian organisation fulfilling the required conditions of impartiality and non-discrimination is able to remedy this situation, relief actions must take place'.[151] Conversely, if there is no risk for the survival of the civilian population, consent can be lawfully refused.[152] On the other hand, part of the scholarship propounds that the denial of consent would be arbitrary also when there is no risk of starvation for the civilian population. According to the ICRC Commentary to Article 3 of the GC, 'the assessment remains context-specific' and it should be decided on a case-by-case basis.[153] Emanuela-Chiara Gillard has suggested a number of elements that should be taken into consideration, such as the needs of the population, whether other organisations are already providing assistance, the nature of the actors offering their services, compatibility with other obligations under international law, and the location and timeframe of the provision of humanitarian relief.[154]

The provision of humanitarian assistance raises a crucial question: who has to provide consent to the offer of relief? Article 3(2) of the GC states that: '[a]n impartial humanitarian body, such as the International Committee of the Red Cross, may offer its services *to the Parties to the conflict*'.[155] On the other hand, Article 18(2) of the AP II expressly refers to 'the consent of *the High Contracting Party concerned*'. Additional Protocol II seems to follow 'a state-centric approach' that is absent in common Article 3 of the GC.[156] Accordingly,

[148] Dörmann et al (n 128) §833; Spieker (n 129) §38; Gillard (n 130) 356; Barber (n 136) 386.

[149] Dörmann et al (n 128) §835: '[i]nternational law does not provide authoritative clarification on how to interpret the criterion of 'arbitrariness.' This assessment remains context-specific'.

[150] ibid, §835.

[151] Sandoz et al (n 136) §4885; ICRC Customary Study, Rule 55, commentary: '[i]f it is established that a civilian population is threatened with starvation and a humanitarian organization which provides relief on an impartial and non-discriminatory basis is able to remedy the situation, a party is obliged to give consent'. See also Lattanzi (n 128) 250: '[t]he consent requirement stipulated in Article 18(2) AP II cannot prevent humanitarian relief in order to ensure the basic needs of a population or parts of it suffering from a lack of supplies essential for its survival during a NIAC'.

[152] Lattanzi (n 128) 244.

[153] Dörmann et al (n 128) §835.

[154] Gillard (n 130) 362–63.

[155] Emphasis added.

[156] Lattanzi (n 128) 250.

some scholars conclude that the consent of the state is always necessary, even when humanitarian relief should be provided in territories under the control of the opposition. Nevertheless, this position has been criticised for a number of reasons. Indeed, concluding that only the state party to the conflict would be entitled to provide consent would deviate 'from the principle of the equality of the belligerents'.[157] Moreover, Additional Protocol II expressly 'develops and supplements Common Article 3 to the Geneva Conventions of 12 August 1949 without modifying its existing conditions of application' (Article 1(1) of the AP II). Therefore, Article 18(2) of the AP II should be interpreted in conformity with common Article 3(2) of the GC.[158]

Requiring consent by the state party to the conflict poses a further conundrum. As explained in the previous chapters, during internal conflicts identifying the government capable to speak on behalf of the state is not an easy task. This is particularly true in NIACs that fall within the scope of Additional Protocol II, which is applicable to conflicts where the opposition group exercises territorial control and is able to 'carry out sustained and concerted military operations and to implement [the] Protocol' (Article 1(2) of the AP II). In light of the uncertainty related to identifying the de jure government during NIACs, it seems fair to conclude that the drafters did not intend 'to force humanitarian actors to weigh up rival claims'.[159]

V. CONCLUDING OBSERVATIONS

Respect for human rights and humanitarian law has become predominant in the discourse on intervention. At the same time, the way in which power is exercised has turned into a decisive parameter to determine the legitimacy of governments as representative of their own people. Notably, the international community is increasingly looking at gross and systematic violations of human rights and humanitarian law as a parameter to evaluate the legitimacy of governments. The overall picture that results from our analysis is as follows.

Recent state practice raises the question as to whether governments that excessively use force against their own populations would forfeit their power to seek foreign military help. The Libyan and Syrian conflicts do not seem to provide a clear-cut answer: while states seem hesitant to affirm a right to intervene in favour of governments that commit widespread violations of human rights and IHL, they have not explicitly endorsed the contrary view. Nevertheless, this does

[157] F Bugnion, *The International Committee of the Red Cross and the Protection of War Victims* (Macmillan, 2003) 452.

[158] Lattanzi (n 128) 251; Bugnion (n 157) 453.

[159] M Bothe, KJ Partsch, and W Solf, *New Rules for Victims of Armed Conflicts–Commentary on the Two 1977 Protocols Additional to the Geneva Conventions of 1949* (Martinus Nijhoff, 1982) 94 See also Bugnion (n 157) 453–54.

not imply that interventions in favour of governments that excessively use force against their own people are lawful. Under current international law, limits to the possibility to help these governments are twofold. First, an intervention in favour of a government that commits gross and systematic violations of human rights could trigger the responsibility for aiding and assisting the commission of the wrongful act. Second, with specific regard to breaches of humanitarian law, providing help to a government could amount to a violation of the duty to ensure respect for IHL. Notably, this encompasses also an obligation to prevent transfer of arms, if the state can fairly assume that the weapons are going to facilitate violations of IHL.

Part III

Interventions in Favour of Rebels

What does recognition mean?
One can recognize a man as an Emperor or as a Grocer.
Recognition is meaningless without a defining formula.

Winston Churchill

THE LIBYAN AND Syrian conflicts have brought to the fore the issue of the legitimacy of rebels. They introduced an original narrative, whereby governments that commit gross and systematic violations of human rights and humanitarian law against their own population cease to be recognised as a legitimate representative of the people, while this qualification is attributed to certain opposition groups. These considerations are not merely political: not only they have challenged the traditional preference in favour of governments, but they have also led several states to provide weapons, training, and non-lethal help to rebels.

Talking about the legitimacy of rebels and the possibility to intervene in their favour may sound preposterous: since they fight against the government, they appear inherently illegitimate. This is partially due to the traditional narrative pertaining to opposition groups: the centrality of states in international law, the international community's top-down approach, and the reluctance to see any forms of violence permeate international law. Nevertheless, this is increasingly in contrast with an emerging interest towards rebels' legitimacy. On the one hand, armed non-state actors (ANSAs) have manifested the desire to be recognised as legitimate in several cases and this has been one of the main incentives to push for respect of international humanitarian law (IHL) by opposition groups.[1] On the other hand, over the past decades there have been instances when rebels have been recognised as legitimate representatives of their own people and this has raised the question of the consequences for the current legal framework.

Before the nineteenth century, civil wars were considered exclusively internal matters: opposition groups were treated as common criminals, subject to

[1] A Bellal, 'Welcome on Board: Improving Respect for International Humanitarian Law through the Engagement of Armed Non-State Actors' (2016) 19 *Yearbook of International Humanitarian Law* 47.

municipal law, and did not bear any rights or duties at the international level. However, during the nineteenth century state practice changed this approach: armed non-state actors engaging in a violent fight against a government could be recognised as rebels, insurgents or belligerents depending upon their effectiveness and the intensity of the conflict.[2] The recognition of belligerency and insurgency was an essential premise for applying the laws of war. After the Spanish Civil War this practice seldom occurred and since World War II it has been completely abandoned.[3] As noted by Clapham, '[t]oday, these recognition regimes have been replaced by compulsory rules of international humanitarian law which apply when the fighting reaches certain thresholds'.[4] Similarly, the international legal framework regulating interventions in favour of rebels does not depend upon the recognition of belligerency of insurgency. As we shall see, according to the general rule nearly any form of assistance provided to opposition groups could amount to a violation of the ban on the use of force and the principle of non-intervention. Nevertheless, this does not mean that all forms of recognition of rebels disappeared from state practice.

From the 1960s, several national liberation movements (NLMs) were recognised as legitimate representatives of their own people. More recently, a number of states attributed the same definition to the Libyan National Transitional Council (NTC) and the National Coalition for Syrian Revolutionary and Opposition Forces (hereinafter, Syrian Opposition Coalition, SOC). The evaluation of the recognition of rebels as legitimate representatives of their people raises compelling questions as to the development of this practice and the consequences for the current legal framework. Has state practice developed certain criteria to evaluate the legitimacy of rebels? May a government use force against legitimate rebels and could opposition groups use force against the oppressive power? Can foreign countries intervene in favour of legitimate rebels? This part is devoted to addressing these and related dilemmas.

Chapter six sets the basis of the discourse by analysing the legitimacy of rebels in international law. As aforementioned, since the adoption of the UN Charter there have been two instances when opposition groups have been recognised as legitimate representatives of their own people. However, it is doubtful whether this attribution is deemed to have the same meaning in both circumstances. When a number of states recognised the NTC and SOC as legitimate representatives of respectively the Libyan and Syrian peoples, was the choice of terminology a mere coincidence? Or was it a reference to the exercise of the

[2] See eg A Cullen, *The Concept of Non-International Armed Conflict in International Humanitarian Law* (Cambridge University Press, 2010) 5–24; L Moir, *The Law of Internal Armed Conflict* (Cambridge University Press, 2002) 4.

[3] I Dette, *The Law of War* (Cambridge University Press, 2000) 43; HA Wilson, *International Law and the Use of Force by National Liberation Movements* (Clarendon Press, 1988) 27.

[4] A Clapham, *Human Rights Obligations of Non-State Actors* (Oxford University Press, 2006) 272.

right to self-determination? The ultimate aim is to investigate whether there are common criteria or if the recent narrative brought about a break with the past.

Chapter seven addresses the consequences of recognising rebels as legitimate representatives of their people. Specifically, this issue is analysed from a two-fold angle. First, it examines the use of force by the government against legitimate rebels. The crucial question is whether the traditional presumption that the government can forcibly react against opposition groups has been at least partially reversed. Does the legitimacy of rebels prevent the government from using force against them? Second, this chapter seeks to investigate whether, *de jure condendo*, the understandable reluctance to address non-state violence in terms of right could be overridden. Although a right to use force against the state has never been generally recognised for opposition groups, the second part of the chapter examines when, if ever, non-state violence could be recognised as legitimate and what practical implications this might have.

Finally, chapter eight focuses on foreign interventions in favour or against legitimate opposition groups. Both before and after the adoption of the UN Charter there have been cases when states recognised rebels. Interestingly, qualifying rebels as legitimate triggered discussions as to the possibility to intervene in favour of opposition groups. Does their legitimacy change the traditional rules governing interventions in internal conflicts? The question as to whether human rights affect the instances when it is lawful to assist rebels also emerged during the Libyan conflict. Following Security Council Resolution 1793, a number of countries intervened to protect civilians against the government.[5] The Resolution was interpreted by the intervening states as an authorisation to provide direct support to the opposition groups fighting against the Gaddafi regime. Again, it seems that human rights considerations entered discourses on the use of force. We shall see if this entailed a change in the current legal framework.

[5] S/RES/1973 (2011), 17 March 2011.

6

Legitimacy of Rebels in International Law

I. NATIONAL LIBERATION MOVEMENTS AS LEGITIMATE REPRESENTATIVES OF A PEOPLE

A. The Evolution of Self-determination: From Principle to Right

SELF-DETERMINATION IS ONE of the most debated concepts in international law, 'one of which poets have sung and for which patriots have been ready to lay down their lives'.[1] While its ideological origins contribute to its ambiguity, it has been a crucial 'driving force' within the international community.[2] The genesis of the principle of self-determination goes back to the 1776 American Declaration of Independence, which established that governments derived 'their just powers from the consent of the governed' and that 'whenever any Form of Government becomes destructive of these ends, it is the Right of the People to alter or to abolish it'.[3] During the French Revolution of 1789, scholars were faced with the challenge of reconciling French expansionism with popular sovereignty.[4] Self-determination was thus articulated in terms of the right of the people to be heard before the annexation of new territories. Although France held plebiscites to confirm territorial annexations, they soon became formal exercises: the presence of the French army during the vote raises doubts as to the free and fair character of those plebiscites.[5]

Notwithstanding France's failure to implement the principle of self-determination in a fair manner, the principle did not fall out of fashion. At the beginning of the nineteenth century, the concept reached Italy, where it was embraced in the struggle to unify the peninsula. Giovanni Mazzini defined it as

[1] JP Humphrey, 'Political and Related Rights' in T Meron (ed), *Human Rights in International Law: Legal and Policy Issues* (Clarendon, 1986) 193. See also T Christakis, *Le Droit à l'Autodétermination en dehors des Situations de Décolonisation* (La Documentation Française, 1999) 15.

[2] A Cassese, *Self-Determination of Peoples: A Legal Reappraisal* (Cambridge University Press, 1995) 1.

[3] D Thürer and T Burri, 'Self-Determination' in *Max Planck Encyclopedia of Public International Law* (Oxford University Press, 2008) §§1–2.

[4] BR Roth, *Governmental Illegitimacy in International Law* (Clarendon Press, 1999) 204.

[5] ibid, 205.

'a political postulate demanding that all nations be allowed freely to choose their status'.[6] According to the Italian politician: '[t]he Countries of the People will rise, defined by the voice of the free, upon the ruins of the countries of the Kings and privileged casts'.[7] In subsequent years the principle of self-determination lost its appeal and it was only during World War I and the Bolshevik Revolution that it returned to the fore on the international scene.[8] On the one hand, Vladimir Lenin theorised self-determination as the decisive basis for the realisation of socialism through the liberation of oppressed people.[9] On the other hand, Woodrow Wilson interpreted the principle as encompassing a right of people to choose freely their own government through democracy.[10] Lenin and Wilson's crucially different interpretations of the concept started a divergence of views between Western countries and the communist bloc that has influenced the debates in the international arena.

Despite the increasing interest in self-determination within the international community, during the two World Wars it remained political in nature and did not attain the status of legal principle.[11] Finally, in 1945 the legal validity of self-determination was recognised. Article 1(2) of the UN Charter mentions among the purposes of the UN the development 'of friendly relations among nations based on respect for the principle of equal rights and self-determination of peoples'. However, the inclusion of the principle in Article 1 – and not in Article 2 of the UN Charter, which establishes binding principles for the UN Member States – suggests that the nature of the concept was still unclear. Indeed, it was only during the decolonisation period that the principle gained momentum and was framed in terms of a right.[12]

In the 1960s the UNGA started recognising the right to self-determination of people who had 'not yet attained independence'.[13] Although the resolutions adopted by the UNGA were criticised for going beyond the content of the UN Charter and de facto re-writing the principle,[14] they reflected the general consent within the international community as to the emergence of

[6] Cassese (n 2) 13.

[7] Quoted in Cassese, ibid.

[8] Roth (n 4) 205; Cassese (n 2) 13.

[9] Cassese (n 2) 14; JA Hofbauer, *Sovereignty in the Exercise of the Right to Self-determination* (Martinus Nijhoff, 2016) 63.

[10] Hofbauer (n 9) 64.

[11] Cassese (n 2) 33.

[12] L Doswald-Beck, 'The Legal Validity of Military Intervention by Invitation of the Government' (1986) 56(1) *British Yearbook of International Law* 201.

[13] Hofbauer (n 9) 72.

[14] For instance, the US Ambassador at the Security Council commented that: 'Resolution 1514(XV) does not authorise the use of force for its implementation. It … cannot overrule the Charter injunctions against the use of armed force.' SCOR, 16th year, 988th meeting, 18 December 1961, §93, quoted in CJR Dugard, 'The Organisation of African Unity and Colonialism: An Inquiry into the Plea of Self- Defence as a Justification for the Use of Force in the Eradication of Colonialism' (1967) 16(1) *The International and Comparative Law Quarterly* 176.

the right to self-determination.[15] UNGA Resolutions 1514(XV) and 1541(XV), adopted on 15 and 16 December 1960, marked a shift in the approach toward self-determination. The first, concerning the concession of independence to colonial countries and people, recognised that: 'all people have a right to self-determination' and that 'by virtue of that right they freely determine their political status and freely pursue their economic, social, and cultural development'.[16] Resolution 1541(XV) was meant to serve as an interpretation of Article 73(e) of the UN Charter;[17] however, its annex, *Principles which should guide Members in determining whether or not an obligation exists to transmit the information called for in Article 73(e) of the Charter of the United Nations*, went beyond its object by clarifying that a Non-Self-Governing Territory (NSGT) maintains its status until 'the territory and its people attain a full measure of self-government'. The resolution explains that, in practical terms, the NSGT status ceases in one of the following ways: '[e]mergence of a new sovereign state; [f]ree association with an independent state; [i]ntegration with an independent state'.[18]

The UNGA resolutions adopted in the 1960s and the UN practice related to self-determination led to the emergence of a set of general standards with regard to decolonisation and the right to self-determination. People under colonial domination, alien occupation, and racist regimes were recognised a right to self-determination, interpreted as the right to 'freely determine their political status and freely pursue their economic, social and cultural development'.[19] However, this right encompassed only its external component, namely 'the choice of the international status of the people and the territory where it lives'.[20] Once this choice was made and the right to self-determination was exercised, it expired. Furthermore, the right belonged only to the people as a whole, thus it did not consider whether a colonial people was composed of different ethnic groups and minorities.[21]

[15] Roth (n 4) 208.

[16] A/RES/1514(L)(XV), 14 December 1960, *Declaration on Granting Independence to Colonial Countries and Peoples*, §2.

[17] UN Charter, Art 73(e) reads as follows: 'Members of the United Nations which have or assume responsibilities for the administration of territories whose peoples have not yet attained a full measure of self-government recognize the principle that the interests of the inhabitants of these territories are paramount, and accept as a sacred trust the obligation to promote to the utmost, within the system of international peace and security established by the present Charter, the well-being of the inhabitants of these territories, and, to this end: … (e) to transmit regularly to the Secretary-General for information purposes, subject to such limitation as security and constitutional considerations may require, statistical and other information of a technical nature relating to economic, social, and educational conditions in the territories for which they are respectively responsible other than those territories to which Chapters XII and XIII apply'.

[18] A/RES/1541(XV), 14 December 1960, *Principles Which Should Guide Members in Determining Whether or nor an Obligation Exists to Transmit the Information Called for under Article 73E of the Charter*, Principle VI.

[19] A/RES/1514(L)(XV) (n 16) §2.

[20] Cassese (n 2) 72.

[21] ibid.

Soon after the emergence of the right to external self-determination, the principle developed an internal dimension.[22] In the words of Cassese, 'internal self-determination means the right to authentic self-government, that is, the right for a people really and freely to choose its own political and economic regime'.[23] It is now well-established that people of independent states have a right to self-determination, as enshrined in Article 1 common to the International Covenant on Civil and Political Rights (ICCPR) and to the International Covenant on Economic, Social and Cultural Rights (ICESCR), which establishes that: '[a]ll peoples have the right of self-determination'. This was endorsed by the Declaration on Friendly Relations:

> By virtue of the principle of equal rights and self-determination of peoples enshrined in the Charter of the United Nations, all peoples have the right freely to determine, without external interference, their political status and to pursue their economic, social and cultural development, and every State has the duty to respect this right in accordance with the provisions of the Charter.[24]

By the end of the decolonisation period, the principle of self-determination was generally recognised as a right. Furthermore, the ICJ in the *East Timor* case held that it attained the status of *erga omnes* rule.[25] James Crawford noted that, although the right undoubtedly qualifies as *lex lata*, it qualifies also as *lex obscura* due to its ambiguous content.[26] First, the self to whom it applies is unclear.[27] Second, its content and the consequences attached to the right are uncertain. In its external dimension, it is generally uncontested that the right to self-determination applies to people under colonial domination, alien occupation, and racist regimes. However, it is debatable whether the principle can find application in other cases, especially whether it grants a right to secession.[28] On the other hand, internal self-determination is meant to guarantee that peoples could choose their political, economic, and cultural status, free from

[22] T Christakis and K Mollard-Bannelier, '*Volenti non fit injuria?* Les Effets du Consentement à l'Intervention Militaire' (2004) 50(1) *Annuaire français de droit international* 119.

[23] Cassese (n 2) 101.

[24] *Declaration on Principles of International Law concerning Friendly Relations and Co-operation among States in accordance with the Charter of the United Nations*, A/RES/25/2625 (XXV), 24 October 1970 (hereinafter Declaration on Friendly Relations).

[25] ICJ, *Timor Leste (Portugal v Australia)*, Judgment (Merits), 30 June 1995, §29. See also ICJ, *Legal Consequences for States of the Continued Presence of South Africa in Namibia (South West Africa) notwithstanding Security Council Resolution 276 (1970)*, Advisory Opinion, 21 June 1971, §52; ICJ, *Western Sahara*, Advisory Opinion, 16 October 1975 (hereinafter *Western Sahara* case), §§54–59.

[26] J Crawford, 'The Right of Self-Determination in International Law: Its Developments and Future' in P Alston (ed), *Peoples' Rights* (Oxford University Press 2001) 10.

[27] Hofbauer (n 9) 19–61.

[28] See eg J Dahlitz, *Secession and International Law: Conflict Avoidance – Regional Appraisals* (Asser Press, 2003); MG Kohen, *Secession: International Law Perspectives* (Cambridge University Press, 2006); D Raič, *Statehood and the Law of Self-Determination* (Martinus Nijhoff, 2002); A Tancredi, *La secessione nel diritto internazionale* (CEDAM, 2001).

external interference. Nevertheless, the scholarship is divided as to whether this equates to a right to democratic governance, or whether it has a different meaning.[29]

A comprehensive analysis of these issues exceeds the scope of this research. Instead, we will focus on the practice developed with regard to national liberation movements representing and fighting for people under colonial domination, alien occupation, and racist regimes. As we shall see, during the decolonisation period NLMs were defined as legitimate representatives of people and such recognition triggered crucial questions with regard to the use of force by and against liberation movements, as well as to the provision of military and non-lethal support to the rebels.

B. National Liberation Movements and the Representativeness Test

The recognition of the right to self-determination of people under colonial domination, alien occupation, and racist regimes raised the question of its implementation. A people per se cannot act at the international level. As noted by Roth: 'just as states are abstractions that are represented by concrete institutions of government, so too are non-self-governing political communities abstractions that can act only through concrete organisations that purport to represent them'.[30] Since the colonial powers did not seem the best candidates to represent the people under their domination, and for good reasons, the international community started recognising NLMs as legitimate representatives of the people struggling for their right to self-determination.

The process that led to the international recognition of NLMs was first and foremost political and historical in character. It was accurately described in the Arbitral Award of 31 July 1989 concerning the delimitation of the maritime boundary between Guinea-Bissau and Senegal:

> Dans un processus de libération nationale il y a toujours à l'origine un petit groupe d'hommes décidés qui s'organise et qui, petit à petit, développe une activité sur les plans intellectuel, politique et militaire jusqu'à obtenir l'indépendance de leur pays. Dans le processus de libération on parvient à un stade où les aspirations du mouvement sont précisées et où il est organisé institutionnellement. … Dans ce processus de formation d'un mouvement de libération nationale, la question

[29] See eg Christakis (n 1) 327, where the author defines the right to internal self-determination as a 'droit de l'ensemble de la population d'un État à un government démocratique'. On the other hand, Vladyslav Lanovoy questions 'whether the choice of a democratic form of government, within the understanding of a multiparty democracy, is yet an additional limitation to the people's exercise of the right to self-determination'. See V Lanovoy, 'Self-determination in International Law: A Democratic Phenomenon or an Abuse of Right?' (2015) 4(2) *Cambridge Journal of International and Comparative Law* 392.

[30] Roth (n 4) 227.

> juridique ne consiste pas à identifier l'instant précis où celui-ci est né en tant que tel. Ce qu'il importe de savoir, c'est à partir de quand son activité a eu une portée internationale. … De telles activités ont une portée sur le plan international à partir du moment où elles constituent dans la vie institutionnelle de l'Etat territorial un événement anormal qui le force à prendre des mesures exceptionnelles, c'est-à-dire lorsque, pour dominer ou essayer de dominer les événements, il se voit amené à recourir à des moyens qui ne sont pas ceux qu'on emploie d'ordinaire pour faire face à des troubles occasionnels.[31]

Once a national liberation movement was sufficiently organised to surface from secrecy and constituted a serious challenge to the colonial power through political or military action, it started to have visibility at the international level. Accordingly, since 1969 the international community, and in particular the UN General Assembly, started recognising national liberation movements as legitimate representatives of peoples and invited them as observers or members of international organisations.[32] Nevertheless, the criteria for choosing which armed groups should have been recognised were ambiguous. How to identify the legitimate representative of people among several NLMs operating in one country? On what bases were NLMs from some territories, and not from others, recognised? The uncertainty surrounding these issues was essentially caused by the politicised environment in which this practice emerged and the legal vacuum in which the decolonisation process took place.

The Economic Commission for Africa was one of the first bodies to address the question of recognition of national liberation movements. Following the expulsion of Portugal and suspension of South Africa from the Commission, Angola, Guinea-Bissau, Namibia, and Mozambique were left without representation. In 1964 the Commission thus consulted the African governments, seeking suggestions on the criteria to identify the new representatives of people. The majoritarian view found that the Organisation of African Unity (OAU) should be the organ in charge of proposing representatives.[33] In 1967 the Economic Commission endorsed this suggestion, thus establishing a practice that would be followed by other UN organs.[34] Accordingly, upon the OAU's suggestion, the UNGA accepted into the Commission the delegates of the National Front for the Liberation of Angola (*Frente Nacional de Libertação de Angola*, FNLA), the African Party for the Independence of Guinea and Cape Verde (*Partido Africano da Independência da Guiné e Cabo Verde*, PAIGC), the South West Africa People's Organization (SWAPO),[35] and the Mozambique Liberation

[31] *Case concerning the delimitation of maritime boundary between Guinea-Bissau and Senegal*, Arbitral Award, 31 July 1989, RIAA, XX, 119, §§50–51.

[32] HA Wilson, *International Law and the Use of Force* (Clarendon Press, 1988) 139.

[33] ibid, 139–40.

[34] ibid, 140.

[35] The UN Council for Namibia had to solve a similar issue. According to the UNGA mandate, the UN Council had to administer the territory of Namibia 'with the maximum possible participation of the people of the Territory'. See A/RES/2248(S–V), 19 May 1967, *Question of South West Africa*. However, one of the major challenges was the presence of more than one group claiming to represent

Front (*Frente de Libertação de Moçambique*, FRELIMO) as representatives of the people in their respective countries.[36] This episode initiated the practice of the United Nations and regional organisations to recognise NLMs as identified by the OAU.

If the OAU was overwhelmingly recognised as the organ in charge of identifying the legitimate representative of people in Africa, the procedure and the criteria used by the Organization were not as clear-cut. Since the establishment of the OAU in 1963, the Liberation Committee was created to provide support and to finance national liberation movements in their struggles for self-determination. It was thus natural that the committee was selected as the one responsible for recognising NLMs. In order to make the assessment, the Liberation Committee would seek information through a mission in the region. These investigations were often conducted in neighbouring countries, thus raising doubts as to the quality of the collected data. Based on the results of the mission, the Committee would present its decision to the Heads of State summit, which had the final say on the matter.[37]

The criteria used to assess the representativeness of the NLMs were not clearly defined and ultimately led to subjective evaluations. Nevertheless, two main criteria emerged from state practice.[38] First, all the liberation movements recognised by the OAU claimed to represent the whole population, and not just certain tribes or particular minorities. Second, control over the bulk of the population was a decisive element for the recognition, while territorial control was considered less important. This circumstance raised some criticism: if territorial control is relatively easily ascertained, control over the population was ultimately a subjective assessment. Furthermore, the practice of recognising only one liberation movement could ignore the political complexity of the situation. As noted by the Venezuelan representative at the UNGA, this approach distorted 'the principle of self-determination of peoples for the benefit of one political party and to the detriment of other political parties and the rest of the population'.[39]

In order to remedy this criticism, the OAU recognised more than one NLM in certain circumstances. For instance, in Angola it recognised the National Liberation Front of Angola (FNLA), the National Union for the Total Independence of Angola (UNITA) and the People's Movement for the Liberation of Angola (MPLA). However, the recognition of three liberation movements ultimately exacerbated the tensions and fuelled the civil war in the country. In spite of the criticism and the issues related to the recognition of national

the Namibian people. Following the precedent set by other UN organs, the UN Council consulted the OAU, which identified SWAPO as the sole representative in South West Africa.

[36] A/RES/2795 (XXVI), 10 December 1971, *Question of the Territories under Portuguese Administration*. See Wilson (n 32) 117; Roth (n 4) 227.

[37] Wilson (n 32) 143.

[38] ibid, 143–45.

[39] Roth (n 4) 230.

liberation movements as legitimate representatives of peoples, the practice did help in most cases to unite the country against colonial domination: recognising a group as the sole representative of the population proved to be crucially instrumental to the struggle for independence.[40]

II. LEGITIMISING REBELS OUTSIDE THE DECOLONISATION CONTEXT: NEW WINE IN OLD BOTTLES?

A. Recognising Opposition Groups as Legitimate Representatives of People: The Cases of Libya and Syria

On 17 December 2010, Mohamed Bouazizi, a 26-year-old Tunisian, refused to pay one of the numerous bribes expected by a government inspector and set himself on fire as an act of protest. Little did he know that his desperate act would initiate a wave of political revolutions in several countries bordering the Mediterranean Sea: the Arab Spring.[41] The common aspiration underpinning this historical movement was the will to achieve freedom and to put an end to the despotic governments that oppressed the populations. The courage of the people who risked their lives to protest was widely admired. Former President Obama commented on the events:

> It's the same kind of humiliation that takes place every day in many parts of the world – the relentless tyranny of governments that deny their citizens' dignity. Only this time something different happened. After local officials refused to hear his complaints, this young man, who had never been particularly active in politics, went to the headquarters of the provincial government, doused himself in fuel, and lit himself on fire.[42]

In Tunisia and Egypt the regime change was reached relatively swiftly and with limited use of force. This raised the hope that similar outcomes could take place in other countries.[43] However, in Libya and Syria the governments harshly repressed the protests and demonstrations, thus triggering the outbreak of internal conflicts,[44] with Syria to become perhaps the worst humanitarian crisis since World War II.[45]

[40] ibid, 233.

[41] R Wright, 'How the Arab Spring Became the Arab Cataclysm' (*The New Yorker*, 15 December 2015).

[42] ibid.

[43] Five years after the outbreak of the Arab Spring, Sarah Leah Whitson commented on the events that took place in Libya, Yemen, and Syria: '[p]erhaps we in the international community, and the people on the ground, were naïve and misled by how easy the Tunisians made it seem. The Egyptians, too, got rid of a dictator. But we underestimated the forces against democracy and rights – and the way in which other forces of repression an d destruction were able to fill the vacuums that the uprisings created'. See ibid.

[44] See ch 5.

[45] Wright (n 41).

In Libya the conflict erupted in 2011, when the repression of peaceful demonstrations led to a wave of armed violence and clashes between the population and the government. As we have seen, the international community quickly reacted, condemning the actions of the government and concluding that the Libyan government forfeited its legitimacy due to gross and systematic violations of human rights and humanitarian law committed during the NIAC.[46] On the other hand, the National Transitional Council, the leading authority of the opposition group, was widely recognised as the legitimate representative of the Libyan people. On 10 March 2011, France was the first country to define the NTC as 'the legitimate representative of the Libyan people'.[47] Soon thereafter several European countries, the US, and the Arab League made similar statements. For instance, the Chair of the Libya Contact Group affirmed that:

> Qadhafi and his regime had lost all legitimacy and he must leave power allowing the Libyan people to determine their own future. … In contrast with the current regime, the TNC is a legitimate interlocutor, representing the aspirations of Libyan people.[48]

The events in Syria unfolded in a similar way. In March 2011, the regime of Al-Assad repressed peaceful demonstrations, triggering the outburst of the internal conflict that is still affecting the country.[49] Several countries affirmed that the Syrian government lost its legitimacy and recognised the Syrian Opposition Coalition as a legitimate representative of the Syrian people.[50] On 13 November 2012, then-French President François Hollande announced that:

> France recognizes the Syrian National Coalition as the sole legitimate representative of the Syrian people and thus as the future provisional government of a democratic Syria which paves the way to put an end to Bashar Assad's regime.[51]

In the same vein, then-Italian Prime Minister Mario Monti affirmed that 'Italy recognizes the coalition as a legitimate representative of the Syrian people'.[52]

[46] See ch 5.

[47] See Statements Made by the Ministry of Foreign and European Affairs Spokesperson (10 March 2011), quoted in S Talmon, 'Recognition of the Libyan National Transitional Council' (2011) 15(16) *ASIL insights*.

[48] See Statement by Foreign Secretary William Hague following the Libya Contact Group meeting in Doha, 13 April 2011, §§2, 7. The Libya Contact Group was created during the London Conference on Libya, which took place on 29 March 2011. Its members are several European and Middle East countries, the United States, and international organisations. According to the statement of the Chair of the London Conference on Libya (29 March 2011), the aim of the group is: 'to provide leadership and overall political direction to the international effort in close coordination with the UN, AU, Arab League, OIC, and EU to support Libya; provide a forum for coordinating the international response on Libya; and provide a focal point in the international community for contact with the Libyan parties'. See C Henderson, 'International Measures for the Protection of Civilians in Libya and Côte D'Ivoire' (2011) 60(3) *International and Comparative Law Quarterly* 776–77; Talmon (n 47).

[49] A Bellal and L Doswald-Beck, 'Evaluating the Use of Force During the Arab Spring' (2011) 14 *Yearbook of International Humanitarian Law* 7.

[50] S Talmon, 'Recognition of Opposition Groups as the Legitimate Representative of a People' (2013) 12(2) *Chinese Journal of International Law* 220.

[51] ibid, 221.

[52] ibid.

Furthermore, the UK noted that: 'a credible alternative to the Assad regime is emerging that has the growing support of the Arab League, the European Union, the United States and an increasing number of other countries' and thus recognised the SOC as the 'sole legitimate representative' of the Syrian people.[53] The US, the European Union, several European countries, Turkey, and the League of Arab States similarly recognised the SOC as the legitimate representative of the Syrian people.[54] In November 2012 the Fourth Ministerial Meeting of the Group of Friends of the Syrian People took place in Marrakech (Morocco). The document summarising the conclusions reached during the meeting contained a section entitled 'Recognizing the National Coalition of Syrian Revolution and Opposition Forces and the mechanisms of achieving democratic transition' which specified that:

> Participants acknowledged the National Coalition as the legitimate representative of the Syrian people and the umbrella organisation under which Syrian opposition groups are acting.[55]

The practice that emerged in Libya and Syria raises crucial questions. What does it mean to recognise a rebel group as a legitimate representative of its own people? This practice recalls the events that took place during the decolonisation period, when national liberation movements were recognised as legitimate representatives of their own people. Would the recognition of the opposition groups in Libya and Syria imply that they are exercising their right to self-determination? What consequences derive from such recognition?

B. Recognition as Legitimate Representatives and Recognition of Governments

When states recognised the Libyan and Syrian rebels as legitimate representatives of their people, they made fairly clear that it fell short of recognition of governments. For instance, on 27 April 2011, in a State Department press briefing, the US Ambassador to Libya specified that:

> On the question of recognition [of the Libyan government], we continue to look at … all the issues with respect to Libya. As I mentioned when I was here the last time, the President has not ruled out anything on all those gamut of issues that we were looking at. Recognition remains a legal and an international obligations issue that we're still studying, and we have not made a definitive determination on that question. But that has not stopped us from doing everything that we could to support the

[53] ibid, 220.
[54] ibid, 220–24.
[55] See The Fourth Ministerial Meeting of The Group of Friends of the Syrian People (Marrakech, 12 December 2012), Chairman's conclusions, available at reliefweb.int/sites/reliefweb.int/files/resources/Chairman's%20conclusions.pdf.

> TNC and the Libyans. So I don't see it as an issue. It's an issue, but it's not the main one that we're dealing with right now.[56]

It was only in mid-2011 that some countries upgraded the recognition of the Libyan NTC as the government of Libya. On 4 April 2011, Italy defined the NTC 'as the country's only legitimate interlocutor on bilateral relations',[57] while France affirmed that the NTC was 'the only holder of governmental authority in the contacts between France and Libya and its related entities'.[58] These statements constitute clear recognition of the Libyan NTC as the de jure government of Libya and show evidence that the previous recognition as 'legitimate representative of a people' was intended to be something else.

The major difference between the two forms of recognition lies in their nature. While the recognition of a new government is a legal step, the second bears mainly a political value. This was clarified, for instance, by the US State Department, when it recognised the Syrian Opposition Coalition as the legitimate representative of the Syrian people:

> This is not a legal step, this is a political step which not only allows us to give the SOC a political lift and to make it clear that they are the primary group that we will be working with, but it also allows us, as I said, to try to better channel the non-lethal assistance that we provide to the political groups that they are working with on the ground in Syria.[59]

While the recognition of a new government entails necessarily the de-recognition of the incumbent government, the recognition as a legitimate representative of the people is a political act that does not generate 'direct legal effects'.[60] In practical terms, this political recognition means that the state intends to enter into relations with the group and support it. Moreover, it seems to indicate that the recognising state considers that the opposition group has the capability to potentially become the new government.[61] On the other hand, it may also be accompanied by a reduction of the political relations with the incumbent government. Nevertheless, the recognising state would still be bound by the ban on the use of force and the principle of non-intervention in the internal affairs of the state vis-à-vis the de jure government.[62]

[56] Gene Cret, US Ambassador to Libya, Special Briefing *The Political Situation in Libya* (27 April 2011), available at 2009-2017.state.gov/p/nea/rls/rm/161878.htm.

[57] Quoted in Talmon (n 47).

[58] ibid.

[59] ibid, 230.

[60] T Ruys, Of Arms, Funding and "Non-Lethal Assistance" – Issues Surrounding Third State Intervention in the Syrian Civil War' (2014) 13(1) *Chinese Journal of International Law* 37.

[61] D Akande, 'Self Determination and the Syrian Conflict – Recognition of Syrian Opposition as Sole Legitimate Representative of the Syrian People: What Does this Mean and What Implications Does it Have?' (*EJIL: Talk!*, 2012), available at www.ejiltalk.org/self-determination-and-the-syrian-conflict-recognition-of-syrian-opposition-as-sole-legitimate-representative-of-the-syrian-people-what-does-this-mean-and-what-implications-does-it-have/.

[62] Ruys (n 60) 37.

C. Legitimate Representatives and the Question of Internal Self-determination

The recognition of certain Libyan and Syrian opposition groups as legitimate representatives of their own people is reminiscent of the practice that emerged during the decolonisation period, when this definition was attributed to national liberation movements. As aforementioned, NLMs were fighting in the exercise of their right to self-determination against colonial domination, alien occupation, and racist regimes and were recognised as representing their peoples' rights. We could thus wonder whether the recognising states considered that the NTC and the SOC were exercising the right to self-determination on behalf of their own people. At first sight, the answer may seem easy: the National Transitional Council and the Syrian Opposition Coalition were not fighting against colonial domination, alien occupation, or racist regimes; therefore, recognising them as legitimate representatives of their own peoples is essentially improper. However, at a closer look the answer seems more nuanced. Notably, it raises a crucial question: can a single people within a state enjoy a right to self-determination against its own government?[63] And if this is the case, could we consider the NTC and the SOC as exercising the right of internal self-determination on behalf of the Libyan and Syrian peoples?

It is well-known that the principle of self-determination presents an external and an internal dimension. The first provides a people with 'the right to determine the international status of the territory' without external interferences.[64] According to part of the scholarship, this right is limited to peoples subjected to colonial domination, alien occupation, or racist regimes, thus it could not be invoked by rebel groups with irredentist aspirations.[65] On the other hand, other authors suggest a less restrictive approach: the right to self-determination would have a dynamic character, hence it would not be limited to instances of decolonisation. These considerations led to propounding the idea of remedial secession, whereby a people that is a victim of gross and systematic violations of human rights perpetrated by the state would have a right to secede as a remedy against such heinous acts.[66]

[63] Talmon (n 50) 236.

[64] Lanovoy (n 29) 391–92.

[65] See eg Christakis (n 1) 39–138; O Corten, *La Rébellion et le Droit International: le Principe de Neutralité en Tension* (Martinus Nijhoff, 2016) 176; D Schindler, 'Le Principe de Non-intervention dans les Guerres Civiles' (1975) 56 *Annuaire de l'Institut de Droit International* 454–55; H Quane, 'The United Nations and the Evolving Right to Self-Determination' (1998) 47(3) *International & Comparative Law Quarterly* 554–56; MN Shaw, 'Peoples, Territorialism and Boundaries' (1997) 8(3) *European Journal of International Law* 481.

[66] See eg A Tancredi, 'A Normative "Due Process" in the Creation of States rough Secession' in MG Kohen (ed), *Secession: International Law Perspectives* (Cambridge University Press, 2006) 171–207; S van den Driest, *Remedial Secession: A Right to External Self-Determination as a Remedy to Serious Injustices?* (Cambridge University Press, 2013); A Buchanan, *Justice, Legitimacy, and Self-Determination: Moral Foundations of International Law* (Oxford University Press, 2004).

Outside the decolonisation context, and potentially with the exception of remedial secession, in already established and independent states peoples enjoy a right to internal self-determination.[67] Article 1 common to the ICCPR and ICESCR establishes that: '[a]ll peoples have the right of self-determination. By virtue of that right they freely determine their political status and freely pursue their economic, social and cultural development'. The Declaration on Friendly Relations helped in specifying the meaning of the provision, by linking the content of the right to the requirement of 'a government representing the whole people belonging to the territory without distinction as to race, creed or color'.[68] In the same vein, the International Court of Justice confirmed that the right to internal self-determination 'requires a free and genuine expression of the will of the peoples concerned'.[69]

If the presence of a government representative of the will of the people is decisive for the exercise of the right to internal self-determination, it is paramount to understand when a government can be deemed to be representative. Could a people choose any form of government, dictatorship included, or does international law limit peoples' freedom of choice?[70] Influenced by the debates on the existence of a right to democratic governance, some authors claim that the government can really represent the will of a people only if it is democratic.[71] According to Franck, internal self-determination would equate to a right to 'free, fair and open participation in the democratic process of governance freely chosen by each state'.[72] This conclusion would emerge from a joint

Arguing against the existence of a right to remedial secession, see eg J Vidmar, 'Remedial Secession in International Law: Theory and (Lack of) Practice' (2010) 6(1) *St Antony's International Review* 37–56.

[67] See eg the Canadian Supreme Court: '[t]he recognized sources of international law establish that the right to self-determination of a people is normally fulfilled through internal self-determination – a people's pursuit of its political, economic, social and cultural development within the framework of an existing state'. *Reference re Secession of Quebec* [1998] SCR (Canada) 217, §126. See E Lieblich, *International Law and Civil Wars: Intervention and Consent* (Routledge, 2013) 222; Lanovoy (n 29) 392.

[68] Declaration on Friendly Relations (n 24) principle V, para 7. See also S van den Driest, '"Pro-Democratic" Intervention and the Right To Political Self-Determination: the Case of Operation Iraqi Freedom' (2010) 57(1) *Netherlands International Law Review* 33.

[69] ICJ, *Western Sahara*, Advisory Opinion, 16 October 1975, §55. Cassese defines internal self–determinations as 'the right to authentic self–government, that is, the right for a people really and freely to choose its own political and economic regime'. See Cassese (n 2) 101.

[70] C Vandewoude, 'The Rise of Self-Determination Versus the Rise of Democracy' (2010) 2 *Goettingen Journal of International Law* 984.

[71] Christakis (n 1) 333–34; Vandewoude (n 70) 992; Y Beigbeder, *International Monitoring of Plebiscites, Referenda and National Elections: Self-Determination and Transition to Democracy* (Martinus Nijhoff, 1994) 18; GH Fox, 'Self-Determination in the Post-Cold War Era: a New Internal Focus?' (1995) 16(3) *Michigan Journal of International Law* 736.

[72] TM Franck, 'The Emerging Right to Democratic Governance' (1992) 86(1) *American Journal of International Law* 50. According to Cassese, 'a general rule is now gradually emerging to the effect that peoples of sovereign states are entitled to internal self-determination, i.e. democratic government'. A Cassese, 'The International Court of Justice and the Right of Peoples to Self-Determination' in V Lowe and M Fitzmaurice (eds), *Fifty Years of the International Court of Justice: Essays in Honour of Sir Robert Jennings* (Cambridge University Press, 1996) 352.

interpretation of Articles 1 and 25 of the ICCPR, which establishes that '[e]very citizen shall have the right and the opportunity ... (b) To vote and to be elected at genuine periodic elections which shall be by universal and equal suffrage and shall be held by secret ballot, guaranteeing the free expression of the will of the electors'.[73]

Nevertheless, this democratic interpretation of Article 25 of the ICCPR does not seem to be universally accepted in scholarship and practice.[74] Moreover, the right to internal self-determination does not impose on peoples the obligation to choose a democratic form of governance.[75] As highlighted by the Human Rights Committee:

> The rights under article 25 are related to, but distinct from, the right of peoples to self-determination. By virtue of the rights covered by article 1(1) peoples have the right to freely determine their political status and to enjoy the right to choose the form of their constitution or government. Article 25 deals with the right of individuals to participate in those processes which constitute the conduct of public affairs.[76]

As explained before,[77] democratic governance is not an established right in international law. Roth correctly notes that: '[a]lbeit paradoxical, it is far from ridiculous that popular sovereignty may amount, as a matter of practical application, to the right to be ruled by domestic thugs', rather than by a democratic government elected through free and fair elections.[78] Consequently, peoples may well exercise their right to internal self-determination by accepting being governed by a regime or a dictatorship: the acquiescence of the bulk of the population would suggest that the type of government reflects the will of the people. However, the scenario changes if the population starts demonstrating against the incumbent government and asks for change. In such an instance, the people is clearly expressing the idea that the government no longer reflects its will. What if the government harshly represses the demonstrations, thus triggering the outbreak of an internal conflict? Would it be possible to conclude that the people is fighting for its right of internal self-determination against the government?

This instance reflects the facts that took place in Libya and Syria, where the NTC and the SOC have been recognised as legitimate representatives of

[73] Christakis (n 1) 333–34; Vandewoude (n 70) 992; Y Beigbeder (n 71) 18.
[74] J Vidmar, 'Remedial Secession in International Law: Theory and (Lack of) Practice' (2010) 6(1) *St Antony's International Review* 37–56.
[75] Lanovoy (n 29) 394.
[76] UN Human Rights Committee, 'General Comment 25: Article 25 (Participation in Public Affairs and the Right to Vote), The Right to Participate in Public Affairs, Voting Rights and the Right of Equal Access to Public Service' 12 July 1996, CCPR/C/21/Rev.1/Add.7. See also J Vidmar, 'Judicial Interpretations of Democracy in Human Rights Treaties' (2014) 3(2) *Cambridge Journal of International and Comparative Law* 535–38.
[77] See ch 3.
[78] BR Roth, *Sovereign Equality and Moral Disagreement: Premises of a Pluralist International Legal Order* (Oxford University Press, 2011) 205.

the whole population. This circumstance raises two questions. First, we could wonder whether the Libyan and Syrian peoples were, and in the case of Syria still are, fighting for their right to self-determination. Second, it is unclear whether recognising the NTC and the SOC as legitimate representatives implies that they were representing their peoples in the exercise of their right to self-determination. Talmon answers negatively to both questions:

> [W]here the term 'people' refers to the population of the State as a whole, it is doubtful that international law attaches legally relevant powers of representation to the fact of 'legitimate representative of a people'. In international law, the representative of a single people constituting a sovereign and independent State is the government of that State irrespective of its actual representativeness.[79]

According to Talmon, the right to internal self-determination would apply to peoples of independent states only when the latter are 'multinational states, i.e. states composed of more than one people. In the case of a single people, the right to self-determination becomes the right of the State and is directed against "external interference" by other States'.[80] Otherwise, he explains, the state and the people constituting it would have a different legal personality. Therefore, the only possible conclusion would be that 'a single people within a State does not enjoy a right of internal self-determination against its own State or government'.[81]

However, this approach does not seem in line with the content of the right to self-determination. Cassese explains – correctly, in the author's view – that 'the right to internal self-determination afforded to the *entire population of a sovereign State* … exists under treaty law by virtue of Article 1 of the 1966 Covenants'.[82] Indeed, Article 1 states that all peoples enjoy a right to 'freely determine their political status'. Limiting the right of self-determination of the *whole people* to a right to be free from external interference would undermine the potential of this right. The people's right to 'determine their political status' (Article 1) implies that the people has a right to choose the form of governance, not only free from external interferences, but also void of any coercion from the incumbent government. Unlike its external dimension, the right to internal self-determination is ongoing,[83] thus allowing the people to 'change or recreate the manifestation of their system of government and administration'.[84] As noted by Paust:

> Where a government engages in a strategy to deny political participation of persons in a process of self-determination and to violate correlative human rights, such

[79] Talmon (n 50) 235.
[80] ibid, 236.
[81] ibid, 235–36.
[82] Cassese (n 2) 102.
[83] See eg UN Human Rights Committee, 'General Comment No. 12: The Right to Self-Determination of Peoples' 13 March 1984, HRI/GEN/1/Rev.9 (Vol I).
[84] van den Driest (n 68) 36.

> government engages, however indirectly, in a process of political oppression ... that violates self-determination and related human rights.[85]

In light of the foregoing, we could conclude that the Libyan and Syrian peoples were fighting for their right to internal self-determination.[86] However, this does not automatically clarify what states meant when they recognised the NTC and the SOC as legitimate representatives of their own peoples. The choice of the terminology could suggest that these opposition groups represent the peoples in the exercise of their right to internal self-determination against their respective governments.[87] However, a thorough analysis of the declarations of the states that have proceeded to the recognition of the NTC and of the SOC suggests otherwise. Indeed, the recognising states have never referred to the right to internal self-determination of the Libyan and Syrian peoples. Instead, the recognition of the NTC and the SOC seems to be based on the fact that the governments had lost legitimacy due to their exercise of power, and that those opposition groups seemed a valid and legitimate alternative.

D. Rebel Groups as Legitimate Representatives of People: New Wine in Old Bottles

The previous sections have shown what *legitimate representative of a people* does not mean in the context of the Libyan and Syrian conflicts. Although it was accompanied by the de-legitimation of the incumbent governments, the recognition of certain opposition groups as legitimate representatives of peoples is not tantamount to recognition of governments.[88] On the other hand, such recognition is different from the recognition of liberation movements during the decolonisation period. Akande described with clarity the doubts raised by the recognition of the NTC and the SOC:

> Something which is not quite a government (or perhaps even a kind of government), not quite a national liberation movement, not quite an insurgent. None of the States that has described the NTC as legitimate representative have stated explicitly that

[85] JJ Paust, 'International Law, Dignity, Democracy, and the Arab Spring' (2013) 46 *Cornell International Law Journal* 10.

[86] This conclusion may raise concerns with regard to its consequences and implications. For instance, according to Talmon '[t]he right of internal self-determination would, in case of dictatorships that systematically and grossly violate human rights, ultimately amount to a right of revolution by a people against its own State'. See Talmon (n 50) 235. Furthermore, Schmitt pointed out that: '[e]ven if the right of self-determination applied in Syria, it remains unsettled whether external states are entitled to provide military aid to peoples fighting for self-determination'. See MN Schmitt, 'Legitimacy versus Legality Redux: Arming the Syrian Rebels' (2014) 7 *Journal of National Security Law & Policy* 115.

[87] Akande (n 61).

[88] Corten (n 65) 246.

they regard this as a legal status. However, they all seem to regard this status as having significance.[89]

The practice that emerged in Libya and Syria may suggest that the recognition of an opposition group as legitimate representative of a people might be a procedural step that precedes the possible recognition of the group as the new government.[90] On the one hand, the NTC was eventually recognised as the new government as soon as the Gaddafi regime was defeated.[91] On the other hand, although Assad is still considered as the de jure government, it has been suggested that the recognition of the SOC as legitimate representative may lead to a recognition of it as the government. For instance, then-French President Hollande affirmed that: 'France recognizes the Syrian National Coalition as the sole representative of the Syrian people and thus as the future provisional government of a democratic Syria'.[92] This and similar declarations would suggest that a new trend is crystallising, whereby the recognition of a group as legitimate representative of its own people could be interpreted as 'a form of intermediary step' which could result in recognition as a new government.[93]

This practice could lead us to wonder why states felt the need to introduce this procedural step, and why in Libya and Syria. As a matter of fact, intermediate situations in which states proceeded to the recognition of rebels had already occurred in the past. The traditional belligerency and insurgency doctrines have allowed states to enter into relations with rebel groups. However, such a relationship was contingent upon rebels' effective control over at least part of state territory. While effectiveness has been a crucial criterion for decades, recent developments show that it has been gradually, but not completely, replaced by the criterion of protection of civilians. In the words of Lieblich, the perception of effectiveness is shifting 'from its traditional understanding as connoting *effective control over territory*, to one which refers to the *effective protection of civilians*'. Therefore, when a government commits gross and systematic violations of human rights and humanitarian law, and thus loses its legitimacy in the eyes of (at least part of) the international community, the opposition might be seen as a valid interlocutor and potential new government.[94] It is thus worth investigating the consequences of these new developments with regard to the use of force by legitimate rebels, the government against which they are fighting, and third states.

[89] D Akande, 'Which Entity Is the Government of Libya and Why Does it Matter?' (*EJIL: Talk!*, 2011), available at www.ejiltalk.org/which-entity-is-the-government-of-libya-and-why-does-it-matter/.

[90] J d'Aspremont, '"Regimes" Legitimacy Crises in International Law: Libya, Syria, and their Competing Representatives' in R Grote and TJ Röder (eds), *Constitutionalism, Human Rights, and Islam after the Arab Spring* (Oxford University Press, 2016) 67.

[91] ibid, 60.

[92] S Erlanger and R Gladstone, 'France Grants Its Recognition to Syria Rebels' (*The New York Times*, 13 November 2012), available at www.nytimes.com/2012/11/14/world/middleeast/syria-war-developments.html.

[93] d'Aspremont (n 90) 67.

[94] Lieblich (n 67) 235.

III. CONCLUDING OBSERVATIONS

From the 1960s, several national liberation movements (NLMs) were recognised as legitimate representatives of their own people. Over the past years, a number of states attributed the same definition to the Libyan National Transitional Council and the National Coalition for Syrian Revolutionary and Opposition Forces. In both cases, the recognition was based on the reasons why they were fighting: on the one hand, NLMs were exercising their right to self-determination against colonial domination, alien occupation, or racist regimes; on the other hand, the Libyan and Syrian rebels were fighting against oppressive powers that lost their legitimacy due to gross and systematic violations of human rights and humanitarian law.

As demonstrated in the previous chapters, the legitimacy of governments tends to be assessed on the basis of the origin and the exercise of power. Conversely, state practice would suggest that the legitimacy of rebels is based on the reasons why they are fighting. Specifically, the perception of legitimacy seems to derive from the fact that the opposition group fights against violations of fundamental human rights. This analysis would thus lead us to conclude that human rights have emerged as a parameter of legitimacy. However, this is not void of risks and raises crucial questions. Notably, we may wonder whether these groups were really representatives of their own peoples. As a matter of fact, the assessment conducted by the international community during the decolonisation period raises serious doubts as to the representativeness of the NLMs. Similarly, it is doubtful whether a thorough assessment was conducted with regard to the representativeness of the NTC and the SOC. Furthermore, using human rights as a parameter of legitimacy could entail dangers to human rights themselves. These risks and doubts will be addressed in the concluding chapter.[95]

[95] See ch 9.

7

Use of Force by and against Legitimate Rebels: Towards the Emergence of a Jus ad Bellum *Applicable to Internal Armed Conflicts?*

I. STATE USE OF FORCE AND LEGITIMATE REBELS

A. Use of Force against National Liberation Movements

NATIONAL LIBERATION WARS are in many ways akin to internal conflicts that see one or more opposition groups opposing the incumbent government. However, they differ as to the purposes pursued with the armed struggle. The exercise of the right to self-determination was seen as paramount to putting an end to situations which were considered substantially unjust – namely colonial dominations, alien occupations, and racist regimes. Thus, the international community, especially developing and socialist countries, started to question the application of the traditional rules regulating the relationship between a government and opposition groups fighting against it. While normally the state can repress a rebellion, admitting the lawfulness of such repression against NLMs would have been tantamount to denying peoples' right to self-determination. Therefore, the majority of the international community and of the scholarship propounded that every state has a duty to refrain from taking action aimed at depriving peoples of their right to self-determination.[1]

Several resolutions adopted by the UNGA from the 1960s contributed to consolidating the prohibition to repress the legitimate struggle of NLMs. First, the Declaration on the Granting of Independence to Colonial Countries and Peoples specifies that:

> All armed action or repressive measures of all kinds directed against dependent peoples shall cease in order to enable them to exercise peacefully and freely their right to complete independence, and the integrity of their national territory shall be respected.[2]

[1] A Cassese, *Self-Determination of Peoples: A Legal Reappraisal* (Cambridge University Press, 1995), 194–97; N Ronzitti, 'Resort to Force in Wars of National Liberation' in A Cassese (ed), *Current Problems of International Law* (Giuffrè, 1975) 320.

[2] A/RES/1514(XV), 14 December 1960, *Declaration on the Granting of Independence to Colonial Countries and Peoples*, §4.

Furthermore, Resolution 2131(XX) clarifies that: '[t]he use of force to deprive peoples of their national identity constitutes a violation of their inalienable rights and of the principle of non-intervention'.[3] In 1966 the UNGA restated this position by affirming that any forcible action which deprives peoples under foreign occupation of their right to self-determination amounts to a violation of the UN Charter.[4] While a minority of states opposed the prohibition to repress peoples' struggle for self-determination,[5] the adoption of the Declaration on Friendly Relations overrode the reticence of these countries:

> Every State has the duty to refrain from any forcible action which deprives peoples referred to in the elaboration of the principle of equal rights and self-determination of their right to self-determination and freedom and independence.[6]

This proposition is reinforced by the specification that: '[t]he use of force to deprive peoples of their national identity constitutes a violation of their inalienable rights and of the principle of non-intervention'.[7]

The provisions enshrined in the aforementioned UNGA resolutions and declarations were confirmed by consistent state practice. Indeed, the international community generally condemned the repression of peoples exercising their right to self-determination. However, states' positions reflected the substantial division which accompanied the Cold War in general and debates on decolonisation in particular: while developing and socialist countries condemned any use of force by the oppressive power, Western countries criticised the repression only inasmuch as it was excessive or disproportionate. In spite of this divergence, the existence of the prohibition to repress any endeavours to exercise the right to self-determination seems now generally accepted.[8]

The provisions at issue raised a doctrinal discussion on the nature of the prohibition. Notably, the legal scholarship was divided as to whether the ban on the use of force by the oppressive power would derive from Article 2(4) of the UN Charter, or whether it is an autonomous ad hoc rule that emerged through custom. The first group of authors starts its reasoning from Article 2(4), which establishes that states cannot use force in their international relations.[9] This qualification has generally been interpreted as

[3] A/RES/2132(XX), 21 December 1965, *Declaration on the Inadmissibility of Intervention in the Domestic Affairs of States and the Protection of Their Independence and Sovereignty*, §3.

[4] A/RES/2160(XXI), 30 November 1966, *Strict Observance of the Prohibition of the Threat or Use of Force in International Relations, and of the Right of Peoples to Self-Determination*, §1(b).

[5] Ronzitti (n 1) 332.

[6] A/RES/2625 (XXV), 24 October 1970, *Declaration on Principles of International Law concerning Friendly Relations and Cooperation among States in accordance with the Charter of the United Nations*, emphasis added.

[7] ibid.

[8] C Gray, *International Law and the Use of Force* (Oxford University Press, 2008) 61.

[9] See G Herczeg, 'The Prohibition of the Threat and Use of Force in Contemporary International Law' in *Questions of International Law* (ILA Hungarian Branch, 1964) 84–85; SV Molodcov, 'The Principle that States should Refrain from the Threat or Use of Force in International Relations' in *WFUNA Seminar* 1965.

meaning *relations among states*. Nevertheless, since the 1960s the relations between the oppressive power and the people exercising their right to self-determination 'have no longer been regarded as internal or municipal, but are seen as coming within the purview of international relations proper'.[10] This would be confirmed by Article 1(4) of the Additional Protocol I, which establishes that armed conflicts in which peoples are fighting against colonial domination, alien occupation, or racist regimes are to be considered international conflicts.[11] Furthermore, Article 2(4) prohibits any use of force which is 'inconsistent with the purposes of the United Nations'. Since Article 1(2) of the UN Charter mentions self-determination of people among the purposes of the UN, it has been argued that Article 2(4) would prevent the armed repression of national liberation struggles.[12]

The majority of the scholarship criticised this approach and argued that the use of force to repress people exercising their right to self-determination is not prohibited by Article 2(4) of the UN Charter, but by an autonomous, ad hoc rule which is customary in nature.[13] Ronzitti noted that Article 2(4) prohibits any use of force 'inconsistent with the purposes of the United Nations'. However, the use of force incompatible with the aims of the United Nations is prohibited insofar as it concerns international relations.[14] These cannot be interpreted as encompassing the relationship between the oppressing power and people fighting for their right to self-determination; instead, it should be limited to the relationships among states.[15] Moreover, none of the UNGA resolutions preventing the use of force to repress the exercise of self-determination mentions Article 2(4) of the UN Charter, thus suggesting that the prohibition under exam derives directly from the principle of self-determination and has emerged through custom. The majority of the scholarship has embraced this position. For instance, Wilson propounded that 'the use of force to deny the free exercise of a people's right to self-determination is contrary to the principles of international law'.[16] In the same vein, Wippman maintained that 'action against national liberation movements constitute[s] a violation of the principle of self-determination'.[17] Ten years later, Gray described this provision as a corollary to the right to self-determination.[18]

[10] Cassese, *Self-Determination of Peoples* (n 1) 196. See also G Abi-Saab, 'Wars of National Liberation and the Laws of War' (1972) 3(3) *Annales d'études internationals* 101–03.
[11] Protocol Additional to the Geneva Conventions of 12 August 1949, and relating to the Protection of Victims of Non-International Armed Conflicts (Protocol II).
[12] Cassese, *Self-Determination of Peoples* (n 1) 96.
[13] Ronzitti (n 1) 330. See also Gray (n 8); D Wippman, 'Military Intervention, Regional Organizations, and Host State Consent' (1996) 7 *Duke Journal of Comparative and International Law* 209–39.
[14] Ronzitti (n 1) 330.
[15] ibid.
[16] HA Wilson, *International Law and the Use of Force by National Liberation Movements* (Clarendon Press, 1988) 135.
[17] Wippman (n 13) 215.
[18] Gray (n 8) 61.

A further issue concerns whether the prohibition to repress the struggle of people exercising their right to self-determination is limited to forcible measures, or if it extends to actions short of the use of force. On the one hand, if we accept that the ban derives from Article 2(4) of the UN Charter, it seems logical that it should be limited to the use of force, thus excluding other means of repression.[19] At the other end of the spectrum, Cassese argued that this view is unsound.[20] Indeed, the prohibition to undertake any 'forcible action' could be interpreted as banning the establishment of 'a repressive regime which does not allow the oppressed people to determine its future status by free means'.[21] The latter position seems to be preferred: if the objective of the prohibition to repress peoples' struggle is to allow them to exercise their right to self-determination, it seems logical that this should encompass any forcible action which would prevent such a goal.

In light of the foregoing, it is now well-settled that colonial, alien, and racist powers are prohibited to repress the actions of a people exercising its right to self-determination. As noted by Roth:

> 'Alien, colonial, and racist domination' (illegal conquests and occupations, colonialism, and apartheid) … have explicitly or implicitly lost the protection of the international peace and security order because they violated broadly held premises about acceptable governance and popular sovereignty.[22]

Therefore, the traditional presumption whereby the government can forcibly react against opposition groups has been at least partially reversed.

B. Excessive Use of Internal Force by the Government Outside the Decolonisation Context

It is commonplace that international law regulates the use of force among states. On the other hand, internal conflicts are beyond the reach of international law, thus they are neither lawful, nor unlawful.[23] The UN Charter and customary rules of *jus ad bellum* focus on regulating international instances of the use of force. 'Thus, for the most part, they provide only minimal guidance, if any, to normative judgments concerning conflicts purely within national boundaries.'[24] On the other hand, over the past decades international law has

[19] Ronzitti (n 1) 321–25.

[20] Cassese, *Self-Determination of Peoples* (n 1) 181.

[21] ibid, 182.

[22] BR Roth, *Sovereign Equality and Moral Disagreement: Premises of a Pluralist International Legal Order* (Oxford University Press, 2011) 157.

[23] See eg M Akehurst: '[t]here is no rule in international law against civil wars' in M Akehurst, *A Modern Introduction to International Law* (Routledge, 1992) 281–82. See also K Samuels, '*Jus Ad Bellum* and Civil Conflicts: A Case Study of the International Community's Approach to Violence in the Conflict in Sierra Leone' (2003) 8(2) *Journal of Conflict & Security Law* 317–18.

[24] JN Moore, 'Introduction' in JN Moore (ed), *Law and Civil War in the Modern World* (Johns Hopkins University Press, 1974) xiii.

increasingly developed and refined the laws of wars applicable to NIACs: IHL, IHRL, ICL, and weapons law all contribute to regulating internal conflicts, pursuing the ultimate aim of lessening the impact of violence on the civilian population.[25] Parallel to the development of the rules regulating NIACs, the increasing concern about the dramatic consequences of internal conflicts on civilians has triggered discussions on humanitarian interventions and the Responsibility to Protect (R2P) doctrine.[26]

It is against this backdrop that the practice which emerged during the 1990s should be read, whereby systematic violations of human rights by the government were overwhelmingly condemned in the international arena.[27] For instance, in 1998 the Security Council denounced 'the use of excessive force by Serbian police forces against civilians'.[28] Furthermore, it condemned 'the continued human rights violations by the Yemeni authorities, such as the excessive use of force against peaceful protestors'.[29] In the same vein, the Commission of Inquiry on Libya found that 'the Government forces engaged in excessive use of force against demonstrators',[30] while the Human Rights Council condemned 'the continued grave and systematic human rights violations by the Syrian authorities, such as arbitrary executions, excessive use of force and the killing and persecution of protesters and human rights defenders'.[31]

In light of this practice, some authors wondered whether we are witnessing the emergence of a new customary rule prohibiting states to use excessive *internal* force against their own population.[32] In the words of Frowein:

> It is no longer inconceivable that a rule of international law will come into existence which prohibits the internal use of the State military with its modern weaponry under certain conditions. … As soon as an internal conflict reaches beyond police action, this would then be of concern to international law not only as a matter of the law of non-international armed conflict, but also with respect to the use of force as such.[33]

[25] R Wedgwood, 'The Use of Force in Civil Disputes' (1996) 26 *Israel Yearbook on Human Rights* 239–41.

[26] Samuels (n 23) 321–22; E Lieblich, *International Law and Civil Wars: Intervention and Consent* (Routledge, 2013) 175–76.

[27] Lieblich (n 26) 179.

[28] S/RES/1160 (1998), 31 March 1998.

[29] S/RES/2014 (2011), 21 October 2011.

[30] Human Rights Council, Report of the International Commission of Inquiry to investigate all alleged violations of international human rights law in the Libyan Arab Jamahiriya (hereinafter, Report of the International Commission of Inquiry for Libya), A/HRC/17/44, 1 June 2011, §99.

[31] Human Rights Council Resolution, *Situation of human rights in the Syrian Arab Republic*, A/HRC/RES/S-17/1, 22-23 August 2011, §1.

[32] C Kreß, 'Major Post-Westphalian Shifts and Some Important Neo-Westphalian Hesitations in the State Practice on the International Law on The Use of Force' (2014) 1(1) *Journal on the Use of Force and International Law* 20.

[33] JA Frowein, 'Globale und regionale Friedenssicherung nach 50 Jahren Vereinte Nationen' (1995) 114 *Zeitschri für Schweizerisches Recht* 269, translated in Kreß (n 32) 20.

During the decolonisation period similar questions triggered passionate discussions among scholars and in international practice. Several UNGA resolutions adopted in the 1960s and 1970s unequivocally maintained that 'every state has a duty to *refrain from any forcible action* which deprives peoples' under colonial domination, alien occupation, or racist regimes of their right to self-determination.[34] However, it was unclear whether such prohibition derived from Article 2(4) of the UN Charter or was established by an autonomous, customary rule.[35] While such discussions fell out of fashion after the 1970s, new debates on the emergence of an internal *jus ad bellum* resurfaced in the 1990s. During the Yugoslavian conflict, the international community in general and the Security Council in particular condemned the use of force by both the government and non-state forces.[36] This practice raised the question as to whether the international community intended to extend the scope of the ban on the use of force to also cover internal conflicts.[37] Similar considerations emerged during the Libyan and Syrian conflicts. The reactions of the Security Council and of several states to these conflicts seem ambivalent on this point. On the one hand, they may be interpreted as prohibiting the use of force by all the parties to the conflict. On the other hand, we may wonder whether the UNSC intended to ban the *excessive* use of force, and not just any instance of violent action committed by the parties to the conflict.[38]

The idea that Article 2(4) of the UN Charter could extend to also covering internal conflicts has not matured into law.[39] The international condemnation of the use of force by Libyan and Syrian state forces against their own population would confirm this view. While the commissions of inquiry for Libya and Syria found that the two governments exercised excessive force against their own populations, the term was not used as to fall within the scope of Article 2(4) of the UN Charter. Rather, it was considered within the human rights framework. Notably, in considering the excessive use of force by governmental forces during the demonstrations, the Commission of Inquiry for Libya specified that the legal framework encompasses the ICCPR and the Code of Conduct for Law Enforcement Officials and the Basic Principles on

[34] *Declaration on Principles of International Law concerning Friendly Relations and Co-operation among States in accordance with the Charter of the United Nations*, A/RES/25/2625 (XXV), 24 October 1970 (hereinafter Declaration on Friendly Relations), emphasis added.

[35] Ronzitti (n 1) 330.

[36] See eg S/RES/876 (1993), 19 October 1993, §4; S/RES/1125 (1997), 6 August 1997, §6; S/RES/1311 (2000), 28 July 2000, §5.

[37] O Corten, *The Law against War: The Prohibition on the Use of Force in Contemporary International Law* (Hart Publishing, 2010) 131.

[38] O Corten, *La Rébellion et le Droit International: le Principe de Neutralité en Tension* (Martinus Nijhoff, 2016) 134–39.

[39] See eg ibid, 130; G Nolte, *Eingreifen auf Einladung: zur völkerrechtlichen Zulässigkeit des Einsatzes fremder Truppen im internen Konflikt auf Einladung der Regierung* (Springer, 1999) 204.

the Use of Force and Firearms by Law Enforcement Officials, and concluded that there is:

> [S]ufficient evidence to suggest that the Government forces engaged in excessive use of force against demonstrators, at least in the early days of the protests, leading to significant deaths and injuries. ... Such actions represented a serious breach of a range of rights under the ICCPR including the right to life, the right to security of person, as well as freedom of assembly and freedom of expression.[40]

Similar considerations can be found in subsequent reports on Libya and Syria. Therefore, it seems clear that excessive use of force by governmental forces is not considered in terms of *jus ad bellum*. Instead, the common denominator is the emphasis on gross and systematic violations of human rights and humanitarian law.[41] Therefore, in order to limit state use of internal force, international practice shows a preference for international human rights law, IHL, and international criminal law.[42] These findings confirm the traditional approach: the monopoly on the use of force is a state prerogative and the ban on the use of force applies only among states in their international relations. Nevertheless, this conclusion leaves open a further question: while governments have the right to use force to repress an internal conflict, and it is only the *excessive* use of force that is prohibited, does international law have something to say about the beginning of an internal conflict? In other words, can states start an internal conflict?

The Libyan and Syrian conflicts may help with addressing this issue. In both countries, the regimes violently repressed peaceful protests and their actions were condemned by the international community.[43] At the same time, as a reaction to the violent governmental repression the Libyan and Syrian peoples started to organise themselves into rebel groups. Before the outbreak of a NIAC, the relevant legal framework is human rights law and law enforcement.[44] The human right to life is enshrined in Article 6(1) of the ICCPR[45] and has a customary nature. It is well-known that this right is not absolute. For instance,

[40] Report of the International Commission of Inquiry for Libya (n 30) §99.

[41] See eg on Libya, S/RES/1970 (2011), preamble, §2: '*[d]eploring* the gross and systematic violation of human rights, including the repression of peaceful demonstrators'; S/RES/1973 (2011), 17 March 2011, preamble, §4: '*[c]ondemning* the gross and systematic violation of human rights, including arbitrary detentions, enforced disappearances, torture and summary executions'. On Syria, see eg A/RES/67/262, 4 June 2013, *The situation in the Syrian Arab Republic*, preamble, §5: '[e]xpressing grave concern at the continuing escalation of violence in the Syrian Arab Republic, in particular the continued widespread and systematic gross violations and abuses of human rights and violations of international humanitarian law'.

[42] Kreß (n 32) 25.

[43] A Bellal and L Doswald-Beck, 'Evaluating the Use of Force During the Arab Spring' (2011) 14 *Yearbook of International Humanitarian Law* 5–7.

[44] ibid, 15.

[45] At the regional level see eg American Convention on Human Rights, Art 4(1); and Arab Charter on Human Rights 2004, Art 5(2).

states could exceptionally use lethal force to maintain public order and to protect the rights and freedom of others.[46] The UN Basic Principles on the Use of Force and Firearms by Law Enforcement Officials[47] detail the standards that should be respected in the context of peaceful protests. Notably, the recourse to force would be lawful only 'if other means remain ineffective or without any promise of achieving the intended result'. Furthermore, Principle 10 establishes that:

> In the dispersal of violent assemblies, law enforcement officials may use firearms only when less dangerous means are not practicable and only to the minimum extent necessary. Law enforcement officials shall not use firearms in such cases, except under the conditions stipulated in principle 9.

Principle 9 reads as follows:

> Law enforcement officials shall not use firearms against persons except in self-defence or defence of others against the imminent threat of death or serious injury, to prevent the perpetration of a particularly serious crime involving grave threat to life, to arrest a person presenting such danger and resisting their authority, or to prevent his or her escape, and only when less extreme means are insufficient to achieve these objectives. In any event, intentional lethal use of firearms may only be made when strictly unavoidable in order to protect life.

Therefore, under law enforcement standards states can recur to lethal force only in exceptional circumstances. In particular, states

> [M]ust only use the minimum necessary force in pursuit of a legitimate objective (including arrest whenever possible); and must only use force in proportion to the harm sought to be avoided. … Potentially lethal force (e.g. firearms or certain less-lethal weapons) may only be used where there is an imminent threat to life or of serious injury (i.e. a potentially life-threatening act). In any event, intentional lethal use of force (which use of artillery clearly is) is only lawful when strictly unavoidable to protect life.[48]

In conclusion, under human rights law states would be prohibited from starting an internal conflict. This would find confirmation in UNSC and states' reactions to the violent repression of demonstrations in Libya and Syria. For instance, in Resolution 1970 (2011) the Security Council deplored 'the gross and systematic violation of human rights, including the repression of peaceful demonstrators', demanded 'an immediate end to the violence and call[ed] for steps to fulfil the legitimate demands of the population'.[49] Similarly,

[46] Bellal and Doswald-Beck (n 43) 15.

[47] Basic Principles on the Use of Force and Firearms by Law Enforcement Officials, Adopted by the Eighth United Nations Congress on the Prevention of Crime and the Treatment of Offenders, Havana, Cuba, 1990.

[48] C Redaelli and S Casey-Maslen, 'Protecting Civilians in Populated Areas during the Conduct of Hostilities after the *Gotovina* Case' in *The War Report: Armed Conflict in 2013* (Oxford University Press, 2014) 468.

[49] S/RES/1970 (2011) (n 41).

the international community overwhelmingly condemned the use of force against the population in Syria and the attacks against the protesters.[50] It is interesting to note that international human rights law prohibits states from starting an internal conflict, while the same ban does not apply to the population.

II. LEGITIMATE REBELS AND THE USE OF FORCE

A. The Right to Rebel under International Law

The idea that rebels may have a right to revolt against the state, at least under certain circumstances, is not a new one. In the Middle Ages some scholars suggested that people had a right to react against an oppressive and abusive tyrant.[51] However, it was only in the sixteenth century that the idea was thoroughly developed in the scholarship. The Spanish Jesuit Suárez, for instance, propounded that the people could overthrow the sovereign. Since the power of the prince descends from God, the sovereign cannot exercise it as it pleases. Notably, he has to respect the population under its power. Should he turn into a tyrant and oppress his own people, they could overthrow him.[52] In subsequent years, the idea of a right to rebel was secularised. In the seventeenth century, Pufendorf propounded that the right to revolt against a tyrant derived from the inherent right to individual self-defence.[53] Similarly, Vattel maintained that people subject to a tyranny have the right to resist their sovereign: 'those monsters who, under the title of sovereigns, render themselves the scourges and horror of the human race … are savage beasts, whom every brave man may justly exterminate from the face of the earth'.[54]

Discourses on the right to rebel fell out of fashion during the nineteenth century and it was only during the decolonisation period that similar discussions resurfaced among legal scholars.[55] More recently, the outbreak of revolutions

[50] UN Human Rights Council, *The Human Rights Situation in the Syrian Arab Republic*, 2 December 2011, A/HRC/RES/S–18/1; UNGA Third Committee, Situation of Human Rights in the Syrian Arab Republic, A/C.3/66/L.57/Rev.1, adopted by the Third Committee on 22 November 2011. See Bellal and Doswald-Beck (n 43) 19.

[51] See ch 1.

[52] F Suárez, *Selections from three works of Francisco Suárez, S.J.: De legibus, ac Deo legislatore, 1612, Defensio fidei catholicae, et apostolicae adversus anglicanae sectae errores, 1613, De triplici virtute theologica, fide, spe, et charitate, 1621* (Clarendon Press, 1944).

[53] S von Pufendorf, *Le devoir de l'Homme et du Citoyen selon la Loi Naturelle* (Presses universitaires de Caen, 1998) 721–22.

[54] E Vattel, *Le droit des gens ou Principes de la loi naturelle appliqués à la conduite et aux affaires des nations et des souverains* (London, 1758) ii. iv, §56.

[55] F Mégret, 'Le droit international Peut-il Etre un Droit de Résistance? Dix Conditions pour un Renouveau de l'Ambition Normative Internationale' (2008) 39(1) *Revue Études Internationales* 53.

in Libya and Syria started as peaceful protests violently repressed by the government.[56] The harsh reactions against the protests and the gross and systematic violations of human rights and – when applicable – humanitarian law led the international community to condemn such actions and to conclude that the Libyan and Syrian governments were no longer legitimate representatives of their own people. On the other hand, such legitimacy was attributed to the rebels fighting against them. It is thus interesting to reflect on whether legitimate opposition groups fighting against illegitimate governments might have a right to use force against the oppressive power.

The dominant view among contemporary legal scholars is that international law is indifferent to rebellions. While IHRL would prevent states from starting an internal conflict, the same is not true for rebels: insurgencies are neither allowed, nor prohibited.[57] The reason for this silence can be found in the very essence of rebellions. A rebel is someone who opposes the power and essentially threatens the very existence of state power. It is thus natural that domestic law outlaws rebellions and considers opposition groups as criminals or terrorists: 'comment le droit peut-il en même temps poser la règle et énoncer les circonstances légitimes de sa violation?'[58] Nevertheless, the right to rebel has received express, albeit sporadic, recognition at the domestic level: several constitutions recognise the people's right to rebel. For instance, Article 20(4) of the German Basic Law (1968) provides that: '[a]ll Germans shall have the right to resist any person seeking to abolish this constitutional order, if no other remedy is available'. Moreover, according to the Portuguese Constitution of 1976 '[e]veryone shall possess the right to resist any order that infringes their rights, freedoms or guarantees and, when it is not possible to resort to the public authorities, to use force to repel any aggression'. Similarly, constitutions of a number of states worldwide recognise the right to rebel.[59]

At the regional level, Article 2(2) of the European Convention of Human Rights establishes that '[d]eprivation of life shall not be regarded as inflicted in contravention of this Article when it results from the use of force which is no more than absolutely necessary: … (c) in action lawfully taken for the purpose of quelling a riot or insurrection'. The Arab world seems more open to rebellions: the Universal Islamic Declaration on Human Rights (1981) acknowledges that '[e]very individual and every people has the inalienable

[56] Bellal and Doswald-Beck (n 43) 11.

[57] M Dubuy, 'Le Droit de Résistance à l'Oppression en Droit International Public: Le Cas de la Résistance à un Régime Tyrannique' (2014) 32(1) *Civitas Europa* 144.

[58] Mégret (n 55) 40; Corten (n 38) 71.

[59] See eg Ukrainian Constitution 1996, Art 55; Constitution of Estonia 1992, Art 54; Constitution of Peru 1979, Art 82; Constitution of Uganda 1995, Art 3; Constitution of Timor Leste 2002, Art 11. See also T Honoré, 'The Right to Rebel' (1988) 8(1) *Oxford Journal of Legal Studies* 42; Mégret (n 55) 54.

right to freedom … and shall be entitled to struggle by all available means against any infringement or abrogation of this right'.[60] Similarly, the Arab Charter on Human Rights 2004 affirms that 'all peoples have the right to resist foreign occupation'.[61] Last but not least, Article 20(2) of the African Charter of Human and Peoples' Rights 1981 recognises that 'colonized or oppressed peoples shall have the right to free themselves from the bonds of domination by resorting to any means recognized by the international community'.[62] While this could be interpreted as a reaffirmation of the right to self-determination, thus recognising a right to resist to people under colonial domination, alien occupation, or racist regimes,[63] other authors see this provision as innovative: the reference to all the 'oppressed people' may suggest a broader reading of the article.[64]

At the international level there is no explicit recognition of a right to rebel. The only exception is the preamble of the Universal Declaration of Human Rights, which establishes that 'whereas it is essential, if man is not to be compelled to have recourse, as a last resource, to rebellion against tyranny and oppression, that human rights should be protected by the rule of law'. While drafting the Declaration, discussions emerged as to whether such a right should have been recognised in an ad hoc article. However, the drafters preferred to include it in the preamble for fear that a right to revolt would have excessively destabilised governments.[65] Successive human rights treaties do not recognise such a right.

Although the majority of scholars agree that international law neither allows nor prohibits rebellions,[66] during the decolonisation period the international community wondered whether NLMs had a right to embrace arms

[60] Universal Islamic Declaration on Human Rights 1981, Art II. See also A Marsavelski, 'The Crime of Terrorism and the Right to Revolution' (2013) 28 *Connecticut Journal of International Law* 274–75.

[61] Arab Charter on Human Rights 2004, Art 2(4). See also Dubuy (n 57) 151.

[62] S Murphy, 'Unique in International Human Rights Law: Article 20(2) and the Right to Resist in the African Charter on Human and Peoples' Rights' (2011) 11(2) *African Human Rights Journal* 465–94.

[63] Corten (n 38) 240.

[64] Murphy (n 62) 473.

[65] J Morsink, *The Universal Declaration of Human Rights: Origins, Drafting, and Intent* (University of Pennsylvania Press, 1999) 312; S Karagiannis, 'Qu'est-il, en droit international, le droit à la résistance devenu?' (2008) 76 *Revue trimestrielle de droits de l'homme* 957.

[66] See eg R Pinto: '[l]es fomenteurs de la guerre civile ne portent atteinte à aucune règle du droit des gens qui interdirait à une partie de la population d'un Etat de prendre les armes contre le gouvernement établi … L'investiture des gouvernants au sein de la société politique étatique est affaire purement interne.' See R. Pinto, 'Les règles du droit international concernant la guerre civile,' in *Collected Courses of the Hague Academy of International Law* (Martinus Nijhoff, 1965) 466. Similarly, Yoram Dinstien maintains that: '[t]here is no international legal right to rebellion, and international law does not deny the entitlement of the incumbent Government to stamp out an insurgency by force'. See Y Dinstein, *Non-International Armed Conflicts in International Law* (Cambridge University Press, 2014) 5.

against the colonial, alien, or racist power. Moreover, the recognition of the opposition groups in Libya and Syria as legitimate representatives of the people raises the question as to whether such a qualification implies a recognition of their right to embrace arms against the regimes of Gaddafi and Assad. More generally, we could wonder whether the commission of gross and systematic violations of human rights and humanitarian law against the population could potentially raise a right to react against the government.

B. National Liberation Movements and the 'Legal Entitlement' to Use Force

The emergence of the right to self-determination in the 1960s brought about significant changes in the traditional legal framework regulating the use of force. On the one hand, a norm emerged whereby colonial, occupying, or racist powers could not repress the people exercising their right to self-determination. On the other hand, persistent denial of peoples' aspirations to self-determination triggered a lively debate on the remedies at their disposal: the question of whether NLMs had the right to use force against oppressive powers has gripped scholarship and practice for a long time. In order to strengthen the role of NLMs and to make their struggle more effective, several developing and socialist countries argued that the liberation movements could use force in the exercise of their right to self-determination. If colonial domination, alien occupation, and racist regimes are contrary to the right to self-determination, and if these struggles are legitimate because of the heinous and unacceptable nature of these situations, then liberation movements should have the right to use force. However, Western countries rejected this proposition and insisted that the struggle should be peaceful in nature.

The idea that NLMs could lawfully engage in armed conflicts against the oppressive powers was put forward for the first time in 1964, when the Conference of Jurists of Afro-Asian Countries explicitly recognised that: '[a]ll struggles undertaken by the peoples for their national independence or for the restitution of the territories or occupied parts thereof, including armed struggle, are entirely legal'.[67] Similar conclusions were reached by the Conference of Non-Aligned Countries, held in Cairo in 1964, which acknowledged that: '[c]olonized peoples may legitimately resort to arms to secure the full exercise of their right to self-determination and independence if the colonial powers persist in opposing their natural aspirations'.[68] The year after, developing countries

[67] Conference of Jurists of Afro-Asian Countries, Conakry (Guinea), 1964.

[68] 2nd Summit Conference of Heads of State or Government of the Non-Aligned Movement, Cairo (Egypt), 10 September 1964.

brought this idea before the UN General Assembly, triggering a longstanding debate on the use of force by liberation movements. The fracture within the UNGA is reflected in the resolutions adopted in that period: when it came to the use of force by NLMs, their wording was extremely cautious, resulting often in a 'deliberate ambiguity' aimed at obtaining a consensus.[69]

One clear example is Resolution 2105(XX), whose ambivalent wording reflects the profound division within the UNGA. Criticising the negative attitude of Portugal and South Africa, 'which refused to recognise the right of colonial people to independence',[70] the UNGA recognised:

> The *legitimacy of the struggle* by the peoples under colonial rule to exercise their right to self-determination and independence and invites all States to *provide material and moral assistance* to the national liberation movements in colonial territories.[71]

The generic use of the term 'struggle' – without specifying whether it was meant to cover also forcible action – characterised the majority of the resolutions adopted by the UNGA and fuelled lively debates as to its meaning. The need to reach a compromise and the derived ambiguity of the resolutions was reflected also in the debates that took place within the Security Council. For instance, Resolution 232 (1966) on Southern Rhodesia reaffirmed 'the inalienable right of the people of Southern Rhodesia to freedom and independence in accordance with the Declaration [on Colonialism] ... and recognise[d] the *legitimacy of their struggle* to secure the enjoyment of their rights'.[72] Yet again, the nature of the struggle was deliberately uncertain.[73]

The 1970s witnessed a slight change, when a number of UNGA resolutions showed more openness to the idea of the legitimacy of an armed struggle by NLMs. For instance, in 1970 Resolution 2708 (XXV) reaffirmed the General Assembly's 'recognition of the legitimacy of the struggle of the colonial peoples and peoples under alien domination to exercise their right to self-determination and independence by all means at their disposal'.[74] However, several Western countries voted against the resolution or abstained. Similarly, three years later Resolution 3070 (XXVIII) recognised '[t]he legitimacy of peoples' struggle for liberation from colonial and foreign domination and alien subjugation by all available means, *including armed struggle*'.[75] Again, Western states opposed the idea of the legitimacy of an armed struggle with five votes against the resolution

[69] Gray (n 8) 60.

[70] A/RES/ 2105(XX), 20 December 1965, *Implementation of the Declaration on the Granting of Independence to Colonial Countries and Peoples*, preamble.

[71] ibid, §10, emphasis added.

[72] S/RES/232 (1966), 16 December 1966.

[73] Wilson (n 16) 96.

[74] A/RES/2708(XXV), 14 December 1970, *Implementation of the Declaration on the Granting of Independence to Colonial Countries and Peoples.*

[75] A/RES/3070(XXVIII), 30 November 1973, *Importance of the Universal Realization of the Right of Peoples to Self-determination and of the Speedy Granting of Independence to Colonial Countries and Peoples for the Effective Guarantee and Observance of Human Rights.*

and 28 abstentions. These instances clearly show that consensus could not be reached when the struggle was defined as *armed*. On the contrary, resolutions that maintained an ambiguous wording could be adopted by consensus.

This is further confirmed by the Declaration on Friendly Relations, which established that:

> In their *actions against*, and *resistance to*, such forcible action in pursuit of the exercise of their right to self-determination, such peoples are entitled to seek and to receive support in accordance with the purposes and principles of the Charter.[76]

Clearly, 'action against' and 'resistance to' an oppressive power does not qualify the struggle, thus leaving open the debate on the use of force by NLMs. Similarly, the adoption by consensus of the Definition of Aggression was made possible by the ambiguity of the resolution and the avoidance of any terms alluding to the use of force.[77] Article 7 of the resolution reads as follows:

> Nothing in this Definition, and in particular article 3, could in any way prejudice the right to self-determination, freedom and independence … nor the right of these peoples to struggle to that end and to seek and receive support, in accordance with the principles of the Charter and in conformity with the above-mentioned Declaration.

The ambiguity of the UNGA resolutions fuelled doctrinal debates on the issue. Some authors interpreted the aforementioned paragraph as authorising liberation movements to use force against the colonial powers. For instance, Abi-Saab propounded that:

> Armed resistance to forcible denial of self-determination – by imposing or maintaining by force colonial or alien domination – is legitimate according to the Declaration [on Friendly relations]. In other words, liberation movements have a *jus ad bellum* under the Charter.[78]

In the same vein, Eide maintained that the Resolution 'makes it clearer than before that armed struggle for self-determination is legitimate'.[79] At the other end of the spectrum, other scholars highlighted the ambiguity of the Resolution and concluded that the Declaration on Friendly Relations could not be interpreted as allowing the use of force by NLMs. Between the two extremes, Wilson offers an interesting interpretation: the Declaration would allow NLMs to recur to forcible action when the oppressive power uses force against them. This is clearly different from affirming that liberation movements are allowed to use force, as such a possibility would only be a last resort in case the colonial power recurs to force first.[80]

[76] Emphasis added.
[77] Wilson (n 16) 103.
[78] Abi-Saab (n 10) 100.
[79] A Eide, 'Sovereign Equality Versus Global Military Structure: Two Competing Approaches to World Order' in A Cassese (ed), *New Humanitarian Law of Armed Conflict* (Editoriale Scientifica, 1979) 25.
[80] Wilson (n 16) 99.

During the following years, resolutions adopted by the UNGA and UNSC continued to mirror the division within the international community. The UN instruments could pass by consensus only when they used ambiguous terms. This was the only way to reconcile the two opposite visions that divided the international community.[81] The legal bases underpinning the position of Western countries were clear: under international law non-state actors do not enjoy a right to use force against the state. Therefore, the term 'struggle' mentioned in the UN resolutions could refer only to peaceful forms of resistance.[82] On the other hand, states in favour of the use of force by NLMs put forward several arguments to support their claims: their calls were not grounded only on political considerations and on the legitimacy of national liberation movements.

First, the right to self-defence was invoked to reconcile the armed enforcement of self-determination by NLMs with the UN Charter system. Some proponents of this position maintained that such a right descended from the original colonial invasion. This is for instance the justification put forward by India when it annexed Goa in 1954. In order to provide the legal basis of its action before the Security Council, India claimed that it was exercising its right to collective self-defence against the armed attack perpetrated by Portugal in 1510.[83] However, such a position is subject to two solid counterarguments. First, at the time when Portugal annexed Goa, the acquisition of territory by force was not prohibited and thus provided a good title.[84] Furthermore, Wright wonders 'when does the inherent right of self-defense merge into a dispute about possession or title to a territory?'.[85] In other words, the question is how long the right to self-defence persists after the armed attack. The wording of Article 51 of the UN Charter, which requires that the state under attack should report *immediately* to the Security Council the measures undertaken, would suggest a short temporal interval between the armed attack and the reaction in self-defence.[86] Hundreds of years of acquiescence from the international community in general and Goa's population in particular would suggest that the right to self-defence had expired.[87]

[81] ibid.

[82] See eg CJR Dugard, 'The Organisation of African Unity and Colonialism: An Inquiry into the Plea of Self-Defence as a Justification for the Use of Force in the Eradication of Colonialism' (1967) 16(1) *The International and Comparative Law Quarterly* 157–90; RE Gorelick, 'Wars of National Liberation: *Jus Ad Bellum*' (1979) 11(1) *Case Western Reserve Journal of International Law* 71–93.

[83] Q Wright, 'The Goa Incident' (1962) 56 *American Journal of International Law* 622.

[84] ibid, 623.

[85] ibid.

[86] I Brownlie, *International Law and the Use of Force by the States* (Oxford University Press, 1991) 255, 273–74.

[87] Gorelick (n 82) 78–79; Dugard (n 82) 168–70. At the UNSC, a resolution condemning the action of India failed to be adopted due to the veto of Russia. On the other hand, a resolution proposed by Russia which invited Portugal to cooperate with India to terminate its colonial domination in Goa was rejected by Western countries. Wright (n 83) 617; A Cassese, 'Le droit international et la question de l'assistance aux mouvements de libération nationale' (1986) 19 *Revue belge de droit international* 314.

Other scholars suggested that colonial domination constitutes permanent aggression per se and could thus trigger the application of Article 51 of the UN Charter. This position was put forward by developing and soviet countries during the deliberations on the Declaration of Friendly Relations and the Definition of Aggression. For instance, the Syrian delegate affirmed that:

> His delegation believed that the right to self-defence should be interpreted in the widest possible sense and should cover the use of force by peoples who were oppressed, colonised or expelled from the land of their birth.[88]

However, this liberal and broad interpretation of Article 51 of the UN Charter found opposition from several Western and Latin American countries, as well as numerous scholars. First, they claimed that the right to self-defence should pertain only to states. Although NLMs attained a status separate from that of the oppressing powers, this does not imply that Article 51 applies to them. Furthermore, granting the right to self-defence could lead to undesirable consequences, namely to the escalation and proliferation of conflicts.[89]

Another part of the scholarship suggested that the right to self-defence could emerge only when the colonial power was oppressing the people through forcible means. Abi-Saab maintained that such interpretation would derive directly from the Declaration on Friendly Relations, wherein it states that:

> Every State has the duty to refrain from any forcible action which deprives peoples … of their right to self-determination and freedom and independence. In their action against, and resistance to, such forcible action in pursuit of the exercise of their right to self-determination, such peoples are entitled to seek and receive support in accordance with the purposes and principles of the Charter.[90]

According to Abi-Saab, this paragraph would suggest that 'armed resistance to forcible denial of self-determination – by imposing or maintaining by force colonial or alien domination – is legitimate under the Charter according to the Declaration'.[91] By limiting the interpretation of armed attack and of the scope of application of Article 51 UN Charter, this interpretation aimed at responding to the criticism by Western states. However, it is exactly for this reason that developing and socialist countries did not embrace it. Furthermore, Western and Latin American countries continued to oppose the application of the right to self-defence to colonial situations. Eventually, the idea was definitively abandoned.[92]

[88] See eg Dugard (n 82); Gorelick (n 82).
[89] Cassese (n 87) 315.
[90] Declaration on Friendly Relations (n 34), emphasis added.
[91] G Abi-Saab, 'Wars of National Liberation in the Geneva Conventions and Protocols' (1979) 165 *Collected Courses of the Hague Academy of International Law* 371–72.
[92] Cassese (n 87) 315.

Although NLMs' right to self-defence was not acknowledged by the international community, developing and socialist countries did not give up on the idea of the legality of using force against an oppressive power. Notably, it was suggested that liberation movements have a right to use force against colonial domination, alien occupation, and racist regimes. This right would derive from a new, autonomous rule, customary in nature, which constitutes an exception to the ban on the use of force.[93] This position rests on the assumption that Article 2(4) of the UN Charter would apply to NLMs. Liberation movements, the argument goes, attained an international personality separate and distinct from the one of the oppressive power. As a result, they would be bound by Article 2(4). However, the firm opposition of Western countries to recognise such a right would constitute sound proof that such an exception did not attain the status of customary law.[94]

Despite the numerous endeavours to justify the right to the use of force by liberation movements, no agreement was ever reached within the international community. While developing and socialist countries strenuously pushed in that direction, Western and Latin American states never accepted the idea of the legality of armed struggles to exercise the right to self-determination. In light of the debates between the two blocs, it does not seem possible to conclude for the existence of the right, nor for the ban on using force by NLMs. Nevertheless, the resolutions by the UNGA expressly recognising the legitimacy of armed struggle by liberation movements may lead us to prefer a more nuanced conclusion. We can thus conclude with Cassese that: 'liberation movements have been given a *legal entitlement* that is less than a *right* proper but more than the *absence of any authorization whatsoever*'.[95] Therefore, unlike traditional rebellions, national liberation wars are not 'left in a legal vacuum'.[96] Instead, the legitimacy of the fight is acknowledged by the international legal order and recognised in the form of a '*licence* to use force'.[97]

C. Is there a Right to Individual or Collective Self-defence against Excessive State Use of Force?

The idea of a right to self-defence for opposition groups was first propounded with regard to national liberation movements. The most interesting position for our discourse is the one suggested by Abi-Saab, who propounded that such a right would emerge when the government is denying by force a people's right

[93] Abi-Saab (n 91) 374; SN MacFarlane, *Superpower Rivalry & Third World Radicalism: The Idea of National Liberation* (Johns Hopkins University Press, 1985).

[94] Wilson (n 16) 133–34; Ronzitti (n 1) 350–51.

[95] Cassese *Self-Determination of Peoples* (n 1) 153.

[96] ibid.

[97] ibid.

to self-determination. The right to self-defence would thus arise as a response to the use of force by the government. In Libya and Syria, peaceful protests were violently and forcibly repressed by the government. Understandably, the population reacted against such heinous acts, which allegedly amounted to crimes against humanity.[98] Could this instance be interpreted as an act of self-defence?

Article 51 of the UN Charter provides that states can act in individual or collective self-defence against an armed attack. Would it be possible to imagine the application of this provision to the relationship between the state and its own people? This idea was suggested by a minority of scholars, who interpreted the Arab Spring as 'a response by large segments of the citizenry to *internal aggression* by their own governments'.[99] This interpretation could suggest that the heinous violations of human rights committed against the protesters may amount to an armed attack against which the population may have a right to react in self-defence. As a matter of fact, Security Council Resolution 1973 (2011) authorised the use of force 'to protect civilians and civilian populated areas under threat of *attack* in the Libyan Jamahiriya, including Benghazi'.[100] However, there are no signs that here the term *attack* would mean an armed attack triggering Article 51 of the UN Charter. More generally, the application of Article 2(4) of the UN Charter to non-international armed conflicts has been unequivocally excluded, thus ruling out the possibility to extend the scope of application of Article 51 to non-state actors.

Ben Saul suggested an alternative approach, whereby a group's right to self-defence against governments committing heinous atrocities could be inferred by analogy from the individuals' right to self-defence.[101] The ICTY has recognised that individuals have a right to use violence in self-defence, and that such a right now forms part of the general principles of criminal law.[102] Article 31 of the Rome Statute excludes criminal responsibility when '[t]he person acts reasonably to defend himself or herself or another person … against an imminent and unlawful use of force in a manner proportionate to the degree of danger to the person or the other person'.[103] Thus it would not seem preposterous to suggest that the gross and systematic violations of human rights committed by the government, in particular the excessive use of force against the population,

[98] Bellal and Doswald-Beck (n 43) 20.

[99] J Nyamuya and A Coleman, 'Changing The Guard – The Price of Democracy: Lessons from the Arab Spring on Constitutionalism' in G Wilson and C Panara (eds), *The "Arab Spring": New Patterns for Democracy and International Law* (Martinus Nijhoff, 2013) 3.

[100] S/RES/1973 (2011), 17 March 2011, §4, emphasis added. See Bellal and Doswald-Beck (n 43) 21.

[101] B Saul, 'Defending "Terrorism": Justifications and Excuses for Terrorism in International Criminal Law' (2006) 25 *Australian Yearbook of International Law* 203.

[102] ICTY, *Prosecutor v Kordić & Čerkez*, Judgment, Trial Chamber (IT-95-14/2-T) 26 February 2001, §449.

[103] Rome Statute of the International Criminal Court 1998, Art 31(1)(c).

constituted an armed attack and could hence trigger a group's right to self-defence. However, this conclusion would neglect to consider one of the main requirements of individual self-defence, namely that 'an act remains defensive as long as it is a reasonable and proportionate response to imminent, unlawful force'.[104] Saul correctly notes that:

> Self-defence does not confer a license to use violence in a strategic way in protest at a generalized policy of State oppression. Where an oppressive government threatens imminent and internationally unlawful force, affected individuals may exercise self-defence against the State agents or officials implementing the policy, such as the police, security services, or paramilitaries.[105]

In sum, the actions of Libyan and Syrian protesters against the excessive governmental use of force could not be justified as self-defence under the current legal framework. Nonetheless, Bellal and Doswald-Beck wondered whether this conclusion should be revised:

> [I]t is worth considering whether the international community should call for an exception in cases of violence in the form of individual or even collective self-defence. The present situation in non-international conflicts is the equivalent of punishing a State for exercising its right to self-defence against the unlawful aggression of another State. This would be manifestly absurd in an inter-State context. Total freedom for a government to treat its citizens as it wishes has long since disappeared and the reaction to the violence in Syria, even by the Arab League which imposed sanctions, shows that attitudes are changing.[106]

D. Do Legitimate Opposition Groups Enjoy a Right to Rebel against Excessive State Use of Force?

Could excessive state use of force ground a right to rebel against the perpetrator of such actions, namely the government? Corten defines this instance as *remedial rebellion*, whereby the insurrection would be a reaction to grave violations of human rights committed against the population; the government would thus have to step down and leave the power to the opposition group.[107] This issue is particularly interesting if we think of the Libyan and Syrian conflicts: the recognition of certain opposition groups as legitimate representatives of the people could lead us to wonder whether the international community intended to recognise that they have an actual right to rebel.[108]

[104] Saul (n 101) 203.
[105] ibid.
[106] Bellal and Doswald-Beck (n 43) 22–23.
[107] Corten (n 38) 248.
[108] ibid.

The idea that it would be pointless to recognise fundamental human rights for individuals, without granting them a right to rebel against violations of fundamental human rights, is not new. Already in 1983 Paust suggested that:

> Revolution is actually one of the strategies available to a people for the securing of authority, national self-determination and a relatively free and equal enjoyment of the human right of all persons to participate in the political processes of their society.[109]

Five years later, Honoré suggested that 'unless in certain conditions we have the right to rebel, much talk on human rights can be dismissed as empty rhetoric'.[110] In his view, the right to rebel should be a secondary right, triggered when 'a wrong has been committed. Its point is to provide remedy in the event of the violation on a large scale of primary rights like the right to freedom from arbitrary arrest'.[111]

Interestingly, the idea that there are instances when violations of human rights are so widespread and heinous that it is impossible to remain watching, and that action should be taken to stop such atrocities, has received vast support vis-à-vis foreign interventions. The question on how to react to heinous crimes was famously addressed by former UN Secretary General Kofi Annan before the General Assembly:

> If humanitarian intervention is, indeed, an unacceptable assault on sovereignty, how should we respond to a Rwanda, to a Srebrenica – to gross and systematic violations of human rights that affect every precept of our common humanity?[112]

In response to this challenge, the government of Canada established the International Commission on Intervention and State Sovereignty (ICISS), whose report on the Responsibility to Protect triggered copious discussions on the interventions to stop atrocities.[113]

As aforementioned, during the Middle Ages several scholars maintained that states had a right to wage war in order to protect a foreign population against a tyrant, and some authors added that such a possibility could have been envisaged only if a corresponding right to rebel was granted to the population. Although discussions on humanitarian intervention and R2P did not trigger a similar debate, Mégret suggests strong arguments in favour of

[109] JJ Paust, 'Human Right to Participate in Armed Revolution and Related Forms of Social Violence: Testing the Limits of Permissibility' (1983) 32(2) *Emory Law Journal* 580. See *contra* K Obse, 'The Arab Spring and the Question of Legality of Democratic Revolution in Theory and Practice: A Perspective Based on the African Union Normative Framework' (2014) 27(4) *Leiden Journal of International Law* 823.

[110] Honoré (n 59) 34.

[111] ibid, 38.

[112] International Commission on Intervention and State Sovereignty (ICISS), *The Responsibility to Protect* (International Development Research Centre 2001), vii.

[113] ibid.

the recognition of a right to rebel against gross and systematic violations of human rights.[114] First, instances such as the success of the Rwanda Patriotic Front would suggest that historically peoples have been more successful than foreign countries in halting mass atrocities.[115] Second, victims are the ones with the strongest interest in reacting to such heinous crimes, thus their resistance is likely to occur. Finally, '[t]he great strength of local civil society is that it is in a sense always already there, and that its efforts at resistance will often have begun in direct response to patterns of violence'.[116] There are thus compelling reasons to grant peoples a right to react against gross and systematic violations of human rights. Mégret notes that:

> All in all, the resistance paradigm offers a view of fighting atrocities that is more decentralized, bottom-up, empowering, people-based and spontaneous, where international intervention runs the risk of being centralized, top-down, paternalistic, state-based and institutional.[117]

Nevertheless, it is extremely unlikely that international law will ever recognise a right to rebel. With specific regard to the Libyan and Syrian conflicts, we could conclude that recognising the legitimacy of the NTC and the SOC was tantamount to acknowledging the legitimacy of their struggles. However, nothing seems to suggest that states went as far as recognising a right to rebel against Gaddafi's and Assad's regimes. Therefore, similar to national liberation movements fighting against colonial domination, alien occupation, and racist regimes, legitimate rebel groups fighting against gross and systematic violations of fundamental human rights do not enjoy a right to rebel.

III. CONCLUDING OBSERVATIONS

From the analysis conducted so far it seems that the traditional rules regulating the use of force between state forces and rebel groups have not been drastically changed. The scope of application of the ban on the use of force, enshrined in Article 2(4) of the UN Charter, is limited to the international relations among states. Therefore, it does not address the use of force by opposition groups, nor by the government. Consequently, rebel groups do not enjoy a right to self-defence against heinous violations of human rights committed by the state. Similarly, international law does not grant legitimate rebels a right to use force against such violations, not even when no other means are available. The only change to traditional international law concerns the decolonisation period,

[114] Mégret (n 55); F Mégret, 'Beyond the 'Salvation' Paradigm: Responsibility To Protect (Others) vs the Power of Protecting Oneself' (2009) 40(6) *Security Dialogue* 575–95.
[115] Mégret 'Beyond the 'Salvation' Paradigm' (n 114) 583.
[116] ibid, 584.
[117] ibid; Mégret (n 55) 51–52.

whereby the oppressive power was banned from using force to prevent or repress peoples' exercise of their right to self-determination. As we shall see, the corollary of this provision was that foreign countries could not provide help to the oppressive power.

Apart from this exception, *de lege lata* international law has not undergone drastic changes following the recognition of rebels as legitimate representatives of peoples. Nevertheless, *de lege ferenda* we may wonder whether the traditional approach that identifies effectiveness as the pivotal criterion in international law seems to be challenged by the practice that emerged during the decolonisation period, and more recently in Libya and Syria. Notably, it seems that the traditional indifference of *jus ad bellum* towards internal conflicts is at times inadequate to address certain circumstances. The recognition of rebels as legitimate representatives of people may be the expression of a need to have more flexible rules vis-à-vis non-state actors. However, a development in this direction would not be void of risks, which will be highlighted in the conclusions of this work.[118]

[118] See ch 9.

8

Interventions in Favour of Rebels and Human Rights

I. REBELS' RECOGNITION AND FOREIGN INTERVENTIONS

A. The Prohibition to Intervene in Favour of Opposition Groups in the UN Charter Era

THE BAN ON the use of force enshrined in Article 2(4) of the UN Charter and the principle of non-intervention in the internal affairs of states outlaw interventions in internal conflicts. In the previous chapters we have seen that there are exceptions to such a prohibition, namely if the force is used in self-defence (Article 51 of the UN Charter), if the UNSC authorises the intervention (Chapter VII of the UN Charter), and if the government invites a foreign country to intervene.[1] It is thus apparent that interventions in favour of opposition groups are prima facie unlawful. This is confirmed by the UNGA Declaration on Friendly Relations, which establishes that:

> Every State has a duty to refrain from organising, instigating, assisting or participating in acts of civil strife or terrorist acts in another State or in organised activities within its territory directed towards the commission of such acts, when the acts referred to in the present paragraph involve a threat or use of force.[2]

The Declaration specifies also that 'no State shall organise, assist, foment, finance, incite or tolerate subversive, terrorist or armed activities directed towards the violent overthrow of the regime of another State, or interfere in civil strife in another state'.[3] Similarly, the Declaration on the Enhancement of the

[1] In the previous chapters we have seen that interventions upon invitation of the government are lawful, at least under certain circumstances. Therefore, an intervention in favour of the rebels may be lawful if the opposition groups became the new government.

[2] A/RES/2625 (XXV), 24 October 1970, *Declaration on Principles of International Law concerning Friendly Relations and Cooperation among States in accordance with the Charter of the United Nations* (hereinafter Declaration on Friendly Relations), principle §1.9.

[3] Declaration on Friendly Relations, principle §3.2. See also O Corten, *The Law against War: The Prohibition on the Use of Force in Contemporary International Law* (Hart Publishing, 2010) 129–30; E Lieblich, *International Law and Civil Wars: Intervention and Consent* (Routledge, 2013) 238.

Effectiveness of the Principle of Refraining from the Threat or Use of Force in International Relations specifies that:

> States shall fulfil their obligations under international law to refrain from organizing, instigating, or assisting or participating in paramilitary, terrorist or subversive acts, including acts of mercenaries, in other States, or acquiescing in organized activities within their territory directed towards the commission of such acts.[4]

Although the Declaration is a UNGA Resolution, and thus not binding, the ICJ in the *Nicaragua* case affirmed that 'the adoption by States of this text affords an indication of their *opinio juris* as to customary international law on the question'.[5] The Court then reaffirmed these obligations in a famous passage:

> [I]t is difficult to see what would remain of the principle of non-intervention in international law if intervention, which is already allowable at the request of the government of a State, were also to be allowed at the request of the opposition. This would permit any State to intervene at any moment in the internal affairs of another State, whether at the request of the government or at the request of its opposition. Such a situation does not in the Court's view correspond to the present state of international law.[6]

Furthermore, in the *Congo* case the ICJ confirmed this *dictum* when it concluded that Uganda violated the ban on the use of force by intervening in favour of rebel groups in the DRC.[7] It appears from all the above that interventions in favour of opposition groups are generally unlawful.[8] Contemporary state practice confirms this conclusion. Indeed, states have never explicitly claimed the existence of a right to intervene in an internal conflict upon invitation of the rebels.[9]

It is generally uncontested that sending state forces against a foreign government constitutes a violation of the ban on the use of force and the principle of non-intervention;[10] furthermore, it can amount to an armed attack and thus trigger the right to self-defence under Article 51 of the UN Charter.[11]

[4] A/RES/42/22, 18 November 1987, *Declaration on the Enhancement of the Effectiveness of the Principle of Refraining from the Threat or Use of Force in International Relations*, §6.

[5] ICJ, *Military and Paramilitary Activities in and against Nicaragua, (Nicaragua v United States of America)*, Judgment (Merits), 27 June 1986 (hereinafter *Nicaragua* case), §191. See also ICJ, *Armed Activities in the* Congo (Democratic Republic of Congo v Uganda), Judgment (Merits), 19 December 2005 (hereinafter *Congo* case), §162; ICJ, *Legality of the Threat or Use of Nuclear Weapons*, Advisory Opinion, 8 July 1996, §70.

[6] *Nicaragua* case, §246.

[7] *Congo* case, §162–65. See also Corten (n 3) 260.

[8] CJ Le Mon, 'Unilateral Intervention by Invitation in Civil Wars: The Effective Control Test Tested' (2003) 35(3) *New York University Journal of International Law and Politics* 750.

[9] One exception is the case of intervention in favour of national liberation movements during the decolonisation period. See also C Gray, *International Law and the Use of Force* (Oxford University Press, 2008) 105.

[10] P Kunig, 'Intervention, Prohibition of' in *Max Planck Encyclopedia of Public International Law* (Oxford University Press, 2008) §24.

[11] See ch 2.

However, indirect interventions in favour of rebels are more problematic. The crucial question is whether training, arming, equipping, and funding rebels amount to violations of the ban on the use of force and/or the principle of non-intervention.

The first issue regards arming and training rebels. Although 'on its face, Article 2(4) UN Charter would not seem to reach the mere arming of rebels',[12] the ICJ in the *Nicaragua* case clarified that arming and training would amount to a threat or use of force.[13] This conclusion raises the question of state response to such violation of Article 2(4) of the UN Charter. Would arming opposition groups amount to an armed attack and trigger the right to self-defence of the victim state? Few states answered positively. For instance, in 2012 the Legal Adviser to the US State Department clarified that: 'the inherent right of self-defense potentially applies against any illegal use of force. In our view, there is no threshold for a use of deadly force to qualify as an "armed attack" that may warrant a forcible response'.[14] Nonetheless, this position does not reflect the majoritarian view. Indeed, according to the prevailing approach endorsed by the ICJ, 'less grave forms of the use of force' – such as providing weapons and training rebels – do not amount to armed attacks. Therefore, even if training and providing weapons to opposition groups qualify as a use of force, it does not amount to an armed attack and hence does not trigger the right to self-defence.[15]

Furthermore, states tend to provide help to rebels in the form of non-lethal assistance and funding. The scope of the principle of non-intervention covers these instances: according to the 1965 Declaration on the Inadmissibility of Intervention: 'no State shall organize, assist, foment, finance, incite or tolerate subversive, terrorist or armed activities directed towards the violent overthrow of the regime of another State'. Similarly, the ICJ in the *Nicaragua* case affirmed that: 'the mere supply of funds to the *contras*', while it 'does not in itself amount to a use of force', undoubtedly amounts to 'an act of intervention in the internal affairs of Nicaragua'.[16] Nonetheless, the principle of non-intervention, as interpreted by the UNGA resolutions and the ICJ case law, leaves some issues unresolved. For instance, during the Libyan and Syrian conflicts the question emerged as to whether states could purchase natural resources (such as crude oil) from opposition groups.[17] At the other end of the spectrum, the ICJ specified

[12] MN Schmitt, 'Legitimacy versus Legality Redux: Arming the Syrian Rebels' (2014) 7 *Journal of National Security Law & Policy* 141.

[13] *Nicaragua* case, §228. See also A Clapham, 'Weapons and Armed Non-state Actors' in S Casey-Maslen (ed), *Weapons Under International Human Rights Law* (Cambridge University Press, 2014) 163–96; T Ruys, 'Of Arms, Funding and "Non-Lethal Assistance" – Issues Surrounding Third State Intervention in the Syrian Civil War' (2014) 13(1) *Chinese Journal of International Law* 32.

[14] Schmitt (n 12) 142–43.

[15] ibid.

[16] *Nicaragua* case, §228; Ruys (n 13) 48.

[17] Ruys (n 13) 50.

that providing strictly humanitarian assistance 'cannot be regarded as unlawful intervention, or as in any other way contrary to international law'.[18] It is beyond the scope of this work to discuss such dilemmas. Here it suffices to conclude that, generally speaking, interventions in favour of opposition groups are prohibited by the ban on the use of force and the principle of non-intervention in the internal affairs of the state.[19]

B. Recognition of an Insurgent Government

Since the adoption of the UN Charter, the recognition of belligerency and insurgency has been 'abandoned'.[20] On the other hand, the ban on the use of force and the principle of non-intervention have outlawed virtually any forcible and non-lethal forms of intervention in favour of rebel groups.[21] Nevertheless, once the opposition group has attained the status of new government, it can speak on behalf of the state and lawfully ask for foreign intervention. Despite several states that embrace the Estrada doctrine and claim to recognise only states and not governments, there are instances when this is not possible.[22] One such case is undoubtedly when a rebel group claims to have attained the status of government. This exercise is particularly problematic if we consider, as Talmon noted, that 'international law determines what a government is, but not who the government of a particular state is'.[23] Therefore, the crucial question concerns the criteria for recognising a new government.

Traditionally, an entity which wields 'effective power, with a reasonable perspective of permanency, over the whole – or practically the whole – territory of the state' is considered as the government.[24] Peterson suggested the reason why the effectiveness criterion has been considered: 'the one condition necessary for recognition stems from the very definition of a government as those who rule the state, maintain internal order, and carry out international relations on the state's behalf'.[25] The value of this criterion lies in its objectivity: effectiveness

[18] *Nicaragua* case, §242; Kunig (n 10) §9; O Corten, *La Rébellion et le Droit International: le Principe de Neutralité en Tension* (Martinus Nijhoff, 2016) 168–70.

[19] For an analysis of what exactly is intervention, training, financing, arming, see ch 2.

[20] I Dette, *The Law of War* (Cambridge University Press, 2000) 43; A Clapham, *Human Rights Obligations of Non-State Actors* (Oxford University Press, 2006) 272; HA Wilson, *International Law and the Use of Force by National Liberation Movements* (Clarendon Press, 1988) 27.

[21] Lieblich (n 3) 232; Y Dinstein, *Non-International Armed Conflicts in International Law* (Cambridge University Press, 2014) 102.

[22] See ch 3.

[23] S Talmon, 'Recognition of Opposition Groups as the Legitimate Representative of a People' (2013) 12(2) *Chinese Journal of International Law* 233.

[24] H Lauterpacht, *Recognition in International Law* (Cambridge University Press, 1947) 98.

[25] MJ Peterson, *Recognition of Governments: Legal Doctrine and State Practice, 1815–1995* (Palgrave MacMillan, 1997) 36.

does not imply any considerations as to the *legitimacy* of the government and thus excludes any non-factual assessment. Nevertheless, it has been argued by Roth that the effectiveness doctrine could be 'perceived as little more than an imprimatur for "might makes right"'.[26] Furthermore, we have seen that recent state practice would suggest that a democratically elected but ineffective government is preferred over an effective but undemocratic one. However, lacking a democratic alternative, effective control over territory and population remains the preferred criterion to identify the authority capable to speak and act on behalf of the state.

Due to the lack of clear-cut rules regulating the recognition of new governments, this issue is strictly intertwined with the question of who grants such recognition in a particular circumstance. Absent collective mechanisms and certain criteria to recognise new governments, the practice is prone to abuses. In particular, a premature recognition could amount to unlawful intervention in itself.[27] Frowein suggested that: '[w]here there are still two competing governments, recognition of the revolutionary government as the government of the State is unlawful unless it has established its authority to such an extent that the outcome of the conflict is clear and the former government's authority is reduced to a negligible area'.[28] The rationale underpinning this conclusion lies in the risk that government recognition is granted as a pretext for foreign intervention, justified by the invitation of the newly recognised government.[29] It is thus understandable why traditionally effective control has been the preferred criterion. Nevertheless, as we shall see, state practice has nuanced the discourse by introducing other forms of recognition. Notably, over the last decades there have been instances when states have recognised opposition groups as legitimate representatives of people, and have engaged with rebels as a result. The next paragraphs will be devoted to investigating the meaning and implications of this practice.

II. HELPING REBELS IN THE EXERCISE OF THEIR RIGHT TO SELF-DETERMINATION

A. Interventions in Favour of National Liberation Movements

A crucial question that emerged during the decolonisation period was whether and to what extent third states could intervene in national liberation wars.

[26] BR Roth, *Sovereign Equality and Moral Disagreement: Premises of a Pluralist International Legal Order* (Oxford University Press, 2011) 170.

[27] Dinstein (n 21) 99.

[28] JA Frowein, 'Recognition' in *Max Planck Encyclopedia of Public International Law* (Oxford University Press, 2010) §15.

[29] ibid, §15. See also Lieblich (n 3) 244.

As we have seen, interventions in favour of the incumbent government are generally lawful, while helping the rebels would violate the ban on the use of force and/or the principle of non-intervention in the internal affairs of the state. Situations of colonial domination, alien occupation, and racist regimes led to crucial changes as to the possibility of using force by liberation movements fighting for their right to self-determination. On the one hand, a customary rule emerged establishing that the oppressive power could not repress instances of self-determination by colonial or foreign people or racial groups.[30] On the other hand, the NLMs were deemed 'legally entitled' to use force.[31] What about the involvement of foreign states in national liberation wars?

With regard to intervention in favour of the colonial power, both the Security Council and the General Assembly expressed the view that foreign assistance aimed at repressing a national liberation struggle amounted to a violation of the right to self-determination.[32] This was clearly stated in the Declaration on Friendly Relations, which established that:

> Every State has the duty to refrain from any forcible action which deprives peoples referred to in the elaboration of the principle of equal rights and self-determination of their right to self-determination and freedom and independence.[33]

The traditional presumption that the incumbent government can lawfully ask for foreign intervention in order to repress a rebellion was thus reversed.[34] Having clarified that colonial powers lose their consent capacity, the Declaration on Friendly Relations took a step further and addressed the issue of intervention in favour of national liberation movements:

> In their actions against, and resistance to, such forcible action in pursuit of the exercise of their right to self-determination, such peoples are entitled to seek and to receive support in accordance with the purposes and principles of the Charter.[35]

[30] A Cassese, *Self-Determination of Peoples: A Legal Reappraisal* (Cambridge University Press, 1995) 194.

[31] ibid, 153.

[32] BR Roth, *Governmental Illegitimacy in International Law* (Clarendon Press, 1999) 212.

[33] *Declaration on Principles of International Law concerning Friendly Relations and Co-operation among States in accordance with the Charter of the United Nations*, A/RES/25/2625 (XXV), 24 October 1970 (hereinafter Declaration on Friendly Relations), §1.

[34] Other resolutions by the UNGA and UNSC established that states could not provide any assistance to colonial powers. See eg A/RES/2105(XX), 20 December 1965, *Implementation of the Declaration on the Granting of Independence to Colonial Countries and Peoples*, §11, which requested 'all States and international institutions … to withhold assistance of any kind to the Governments of Portugal and South Africa until they renounce their policy of colonial domination and racial discrimination'. In the same vein, UNSC Resolution 180 requested 'States to take all measures to prevent the sale and supply of arms and military equipment to the Portuguese Government for use in colonial repression'. See D Wippman, 'Military Intervention, Regional Organizations, and Host State Consent' (1996) 7(1) *Duke Journal of Comparative and International Law* 215; Lieblich (n 3) 221; Roth (n 32) 212.

[35] Declaration on Friendly Relations (n 33) §5.5. See also A/RES/2105(XX), 20 December 1965, *Implementation of the Declaration on the Granting of Independence to Colonial Countries and Peoples*, §10: '[t]he UNGA … recognizes the legitimacy of the struggle by the peoples under colonial

This disposition was reaffirmed by the Definition of Aggression, whereby the UNGA propounded that:

> Nothing in this Definition, and in particular article 3, could in any way prejudice the right to self-determination, freedom and independence ... nor the right of these peoples to struggle to that end and to seek and receive support, in accordance with the principles of the Charter and in conformity with the above-mentioned Declaration.[36]

These and other resolutions of the General Assembly highlight a general agreement within the international community on the possibility to provide support to NLMs.[37] This conclusion appears in line with the idea that national liberation wars are different from *common rebellions*: not only were the struggles recognised as legitimate by the international community, but also the nature of national liberation wars was equated to international armed conflicts.[38] However, the character of the support that could be lawfully provided to NLMs remained unclear: could third states provide forcible assistance to liberation movements, or should the help be non-lethal in nature?

The ambiguity of the General Assembly resolutions, which mentioned the possibility to provide support to NLMs without specifying its nature, reflected the fracture of the international community on this point. Notwithstanding the numerous attempts by developing and socialist countries to affirm that liberation movements had a right to self-defence against the oppressive power, Western countries never accepted this idea. Therefore, third countries could not intervene under the umbrella of the right to collective self-defence.[39] Developing and socialist states thus put forward another legal basis to justify military interventions in favour of NLMs. If liberation movements enjoy a status distinct and separate from the colonial power,[40] and if they can lawfully use force against such a power, then it is only logical that they can also invite foreign countries to intervene in their favour.[41] However, Western states have always opposed such a

rule to exercise their right to self-determination and independence and invites all States to provide *material and moral assistance* to the national liberation movements in colonial territories', emphasis added.

[36] A/RES/3314, 14 December 1974, *Definition of Aggression*, Art 7.

[37] See eg A/RES/2189(XXI), 13 December 1966, *Implementation of the Declaration on the Granting of Independence to Colonial People*; A/RES/2426 (XXIII), 18 December 1968, *Implementation of the Declaration on the Granting of Independence to Colonial Countries and Peoples by the Specialized Agencies and the International Institutions Associated with the United Nations*; A/RES/2704 (XXV), 14 December 1970, *Implementation of the Declaration on the Granting of Independence to Colonial People*. See also A Cassese, 'Le Droit International et la Question de l'Assistance aux Mouvements de Libération Nationale' (1986) 19 *Revue belge de droit international* 315–16.

[38] Protocol Additional to the Geneva Conventions of 12 August 1949, and relating to the Protection of Victims of Non-International Armed Conflicts (Protocol II), 1977, Art 1(4).

[39] A Tanca, *Foreign Armed Intervention in Internal Conflict* (Martinus Nijhoff, 1993) 106; Cassese (n 30) 199.

[40] Declaration on Friendly Relations (n 33) §5.6.

[41] Cassese (n 37) 318–19.

conclusion. As mentioned before, they have always rejected the idea that NLMs could engage in armed activities against the oppressive power. Consequently, third states could not provide them with forcible help.[42]

The ICJ in the *Nicaragua* case addressed the issue, where it affirmed that:

> There have been in recent years a number of instances of foreign intervention for the benefit of forces opposed to the government of another State. The Court is not here concerned with the process of decolonization; this question is not in issue in the present case. It has to consider whether there might be indications of a practice illustrative of belief in a kind of general right for States to intervene, directly or indirectly, with or without armed force, in support of an internal opposition in another State, whose cause appeared particularly worthy by reason of the political and moral values with which it was identified. For such a general right to come into existence would involve a fundamental modification of the customary law principle of non-intervention.[43]

Although the *dictum* did not clarify the controversy, it seems to suggest that national liberation struggles are an exception to the general rule prohibiting armed interventions in favour of opposition groups. Judge Schwebel vehemently criticised this idea in his dissenting opinion: while it is generally accepted that NLMs enjoy a right to struggle in the exercise of their right to self-determination, 'what is *not* universally recognized and what is *not* universally accepted is any right of such peoples to foreign assistance or support which constitutes intervention'.[44] Furthermore, he added that:

> [I]t is lawful for a foreign State or movement to give to a people struggling for self-determination moral, political and humanitarian assistance; but it is not lawful for a foreign State or movement to intervene in that struggle with force or to provide arms, supplies and other logistical support in the prosecution of armed rebellion.[45]

Notwithstanding the numerous attempts of developing and socialist countries to legally justify the provision of military assistance to NLMs, Western and Latin American states never accepted such a possibility. Therefore, although it is generally uncontested that third states could provide non-lethal help to NLMs, the question of military interventions in their favour remained unresolved.[46]

B. Interventions Outside the Decolonisation Context

Outside the decolonisation context, studies on the right to self-determination have focused mainly on secession and the right to democratic entitlement.

[42] ibid.
[43] *Nicaragua* case, §206.
[44] *Nicaragua* case, dissenting Opinion by Judge Schwebel, §180. See also Lieblich (n 3) 222; Gray (n 9) 63.
[45] Judge Schwebel, Dissenting Opinion (n 44) §180.
[46] Cassese (n 30) 199–200.

The question as to whether people fighting in the exercise of their right to self-determination can receive foreign support, however, has received scant attention. As a matter of fact, outside the decolonisation cases there is no practice supporting the idea that foreign countries can provide assistance to people exercising their right to self-determination. This seems understandable, if we consider that the right to provide military support to NLMs did not attain the status of customary law and remained a controversial and debatable issue during the latter half of the twentieth century. After a few decades of silence, the question of intervention in favour of opposition groups exercising their right to self-determination emerged again during the Syrian and Libyan conflicts, when some authors wondered whether it would have been possible to justify interventions in favour of the Libyan National Transitional Council (NTC) and the Syrian Opposition Coalition (SOC) on the basis of the fact that they were exercising their right to self-determination.[47]

As aforementioned, it could be possible to affirm that the Libyan and Syrian rebels were and are fighting in the exercise of their right to internal self-determination. Indeed, when a government denies the people's right to 'determine their political status' (Article 1 of the ICCPR and ICESCR), thus engaging in political oppression,[48] it violates the right to internal self-determination of its own people. Could foreign countries provide military assistance to the rebels on such a basis? It is submitted that this should not be the case for several reasons.

First, during the decolonisation context the question of the provision of military assistance to NLMs remained unresolved. The fracture between developing and socialist countries, on the one hand, and Western and Latin American states, on the other, was reflected in the ambiguity of the General Assembly resolutions, which generically mentioned the possibility of providing assistance to NLMs without further specifying the means and modalities of such help.[49] Second, even if we admitted that liberation movements enjoy a right to receive foreign support in their struggles against oppressive powers, it would be difficult to maintain that such a possibility also applies to people exercising their right to internal self-determination, which is the case in Libya and Syria.[50] Furthermore, it would be paradoxical if Western countries, which strenuously opposed the idea of military help to NLMs, based their support to the NTC and the SOC on the right to self-determination of the Libyan and Syrian peoples.[51]

[47] See eg Ruys (n 13) 34–36, Schmitt (n 12) 154–55.

[48] JJ Paust, 'International Law, Dignity, Democracy' (2013) 46(1) *Cornell International Law Journal* 10.

[49] Ruys (n 13) 34–35.

[50] Schmitt (n 12) 155.

[51] ibid.

Besides the aforementioned legal considerations, there is a further powerful reason against the possibility to intervene in favour of opposition groups fighting for their right to self-determination. As noted by Akande:

> [I]f the rule which permits foreign support to those fighting for self-determination were extended to cases like Syria, i.e. cases of opposition forces fighting against the government of an independent State, this exception to the principle of non-intervention and the prohibition of the use of force, threatens to swallow up the rule.[52]

Indeed, this could lead to a situation where foreign countries would start using the recognition of rebels as legitimate representatives of people instrumentally, to the sole end of helping a specific opposition group. Therefore, granting to people exercising their right to self-determination, and to the opposition groups representing them, a right to receive foreign military support could potentially erode the principle of non-intervention.

III. RESPONSIBILITY TO PROTECT AND INTERVENTIONS IN FAVOUR OF REBELS

A. Responsibility to Protect and the Military Intervention in Libya

The 1990s are known as 'the era of humanitarian intervention'.[53] On the one hand, the international community showed an increasing interest towards the protection of human rights. States using excessive internal force were overwhelmingly condemned in the international arena:[54] the military actions of the Russian government in Chechnya, of Turkey against the Kurdistan Workers' Party (*Partiya Karkerên Kurdistanê*, PKK), and of the Federal Republic of Yugoslavia in Kosovo were widely criticised and in the third case led to a military intervention by NATO.[55] On the other hand, with the end of the Cold War the Security Council saw a crucial increase in its activity. While between its inception and 1989 the UNSC had adopted 646 resolutions, between 1990 and 1999 the Security Council adopted 638 resolutions.[56] Once the factor

[52] D Akande, 'Self Determination and the Syrian Conflict – Recognition of Syrian Opposition as Sole Legitimate Representative of the Syrian People: What Does this Mean and What Implications Does it Have?' (*Ejil:Talk!*, 2012), available at www.ejiltalk.org/self-determination-and-the-syrian-conflict-recognition-of-syrian-opposition-as-sole-legitimate-representative-of-the-syrian-people-what-does-this-mean-and-what-implications-does-it-have/.

[53] L Glanville, *Sovereignty and the Responsibility to Protect: A New History* (University of Chicago Press, 2014) 181.

[54] Lieblich (n 3) 179.

[55] C Kreß, 'Major Post-Westphalian Shifts and Some Important Neo-Westphalian Hesitations in the State Practice on the International Law on The Use of Force' (2014) 1(1) *Journal on the Use of Force and International Law* 20.

[56] Glanville (n 53) 181.

that had paralysed the UNSC for decades was removed, the Council started participating in the international debate on civilian protection. Notably, it developed a thematic agenda which encompassed demand of respect for the relevant provisions of IHL, disarmament issues, and responses to emergencies.[57] This led the UNSC to authorise military interventions for humanitarian purposes, such as the operations in Eastern Zaire (1996), East Timor (1999), and Somalia (1992–94). Interestingly, none of these operations took place against the will of the incumbent government.[58]

Notwithstanding the activism of the Security Council, the failure to react in a timely and effective manner to the Rwandan genocide (1994) and to prevent the massacre that took place in Srebrenica (1995) questioned the capacity of the UNSC to enhance civilian protection. In light of these events the former UN Secretary General Kofi Annan invited the international community to engage with a crucial dilemma:

> If humanitarian intervention is, indeed, an unacceptable assault on sovereignty, how should we respond to a Rwanda, to a Srebrenica – to gross and systematic violations of human rights that offend every precept of our common humanity?[59]

The Canadian government accepted the challenge and established the International Commission on Intervention and State Sovereignty, which produced the well-known report on *The Responsibility to Protect*. The ICISS hoped that the change of terminology from 'humanitarian intervention' to 'responsibility to protect' would help reframe the debate, shifting the focus from the rights of states to the protection of the people under their jurisdiction.[60] Although this attempt was criticised by some scholars as a mere 'rhetorical trick,'[61] the idea

[57] Security Council Report, *Protection of Civilians*, Cross-Cutting Report 2008 no 2, 14 October 2008, New York. See also JM Lehmann, 'All Necessary Means to Protect Civilians: What the Intervention in Libya Says About the Relationship Between the *Jus in Bello* and the *Jus ad Bellum*' (2012) 17(1) *Journal of Conflict and Security Law* 122; AJ Bellamy and PD Williams, 'The New Politics of Protection? Côte d'Ivoire, Libya and the Responsibility to Protect' (2011) 87(4) *International Affairs* 827.

[58] Glanville (n 53) 182.

[59] *We the Peoples: The Role of the United Nations in the 21st Century*, Report of the Secretary General, A/54/2000, 27 March 2000, at 48, §§217–19. See also *In Larger Freedom: Towards Development, Security and Human Rights for All*, Report of the Secretary General, A/59/2005, 21 March 2005, §135; *Uniting our Strengths: Enhancing United Nations Support for the Rule of Law*, Report of the Secretary General, A/61/636–S/2006/980, 14 December 2006, §6. See also Glanville (n 53) 189.

[60] International Commission on Intervention and State Sovereignty (ICISS), *The Responsibility to Protect* (International Development Research Centre 2001) 16–18. See Glanville (n 53) 191. For a critique to this approach, see C Stahn, 'Responsibility to Protect: Political Rhetoric or Emerging Legal Norm?' (2007) 201(1) *American Journal of International Law* 102: '[t]he commission thus used a rhetorical trick: it flipped the coin, shifting the emphasis from a politically and legally undesirable right to intervene for humanitarian purposes to the less confrontational idea of responsibility to protect'.

[61] Stahn (n 60) 102.

of R2P gained momentum in the 2000s. Notably, in 2005 it was endorsed by the General Assembly in the World Summit Outcome document, which established the primary responsibility of each individual state 'to protect its population from genocide, war crimes, ethnic cleansing, and crimes against humanity'.[62] Furthermore, it recognised a parallel, subsidiary responsibility of the international community to use 'appropriate diplomatic, humanitarian and other peaceful means' to help protect populations from such heinous crimes. Should these measures be deemed insufficient, the World Summit Outcome document envisages the possibility of a collective military action with the authorisation of the Security Council.[63]

The events that unfolded in Libya in 2011 should be read against this backdrop. Since the outbreak of the revolution, it was clear that the situation constituted a serious threat to civilians. Gaddafi made clear his intentions when he affirmed that 'officers have been deployed in all tribes and regions so that they can purify all decisions from these cockroaches' and that 'any Libyan who takes arms against Libya will be executed'.[64] On 22 February 2011, the UN High Commissioner for Human Rights called for the cessation of 'widespread and systematic attacks against the civilian population' which 'may amount to crimes against humanity'.[65] The same day, the UN Secretary General's Special Adviser on the Prevention of Genocide, Francis Deng, and Special Adviser on the Responsibility to Protect, Edward Luck, expressed their concerns regarding the '[w]idespread and systematic attacks against civilian populations by military forces, mercenaries, and aircraft' which 'are egregious violations of international human rights and humanitarian law' and 'may well constitute crimes against humanity, for which national authorities should be held accountable'.[66] They then reminded the Libyan authorities that 'the heads of State and Government at the 2005 World Summit pledged to protect populations by preventing genocide, war crimes, ethnic cleansing, and crimes against humanity, as well as their incitement'.[67] Four days later, the Human Rights Council dispatched a commission of inquiry and asked the General Assembly to suspend Libya from the Council.[68] The General Assembly acted accordingly on 1 March 2011.[69]

[62] A/RES/60/1, 24 October 2005, *World Summit Outcome*, §138.

[63] ibid, §139. See Glanville (n 53) 197; Kreß (n 55) 19.

[64] ABC Staff, 'Defiant Gaddafi issues chilling call' (*ABC*, 23 February 2011), available at www.abc.net.au/worldtoday/content/2011/s3146582.htm.

[65] S Nebehay, 'Libya Attacks May Be Crimes against Humanity: U.N.' (*Reuters*, 22 February 2011), available at www.reuters.com/article/us-libya-protests-rights/libya-attacks-may-be-crimes-against-humanity-u-n-idUSTRE71L4Z020110222.

[66] United Nations Press Release, *UN Secretary-General Special Adviser on the Prevention of Genocide, Francis Deng, and Special Adviser on the Responsibility to Protect, Edward Luck, on the Situation in Libya*, 22 February 2011.

[67] ibid.

[68] Human Rights Council, *Situation of human rights in the Libyan Arab Jamahiriya*, A/HRC/S-15/1, 25 February 2011, §§11 and 14.

[69] United Nations Press Release, *General Assembly Suspends Libya from Human Rights Council*, 1 March 2011.

Similar concerns were expressed by regional organisations. On 22 February, the League of Arab States suspended Libya until the end of the violence.[70] The day after, the African Union's Peace and Security Council condemned 'the indiscriminate and excessive use of force and lethal weapons against peaceful protestors, in violation of human rights and International Humanitarian Law, which continues to contribute to the loss of human life and the destruction of property'.[71] At the same time, a number of NGOs called for a stop to the violence in Libya.[72] The International Crisis Group issued several reports in which it condemned 'Libya's resort to state violence against civilians' and recommended the adoption of urgent steps, such as the imposition of 'targeted sanctions against Muammar Qaddafi and family members' and of 'an international embargo to prevent the sale and delivery of any military equipment or support to Libyan security'.[73] Human Rights Watch expressed similar concerns in its numerous communiqués on the issue.[74]

Concurrently, the UNSC held several consultations which resulted in the adoption of Resolution 1970 (2011), which recalled 'the Libyan authorities' responsibility to protect its population' and highlighted that 'the widespread and systematic attacks currently taking place in the Libyan Arab Jamahiriya against the civilian population may amount to crimes against humanity'.[75] Furthermore, the UNSC referred the situation to the Prosecutor of the International Criminal Court, established an arms embargo, and imposed a travel ban and asset freeze on the individuals listed in the Annexes of the Resolution. Nevertheless, these provisions proved unable to stop the mass atrocities that were taking place in the country. At the same time, both the Gulf Cooperation Council and the Organization of the Islamic Conference invited the UNSC to 'take all necessary measures to protect civilians, including enforcing a no-fly zone over Libya'.[76] On 12 March 2011, the League of Arab States called on the Security Council to:

> [I]mpose immediately a no-fly zone on Libyan military aviation, and to establish safe areas in places exposed to shelling as a precautionary measure that allows the protection of the Libyan people and foreign nationals residing in Libya, while respecting the sovereignty and territorial integrity of neighbouring States.[77]

[70] Bellamy and Williams (n 57) 839.

[71] AU document PSC/PR/COMM(CCLXI), *Communiqué*, 23 February 2011.

[72] M-J Domestici-Met, 'Protecting in Libya on Behalf of the International Community' (2011) 3(3) *Goettingen Journal of International Law* 867.

[73] International Crisis Group, 'Immediate International Steps Needed to Stop Atrocities in Libya', Statement, 22 February 2011.

[74] Human Rights Watch, 'Libya: Governments Should Demand End to Unlawful Killings', 20 February 2011.

[75] S/RES/1970 (2011), 26 February 2011, preamble.

[76] MN Schmitt, 'Wings over Libya: The No-Fly Zone in Legal Perspective' (2011) 36 *Yale Journal of International Law Online* 55–57; Bellamy and Williams (n 57) 841.

[77] Council of the League of Arab States, Resolution 7360, 12 March 2011, §1.

Furthermore, it invited the UNSC to 'provide the Libyan people with … the necessary protection from the serious violations and grave crimes committed by the Libyan authorities'.[78]

The calls for the establishment of a no-fly zone and for the protection of civilians framed the discussion within the UNSC. Indeed, debates focused in particular on whether to authorise a military intervention in Libya and on the establishment of a no-fly zone. Notably, Russia, China and three non-permanent members (India, Brazil, and Germany) were sceptical about the possibility of authorising military operations. Questions were raised on the modalities of the intervention and on the enforcement of a no-fly zone. Furthermore, Brazil wondered whether an intervention would have had the effect of changing the domestic nature of the conflict, with the risk of prolonging the fight.[79] Notwithstanding these concerns, on 17 March the Security Council adopted Resolution 1973 (2011) with ten votes in favour and five abstentions (Brazil, China, Germany, India, Russia). Having determined that 'the situation in the Libyan Arab Jamahiriya continues to constitute a threat to international peace and security',[80] the UNSC authorised:

> Member States that have notified the Secretary-General, acting nationally or through regional organizations or arrangements, and acting in cooperation with the Secretary-General, to take all necessary measures … to protect civilians and civilian populated areas under threat of attack in the Libyan Arab Jamahiriya, including Benghazi, while excluding a foreign occupation force of any form on any part of Libyan territory; …
>
> Authoriz[ed] Member States that have notified the Secretary-General and the Secretary-General of the League of Arab States, acting nationally or through regional organizations or arrangements, to take all necessary measures to enforce compliance with the ban on flights imposed by paragraph 6 above.[81]

The Resolution was interpreted as authorising the use of force in Libya.[82] On 19 March 2011, France launched an air attack against a governmental military convoy that was approaching Benghazi. Soon thereafter, the 'Operation Unified Protector' passed under NATO's command and saw the participation of the US,

[78] ibid, §2.

[79] Bellamy and Williams (n 57) 843–44.

[80] S/RES/1973 (2011), 17 March 2011, preamble.

[81] ibid, §§4 and 8.

[82] It is overwhelmingly accepted that the expression 'all the necessary measures' encompasses military operations. This is confirmed by other instances where the UNSC authorised the use of force by inviting states to use 'all the necessary means'. See eg S/RES/794 (1992), 3 December 1992, on Somalia; S/RES/929 (1994), 22 June 1994, on Rwanda; S/RES/1264 (1999), 15 September 1999, on East Timor; S/RES/1464 (2003), 4 February 2003, on Côte d'Ivoire. See also Corten (n 3) 260, 312; P Thielbörger, 'The Status and Future of International Law after the Libya Intervention' (2012) 4(1) *Goettingen Journal of International Law* 20; R Van Steenberghe, 'L'emploi de la Force en Libye: Question de Droit International et de Droit Belge' (2011) 26(6444) *Journal des Tribunaux* 533; Schmitt (n 76) 47–48; Lehmann (n 57) 130.

the UK, Belgium, France, Canada, Denmark, Italy, the Netherlands, Norway, Spain, Qatar and the United Arab Emirates.[83] During the first stages of the intervention, the main objective was to protect the civilians in Benghazi. This was reflected in the statement of US President Barack Obama:

> We struck regime forces approaching Benghazi to save that city and the people within it. We hit Qaddafi's troops in neighbouring Ajdabiya, allowing the opposition to drive them out. … The task that I assigned our forces – to protect the Libyan people from immediate danger, and to establish a no-fly zone – carries with it a U.N. mandate and international support.[84]

However, from April 2011 the coalition of intervening states started targeting governmental forces and infrastructures, regardless of whether they constituted a direct threat to the civilian population. Soon it was apparent that the real objective of the operation was overthrowing Gaddafi's regime, which was deemed illegitimate. Moreover, some states went as far as providing direct help to the Libyan rebels.[85]

With Resolution 1973, for the first time the UNSC authorised an armed intervention within a state, against its will, for the purpose of protecting civilians.[86] Since the adoption of the UN Charter, there had been cases when individual states or coalitions forcibly intervened in other countries.[87] The Security Council Resolution thus constitutes a landmark decision. However, the modalities and the consequences of the intervention raised serious and well-founded doubts with regard to the risk of abuses and the capacity to improve the situation on the ground.[88] Crucially, the military operation in Libya highlighted that noble intentions may in reality be used to pursue other objectives and that it is only a small step from protecting civilians to helping the rebels in their struggle against the government.[89]

B. Responsibility to Protect and Regime Change: From Protecting Civilians to Helping Rebels

Since the 1990s, humanitarian interventions have raised many fundamental questions. Debates on the existence of a right to unilateral intervention for

[83] O Corten and V Koutroulis, 'The Illegality of Military Support to Rebels in the Libyan War: Aspects of *Jus contra Bellum* and *Jus in Bello*' (2013) 18(1) *Journal of Conflict and Security Law* 59.

[84] US White House, Office of the Press Secretary, 'Remarks by the President in Address to the Nation on Libya' (28 March 2011), available at obamawhitehouse.archives.gov/the-press-office/2011/03/28/remarks-president-address-nation-libya.

[85] Corten (n 18) 166.

[86] Bellamy and Williams (n 57) 825.

[87] Glanville (n 53) 205.

[88] Corten (n 18) 168.

[89] RR Janik, 'You Can't Have One Without the Other, Can You? Assessing the Relationship between the Use of Force in the Name of Human Rights and Regime Change' (2015) 6 *Czech Yearbook of Public & Private International Law* 223.

humanitarian reasons outside the UN Charter framework have gripped theory and practice for a long time. From NATO's intervention in Kosovo in 1999 to the recent US military operations in Syria as a reaction to the use of chemical weapons against the civilian population in 2017–18, attempts to establish a right to humanitarian intervention without an express authorisation of the Security Council proved fruitless.[90] On the other hand, interventions authorised by the UNSC under the R2P framework have proved equally controversial. Indeed, the intervention in Libya has emphasised the risk of abuses and has raised significant dilemmas with regard to the use of force in the name of human rights, regime change, and the possibility to help rebels for humanitarian reasons.

As aforementioned, on 17 March 2011 the Security Council adopted Resolution 1973, which allowed states to use 'all the necessary measures … to protect civilians and civilian populated areas under threat of attack in the Libyan Arab Jamahiriya'.[91] The same day, Gaddafi warned the population in Benghazi: 'We are coming tonight', he said, 'You will come out from inside. Prepare yourselves from tonight. We will find you in your closets.'[92] On 19 March 2011, the French air force attacked Libyan military tanks approaching Benghazi. A few days later, the operation passed to the hands of NATO. While at first the military operation was exclusively aimed at protecting civilians, in late April the coalition of intervening states started targeting governmental personnel and infrastructure, even when this was not strictly necessary to protect the civilian population.[93] As explained by Corten and Koutroulis:

> [T]he declared objective of the operation had shifted from the prevention of immediate danger to civilians in some cities threatened by the army (1), to the destruction of the military and economic infrastructure of the regime (2), to be followed by change of regime (3), through military support for the rebels (4).[94]

It is generally uncontested that Resolution 1793 served as the sole legal basis for the intervention. As a matter of fact, no intervening state suggested otherwise, nor did it invoke any other legal basis, such as a right to intervene in the name of human rights.[95] On the contrary, the intervening states claimed that overthrowing Gaddafi was instrumental to protecting civilians: the latter could not happen without the former.[96] At the same time, they affirmed that Gaddafi

[90] ibid, 230.

[91] S/RES/1973 (2011), §4.

[92] Reuters Staff, 'Gaddafi tells Benghazi his army is coming tonight' (*Reuters*, 17 March 2011), available at www.reuters.com/article/us-libya-gaddafi-address/gaddafi-tells-benghazi-his-army-is-coming-tonight-idUSTRE72G7B220110317.

[93] Corten and Koutroulis (n 83) 68.

[94] ibid, 69.

[95] See eg 'Supporting the Libyan National Transitional Council' written statement by UK Foreign Secretary William Hague to the British Parliament (13 May 2011), available at www.gov.uk/government/news/supporting-the-libyan-national-transitional-council.

[96] See eg the interview of French Minister of Foreign Affairs Alain Juppé in which he affirmed that: '[i]l n'y a pas de changement de stratégie, nous sommes toujours dans la stricte application

lost his legitimacy due to the heinous crimes committed against the population and should thus relinquish power to the NTC, recognised as the legitimate representative of the Libyan people. The Council of the European Union unequivocally expressed this position, where it welcomed:

> [T]he emphasis of the Chairs' Conclusions on the need to intensify the political, military and economic pressure on the Kadhafi regime in fulfilment of UNSCRs 1970 and 1973. The Council reiterates its call for an immediate and genuine ceasefire, the fact that *Colonel Kadhafi has lost legitimacy and that he must relinquish power immediately*. Colonel Kadhafi remains a threat to the Libyan people.[97]

Although the intervening states claimed that they were acting within the limits set by Resolution 1793, the link between civilian protection and regime change was criticised by a number of international organisations and individual countries. For instance, the Peace and Security Council of the African Union specified in a communiqué that the objective of the Resolution is 'solely to ensure the protection of the civilian population' and thus urged 'all involved to refrain from actions, including military operations targeting Libyan Senior Officials and socio economic infrastructure, that would further compound the situation and make it more difficult to achieve international consensus on the best way forward'.[98] Similar concerns were raised by the Secretary-General of the Organization of the Islamic Conference, who emphasised that the aim of Resolution 1793 is the protection of civilians and 'urged the International Community to remain within the limits of the mandate given by the Security Council in these resolutions while dealing with the Libyan crisis'.[99] Several countries openly denounced the overthrowing of the Libyan regime as exceeding the mandate of the UNSC Resolution. Notably, Russia affirmed that 'the Council's mandate for conducting the operation in Libya was disregarded',[100] while China made clear that it was 'not in favour of any arbitrary interpretation of the Council's resolutions or of any actions going beyond those mandated by the Council'.[101]

des résolutions du Conseil de sécurité qui prévoient de mettre en œuvre les moyens nécessaires pour protéger les populations. Protéger les populations, ce n'est pas simplement neutraliser les blindés ou les avions de Kadhafi, c'est aussi affaiblir ses capacités militaires, ses postes de commandement, ses réseaux d'approvisionnement. C'est, donc, dans cet esprit que nous avons mis en place ce dispositif qui nous permettra d'avoir des frappes plus ciblées, plus proches des réalités du terrain. La résolution 1973 prévoit que l'on peut utiliser tous les moyens pour protéger les populations. Évidemment, pour protéger les populations, on l'a bien vu à Misrata, il faut casser la force militaire de Kadhafi et donc s'attaquer aux postes de commandement, aux infrastructures ou aux réseaux d'approvisionnement de ses troupes'. 'Libye: Entretien du Ministère d'Etat, Ministre des Affaires étrangères et européennes, Alain Juppé, avec "Radio France International"' (23 May 2011).

[97] Council of the European Union, Council conclusions on Libya, 3091st Foreign Affairs Council Meeting, Brussels, 23 May 2011, §2, emphasis added.

[98] African Union, Peace and Security Council, 268th meeting, Addis Ababa, 10 March 2011, PSC/PR/COMM.2(CCLXV).

[99] Secretary-General of the Organization of the Islamic Conference, 'Ihsanoglu: Political solution to the Libyan crisis is the only way to bring lasting peace to Libya' 7 May 2011.

[100] UNSC Verbatim Record, UN Doc S/PV/6620, §3, 16 September 2011.

[101] UNSC Verbatim Record, UN Doc S/PV/6528, §10, 4 May 2011. In the same vein, Algeria, Bolivia, Cuba, Mauritania, Nicaragua, Nigeria, South Africa, and Venezuela did not accept the

As a matter of fact, concerns regarding the vague terms and conditions of the authorisation to use force were expressed already during the UNSC meeting that led to the adoption of Resolution 1793. Notably, the abstaining countries were worried by the lack of 'clarity about details of enforcement measures, including who will participate and with what assets, and how these measures will exactly be carried out',[102] thus implicitly recognising that 'a margin of interpretation was left to the intervening states'.[103] This would find confirmation in the comparison between Resolution 1793 and Resolution 1795 on Côte d'Ivoire, where the UNSC unanimously authorised the use of all necessary means 'to protect civilians under *imminent threat* of physical violence'.[104] The fact that Resolution 1793 allowed the use of force to protect 'civilians and civilian populated areas under threat of attack' suggests that in the case of Libya the authorisation was broader. Nevertheless, this does not necessarily imply that Resolution 1793 authorised the overthrowing of Gaddafi. This would be the case only if overthrowing Gaddafi was indeed necessary to protect the civilian population 'under threat of attack'.[105]

According to the ICJ, 'whether a measure is necessary [is not] purely a question for the subjective judgment of the party; the text does not refer to what the party "considers necessary"'.[106] In the same vein, the resolution on 'Authorization of the Use of Force by the United Nations' by the Institut de droit international clarifies that '[t]he objectives, scope and modes of control of each authorization should be strictly interpreted and implemented' (Article 9) and that '[i]n no case may a previous authorization be invoked for any purpose beyond its specific objectives, time and scope' (Article 10).[107] The general meaning attributed to the necessity requirement would thus suggest that linking protection of civilians and regime change would override the limits of the UNSC authorisation. This would be confirmed by the fact that, 'when the Security Council decides to target a government, it clearly states as much in the relevant resolution'.'[108] This was the case in Haiti, where the UNSC authorised States to use 'all necessary means to facilitate the departure from Haiti of the military leadership'.[109] It seems therefore clear that Resolution 1793 did not imply the possibility to overthrow the Libyan regime as a mean to protect the civilian population.

extensive interpretation of Resolution 1973 by the intervening countries. See Corten and Koutroulis (n 83) 76; Bellamy and Williams (n 57) 847.

[102] UNSC Verbatim Record, UN Doc S/PV/6498, 17 March 2011, at 6.

[103] Corten and Koutroulis (n 83) 70.

[104] S/RES/1795 (2011), 30 March 2011, §6, emphasis added. See Bellamy and Williams (n 57) 835.

[105] S/RES/1973 (2011), §4.

[106] *Nicaragua* case, §282.

[107] Institut de Droit International, *Present Problems of the Use of Force in International Law: Sub-group D – Authorization of the Use of Force by the United Nations*, Session de Rhodes, 9 September 2011.

[108] Corten and Koutroulis (n 83) 72.

[109] S/RES/940 (1994), 31 July 1994, §4.

As aforementioned, the intervening states did not limit themselves to targeting the Libyan governmental forces, but went as far as providing military support to the rebels.[110] This has raised a further question, namely whether helping opposition groups could be justified on humanitarian grounds. As explained by Akande, in principle helping rebels could fall within the mandate of the UNSC Resolution:

> Under international law States may use force either directly (through their own armed forces) or indirectly (by providing support to non-State groups) … If a State is authorized to use force it may choose to do so directly or indirectly. This may include providing support or arms or other assistance to non-State groups in order to fulfill the mandate.[111]

Nevertheless, providing military help to the NTC raises three crucial problems. First, as for the overthrowing of the Libyan regime, in order to be lawful the assistance to rebels should be necessary to protect the civilian population. This could be the case if Resolution 1793 did permit a regime change. However, as explained before this interpretation goes too far. Second, providing assistance to rebels raises a further problem: even if it were possible to justify the provision of weapons and the military support to the NTC, it would be extremely difficult for the intervening states to make sure that the weapons and military support would be used by the rebels only for the specific end of protecting civilians, and not for pursuing other objectives.[112] Lastly, the support provided to the rebels may amount to a violation of IHL, namely the obligation to ensure respect for humanitarian law.[113] It is beyond the scope of this work to analyse in depth the personal and material scope of application of this provision. Here it suffices to say that the duty to abstain from supporting a party to a conflict that commits violations of IHL is well-settled.[114] The International Commission of Inquiry on Libya found compelling evidence that the Libyan rebel forces 'committed serious violations, including war crimes and breaches of international human rights law'.[115] Since these violations were known at the time of the foreign intervention

[110] See eg the statement by UK Foreign Secretary William Hague following the Libya Contact Group meeting in Doha, 13 April 2011, §8: '[p]articipants in the Contact Group agreed to continue to provide support to the opposition, including material support, consistent with UNSCRs 1970 and 1973 (2011) and the delivery of humanitarian aid to agencies able to deliver it effectively including the UN, humanitarian agencies and the opposition', Libya Contact Group Doha, 13 April 2011, Chair's statement, available at www.nato.int/nato_static_fl2014/assets/pdf/pdf_2011_04/20110926_110413-Libya-Contact_-Group-Doha.pdf. See also Human Rights Watch, *World Report 2012*, New York, 2012, at 596.

[111] D Akande, 'Does SC Resolution 1973 Permit Coalition Military Support for the Libyan Rebels?' (*EJIL: Talk!*, 2011), available at www.ejiltalk.org/does-sc-resolution-1973-permit-coalition-military-support-for-the-libyan-rebels/.

[112] Clapham (n 13) 163–96; Akande (n 111).

[113] Corten and Koutroulis (n 83) 78. For the legal basis of this provision, see ch 5.

[114] Corten and Koutroulis (n 83) 85.

[115] Human Rights Council, 'Report of the International Commission of Inquiry on Libya,' 8 March 2012, A/HRC/19/68, at 1.

in Libya[116] and since the intervening states 'did not exert their influence, to the degree possible, to stop violations' of *jus in bello*,[117] the support provided to the opposition groups amounted to a violation of the obligation to ensure respect for humanitarian law.

Resolution 1793 and the subsequent intervention in Libya highlight the difficulties of protecting the civilian population through a military operation. Notably, it shows how the prima facie impartial nature of humanitarian interventions could be de facto artificial. The position adopted by Russia – it has used or threatened to use the veto against a military intervention in Syria – is thus understandable: the Libyan case showed the risk of abuses pertaining to interventions carried out in the name of human rights.[118] Against this backdrop, it is of some interest to mention a paper submitted to the UNSC by Brazil, called 'Responsibility while Protecting'.[119] The paper aims at addressing the issues that emerged during the intervention in Libya as to the scope and modalities of the military operation. First, it acknowledges that

> There is a growing perception that the concept of the responsibility to protect might be misused for purposes other than protecting civilians, such as regime change. This perception may make it even more difficult to attain the protection objectives pursued by the international community.[120]

Then, the paper makes the case for the need to establish clear and specific criteria to guide and limit the scope of the intervention. Furthermore, it emphasises that '[e]nhanced Security Council procedures are needed to monitor and assess the manner in which resolutions are interpreted and implemented to ensure responsibility while protecting'.[121] Inasmuch as the 'Responsibility while Protecting' paper constitutes 'a constructive critique of the practical implementation of R2P',[122] its value should not be belittled. Nevertheless, the ideas advanced by Brazil proved incapable of guiding the discussion on the Syrian crisis within the Security Council. Furthermore, it leaves unanswered a decisive question: when a government commits heinous crimes against its own people, how is it possible to

[116] See eg UN News Centre, 'Libya: UN Alarmed at Reports of Violence against sub-Saharan Migrants' (8 March 2011), available at news.un.org/en/story/2011/03/368362-libya-un-alarmed-reports-violence-against-sub-saharan-migrants.

[117] J-M Henckaerts and L Doswald-Beck, *Customary International Humanitarian Law*, vol I (Cambridge University Press, 2005) Rule 144.

[118] O Corten and A Verdebout, 'Les interventions militaires récentes en territoire étranger: vers une remise en cause du *jus contra bellum*?' (2014) LX *Annuaire Français de Droit International* 168.

[119] 'Responsibility while Protecting: Elements for the Development and Promotion of a Concept', letter dated 9 November 2011 from the Permanent Representative of Brazil to the United Nations addressed to the Secretary-General, A/66/151–S/2011/701, 9 November 2011 (hereinafter, 'Responsibility while Protecting').

[120] ibid, §10.

[121] ibid, §11(d) and (h). See also M Tourinho, O Stuenkel and S Brockmeier, 'Responsibility while Protecting: Reforming R2P Implementation' (2016) 30(1) *Global Society* 138.

[122] ibid, 143.

protect civilians without weakening the government and thus without facilitating a regime change?[123]

C. Humanitarian Intervention without Regime Change

The military intervention in Libya raised the question of the possibility of using force for humanitarian reasons against the government without helping the opposition groups. The Syrian conflict is particularly interesting in this regard. As aforementioned, the events in Libya and Syria unfolded in a similar fashion and were both characterised by widespread violence against the civilian population. However, unlike the Libyan conflict, the chances that the Security Council would authorise a military intervention to protect the Syrian population are nearly non-existent. Indeed, Russia has vetoed several resolutions on Syria and will plausibly prevent the UNSC from adopting more forceful measures.[124] While it is undeniable that this position is politically motivated, especially if we consider Russian support to the Assad government, this approach is also consonant with Russian scepticism regarding the intervention in Libya in particular and the R2P doctrine more generally.

While the possibility of intervening was already discussed during the early stages of the conflict, the use of chemical weapons proved to be a 'game changer'.[125] Between March and August 2013 several chemical weapons attacks took place in Syria, with dramatic consequences for the civilian population.[126] The international community reacted harshly; for instance, President Obama stated that:

> Horrific as it is when mortars are being fired on civilians and people are being indiscriminately killed, to use potential weapons of mass destruction on civilian populations crosses another line with respect to international norms and

[123] Bellamy and Williams (n 57) 848. An interesting endeavour to develop clear guidance in military operations aimed at protecting the civilian population against heinous violations of human rights and IHL is represented by the *Mass Atrocity Response Operations (MARO): A Military Planning Handbook*. The manual was developed for the US military and illustrates ways to 'to halt widespread and systematic use of violence by state or non-state armed groups against non-combatants'. See S Sewall, D Raymond and S Chin, *Mass Atrocity Response Operations (MARO): A Military Planning Handbook* (Centre for Human Rights Policy, Harvard Kennedy School, and the US Army Peacekeeping and Stability Operations Institute, Cambridge (MA), 2010).

[124] See A Bell, 'Syria, Chemical Weapons, and a Qualitative Threshold for Humanitarian Intervention' (*Just Security*, 2018), available at www.justsecurity.org/54665/syria-chemical-weapons-international-law-developing-qualitative-threshold-humanitarian-intervention/.

[125] BBC Staff, 'Barack Obama warns Syria chemical arms a "game changer"' (*BBC*, 26 April 2013), available at www.bbc.com/news/world-middle-east-22318749. See also D Akande, 'Does Use of Chemical Weapons Justify Intervention in Syria?' (*EJIL: Talk!*, 2013), available at www.ejiltalk.org/does-use-of-chemical-weapons-justify-intervention-in-syria/.

[126] BBC Staff, 'Syria chemical weapons allegations' (*BBC*, 31 October 2013), available at www.bbc.com/news/world-middle-east-22557347; BBC Staff, 'Syria chemical attack: What we know' (*BBC*, 24 September 2013), available at www.bbc.com/news/world-middle-east-23927399.

> international law. … All of us, not just the United States, but around the world, have to recognise how we cannot stand by and permit the systematic use of weapons like chemical weapons on civilian populations.[127]

By August 2013, it seemed quite clear that the US and the UK were going to intervene in Syria as a reaction to the use of chemical weapons.[128] However, ultimately the intervention did not take place.[129] Bowing to international pressure, in September 2013 Syria acceded to the 1992 Chemical Weapons Convention[130] and committed to provisionally applying the treaty before its entry into force. At the same time, the US and Russia submitted the Framework for Elimination of Syrian Chemical Weapons to the Members of the Executive Council of the Organization for the Prohibition of Chemical Weapons, where the two countries expressed 'their joint determination to ensure the destruction of the Syrian chemical weapons program (CW) in the soonest and safest manner'.[131] Accordingly, the removal of chemical weapons in Syria began soon thereafter.[132] Although these positive steps raised the hope that no other chemical attacks would happen in the future, on 4 April 2017 the nerve agent sarin was used to attack Khan Sheikhoun, a rebel-held town, and resulted in the deaths of about 80 people.[133] Two days later, the US launched military airstrikes against 'Syrian fighter jets, hardened aircraft shelters, radar equipment, ammunition bunkers, sites for storing fuel and air defense systems'.[134] On 7 April 2018, at least

[127] BBC Staff (n 125).

[128] See eg the remarks delivered on 31 August 2013 by President Obama: '[n]ow, after careful deliberation, I have decided that the United States should take military action against Syrian regime targets. This would not be an open-ended intervention. We would not put boots on the ground. Instead, our action would be designed to be limited in duration and scope. But I'm confident we can hold the Assad regime accountable for their use of chemical weapons, deter this kind of behavior, and degrade their capacity to carry it out'. See B Obama, 'Barack Obama statement on US intervention in Syria – full text' (*The Guardian*, 31 August 2013), available at www.theguardian.com/world/2013/aug/31/barack-obama-statement-us-intervention-syria. See also D Akande, 'The Legality of Military Action in Syria: Humanitarian Intervention and Responsibility to Protect' (*EJIL: Talk!* 2013), available at www.ejiltalk.org/humanitarian-intervention-responsibility-to-protect-and-the-legality-of-military-action-in-syria/.

[129] BBC Staff, 'Syria crisis: Cameron loses Commons vote on Syria action' (*BBC*, 30 August 2013), available at www.bbc.com/news/uk-politics-23892783; BBC Staff, 'Syria crisis: Barack Obama puts military strike on hold' (*BBC*, 11 September 2013), available at www.bbc.com/news/world-us-canada-24043751.

[130] Convention on the Prohibition of the Development, Production, Stockpiling and Use of Chemical Weapons and on Their Destruction, 30 November 1992.

[131] Framework for Elimination of Syrian Chemical Weapons, Joint National Paper by the Russian Federation and the United States of America, EC-M-33/NAT.1, 17 September 2013.

[132] A. Conte, 'The Responsibility to Protect, and Syria' in S Casey-Maslen (ed), *The War Report: Armed Conflict in 2013* (Oxford University Press, 2014) 447.

[133] BBC Staff, 'Syria chemical "attack": What we know' (*BBC*, 26 April 2017), available at www.bbc.com/news/world-middle-east-39500947.

[134] MR Gordon, H Cooper and MD Shear, 'Dozens of U.S. Missiles Hit Air Base in Syria' (*The New York Times*, 6 April 2017), available at www.nytimes.com/2017/04/06/world/middleeast/us-said-to-weigh-military-responses-to-syrian-chemical-attack.html.

40 people were killed by a chemical attack in Douma, 'the last rebel-held town in the Eastern Ghouta region'.[135] One week later, the US, the UK, and France engaged in airstrikes against the Assad regime.[136]

The US and France did not provide any legal arguments to justify the intervention: President Trump claimed that the aim of the airstrikes was 'to establish a strong deterrent against the production, spread, and use of chemical weapons',[137] while President Macron maintained that the intervention was directed only at the chemical weapons arsenal of the Syrian government.[138] On the contrary, the UK explicitly relied on humanitarian intervention and maintained that: '[t]he UK is permitted under international law, on an exceptional basis, to take measures in order to alleviate overwhelming humanitarian suffering. The legal basis for the use of force is humanitarian intervention'.[139]

Legal scholarship engaged in dynamic debates on the legality of the interventions and on the possibility of using force as a consequence of chemical weapons attacks against the civilian population. On the one hand, few authors noted that, notwithstanding the legal basis provided by the UK, in light of its nature and scope, the intervention could amount to armed reprisals.[140] The Institut de

[135] BBC Staff, 'Syria war: What we know about Douma "chemical attack"' (*BBC*, 16 April 2018), available at www.bbc.com/news/world-middle-east-43697084.

[136] J Borger and P Beaumont, 'Syria: US, UK and France launch strikes in response to chemical attack' (*The Guardian*, 14 April 2018), available at www.theguardian.com/world/2018/apr/14/syria-air-strikes-us-uk-and-france-launch-attack-on-assad-regime.

[137] Q Jurecic, 'Transcript: President Trump's Remarks on Syria Airstrikes' (*Lawfare*, 13 April 2018), available at www.lawfareblog.com/transcript-president-trumps-remarks-syria-airstrikes.

[138] President Macron stated that: '[j]'ai donc ordonné aux forces armées françaises d'intervenir cette nuit, dans le cadre d'une opération internationale menée en coalition avec les Etats-Unis d'Amérique et le Royaume-Uni et dirigée contre l'arsenal chimique clandestin du régime syrien. Notre réponse a été circonscrite aux capacités du régime syrien permettant la production et l'emploi d'armes chimiques. Nous ne pouvons pas tolérer la banalisation de l'emploi d'armes chimiques, qui est un danger immédiat pour le peuple syrien et pour notre sécurité collective. C'est le sens des initiatives constamment portées par la France au Conseil de Sécurité des Nations unies'. See 'Communiqué de presse du Président de la République sur l'intervention des forces armées françaises en réponse à l'emploi d'armes chimiques en Syrie' (14 Avril 2018), available at www.elysee.fr/communiques-de-presse/article/communique-de-presse-du-president-de-la-republique-sur-l-intervention-des-forces-armees-francaises-en-reponse-a-l-emploi-d-armes-chimiques-en-syrie/.

[139] 'Syria action – UK government legal position' (Policy Paper, 14 April 2018), available at www.gov.uk/government/publications/syria-action-uk-government-legal-position/syria-action-uk-government-legal-position. The UK suggested already in 2013 that humanitarian intervention would have offered the legal basis to intervene in Syria following the use of chemical weapons by the government. See 'Chemical weapon use by Syrian regime: UK government legal position' (29 August 2013), Policy Paper, available at www.gov.uk/government/publications/chemical-weapon-use-by-syrian-regime-uk-government-legal-position/chemical-weapon-use-by-syrian-regime-uk-government-legal-position-html-version.

[140] This position could be fostered by a statement by President Macron, in which he affirmed that 'the use of chemical weapons in Syria is a red line for France and would result in reprisals'. See Reuters Staff, 'Chemical weapons a red line in Syria, says France's Macron' (*Reuters*, 29 May 2017), available at uk.reuters.com/article/uk-france-russia-syria-macron-idUKKBN18P1OQ. See also M Hakimi, 'Macron's Threat of Reprisals and the *Jus ad Bellum*' (*EJIL: Talk!*, 2017), available at www.ejiltalk.org/macrons-threat-of-reprisals-and-the-jus-ad-bellum/.

Droit International defines reprisals as 'des mesures de contrainte, dérogatoires aux règles ordinaires du Droit des Gens, prises par un Etat à la suite d'actes illicites commis à son préjudice par un autre Etat et ayant pour but d'imposer à celui-ci, au moyen d'un dommage, le respect du droit'.[141] Since the interventions in Syria seem to be punitive and deterrent, they could be considered as reprisals.[142] Nevertheless, the authors that suggested this view noted that forcible reprisals not authorised by the Security Council would be unlawful under positive interventional law.[143]

On the other hand, the overwhelming majority of scholars engaged in discussions on the legality of humanitarian interventions. A number of authors have held that military interventions for humanitarian reasons are lawful under international law. For instance, Koh maintained that 'international law has evolved sufficiently to permit morally legitimate action to prevent atrocities by responding to the deliberate use of chemical weapons'.[144] Ohlin criticised the idea that 'stopping international conflicts is the most important goal of the international legal system':[145] the aim of the UN Charter should not be limited to preventing international armed conflicts, but it should also protect other values. Therefore, he concludes that there might be times when the use of force without the UNSC's authorisation would be necessary and lawful.[146] At the other end of the spectrum, the majoritarian view endorses the idea that humanitarian interventions

[141] Institut de Droit International, *Régime des représailles en temps de paix*, Session de Paris, 19 October 1934, Art 1. See also M Ruffert, 'Reprisals' in *Max Planck Encyclopedia of Public International Law* (Oxford University Press, 2015) §7.

[142] C Stahn, 'Syria and the Semantics of intervention, aggression and punishment: On "red lines" and "blurred lines"' (2013) 11(5) *Journal of International Criminal Justice* 970.

[143] M Milanovic, 'The Syria Strikes: Still Clearly Illegal' (*EJIL: Talk!*, 2018), available at www.ejiltalk.org/the-syria-strikes-still-clearly-illegal/; S Darcy, 'Military force against Syria would be a reprisal rather than humanitarian intervention, but that doesn't make it any more lawful' (*EJIL: Talk!*, 2013), available at www.ejiltalk.org/military-force-against-syria-would-be-a-reprisal-rather-than-humanitarian-intervention-but-that-doesnt-make-it-any-more-lawful/; A Zammit Borda, 'The Precedent Set by the US Reprisal Against the Use of Chemical Weapons in Syria' (*EJIL: Talk!*, 2017), available at www.ejiltalk.org/the-precedent-set-by-the-us-reprisal-against-the-use-of-chemical-weapons-in-syria/; M Hakimi, 'The Attack on Syria and the Contemporary *Jus ad Bellum*' (*EJIL: Talk!*, 2018), available at www.ejiltalk.org/the-attack-on-syria-and-the-contemporary-jus-ad-bellum/; ME O'Connell, 'Unlawful Reprisals to the Rescue against Chemical Attacks?' (*EJIL: Talk!*, 2018), available at www.ejiltalk.org/unlawful-reprisals-to-the-rescue-against-chemical-attacks/.

[144] HH Koh, 'Syria and the Law of Humanitarian Intervention (Part II: International Law and the Way Forward)' (*EJIL: Talk!*, 2013), available at www.ejiltalk.org/syria-and-the-law-of-humanitarian-intervention-part-ii-international-law-and-the-way-forward/. See also HH Koh, 'The War Powers and Humanitarian Intervention' (2016) 53(4) *Houston Law Review* 971–1033.

[145] D Ohlin, 'Two Visions of the UN Charter' (*Opinio Juris*, 2017), available at opiniojuris.org/2017/04/13/two-visions-of-the-un-charter/.

[146] See also J Trahan, 'The Narrow Case for the Legality of Strikes in Syria and Russia's Illegitimate Veto' (*Opinio Juris*, 2018), available at opiniojuris.org/2018/04/23/the-narrow-case-for-the-legality-of-strikes-in-syria-and-russias-illegitimate-veto/; D Bethlehem, 'Stepping Back a Moment – The Legal Basis in Favour of a Principle of Humanitarian Intervention' (*EJIL: Talk!*, 2013), available at www.ejiltalk.org/stepping-back-a-moment-the-legal-basis-in-favour-of-a-principle-of-humanitarian-intervention/; K Anderson, 'Legality of Intervention in Syria in Response to Chemical Weapon Attacks' (2013) 17(21) *ASIL insights*.

are still unlawful under the current legal framework,[147] while some scholars wonder whether they could be 'illegal but legitimate'.[148] Despite attempts to provide a legal justification for the use of force in Syria, it is fairly clear that unilateral humanitarian interventions are not part of positive international law and that the military actions against Syria amounted to a violation of the ban on using force.

Concluding that humanitarian interventions are unlawful is not the end of the story. Indeed, their illegality notwithstanding, the interventions in Syria are interesting inasmuch as they do not seem to have helped the opposition groups in their fight against the government. This would prove that it is possible to have interventions grounded on humanitarian considerations and that do not facilitate or result in regime change. Nevertheless, we may wonder whether the use of force by the US, the UK, and France achieved the hoped-for objective. As a matter of fact, the 2017 airstrikes did not prevent the chemical attack that took place the next year. Therefore, it is at least doubtful whether this time they will succeed in preventing future use of chemical weapons against the population.

IV. CONCLUDING OBSERVATIONS

With the adoption of the UN Charter and the development of the principle of non-intervention through UN General Assembly resolutions and state practice, nearly any forms of forcible or non-lethal interference in favour of rebels have been outlawed. Nevertheless, the limits of such a ban had already emerged in the 1960s.

As the existence of colonial dominations, alien occupations, and racist regimes started being perceived as heinous and unjust, the international community wondered whether the legal framework should have been adapted in light of the singularities of the decolonisation process. While the struggle of National Liberation Movements was overwhelmingly recognised as legitimate, the question of the practical implications of such recognition was highly divisive. Nevertheless, the international community agreed on a number of issues which departed from the legal framework established by the UN Charter. In particular, with regard to foreign intervention it was generally uncontested that people subjected to colonial domination, alien occupation, and racist regimes

[147] See eg M Hayashi, 'Reacting to the Use of Chemical Weapons: Options for Third States' (2014) 1(1) *Journal on the Use of Force and International Law* 117; A Henriksen and M Schack, 'The Crisis in Syria and Humanitarian Intervention' (2014) 1(1) *Journal on the Use of Force and International Law* 122–47; M Milanović, 'The Clearly Illegal US Missile Strike in Syria' (*EJIL: Talk!*, 2017), available at www.ejiltalk.org/the-clearly-illegal-us-missile-strike-in-syria/comment-page-1/.

[148] M Milanović, 'Illegal But Legitimate?' (*EJIL: Talk!*, 2017), available at www.ejiltalk.org/illegal-but-legitimate/; R Goodman, 'Humanitarian Military Options for Syrian Chemical Weapons Attack: "Illegal but Not Unprecedented"' (*Just Security*, 2017), available at www.justsecurity.org/39658/humanitarian-military-options-syrian-chemical-weapons-attack-illegal-unprecedented/.

had a right to receive (at least non-lethal) assistance from third countries, while no help could have been provided to the oppressive power. This crucial divergence with the traditional rule, which establishes that interventions in favour of rebels are unlawful, stems from the reasons why NLMs exist: it is the legitimacy of cause that led to a change of the general rules governing foreign interventions.

Similarly, the intervention in Libya and the subsequent overthrowing of Gaddafi should be read in light of the discourses on legitimacy of the NTC. While France and its allies were preparing to intervene to protect the Libyan population, they affirmed that Gaddafi had lost his legitimacy due to the heinous crimes committed against the population. At the same time, they recognised the NTC as the legitimate representative of the Libyan people and as legitimate interlocutor. These considerations raise pivotal questions as to the interrelations between legitimacy, R2P, and regime change. What is the role of sovereignty against this backdrop? Are we witnessing a shift towards a preference of legitimacy over effectiveness? And how could this affect the current legal framework? These dilemmas will be addressed in the concluding chapter. For the moment, we can agree with Lieblich that:

> The more a government violates the principle of protection, the international community might be more willing to give credit to relatively ineffective opposition groups, as potential fulfillers of the responsibility to protect.[149]

[149] Lieblich (n 3) 235.

9

Conclusions

THE OBJECTIVE OF the present work has been to analyse how the human rights paradigm has affected the legal framework regulating foreign armed interventions in internal conflicts. The conventional approach holds that providing help to opposition groups is always unlawful. On the other hand, the question of interventions in favour of the government is highly divisive. Some scholars argue that interventions in civil wars upon invitation of the government are unlawful. Others maintain that these interventions are allowed only if the government exercises effective control over territory and population.[1] Yet others propound that democratic legitimacy, and not effectiveness, is the determining criterion to identify the authority capable of asking for foreign interventions.

The argument that I have advanced challenges this traditional approach and demonstrates that human rights have been affecting *jus ad bellum* in a pervasive and profound fashion. The analysis conducted so far has established an emerging pattern with respect to foreign interventions in internal conflicts: while the effectiveness doctrine no longer reflects the current legal framework, legitimacy is emerging as a possible alternative with regard to interventions in favour of governments and rebels alike. Specifically, the pattern suggests that human rights are being used as a parameter of legitimacy. This chapter will provide the conclusions of this research and will contextualise them in light of two recurring concepts that have permeated this study: effectiveness and legitimacy. It will further highlight the dangers of the emerging legitimacy framed in terms of human rights.

I. THE SHIFT FROM LEGITIMACY TO EFFECTIVENESS AND BACK

A. Interventions by Invitation between Effectiveness and Legitimacy

Interventions upon invitation have always been a common practice in international relations. It is generally uncontested that a state can consent to the

[1] A minority view maintains that foreign countries have a duty to abstain from interfering in internal conflicts (abstentionism approach). However, Part II has demonstrated that this view is not confirmed in state practice.

use of force by a foreign country within its borders. Furthermore, in order to be valid the invitation needs to come from an organ capable of speaking on behalf of the state, normally the government. However, as discussed in Part II, identifying who has the authority to invite foreign forces during an internal conflict could be a difficult task. Since the adoption of the UN Charter, scholars have suggested three approaches to determine when, if ever, interventions upon invitation are lawful. First, proponents of the abstentionism approach have claimed that interventions in civil wars are unlawful, inasmuch as they are contrary to the principle of non-intervention and the right to self-determination of peoples. Yet, as demonstrated above, this suggestion does not reflect current state practice. Second, according to the effectiveness doctrine a government has consent power only if it exercises effective control over the territory and population. Worried that this approach would ultimately endorse a 'might makes right' narrative, a number of authors propounded a third approach: that democratic governments are legitimate and should thus be preferred over effective ones. This contraposition between effectiveness and legitimacy is grounded in arguments with deep historical roots: over the centuries, the criteria to recognise governments have constantly shifted from legitimacy to effectiveness and back.

In the Middle Ages, sovereign authority was legitimised by God's investiture. In the thirteenth century, a number of Italian and French jurists started challenging the temporal role of the Church and propounded the idea that the king represents the supreme authority in his own kingdom. These discussions led to the emergence of the idea of the absolute sovereign: Christendom, once a single polity, started being fragmented into sovereign entities. Yet this did not mark the end of legitimacy: although *legibus soluto* within his reign, the legitimacy of the king still derived from divine and dynastic rights. This approach is clearly described by Cranston: '[t]he King … is King by Divine Right and ancient prescription, and nothing any living person does or says can alter that reality. The King is not King because he does anything, or because he is thought to be something, but because he is something'.[2] In the sixteenth century, some authors started regarding legitimacy with scepticism and diffidence. Accordingly, effectiveness emerged as a viable alternative to legitimacy. Prominent authors such as Grotius, Pufendorf, and Vattel supported the effectiveness doctrine: in a time when legitimacy derived from God, preferences for de facto control over a territory and population represented a clear stand against any forms of divine and dynastic legitimacy.

The American and French revolutions changed the terms of the debate: governments derived their power from the will of the people; popular sovereignty was hence established as a criterion to identify the legitimate authority. Accordingly, their representatives were responsible for guaranteeing the rights

[2] M Cranston, 'From Legitimism to Legitimacy' in A Moulakis (ed), *Legitimacy/Légitimité: Proceedings of the Conference Held in Florence, June 3-4, 1982* (Walter de Gruyter, 1986) 39.

of man and citizens. Worried about the shift from the sovereignty of the sovereign to popular sovereignty, conservative European monarchies initiated the Holy Alliance (1815–48), a coalition which sponsored the principle of armed intervention in order to re-establish monarchies overthrown by the rebels.[3] However, when the Congress of Vienna (1815) ended the Napoleonic era and determined the beginning of a new international order, the Holy Alliance and its interventionism approach lost relevance.

The early twentieth century witnessed, once again, a shift from legitimacy to effectiveness. Arbitral decisions such as the *Dreyfus* (1901) and the *Tinoco Concessions* (1923) cases propounded the idea that an effective government ought to be considered as the authority representing the state, regardless of the means used to gain power. In the same vein, all through the twentieth century prominent scholars, such as Kelsen, Lauterpacht, and Wippman, supported the effectiveness doctrine. In summary, since the adoption of the UN Charter effectiveness has been the default criterion to identify the government: authority derives from effective control over the territory and population, facts that are generally easily ascertained and that do not entail qualitative considerations. Nevertheless, as much as in the past divine and monastic legitimacy generated a quest for effectiveness, the de facto test triggered a shift towards democratic legitimacy.

As these results show, the recognition of governments has always shifted between legitimacy and effectiveness and this has significantly affected interventions upon invitation. Indeed, if consent to a foreign military intervention should come from an organ capable of speaking and acting for the state, the question of the criteria to identify the government is decisive. While the effectiveness doctrine reflected the majoritarian position during the last century, since the 1990s some scholars have noted a pro-democratic shift in the international legal framework. Notably, they claimed that democratic governments are legitimate and should thus be capable of inviting foreign forces, even when they do not exercise effective control over the territory and population. Where do we stand now? From the analysis conducted in the second part of this research, the following conclusions emerge:

- Legitimacy of origin. Democratic governments – ie endorsed by free and fair elections – are recognised even if they do not exercise effective control over the territory and population, and even when an effective but undemocratic

[3] D Zacharias, 'Holy Alliance (1815)' in *Max Planck Encyclopedia of Public International Law* (Oxford University Press, 2007) §1; G Ferrero, *Problems of Peace: From the Holy Alliance to the League of Nations* (The Knickerbocker Press, 1919) 6–28; BR Roth, *Governmental Illegitimacy in International Law* (Clarendon Press, 1999) 142–43; D Rodogno, *Against Massacre: Humanitarian Interventions in the Ottoman Empire, 1815–1914* (Princeton University Press, 2012) 20. See also AG Stapleton, *Intervention and Non-intervention; or, The Foreign Policy of Great Britain from 1790 to 1865* (J Murray, 1866) 28: 'they [the members of the Holy Alliance] acted as a sort of European police, first, as far as possible to prevent any popular outbreak but if that failed, then to join in suppressing it in every country where it might happen to triumph'.

alternative is available. This conclusion is valid in cases when the democratic government has exercised power for some time before being overthrown (eg Sierra Leone, 1997; Haiti, 1990-94; Honduras, 2009) as well as when the government has never been in power (eg Côte d'Ivoire, 2010, and The Gambia, 2017). Therefore, state practice suggests that free and fair elections constitute a legitimate source of power that provides legitimacy to newly elected, but beleaguered, governments. Accordingly, democratic but ineffective governments are deemed to have the capacity to consent to foreign interventions in their favour.

- Effectiveness. The preference for democratic governments is not absolute: undemocratic governments – ie governments that have reached power through coups d'état, through elections which were not free and fair, or whose leaders refused to step down after losing elections – are recognised as de jure governments if there is no democratic alternative. Therefore, in such circumstances they can invite foreign countries to quell an insurrection.
- Legitimacy of exercise. Regardless of the way in which they obtained power, governments that commit gross and systematic violations of human rights and humanitarian law against their own populations may lose legitimacy. On the other hand, certain opposition groups fighting against them could be defined as legitimate representatives of their people (eg, Libya and Syria, 2011). Therefore, the way in which power is exercised can have a disqualifying function. Nevertheless, this does not necessarily entail a loss of consent power. Although over the last two decades there has been a growing hesitation by states to intervene in favour of governments that commit heinous crimes against their own populations, in positive international law illegitimate governments did not lose the capacity to ask for foreign interventions. In any case, intervening states could incur responsibility for complicity in the commission of violations of human rights and humanitarian law or could violate the obligation to ensure respect for IHL.

This analysis highlights that legitimacy is resurfacing and that human rights have emerged as a parameter of legitimacy. Specifically, the preference for democratic governments has been framed in terms of rights: on the one hand, it has been grounded in the emerging right to democratic governance; on the other hand, it is deemed to reflect and protect the right to internal self-determination of people. Furthermore, heinous violations of human rights and International Humanitarian Law (IHL) could lead to disqualifying a government once considered legitimate.

B. Legitimacy of Rebels and Human Rights

None would deny that interventions in favour of opposition groups are unlawful in positive international law. However, the recognition of opposition groups as legitimate representatives of the people shows that there are instances when states would be willing to interact with rebels and possibly assist them. Perhaps this practice will turn out to be a limited one and will not be replicated beyond the Libyan and Syrian conflicts. Nevertheless, this does not necessarily imply that it cannot have a more general relevance. Indeed, over the past decades there have been cases when states have recognised rebels as legitimate and this recognition has led to discussions on the admissibility of foreign interventions in their favour.

International law has never completely ignored opposition groups: in different historical periods, it has addressed their legitimacy. However, it has done so in a limited fashion, regulating specific situations, instead of adopting a more coherent and comprehensive approach. The reason might be found in the traditional narrative pertaining to rebels: since they oppose the government, they appear inherently illegitimate. This is understandable: arguably, international law is first and foremost a validation of sovereignty. States are the primary actors of the international legal order: although there has been a shift from sovereign rights to human rights, and although individuals are playing a more relevant role at the international level, states largely remain the protagonists in the international arena. It would thus be a critical inconsistency if international law protected both sovereignty and the right to rebel against it. However, legitimising opposition groups at the international level might appear less paradoxical than it seems at first sight. This work has highlighted that sovereignty has never been absolute. Specifically, over the centuries some scholars have propounded that the way in which the ruler exercises his power could weaken the rights attached to sovereignty, such as protection from foreign interventions. At times, these considerations led to granting legitimacy to opposition groups.

Since the Middle Ages, some scholars have supported the legitimacy of resistance to oppression. For instance, Francisco Suárez wrote about the right to rebel against a tyrant and claimed that people could depose the sovereign if he was excommunicated by the Pope. For Pufendorf, the right to rebel against a repressive sovereign would derive from the right to self-defence. In the same vein, Vattel supported the idea that a people could embrace arms against an oppressive power. This point is particularly significant: Pufendorf and Vattel supported the effectiveness doctrine against divine and monarchic legitimacy. Furthermore, Vattel famously articulated the principle of non-intervention as a corollary of state sovereignty. However, they did not see this contrasting with the recognition of a right to embrace arms against a tyrant.

During the nineteenth century, the idea that rebels could legitimately use force against an oppressive regime faded away. Inasmuch as governmental legitimacy was supplanted by the effectiveness doctrine, discourses on the legitimacy of opposition groups fell out of fashion. Nevertheless, this does not mean that the international legal framework did not allow any forms of interaction with rebels: under certain circumstances, states could resort to recognition of belligerency or insurgency. Following the recognition of belligerency, all the parties to the conflict were granted belligerents' rights. Furthermore, this practice triggered the law of neutrality: the state recognising the opposition group could not provide support to any of the parties to the conflict. The recognition of belligerency and insurgency did not derive from considerations on the legitimacy of opposition groups: the reasons why they were fighting were irrelevant and the assessment was based on mere factual criteria, such as the intensity of the conflict and territorial control.

The adoption of the UN Charter reinforced the prohibition to intervene in favour of opposition groups. In positive international law, providing military or non-lethal assistance to rebels amounts to a violation of the principle of non-intervention in the internal affairs of the state and, in case of forcible help, of the ban on the use of force. At the same time, the acknowledgement of the right to self-determination in positive international law (Article 1 of the ICCPR and ICESCR) provided further support to the prohibition to interfere in internal conflicts: every people enjoys a right to decide its form of government free from external interference. Against this backdrop, part of the scholarship embraced the abstentionism approach and supported the idea that foreign countries should remain neutral and should avoid intervening in internal conflicts in any way. Nevertheless, this idea is contradicted by the practice that emerged during the decolonisation period, when national liberation movements were recognised as legitimate representatives of their own peoples. More recently, a number of Libyan and Syrian opposition groups were recognised as legitimate representatives, while their respective governments were deemed illegitimate.

Similar to the recognition of governments, the criteria to determine the legitimacy of rebels and their right to receive external support have shifted from a human rights-based legitimacy to effectiveness and back. Specifically, this study suggests that the legitimacy of rebels has been framed in terms of rights and this has affected the rules governing the use of force by, against, and in favour of the opposition groups. Specifically, since the adoption of the UN Charter there have been two situations when rebels have been recognised as legitimate:

i. National Liberation Movements

- Legitimacy of origin. During the decolonisation period, national liberation movements were recognised as legitimate representatives of their own people. This qualification was framed in terms of rights and derived from the fact that they were exercising their right to self-determination against colonial domination, alien occupation, or racist regimes.
- Use of force by NLMs. While UNGA resolutions acknowledge that NLMs have a right to struggle, the international community has never reached an agreement as to whether this could be military in nature. Even if liberation movements did not have a right to use force, forcible struggle was not prohibited either. Accordingly, they had a *legal entitlement* to use force against the oppressive power.

- Use of force against NLMs. Since colonial domination, alien occupation, and racist regimes are considered heinous situations, there was a general agreement on the prohibition to repress the struggle of national liberation movements, as well as to provide assistance to the oppressive power.
- Intervention in favour of NLMs. The issue of foreign assistance is controversial: although it is generally uncontested that third states could provide non-lethal help to NLMs, military interventions in their favour remained unlawful.

ii. Opposition Groups Fighting against Illegitimate Governments

- Legitimacy of origin. Recently, Libyan and Syrian rebels were recognised as a legitimate representative of peoples in their fight against their respective governments. Again, the recognition was grounded on the reasons why they were fighting – rebellion against an illegitimate government – and framed in terms of human rights – the government forfeits its legitimacy due to the commission of gross and systematic violations of human rights and humanitarian law against its own population.
- Use of force against legitimate rebels. Outside the decolonisation context, there is a general presumption that the government can forcibly react against opposition groups. However, the situation changes when the government uses excessive force against the population, thus triggering an internal conflict: human rights and law enforcement standards point to the conclusion that states are prohibited from starting a NIAC. Nevertheless, this does not prevent third states from intervening in favour of illegitimate governments, unless the help triggers a responsibility for complicity in the commission of violations of human rights and humanitarian law or amounts to a violation of the obligation to ensure respect for IHL.
- Use of force by legitimate rebels. The recognition of legitimacy of the Libyan and Syrian rebels did not lead to discussions on their right to use force against the government. Therefore, the general rule applies: their rebellion is neither prohibited nor allowed in positive international law.
- Intervention in favour of legitimate rebels. States that recognised the Libyan and Syrian rebels as legitimate representatives discussed the possibility of intervening in their favour. While in Libya the intervention effectively turned into open assistance to the rebels, in Syria a number of states provided weapons and other non-lethal assistance to certain opposition groups. However, this is not sufficient to claim that interventions in favour of legitimate rebels are lawful.

In summary, human rights have emerged as the parameter to assess the legitimacy of rebels. While during the 1960s and 1970s the right to self-determination provided the basis of the legitimacy of national liberation movements, since the

1990s the focus has been on gross and systematic violations of human rights and humanitarian law. When a government commits such heinous crimes against its own population, it forfeits its legitimacy, while certain opposition groups fighting against it are recognised as legitimate representative of peoples.

II. THE DANGERS OF LEGITIMACY

A. Legitimacy, Democracy, and the Dangers to the Right to Self-determination

In 1980 Walzer proposed an intellectual experiment. He suggested imagining that in Algeria a group of revolutionaries comes to power in order to create a democratic and secular state, which turns into 'a military dictatorship and a religious "republic", without civil and political liberties, and brutally repressive'.[4] Walzer then imagined that Sweden possesses a 'wondrous chemical which, if introduced into the water supply of Algeria, would turn all Algerians, elites and masses, into Swedish-style social democrats'.[5] They would forget their former views and would be able to create a new democratic regime. Should Sweden use the chemical? This intellectual exercise highlights the dangers and limits of the emergence of a democratic legitimacy. In particular, it raises crucial questions with regard to the relationship between democracy and self-determination.

Popular sovereignty gained momentum during the American and French revolutions and is now a well-established principle. Its internal dimension essentially establishes that 'the will of the people shall be the basis of the authority of government' (Article 21(3) of the Universal Declaration of Human Rights). The right to internal self-determination is an expression of popular sovereignty, inasmuch as it posits that peoples enjoy a right to determine their political status (Article 1 of the ICCPR and ICESCR). However, the question has been and still is how to implement such a right? Part of the scholarship has suggested that internal self-determination should be interpreted as embodying a right to democracy. While this work has demonstrated that such a right does not exist in positive international law, it did point to the conclusion that democratic governments, ie governments endorsed by free and fair elections, are deemed legitimate and preferred over effective but undemocratic authorities. Is this conclusion a welcome development of the current legal framework?

The above chapters have shown that international law does not impose democracy as a form of government. It suffices to think of several undemocratic regimes that hold seats within international organisations to conclude that 'the

[4] M Walzer, 'The Moral Standing of States: A Response to Four Critics' (1980) 9(3) *Philosophy & Public Affairs* 226.

[5] ibid.

choice of a political, economic, social and cultural system, and the formulation of foreign policy',[6] should be decided freely by the people without external interference or imposition. The absence of a rule that imposes democracy should not be lamented. Indeed, claiming otherwise would deprive people of the right to find their own path. Nevertheless, while positive international law does not mandate the choice of a particular governing system, it does prescribe that the right to self-determination should be exercised in a free and fair way. As a matter of fact, the right to free and fair elections is a pivotal part of the right to political participation, as acknowledged in Article 25 of the ICCPR. Nevertheless, upon a closer look we might wonder whether free and fair elections guarantee the expression of popular will and ensure democratic outcomes. Indeed, electoral democracy could yield to the 'tyranny of the majority', namely the ability of the majority 'to abuse its authority without compromise'.[7] This would be particularly problematic when the majority uses its power against the minority. Furthermore, voters' decision-making is complex and could raise doubts as to whether the electoral process can ensure the protection of the right to self-determination, or whether it could lead to arbitrary and undemocratic results.

Some may argue that, notwithstanding its imperfections and flaws, democracy probably constitutes the system of government that best respects the right to self-determination and popular will. This position was famously propounded by Churchill in 1947, when he affirmed that:

> Many forms of Government have been tried, and will be tried in this world of sin and woe. No one pretends that democracy is perfect or all-wise. Indeed it has been said that democracy is the worst form of Government except for all those other forms that have been tried from time to time.[8]

Yet, the point of self-determination is exactly to allow peoples to freely decide whether they agree with Churchill or not. In other words, popular sovereignty ultimately amounts to the right to be ruled by a representative government, but not necessarily a democratic one. Undoubtedly, representativeness could be assessed through free and fair elections. However, we could wonder whether the lack of electoral mandate would automatically imply that the government is not representative. Does the acquiescence of the population mean that the government represents their will? We can think of several reasons why a people might prefer to be subjected to a dictatorship instead of embracing arms to change the political system: none would start a civil war lightly, and the status quo might seem preferable to the disruptive potential of an armed conflict. If a

[6] ICJ, *Military and Paramilitary Activities in and against Nicaragua, (Nicaragua v United States of America)*, Judgment (Merits), 27 June 1986, §205.

[7] R Miller, 'Self-Determination in International Law and the Demise of Democracy?' (2003) 41(3) *Columbia Journal of Transnational Law* 634.

[8] Speech of 11 November 1947 in the House of Commons. See W Churchill, *His Complete Speeches 1897-1963* (Chelsea House Publishers, 1974) 7566.

people makes peace with an unwanted regime, the latter may well be considered representative of the popular will. This would not mean that the situation is ideal, but only that, in a specific moment in time, a people decides to accept an undemocratic regime.

This conclusion raises a further dilemma with regard to the practice of recognising opposition groups as legitimate representatives of a people. Although decolonisation struggles are an expression of the right to *external* self-determination, and possibly the most uncontested one, it is questionable whether the emancipation of colonies from the oppressive powers respected also the right to *internal* self-determination, ie the right of a people to freely choose its own political system. Indeed, the criteria used to identify the national liberation movements representative of the people were highly subjective and did not guarantee that the NLMs reflected the preference of the people. Similar doubts rise with regard to the practice that emerged in Libya and Syria: do the NTC and SOC really reflect the popular will? As a matter of fact, it appears that the military capability and probability of success of a specific opposition group is used as a parameter to verify its claim to represent the people, without an endeavour to assess the actual will of the population.

Assessing the real will of the people is extremely difficult and we may wonder whether it is feasible, or whether this assessment will always be flawed. While the transition from state sovereignty to popular sovereignty is commendable, it risks overlooking that the idea of a people is an abstraction, as much as is the idea of a state. Therefore, the question of how to respect the will of the people concretely remains an open one. In the absence of universally accepted criteria to solve this dilemma, answering this question ultimately requires making a choice based on the values and objectives that we believe international law should encourage and promote.

B. The Dangers to Human Rights and Humanitarian Law

A key finding of this study is that human rights have emerged as a parameter of legitimacy. On the one hand, governments that commit gross and systematic violations of human rights may lose their legitimacy; on the other hand, certain opposition groups fighting against such violations or struggling in the exercise of their right to self-determination have been recognised as legitimate representatives of their people. At first sight, linking legitimacy and human rights might seem a positive development: the enjoyment of human rights is one of the founding values of the UN system, and arguably of the international community. However, a closer look reveals the dangers of this approach.

Part III has shown that the legitimacy of opposition groups is assessed on the basis of the reasons why they are fighting and that this assessment is tied to human rights considerations. Nevertheless, the legitimacy of rebels was not necessarily conditional upon the protection of human rights. While liberation movements were considered legitimate because they were fighting for their right to self-determination, it is at least doubtful whether they reflected the actual will of the people they were deemed to represent.[9] Similarly, the Libyan and Syrian rebels were recognised as legitimate representatives of their people because they were fighting against governments that committed gross and systematic violations of human rights and humanitarian law. However, the Commissions of Inquiry on Libya and Syria demonstrated extensively that opposition groups engaged in the commission of similar violations.[10] Therefore, we face a paradoxical situation, whereby the legitimacy of rebels is based on the circumstance that they are fighting against the violation of fundamental human rights. However, this assessment is not affected by the fact that they violate the very same human rights that ground their legitimacy.[11]

[9] As explained above, the OAU was overwhelmingly recognised as the organ in charge of identifying the legitimate representative of people in Africa. However, the procedure and the criteria used by the Organization were not clear-cut. The OAU Liberation Committee was responsible for recognising NLMs. In order to make the assessment, the Liberation Committee would seek information through a mission in the region. Nevertheless, these investigations were often conducted in neighbouring countries, thus raising doubts as to the quality of the collected data. As for the criteria used to assess the representativeness of the NLM, they were not clearly defined and ultimately led to subjective evaluations. Furthermore, the practice of recognising only one liberation movement ignored the political complexity of some situations. In order to remedy this criticism, the OAU recognised more than one NLM in certain circumstances, such as in Angola. However, the recognition of more than one liberation movement ultimately fuelled the conflict in the interested country.

[10] The International Commission of Inquiry on Libya found that opposition groups 'committed serious violations, including war crimes and breaches of international human rights law' ('Report of the International Commission of Inquiry on Libya', Human Rights Council, A/HRC/19/68, 8 March 2012, §1). Similarly, the Independent International Commission of Inquiry on Syria has concluded that armed groups have engaged in violations of human rights, such as summary executions, arbitrary arrests, torture, and enforced disappearances ('Human rights abuses and international humanitarian law violations in the Syrian Arab Republic, 21 July 2016-28 February 2017', Human Rights Council, A/HRC/34/CRP.3, 10 March 2017).

[11] The legal scholarship is presently divided as to whether armed groups are bearers of human rights obligations in positive international law. The traditional approach to international law is that only states can breach IHRL, whereas non-state armed groups can simply commit criminal acts under domestic law. This approach stands on the assumption that 'anywhere on this globe there exists a governmental organization which controls the relevant territory' (C Tomuschat, 'The Applicability of Human Rights Law to Insurgent Movements' in H Fischer, U Froissart, W Heintschel von Heinegg and C Raap (eds), *Krisensicherung und humanitärer Schutz: Festschrift fur Dieter Fleck* (Berliner Wissenschafts-Verlag, 2004) 574). Therefore, it seems that there is no need to make other entities accountable under IHRL, as states have the responsibility to respect, protect and fulfill human rights of individuals under their jurisdiction. However, there are several instances in which governmental authority is lacking; one of them is when non-state armed groups exercise governmental functions. When rebels control part of the territory and population, the reality of the human rights equation is satisfied: individuals are at the mercy of a power over whose actions the state government is impotent. As a result, non-state armed groups could be considered as de facto governments and thus bound by human rights obligations. The UN practice has increasingly accepted that armed non-state actors are bearers of human rights obligations when they control part of the territory. For instance, the Commission of Inquiry on Libya affirmed that: 'it is increasingly accepted that, where non-state groups exercise de facto control over territory, they must respect fundamental human rights of persons in that territory' ('Report of the International Commission of Inquiry to investigate all alleged violations of international human rights law in the Libyan Arab Jamahiriya', UN Human Rights Council, A/HRC/17/44, 1 June 2011, §72). Similarly, the

This conundrum raises crucial dilemmas not only with regard to the legitimacy of power, but also with reference to the relativity inherent in any form of legitimacy. As long as there will be no general agreement within the international community as to the criteria of legitimacy of governments and rebels, this relativity appears inevitable. Furthermore, the picture is complicated by the essentially political nature of interventions in internal conflicts. Ultimately, the risk is that states would proceed to legitimise or de-legitimise governments and rebels with the specific aim of intervening in their favour or in order to justify the adoption of measures against them.

III. A FINAL WORD

This analysis confirms, as it has been suggested throughout this work, that the human rights paradigm has affected the legal framework regulating foreign armed interventions in internal conflicts. Specifically, we are witnessing a shift from effectiveness to legitimacy, whereby human rights have emerged as a parameter of the latter. Accordingly, democratically elected governments tend to be preferred to undemocratic, but effective, regimes (legitimacy of origin); governments that commit heinous crimes against their own population tend to lose their legitimacy (legitimacy of exercise); while opposition groups that fight against them – or in the exercise of their right to self-determination during the decolonisation period – are deemed legitimate representatives of their people (legitimacy of cause).

In his seminal book *From Apology to Utopia*, Martti Koskenniemi suggests that the fundamental structure of the international legal argument constantly swings between two extremes. On the one hand, scholars tend to adhere as much as possible to international law as it exists in state practice; this approach could be read as apologetic, inasmuch as it bears the risk of describing what states do, as opposed to what states should do. On the other hand, authors focus on behaviours that states ought to adopt; however, their analysis risks suggesting principles that do not reflect international law, thus resulting in a utopian approach to the legal framework. The shift from legitimacy to effectiveness and back, which has characterised discourses on recognition and interventions for

Commission of Inquiry on Syria maintained that: 'Non-state actors … must respect the fundamental human rights of persons forming customary international law (CIL), in areas where such actors exercise de facto control' ('Report of the Independent International Commission of Inquiry on the Syrian Arab Republic', A/HRC/21/50, 16 August 2012, §10). See eg A Clapham, *Human Rights Obligations of Non-State Actors* (Oxford University Press, 2006) 271–316; A Bellal and S Casey-Maslen, 'Enhancing Compliance with International Law by Armed Non-State Actors' (2011) 3(1) *Goettingen Journal of International Law* 176–98. See, *contra*, L Zegveld, *Accountability of Armed Opposition Groups in International Law* (Cambridge University Press, 2002) 40, 148; N Rodley, 'Can Armed Opposition Groups Violate Human Rights?' in KH Mahoney and P Mahoney (eds), *Human Rights in the Twenty-First Century: A Global Challenge* (Martinus Nijhoff, 1993) 313.

centuries, reflects the swing from apology to utopia. Inasmuch as it endorses a 'might makes right' narrative, the effectiveness doctrine would embody an apologetic approach. Conversely, doctrines of legitimacy could be criticised as utopian, insofar as they suggest criteria that are not generally accepted by states (such as democracy) and instead reflect moral choices that are essentially subjective.

The present study has sought to clarify recent developments in the legal framework regulating foreign interventions in armed conflicts. Specifically, it has highlighted that criteria of effectiveness are gradually falling out of fashion, in favour of a human rights-based legitimacy. While drawing attention to the dangers of this trend, this work has demonstrated that historically *jus ad bellum* has been characterised by the contraposition and constant swing between effectiveness and legitimacy. There is reason to believe that similar developments will happen in the years to come.

Bibliography

Abass, A, 'Consent Precluding State Responsibility: A Critical Analysis' (2004) 53(1) *International & Comparative Law Quarterly* 21–1225.

Abe, K, 'Human Rights-ization of International Law: a Critical Analysis of the "Ethical Turn"' (2013) 111(4) *Journal of International Law and Diplomacy* 1–28.

Abi-Saab, G, 'Wars of National Liberation and the Laws of War' (1972) 3(3) *Annales d'études internationales* 93–117.

—— 'Wars of National Liberation in the Geneva Conventions and Protocols' (1979) 165(IV) *Collected Courses of the Hague Academy of International Law* 53–448.

Abiew, FK, *The Evolution of the Doctrine and Practice of Humanitarian Intervention* (Kluwer Law International, 1999).

Abrisketa, J, 'The Right to Humanitarian Aid: Basis and Limitations' in *Reflections on Humanitarian Action: Principles, Ethics and Contradictions* (Pluto Press, 2015) 55–77.

Aceves, WJ, 'Relative Normativity: Challenging the Sovereignty Norm Through Human Rights Litigation' (2001) 25(3) *Hastings International and Comparative Law Review* 261–68.

Acquaviva, G, 'Subjects of International Law: A Power-Based Analysis' (2005) 38(2) *Vanderbilt Journal of Transnational Law* 345–96.

Aguilera-Barchet, B, *A History of Western Public Law Between Nation and State* (Springer, 2015).

Akande, D, 'International Law and the Classification of Conflicts' in E Wilmshurst (ed), *International Law and the Classification of Conflicts* (Oxford University Press, 2012) 32–79.

Akehurst, M, *A Modern Introduction to International Law* (Routledge, 1992).

Aldrich, G, 'The Laws of War on Land' (2000) 94(1) *American Journal of International Law* 42–63.

Alfadhel, KA, 'Toward an Instrumental Right to Democracy' (2018) 112 *AJIL Unbound* 84–88.

Alston, P and Goodman, R, *International Human Rights: The Successor to International Human Rights in Context: Law, Politics and Morals: Text and Materials* (Oxford University Press, 2013).

Amer, R, *The United Nations and Foreign Military Interventions: A Comparative Study of the Application of the Charter* (Avdelningen för freds- och konfliktforskning, 1992).

Anderson, K, 'Legality of Intervention in Syria in Response to Chemical Weapon Attacks' (2013) 17(21) *ASIL insights*.

Anghie, A, *Imperialism, Sovereignty and the Making of International Law* (Cambridge University Press, 2004).

Annan, K and Mousavizadeh, A, *Interventions: A Life in War and Peace* (Penguin Press, 2013).

Aquinas, T, *Summa Theologiae* (Blackfriars, 1972).

Araujo, R, 'Sovereignty, Human Rights, and Self-Determination: The Meaning of International Law' (2000) 24(5) *Fordham International Law Journal* 1477–32.

Arend, AC, *Legal Rules and International Society* (Oxford University Press, 1999).

Arend, AC and Beck, RJ, *International Law and the Use of Force: Beyond the UN Charter Paradigm* (Routledge, 1993).

Arraf, S, 'Libya: Conflict and Instability Continue' in A Bellal (ed), *The War Report: Armed Conflict in 2017* (Geneva Academy of International Humanitarian Law and Human Rights, 2018) 71–91.

Askew, WC, 'Italian Intervention in Spain: The Agreement of March 31 1934 with the Spanish Monarchist Parties' (1952) 24(2) *The Journal of Modern History* 181–83.

Augustine, *De Civitate Dei Contra Paganos* (Loeb Classical, 1960).

Aust, HP, *Complicity and the Law of State Responsibility* (Cambridge University Press, 2011).

Badescu, CG, 'The Responsibility to Protect: Embracing Sovereignty and Human Rights' in N Shawki and M Cox (eds), *Negotiating Sovereignty and Human Rights: Actors and Issues in Contemporary Human Rights Politics* (Ashgate, 2009) 81–98.

Badr, GM, 'The Exculpatory Effect of Self-Defense in State Responsibility' (1980) 10(1) *Georgia Journal of International and Comparative Law* 1–28.

Ballis, W, *The Legal Position of War: Changes in its Practice and Theory from Plato to Vattel* (Springer, 1937).

Bannelier, K and Christakis, T, 'Under the Security Council's Watchful Eyes: Military Intervention by Invitation in the Malian Conflict' (2013) 26(4) *Leiden Journal of International Law* 855–74.

—— 'Military Interventions Against ISIL in Iraq, Syria and Libya, and the Legal Basis of Consent' (2016) 29 *Leiden Journal of International Law* 743–75.

Barber, R, 'Facilitating Humanitarian Assistance in International Humanitarian and Human Rights Law' (2009) 91(874) *International Review of the Red Cross* 371–97.

Bartelson, J, 'Double Binds: Sovereignty and the Just War Tradition' in H Kalmo and Q Skinner (eds), *Sovereignty in Fragments: The Past, Present and Future of a Contested Concept* (Cambridge University Press, 2010) 81–95.

Bassett, TF and Straus, S, 'Defending Democracy in Cote d'Ivoire: Africa Takes a Stand' (2011) 90 *Foreign Affairs* 130–40.

Beale, JH, 'The Recognition of Cuban Belligerency' (1896) 9(6) *Harvard Law Review* 406–19.

Beaufort, D, *La guerre comme instrument de secours ou de punition* (Martinus Nijhoff, 1933).

Beaulac, S, 'The Westphalian Legal Orthodoxy – Myth or Reality?' (2000) 2 *Journal of the History of International Law* 148–77.

Becker Lorca, A, 'Rules for the "Global War on Terror": Implying Consent and Presuming Conditions for Intervention' (2012) 45(1) *New York University journal of international law and politics* 1–95.

Beigbeder, Y, *The Role and Status of International Humanitarian Volunteers and Organizations: The Right and Duty to Humanitarian Assistance* (Martinus Nijhoff, 1991).

—— *International Monitoring of Plebiscites, Referenda and National Elections: Self-Determination and Transition to Democracy* (Martinus Nijhoff, 1994).

—— 'Arms Transfers and International Human Rights Law' in S Casey-Maslen (ed), *Weapons Under International Human Rights Law* (Cambridge University Press, 2014) 448–47.

—— 'Armed Conflict in Libya in 2014' in A Bellal (ed), *The War Report: Armed Conflict in 2014* (Oxford University Press, 2015) 194–201.

—— 'Welcome on Board: Improving Respect for International Humanitarian Law through the Engagement of Armed Non-State Actors' (2016) 19 *Yearbook of International Humanitarian Law* 38–61.

—— *The War Report: Armed Conflicts in 2018* (Geneva Academy of International Humanitarian Law and Human Rights, 2019).

Bellal, A and Casey-Maslen, S, 'Enhancing Compliance with International Law by Armed Non-State Actors' (2011) 3(1) *Goettingen Journal of International Law* 176–98.

Bellal, A and Doswald-Beck, L, 'Evaluating the Use of Force During the Arab Spring' (2011) 14 *Yearbook of International Humanitarian Law* 3–35.

Bellamy, AJ, *Massacres and Morality: Mass Atrocities in an Age of Civilian Immunity* (Oxford University Press, 2012).

Bellamy, AJ and Williams, PD, 'The New Politics of Protection? Côte d'Ivoire, Libya and the Responsibility to Protect' (2011) 87(4) *International Affairs* 825–50.

Bennoune, K, 'Sovereignty vs. Suffering? Re-Examining Sovereignty and Human Rights through the Lens of Iraq' (2002) 13(1) *European Journal of International Law* 243–62.

—— 'Toward a Human Rights Approach to Armed Conflict: Iraq 2003' (2004) 11(171) *UC Davis Journal of International Law and Policy* 172–228.

Bernard, M, *A Historical Account of the Neutrality of Great Britain during the American Civil War* (Applewood Books, 1870).

Bernhardt, R, 'Customary International Law' in *Encyclopaedia of Public International Law* (North-Holland, 1992).

Besson, S, 'Sovereignty' in *Max Planck Encyclopedias of International Law* (Oxford University Press, 2011).

Bethlehem, D, 'Self-Defense against an Imminent or Actual Armed Attack by Nonstate Actors' (2012) 106(4) *American Journal of International Law* 770–77.

Bianchi, A, 'Human Rights and the Magic of *Jus Cogens*' (2008) 19(3) *European Journal of International Law* 491–508.

Bílková, V, 'The Use of Force by the Russian Federation in Crimea' (2015) 75(1) *Zeitschrift für ausländisches öffentliches Recht und Völkerrecht* 27–50.

Bluntschli, JC, *Le Droit International Codifié* (Guillaumin, 1870).

Bodansky, D, 'The Concept of Legitimacy in International Law' in R Wolfrum and V Röben (eds), *Legitimacy in International Law* (Springer, 2008) 309–18.

—— 'Legitimacy in international law and international relations' in JL Dunoff and M. A Pollack (eds), *Interdisciplinary Perspectives on International Law and International Relations: The State of the Art* (Cambridge University Press, 2010) 321–42.

Bodin, J, *Six Books of the Commonwealth* (Blackwell, 1955).

Boison de Chazournes, L, and Condorelli, L, 'Quelques remarques à propos de l'obligation des États de "respecter et faire respecter" le droit international humanitaire "en toutes circonstances"' in *Études et essais sur le droit international humanitaire et sur les principes de la Croix-Rouge en l'honneur de Jean Pictet* (International Committee of the Red Cross, 1984) 17–35.

—— 'De la "Responsabilité de Protéger", ou d'une Nouvelle Parure pour une Notion déjà Bien Établie Reference' (2006) 110(1) *Revue générale de droit international public* 11–18.

Boivin, A, 'Complicity and Beyond: International Law and the Transfer of Small Arms and Light Weapons' (2005) 87(859) *International Review of the Red Cross* 467–96.

Boniface, DS, 'Is There a Democratic Norm in the Americas? An Analysis of the Organization of American States' (2002) 8(3) *Global Governance* 365–81.

Boon, KE, 'Are Control Tests Fit for the Future? The Slippage Problem in Attribution Doctrines' (2014) 15(2) *Melbourne Journal of International Law* 2–48.

Borchard, E, 'War, Neutrality and Non-Belligerency' (1941) 35(4) *American Journal of International Law* 618–25.

Borgia, F, 'The Responsibility to Protect Doctrine: Between Criticisms and Inconsistencies' (2015) 2(2) *Journal on the Use of Force and International Law* 223–37.

Bothe, M, Partsch, KJ and Solf, W, *New Rules for Victims of Armed Conflicts – Commentary on the Two 1977 Protocols Additional to the Geneva Conventions of 1949* (Martinus Nijhoff, 1982).

Bouchet-Saulnier, F, 'Consent to Humanitarian Access: An Obligation Triggered by Territorial Control, not States' Rights' (2013) 96(893) *International Review of the Red Cross* 207–17.

Bowett, DW, 'Self-Determination and Political Rights in the Developing Countries' (1966) 60 *Proceedings of the American Society of International Law at Its Annual Meeting (1921–1969)* 129–35.

—— 'The Interrelation of Theories of Intervention and Self-Defense' in J Norton Moore (ed), *Law and Civil War in the Modern World* (Johns Hopkins University Press, 1974).

—— 'International Law and Economic Coercion' (1976) 16(2) *Vanderbilt Journal of International Law* 245–59.

Breau, S, *The Responsibility to Protect in International Law: An Emerging Paradigm Shift* (Routledge, 2016).

Brehm, M, 'The Arms Trade and States' Duty to Ensure Respect for Humanitarian and Human Rights Law' (2007) 12(3) *Journal of Conflict & Security Law* 359–87.

Brierly, JL, 'International Law and Resort to Armed Force' (1932) 4(3) *The Cambridge Law Journal* 308–19.

—— *The Outlook for International Law* (Clarendon Press, 1944).

Briggs, HW, *The Law of Nations. Cases, documents, and notes* (Appleton-Century-Crofts, 1952).

Brown, D, 'Use of Force against Terrorism after September 11th: State Responsibility, Self-Defense and Other Responses' (2003) 11(1) *Cardozo Journal of International and Comparative Law* 1–54.

Brown, PM, 'Editorial Comment: Undeclared Wars' (1939) 33(3) *American Journal of International Law* 538–41.

Brownlie, I, 'The Use of Force in Self-Defence' (1961) 37 *British Yearbook of International Law* 232–47.
—— *International Law and the Use of Force by the States* (Oxford University Press, 1991).
—— *Principles of Public International Law* (Clarendon Press, 1998).
—— '"International Law and the Use of Force by States" Revisited' (2002) 1(1) *Chinese Journal of International Law* 1–19.
Brunnée, J, 'Consent' *Max Planck Encyclopedia of Public International Law* (Oxford University Press, 2010).
Brunnée, J, and others, 'Slouching Towards New "Just" Wars: The Hegemon After September 11th' (2004) 18(4) *International Relations* 405–23.
Buchan, R, 'Cyber Attacks: Unlawful Uses of Force or Prohibited Interventions?' (2012) 17(2) *Journal of Conflict and Security Law* 212–27.
Buchanan, A, *Justice, Legitimacy, and Self-Determination: Moral Foundations for International Law* (Oxford University Press, 2004).
—— *Human Rights, Legitimacy, and the Use of Force* (Oxford University Press, 2010).
Bugnion, F, *The International Committee of the Red Cross and the Protection of War Victims* (Macmillan, 2003).
Burns, JH 'The Idea of Absolutism' in J Miller (ed), *Absolutism in Seventeenth-Century Europe* (Macmillan, 1990) 21–42.
Byers, MR and Chesterman, S, '"You, the People": Pro-democratic Intervention in International Law' in GH Fox and BR Roth (eds), *Democratic Governance and International Law* (Cambridge University Press, 2000) 259–92.
Byrne, M, 'Consent and the use of force: an examination of "intervention by invitation" as a basis for US drone strikes in Pakistan, Somalia and Yemen' (2016) 3(1) *Journal on the Use of Force and International Law* 97–125.
Camilleri, J, 'Sovereignty Discourse and Practice – Past and Future' in C Sampford and R Thakur (eds), *Re-envisioning Sovereignty: The End of Westphalia?* (Ashgate, 2008) 33–50.
Cannizzaro, E and Palchetti, P, 'Customary International Law on the Use of Force … At a Time of Perplexity' in *Customary International Law on the Use of Force: A Methodological Approach* (Martinus Nijhoff, 2005) 1–8.
Carron, D, 'Transnational armed conflicts: An argument for a single classification of non-international armed conflicts' (2016) 7(1) *Journal of International Humanitarian Legal Studies* 5–31.
Casey-Maslen, S, 'Armed Conflicts in 2012 and Their Impact' in *The War Report: Armed Conflict in 2012* (Oxford University Press, 2013) 3–19.
—— 'Armed conflict in Mali in 2012' in S Casey-Maslen (ed), *The War Report 2012* (Oxford University Press, 2013) 117–26.
—— 'Armed Conflict in Libya in 2014' in S Casey-Maslen (ed), *The War Report: Armed Conflict in 2014* (Oxford University Press, 2015) 194–201.
—— *Jus ad Bellum: The Law on Inter-State Use of Force* (Hart Publishing, 2020).
Casey-Maslen, S and Mattirolo, M, 'Use of Chemical Weapons in the Syrian Conflicts and under International Law' in S Casey-Maslen (ed), *The War Report: Armed Conflict in 2013* (Oxford University Press, 2014) 297–316.
Cassel, D, 'Honduras: Coup d'Etat in Constitutional Clothing?' (2009) 13(9) *The American Society of International Law Insight* 1–13.
Cassese, A, 'Le Droit International et la Question de l'Assistance aux Mouvements de Libération Nationale' (1986) 19 *Revue belge de droit international* 307–26.
—— *Self-Determination of Peoples: A Legal Reappraisal* (Cambridge University Press, 1995).
—— 'The International Court of Justice and the Right of Peoples to Self–Determination' in V Lowe and M Fitzmaurice (eds), *Fifty Years of the International Court of Justice: Essays in Honour of Sir Robert Jennings* (Cambridge University Press, 1996) 351–63.
—— 'The Nicaragua and Tadic Tests Revisited in Light of the ICJ Judgment on Genocide in Bosnia' (2007) 18(4) *European Journal of International Law* 649–68.

—— *Voci Contro la Barbarie: La Battaglia per i Diritti Umani Attraverso i Suoi Protagonisti* (Feltrinelli, 2008).

Cassin, R, 'Vichy or Free France?' (1941) 20 *Foreign Affairs* 102–12.

Castrén, E, *Civil War* (Suomalainen Tiedeakatemia, 1966).

Chadwick, E, 'National Liberation in the Context of Post- and Non-Colonial Struggles for Self-Determination' in *The Oxford Handbook of the Use of Force in International Law Edited* (Oxford University Press, 2015).

Chan, K, 'State Failure and the Changing Face of the Jus ad Bellum' (2013) 18(3) *Journal of Conflict and Security Law* 395–26.

Chan, LS, 'Humanitarian Assistance by International Organisations: A Question of Compulsory Access to Victims' (1991) 1991(2) *Singapore Journal of Legal Studies* 320–47.

Charlesworth, H, 'Democracy and International Law' (2014) 371 *Collected courses of The Hague Academy of International Law* 43–152.

Chesterman, S, *Just War or Just Peace? Humanitarian Intervention and International Law* (Oxford University Press, 2001).

Choquette, RB, 'A Rebuttable Presumption Against Consensual Nondemocratic Intervention' (2015) 55(1) *Columbia Journal of Transnational Law* 138–77.

Christakis, T, *Le Droit à l'Autodétermination en dehors des Situations de Décolonisation* (La Documentation Française, 1999).

—— 'Unilateralisme et Multilatéralisme dans la Lutte contre la Terreur: L'exemple du Terrorisme Biologique et Chimique' in K Bannelier et al (eds), *Le Droit International Face au Terrorisme: après le 11 Septembre 2001* (Pedone, 2003) 159–78.

Christakis, T and Bannelier, K, '*Volenti non Fit Injuria*? Les Effets du Consentement à l'Intervention Militaire' (2004) 50(1) *Annuaire français de droit international* 102–37.

Christenson, GA, 'Jus Cogens: Guarding Interests Fundamental to International Society' (1988) 28(3) *Virginia Journal of International Law* 585–648.

Churchill, W, *His Complete Speeches 1897–1963* (Chelsea House Publishers, 1974).

Cicero, *De Officiis* (Mondadori, 1984).

—— *De Re Publica* (Rizzoli, 2008).

Clapham, A, 'On Complicity' in M Henzelin and R Roth (eds), *Le Droit pénal à l'épreuve de l'internationalisation* (Bruylant, 2001) 241–75.

—— *Human Rights Obligations of Non-State Actors* (Oxford University Press, 2006).

—— 'Weapons and Armed Non-state Actors' in S Casey-Maslen (ed), *Weapons Under International Human Rights Law* (Cambridge University Press, 2014) 163–96.

—— 'The Concept of International Armed Conflict' in A Clapham, P Gaeta, and M Sassòli (eds), *The 1949 Geneva Conventions: A Commentary* (Oxford University Press, 2015) 3–26.

—— 'Article 6. Prohibitions' in S Casey-Maslen, A Clapham, G Giacca, and S Parker (eds), *The Arms Trade Treaty: A Commentary* (Oxford University Press, 2016) 177–243.

—— 'Article 7. Export and Export Assessment' in S Casey-Maslen, A Clapham, G Giacca and S Parker (eds), *The Arms Trade Treaty: A Commentary* (Oxford University Press, 2016) 244–85.

Clark, I, *International Legitimacy in World Society* (Oxford University Press, 2007).

Coleman, K, *A History of Chemical Warfare* (Palgrave MacMillan, 2005).

Combacau, J, 'The Exception of Self-Defense in United Nations Practice' in A Cassese (ed), *The Current Legal Regulation of the Use of Force* (Martinus Nijhoff, 1986) 9–38.

Condorelli, L, 'Les attentats du 11 septembre et leurs suites: Où va le droit international?' (2001) 105(4) *Revue générale de droit international public* 829–48.

Conlon, L, 'Sovereignty vs. Human Rights or Sovereignty and Human Rights?' (2004) 46(1) *Race & Class* 75–100.

Conte, A, 'The Responsibility to Protect, and Syria' in S Casey-Maslen (ed), *The War Report: Armed Conflict in 2013* (Oxford University Press, 2014) 428–53.

Corten, O, 'Breaches and Evolution of Customary International Law' in E Cannizzaro and P Palchetti (eds), *Customary International Law on the Use of Force: A Methodological Approach* (Martinus Nijhoff, 2005) 119–45.

—— 'The controversies over the customary prohibition on the use of force: A methodological debate' (2005) 16(5) *European Journal of International Law* 803–22.
—— 'Human Rights and Collective Security: Is There an Emerging Right of Humanitarian Intervention?' in P Alston and E MacDonald (eds), *Human Rights, Intervention, and the Use of Force* (Oxford University Press, 2008) 87–138.
—— *The Law against War: The Prohibition on the Use of Force in Contemporary International Law* (Hart Publishing, 2010).
—— 'The Russian Intervention in the Ukrainian Crisis: Was Jus Contra Bellum "Confirmed Rather Than Weakened"?' (2015) 2(1) *Journal on the Use of Force and International Law* 17–41.
—— *La Rébellion et le Droit International: le Principe de Neutralité en Tension* (Martinus Nijhoff, 2016).
—— 'Military Operations against "Islamic State" (ISIL or Dae'sh) – 2014' in T Ruys, O Corten and A Hofer (eds), *The Use of Force in International Law: A Case-based Approach* (Oxford University Press, 2018) 873–98.
Corten, O and Klein, P, 'L'assistance Humanitaire face à la Souveraineté des Etats' (1992) *Revue trimestrielle de droits de l'homme* 343–64.
—— 'The Limits of Complicity as a Ground for Responsibility: Lessons Learned from the Corfu Channel Case' in K Bannelier, T Christakis and S Heathcote (eds), *The ICJ and the Evolution of International Law: The Enduring Impact of the "Corfu Channel" Case* (Routledge, 2011) 315–34.
Corten, O and Koutroulis, V, 'The Illegality of Military Support to Rebels in the Libyan War: |Aspects of Jus contra Bellum and Jus in Bello' (2013) 18(1) *Journal of Conflict and Security Law* 59–93.
Corten, O and Verdebout, A, 'Les Interventions Militaires Récentes en Territoire Etranger: Vers une Remise en cause du *Jus contra Bellum*?' (2014) LX *Annuaire Français de Droit International* 135–69.
Cranston, M, 'From Legitimism to Legitimacy' in A Moulakis (ed), *Legitimacy/Légitimité: Proceedings of the Conference Held in Florence, June 3–4 1982* (Walter de Gruyter, 1986) 36–43.
Crawford, J, 'Democracy and International Law' (1994) 64(1) *British Yearbook of International Law* 113–33.
—— 'The Right of Self-Determination in International Law: Its Developments and Future' in P Alston (ed), *Peoples' Rights* (Oxford University Press, 2001).
—— *The International Law Commission's Articles on State Responsibility: Introduction, Text and Commentaries* (Cambridge University Press, 2002).
—— *Brownlie's Principles of Public International Law* (Oxford University Press, 2012).
—— *State Responsibility: The General Part* (Cambridge University Press, 2013).
Crawford, J, and Nicholson, R, 'The Continued Relevance of Established Rules and Institutions Relating to the Use of Force' in M Weller (ed), *The Oxford Handbook of the Use of Force in International Law* (Oxford University Press, 2015) 96–113.
Criddle, EJ, and Fox-Decent, E, *Fiduciaries of Humanity: How International Law Constitutes Authority* (Oxford University Press, 2016).
Cronogue, G, 'Responsibility to Protect: Syria the Law, Politics, and Future of Humanitarian Intervention Post-Libya' (2012) 124(3) *Journal of International Humanitarian Legal Studies* 124–59.
Croxton, D, 'Peace of Westphalia of 1648 and the Origins of Sovereignty' (1999) 21(3) *International History Review* 569–91.
Cubie, D, *The International Legal Protection of Persons in Humanitarian Crises: Exploring the Acquis Humanitaire* (Hart Publishing, 2017).
Cullen, A, 'The Parameters of Internal Armed Conflict in International Humanitarian Law' (2004) 1(1) *University of Miami International & Comparative Law Review* 189–230.
—— 'Key Developments Affecting the Scope of Internal Armed Conflict in International Humanitarian Law' (2005) 183 *Military Law Review* 66–109.
—— *The Concept of Non-International Armed Conflicts in international Humanitarian Law* (Cambridge University Press, 2010).

D'Amato, A, *International Law: Process and Prospect* (Transnational Publishers, 1987).
—— 'The Invasion of Panama Was a Lawful Response to Tyranny' (1990) 84(2) *The American Journal of International Law* 516–26.
d'Aspremont, J, *L'État Non Démocratique en Droit International: Etude Critique du Droit International Positif et de la Pratique Contemporaine* (Pedone, 2008).
—— 'Legitimacy of Governments in the Age of Democracy' (2006) 38(4) *New York University Journal of International Law and Politics* 877–917.
—— 'Mapping the Concepts Behind the Contemporary Liberalization of the Use of Force in International Law' (2010) 31(4) *University of Pennsylvania Journal of International Law* 1089–1149.
—— '"Effectivity" in International Law: Self-empowerment against Epistemological Claustrophobia' (2014) *ASIL Proceedings*.
—— 'Regimes' Legitimacy Crises in International Law: Libya, Syria, and their Competing Representatives' in R Grote and TJ Röder (eds), *Constitutionalism, Human Rights, and Islam after the Arab Spring* (Oxford University Press, 2016) 55–69.
d'Aspremont, J and De Brabandere, E, 'The Complementary Faces of Legitimacy in International Law: The Legitimacy of Origin and the Legitimacy of Exercise' (2011) 34(2) *Fordham International Law Journal* 190–235.
Dahlitz, J, *Secession and International Law: Conflict Avoidance – Regional Appraisals* (Asser Press, 2003).
Damrosch, LF, 'Gross and Systematic Human Rights Violations' in *Max Planck Encyclopedia of Public International Law* (Oxford University Press, 2011).
David, E, *Principes de droit des conflits armeés* (Bruylant, 1994).
de Hoogh, AJJ, 'Articles 4 and 8 of the 2001 ILC Articles on State Responsibility, the Tadic Case and Attribution of Acts of Bosnian Serb Authorities to the Federal Republic of Yugoslavia' (2002) 72 *The British Yearbook of International Law* 255–92.
—— 'Jus Cogens and the Use of Armed Force' in M Weller (ed), *The Oxford Handbook of the Use of Force in International Law* (Oxford University Press, 2015) 1162–86.
de Wet, E, *Military Assistance on Request and the Use of Force* (Oxford University Press, 2019).
de Zayas, A, 'Spanish Civil War (1936–39)' in *Max Planck Encyclopedia of Public International Law* (July) (Oxford University Press, 2013).
Deeks, A, 'Chemical Weapons in Syria: Enough to Justify the Use of Force?' (2013) (2) *Lawfare* 2–3.
Despagnet, F, *Cours de Droit international public* (Larose & Forcel, 1905).
Dette, I, *The Law of War* (Cambridge University Press, 2000).
Devillard, A, 'L'obligation de faire respecter le droit international humanitaire: l'article 1 commun aux Conventions de Genève et à leur Premier Protocole Additionnel, fondement d'un droit international humanitaire de cooperation?' (2007) 20(2) *Revue Québécoise de Droit International*, 75–130.
Dhokalia, RP, 'Civil Wars and International Law' (1971) 11 *Indian Journal of International Law* 219–50.
Dinstein, Y, 'The Right to Humanitarian Assistance' (2000) 53(4) *Naval War College Review* 77–91.
—— *War, Aggression and Self-Defence* (Cambridge University Press, 2011).
—— *Non-International Armed Conflicts in International Law* (Cambridge University Press, 2014).
Dobos, N, 'Rebellion, Humanitarian Intervention, and the Prudential Constraints on War' (2008) 7(2) *Journal of Military Ethics* 102–15.
—— *Insurrection and Intervention: The Two Faces of Sovereignty* (Cambridge University Press, 2012).
Domestici-Met, MJ, 'Protecting in Libya on Behalf of the International Community' (2011) 3(3) *Goettingen Journal of International Law* 861–89.
Donnelly, J, 'State Sovereignty and International Human Rights' (2014) 28(2) *Ethics & International Affairs* 225–38.

Dörmann, K and others, *Commentary on the First Geneva Convention: Convention (I) for the Amelioration of the Condition of the Wounded and Sick in Armed Forces in the Field* (Cambridge University Press, 2016).

Dörmann, K and Serralvo, J, 'Common Article 1 to the Geneva Conventions and the obligation to prevent international humanitarian law violations' (2014) 96(895–896) *International Review of the Red Cross* 707–36.

Dörr, O, 'Prohibition of the Use of Force' in *Max Planck Encyclopedia of Public International Law* (Oxford University Press, 2015).

Dörr, O and Randelzhofer, A, 'Purposes and Principles, Article 2(4)' in B Simma, D E. Khan, G Nolte, A Paulus and N Wessendorf (ed.), *The Charter of the United Nations: A Commentary* I (Oxford University Press, 2012) 200–34.

Doswald-Beck, L, 'The Legal Validity of Military Intervention by Invitation of the Government' (1986) 56(1) *British Yearbook of International Law* 189–252.

Doyle, MW, 'A Few Words on Mill, Walzer, and Nonintervention' (2010) 23(4) *Ethics & International Affairs* 349–69.

Dubuy, M, 'Le Droit de Résistance à l'Oppression en Droit International Public: Le Cas de la Résistance à un Régime Tyrannique' (2014) 32(1) *Civitas Europa* 139–63.

Dugard, CJR, 'The Organisation of African Unity and Colonialism: An Inquiry into the Plea of Self-Defence as a Justification for the Use of Force in the Eradication of Colonialism' (1967) 16(1) *The International and Comparative Law Quarterly* 157–90.

Eagleton, C, *International Government* (The Ronald Press Company, 1957).

Eichensehr, KE, 'Defending Nationals Abroad: Assessing the Lawfulness of Forcible Hostage Rescues' (2008) 48(2) *Virginia Journal of International Law* 451–84.

Eide, A 'Sovereign Equality Versus Global Military Structure: Two Competing Approaches to World Order' in A Cassese (ed), *New Humanitarian Law of Armed Conflict* (Editoriale Scientifica, 1979) 25–41.

Elshtain, JB, 'Just War and Humanitarian Intervention Conference: The Third Annual Grotius Lecture' (2001) 17(1) *American University Law Review* 1–25.

Evans, G, 'The Responsibility to Protect: Rethinking Humanitarian Intervention' in S Ask and A Mark-Jungkvist (eds), *The adventure of peace: Dag Hammarskjöld and the future of the UN* (Palgrave Macmillan, 2006) 298–311.

Ruiz Fabri, H, 'Human Rights and State Sovereignty: Have the Boundaries been significantly Redrawn?' in P Alston and E Macdonald (eds), *Human Rights, Intervention, and the Use of Force* (Oxford University Press, 2008) 33–86.

Falk, RA, 'Janus Tormented: The International Law of Internal War' in NJ Rosenau (ed), *International aspects of civil strife* (Princeton University Press, 1964) 185–248.

—— 'Introduction' in RA Falk and Q Wright (eds), *The International Law of Civil War* (Hopkins, 1971) 1–29.

—— *Revitalizing International Law* (Iowa State University Press, 1989).

Farer, TJ, 'Political and Economic Coercion in Contemporary International Law' (1985) 79(2) *European Journal of International Law* 405–13.

Farhang, C, 'The Notion of Consent in Part One of the Draft Articles on State Responsibility' (2014) 27(01) *Leiden Journal of International Law* 55–73.

Fassbender, B, *The United Nations Charter as the Constitution of the International Community* (Martinus Nijhoff, 2009).

Fauchille, P, *Traité de droit international public* (Rousseau & Cie, 1921).

Ferencz, BB, *Defining International Aggression, the Search for World Peace: A Documentary History and Analysis* (Oceana Publications, 1975).

Ferraro, T., 'The ICRC's Legal Position on the Notion of Armed Conflict Involving Foreign Intervention and on Determining the IHL Applicable to This Type of Conflict' (2015) 97(900) *International Review of the Red Cross* 1227–52.

Ferrero, G, *Problems of Peace: From the Holy Alliance to the League of Nations* (The Knickerbocker Press, 1919).
Fielding, LE, 'Taking the Next Step in the Development of New Human Rights: The Emerging Right of Humanitarian Assistance to Restore Democracy' (1995) 5(2) *Duke Journal of Comparative & International Law* 329–78.
Finnemore, M, *The Purpose of Intervention: Changing Beliefs about the Use of Force* (Cornell University Press, 2003).
Fiore, P, *Le droit international codifié et sa sanction juridique* (Pedone, 1890).
—— 'La science du droit international: Horizons nouveaux' (1909) XVI *Revue Générale de Droit International* 463–81.
Fitzmaurice, GG, 'The Definition of Aggression' (1952) 1(1) *The International and Comparative Law Quarterly* 137–44.
Flasch, O, *The Exercise of Self-Defence Against ISIL in Syria: New Insights on the Extraterritorial Use of Force Against Non-State Actors* 1702 (Taylor & Francis, 2015).
—— 'The Legality of the Air Strikes against ISIL in Syria: New Insights on the Extraterritorial Use of Force against Non-state Actors' (2016) 3(1) *Journal on the Use of Force and International Law* 37–69.
Fleck, D, 'National Sovereignty an International Responsibility: Legal and Policy Aspects' in M Bothe, ME O'Connell and N Ronzitti (eds), *Redefining Sovereignty: The Use of Force after the Cold War* (Transnational Publishers, 2005) 53–64.
Forsythe, DP, *Human Rights in International Relations* (Cambridge University Press, 2006).
Fortin, K, *The Accountability of Armed Groups under Human Rights Law* (Oxford University Press, 2017).
Fox, GH, 'The Right to Political Participation in International Law' in GH Fox and BR Roth (eds), *Democratic Governance and International Law* 17 (Cambridge University Press, 1992) 539–73.
—— 'Self-Determination in the Post-Cold War Era: a New Internal Focus?' (1995) 16(3) *Michigan Journal of International Law* 733–81.
—— 'International Law and the Entitlement to Democracy after War' (2003) 9(2) *Global Governance* 179–97.
—— 'Democracy, Right to, International Protection' in *Max Planck Encyclopedia of Public International Law* (Oxford University Press, 2008).
—— 'Intervention by Invitation' in M Weller (ed), *The Oxford Handbook of the Use of Force in International Law* (Oxford University Press, 2015) 816–40.
Fox, GH and Nolte, G, 'Intolerant Democracies' (2010) 1 *Democratic Governance and International Law* 389–435.
Fox, GH, and Roth, BR, 'The Dual Lives of "The Emerging Right to Democratic Governance"' (2018) 112 *AJIL Unbound* 67–72.
Franck, TM, 'Who Killed Article 2(4)? or: Changing Norms Governing the Use of Force by States' (1970) 64(5) *The American Journal of International Law* 809–37.
_____ 'Some Observations on the ICJ's Procedural and Substantive Innovations' (1987) 81(1) *The American Journal of International Law* 116–21.
_____ 'Legitimacy in the International System' (1988) 82(4) *American Journal of International Law* 705–59.
_____ *The Power of Legitimacy among Nations* (Oxford University Press, 1990).
_____ 'The Emerging Right to Democratic Governance' (1992) 86(1) *American Journal of International Law* 46–91.
_____ 'Legitimacy and the Democratic Entitlement' in GH Fox and BR Roth (eds), *Democratic Governance and International Law* (Cambridge University Press, 2000) 25–47.
_____ 'What Happens Now? The United Nations after Iraq' (2003) 97(3) *The American Journal of International Law* 607–20.
_____ *Recourse to Force: State Action against Threats and Armed Attacks* (Cambridge University Press, 2004).

Frei, N, Stahl, D and Weinke, A (eds), *Human Rights and Humanitarian Intervention: Legitimizing the Use of Force since the 1970s* (Wallstein Verlag, 2017).

Frowein, JA, 'Globale und regionale Friedenssicherung nach 50 Jahren Vereinte Nationen' (1995) 114 *Zeitschri für Schweizerisches Recht* 257–71.

_____ 'Recognition' *Max Planck Encyclopedia of Public International Law* (Oxford University Press, 2010).

Fukuyama, F, *The End of History and the Last Man* (Penguin Books, 1992).

Gaja, G, 'Sul ruolo della Corte internazionale di giustizia nell'accertamento del diritto internazionale' in F Salerno (ed), *Il ruolo del giudice internazionale nell'evoluzione del diritto internazionale e comunitario* (CEDAM, 1995) 233–38.

Gardam, J, *Necessity, Proportionality and the Use of Force by States* (Cambridge University Press, 2004).

Garner, JW, 'Recognition of Belligerency' (1938) 32(1) *The American Journal of International Law* 106–13.

Gasser, HP, 'International Armed Conflicts: Case Studies of Afghanistan, Kampuchea, and Lebanon' (1983) 33(1) *American University Law Review* 145–62.

_____ 'Ensuring Respect for the Geneva Conventions and Protocols: The Role of the Third States and the United Nations' in H Fox and MA Meyer (eds), *Effecting Compliance* (British Institute of International and Comparative Law, 1993) 15–49.

_____ 'International humanitarian law: An introduction' in H Haug (ed), *Humanity for All: The International Red Cross and Red Crescent Movement* (Henry Dunant Institute, 1993) 491–592.

Gazzini, T, *The Changing Rules on the Use of Force in International Law* (Manchester University Press, 2005).

Gillard, EC, 'The Law Regulating Cross-border Relief Operations' (2013) 95(890) *International Review of the Red Cross* 351–82.

Gillroy, JM, *An Evolutionary Paradigm for International Law: Philosophical Method, David Hume, and the Essence of Sovereignty* (Palgrave Macmillan, 2013).

Glanville, L, *Sovereignty and the Responsibility to Protect: A New History* (University of Chicago Press, 2014).

_____ 'The Responsibility to Protect beyond Borders in the Law of Nature and Nations' (2018) 28(4) *European Journal of International Law* 1069–95.

Glassman, A, 'The Evolution of the Prohibition on the Use of Force and Its Conflict with Human Rights Protection: Balancing Equally Forceful Jus Cogens Norms' (2011) 16(2) *UCLA Journal of International Law and Foreign Affairs* 345–80.

Glennon, MJ, *Limits of Law, Prerogatives of Power: Interventionism after Kosovo* (Palgrave, 2001).

_____ 'Why the Security Council Failed' (2003) 82(3) *Foreign Affairs* 16–35.

_____ 'How International Rules Die' (2005) 93(3) *Georgetown Law Journal* 939–91.

_____ 'The Limitations of Traditional Rules and Institutions Relating to the Use of Force' in M Weller (ed), *The Oxford Handbook of the Use of Force in International Law* (Oxford University Press, 2015) 79–96.

Gorelick, RE, 'Wars of National Liberation: Jus Ad Bellum' (1979) 11(1) *Case Western Reserve Journal of International Law* 71–93.

Gozzi, G, 'The "Discourse" of International Law and Humanitarian Intervention' (2017) 30(2) *Ratio Juris* 186–204.

Grado, V, *Guerre Civili e Terzi Stati* (CEDAM, 1998).

Graefrath, B, 'Complicity in the Law of International Responsibility' (1996) 2 *Revue belge de droit international* 371–80.

Grant, TD, *The Recognition of States: Law and Practice in Debate and Evolution* (Praeger Publishers, 1999).

Gratian, *Decretum* (Akademische Druck- u. Verlagsanstalt, 1959).

Gray, C, 'The Use and Abuse of the International Court of Justice: Cases concerning the Use of Force after Nicaragua' (2003) 14(5) *European Journal of International Law* 867–905.

_____ *International Law and the Use of Force* (Oxford University Press, 2018).

Green, J, 'Questioning the Peremptory Status of the Use of Force' (2011) 32(2) *Michigan Journal of International Law* 215–57.

Greenwood, C, 'International Humanitarian Law and the Tadić Case' (1996) 7(2) *European Journal of International Law* 265–83.

Gross, L, 'The Peace of Westphalia 1648–1948' (1948) 42(1) *American Journal of International Law* 20–41.

Grote, R, 'Westphalian System' in *Max Planck Encyclopedia of Public International Law* (Oxford University Press, 2006).

Grotius, H, *De Jure Belli ac Pacis* (Liberty Fund, 2005).

Guimaraes, AF, *The Origins of the Angolan Civil War: Foreign Intervention and Domestic Political Conflict 1961–76* (Palgrave, 1998).

Gutiérrez Baylón, J, 'La no intervención' in EO Rabasa (ed), *Los siete principios básicos de la política exterior de México* (Universidad Nacional Autónoma de México, 2005) 71–87.

Hafner, G, 'Present Problems of the Use of Force in International Law, Sub-Group on Intervention by Invitation' (2011) 74 *Yearbook of Institute of International Law* 181–482.

Hakimi, M, 'Introduction to Symposium on Unauthorized Military Interventions for the Public Good' (2017) 111 *AJIL Unbound* 284–86.

Halberstam, M, 'The Copenhagen Document: Intervention in Support of Democracy' (1993) 34(1) *Harvard International Law Journal* 163–75.

Hallet, R, 'The South Africa Intervention in Angola (1975–1976)' (1979) 77 *African Affairs* 347–56.

Hannikainen, L, *Peremptory Norms (Jus Cogens) in International Law: Historical Development, Criteria, Present Status* (Lakimiesliiton Kustannus/Finnish Lawyers' Publishing Company, 1988).

Hargrove, JL 'The Nicaragua Judgment and the Future of the Law of Force and Self-Defense Source' (1987) 81(1) *The American Journal of International Law* 135–43.

_____ 'Intervention by Invitation and the Politics of the New World Order' in L Damrosch and D Scheffer (eds), *Law and Force in the New World Order* (Westview Press, 1991) 113–26.

Hathaway, OA and others, 'War Manifestos' (2018) 85 *University of Chicago Law Review* 1139–1225.

Hathaway, OA and Shapiro, SJ, *The Internationalists: How a Radical Plan to Outlaw War Remade the World* (Simon & Schuster, 2017).

Hayashi, M, 'Reacting to the Use of Chemical Weapons: Options for Third States' (2014) 1(1) *Journal on the Use of Force and International Law* 80–121.

Heintze, HJ, and Zwitter, J (eds), *International Law and Humanitarian Assistance: A Crosscut through Legal Issues Pertaining to Humanitarianism* (Springer, 2011).

Helal, MS, 'The Unknown Unknowns of Humanitarian War' (2017) 111 *AJIL Unbound* 297–301.

Held, D, *Models of Democracy* (Polity Press, 2006).

Helton, AC, 'The legality of providing humanitarian assistance without the consent of the Sovereign' (1992) 4(3) *International Journal of Refugee Law* 373–75.

Hemleben, SJ, *Plans for World Peace through Six Centuries* (University of Chicago Press, 1943).

Henckaert, JM and Doswald-Beck, L, *Customary International Humanitarian Law* I (Cambridge University Press, 2005).

Henckaerts, JM and others, 'Article 2: Application of the Convention' in K Dörmann, L Lijnzaad, M Sassòli and P Spoerri (eds), *Commentary on the First Geneva Convention: Convention (I) for the Amelioration of the Condition of the Wounded and Sick in Armed Forces in the Field* (International Committee of the Red Cross, 2016) 69–125.

_____ 'Article 3: Conflicts not of an International Character' in K Dörmann, L Lijnzaad, M Sassòli and P Spoerri (eds), *Commentary on the First Geneva Convention: Convention (I) for the Amelioration of the Condition of the Wounded and Sick in Armed Forces in the Field* (Cambridge University Press, 2016) 126–325.

Henderson, C, 'International Measures for the Protection of Civilians in Libya and Côte D'Ivoire' (2011) 60(03) *International and Comparative Law Quarterly* 767–78.

_____ 'Editorial Comment: The Use of Force and Islamic State' (2014) 1(2) *Journal on the Use of Force and International Law* 209–22.

Henkin, L, 'The Reports of the Death of Article 2(4) Are Greatly Exaggerated' (1971) 65(3) *The American Journal of International Law* 544–48.

_____ 'Human Rights and State "Sovereignty"' (1994) 25(1) *Georgia Journal of International and Comparative Law* 31–45.

_____ 'The Mythology of Sovereignty' in R St J Macdonald (ed), *Essays in Honour of Wang Tieya* (Martinus Nijhoff Publishers, 1994) 351–58.

_____ *International Law: Politics and Values* (Martinus Nijhoff, 1995).

_____ 'That "S" Word: Sovereignty, and Globalization, and Human Rights, Et Cetera' (1999) 68(1) *Fordham Law Review* 1–14.

Henriksen, A and Schack, M, 'The Crisis in Syria and Humanitarian Intervention' (2014) 1(1) *Journal on the Use of Force and International Law* 122–47.

Hensel, HM, *The Legitimate Use of Military Force. The Just war Tradition and the Customary Law of Armed Conflict* (Ashgate, 2008).

_____ 'Christian Belief and Western Just War Thought' in HM Hensel (ed), *The Prism of Just War: Asian and Western Perspectives on the Legitimate Use of Military Force* (Ashgate, 2010) 29–86.

Herczeg, G, *The Development of International Law through the Political Organs of the United Nations* (Oxford University Press, 1963).

_____ 'The Prohibition of the Threat and Use of Force in Contemporary International Law' in *Questions of International Law* (ILA Hungarian Branch, 1964).

_____ 'Intervention and International Law' in H Bull (ed), *Intervention in World Politics* (Clarendon Press, 1984) 29–44.

_____ *Problems and Process: International Law and How We Use It* (Clarendon Press, 1994).

Higgins, R, *The Development of International Law through the Political Organs of the United Nations* (Oxford University Press, 1963).

_____ *Problems and Process: International Law and How We Use It* (Clarendon Press, 1994).

Hofbauer, JA, *Sovereignty in the Exercise of the Right to Self-determination* (Martinus Nijhoff, 2016).

Hoffmann, S, 'Hedley Bull and His Contribution to International Relations' (1986) 62(2) *International Affairs* 179–95.

Honoré, T, 'The Right to Rebel' (1988) 8(1) *Oxford Journal of Legal Studies* 34–54.

Hornung, J, 'Civilisés et Barbares' (1885) 17 *Revue de droit international et de législation comparée* 447–70.

Howard, ME, *Restraints on war: studies in the limitation of armed conflict* (Oxford University Press, 1979).

Hui, VT, 'Problematizing Sovereignty: Relative Sovereignty in the Historical Transformation of Inter-State and State-Society Relations' in MC Davis, W Dietrich, B Scholdan and D Sepp (eds), *International Intervention in the Post-Cold War World: Moral Responsibility and Power Politics* (ME Sharpe, 2004) 83–103.

Humphrey, JP, 'Political and Related Rights' in T Meron (ed), *Human Rights in International Law: Legal and Policy Issues* (Clarendon, 1986) 193–204.

Hurrelmann, A, Schneider, S and Steffek, S (eds), *Legitimacy in the Age of Global Politics* (Palgrave Macmillan, 2007).

International Commission on Intervention and State Sovereignty (ICISS), *The Responsibility to Protect* (International Development Research Centre, 2001).

Jackson, M, *Complicity in International Law* (Oxford University Press, 2015).

Jamnejad, M and Wood, M, 'The Principle of Non-intervention' (2009) 22(2) *Leiden Journal of International Law* 345–81.

Janik, R, 'You Can't Have One Without the Other, Can You? Assessing the Relationship between the Use of Force in the Name of Human Rights and Regime Change' (2015) 6 *Czech Yearbook of Public & Private International Law* 223–38.

_____ 'The Responsibility to Protect, Conflict Prevention, and the Ius ad Bellum: What Role for Democracy?' in S Fenkart, H Gärtner and H Swoboda (eds), *Gerechte Intervention? Zwischen Gewaltverbot und Schutzverantwortung* (LIT Verlag, 2017) 167–90.

Jennings, J and Watts, A, *Oppenheim's International Law* (Oxford University Press, 2008).
Jessup, PJ, 'The Estrada Doctrine' (1931) 25(4) *The American Journal of International Law* 719–23.
Jinks, D, 'State Responsibility for the Acts of Private Armed Groups' (2003) 4(1) *Chicago Journal of International Law* 83–95.
Jones, C, *Global Justice: Defending Cosmopolitanism* (Cambridge University Press, 2001).
Kabau, T, 'The Responsibility to Protect and the Role of Regional Organizations: an Appraisal of the African Union's Interventions' (2012) 4(1) *Goettingen Journal of International Law* 49–92.
Kalmo, H, 'A Matter of Fact? The Many Faces of Sovereignty' in H Kalmo and Q Skinner (eds), *Sovereignty in Fragments: The Past, Present and Future of a Contested Concept* (Cambridge University Press, 2010) 114–31.
Kalshoven, F, 'The Undertaking to Respect and Ensure Respect in All Circumstances: From Tiny Seed to Ripening Fruit' (1999) 2 *Yearbook of International Humanitarian Law* 3–61.
Kaplan, T, *Democracy: A World History* (Oxford University Press, 2015).
Karagiannis, S, 'Qu'Est-il, en Droit International, le Droit à la Résistance Devenu?' (2008) 76 *Revue trimestrielle de droits de l'homme* 949–1005.
Karimova, T, 'What amounts to 'a serious violation of international human rights law'? An analysis of practice and expert opinion for the purpose of the 2013 Arms Trade Treaty', Academy Briefing No. 6 (Geneva Academy of International Humanitarian Law and Human Rights, 2014).
Kearney RD and Dalton, RE, 'The Treaty on Treaties' (1970) 64(3) *The American Journal of International Law* 495–561.
Kelsen, H, *Principles of International Law* (Rinehart & Company, 1952).
_____ *The General Theory of Law and State* (Russel and Russel, 1961).
Kho, HH, 'The War Powers and Humanitarian Intervention' (2016) 53(4) *Houston Law Review* 971–1033.
_____ 'Humanitarian Intervention: Time for Better Law' (2017) 111 *AJIL Unbound* 287–91.
Kielsgard, MD, 'Evolving Human Rights Methodology: Have Incursions into State Sovereignty Gone Too Far?' (2013) 22(1) *Tulane Journal of International and Comparative Law* 43–61.
Kinactoğlui, M, 'The Principle of Non-intervention at the United Nations: The Charter Framework and the Legal Debate' (2005) Summer *Perceptions: Journal of International Affairs* 15–39.
Kirkpatrick, JJ and Gerson, A, 'The Reagan Doctrine, Human Rights, and International Law' in L Henkin (ed), *Right v. Might: International Law and the Use of Force* (Council on Foreign Relations Press, 1991) 19–36.
Klabbers, J, 'Intervention, Armed Intervention, Armed Attack, Threat to Peace, Act of Aggression, and Threat or Use of Force: What's the Difference?' in M Weller (ed), *The Oxford Handbook of the Use of Force in International Law* (Oxford University Press, 2015) 488–505.
Klein, K and Corten, O, *Droit d'ingérence ou obligation de réaction? Les possibilités d'action visant à assurer le respect des droits de la personne face au principe de non-intervention* (Bruylant, 1992).
Kohen, MG, *Secession: International Law Perspectives* (Cambridge University Press, 2006).
_____ 'The Principle of Non-intervention 25 Years after the Nicaragua Judgment' (2012) 25(1) *Leiden Journal of International Law* 157–64.
Kolb, R, *Ius contra Bellum: Le Droit International relatif au Maintien de la Paix* (Bruylant, 2009).
Kopelmanas, L, 'The Problem of Aggression and the Prevention of War' (1937) 31(2) *The American Journal of International Law* 244–57.
Koskenniemi, M, 'The Wonderful Artificiality of States' (1994) 88 *American Society of International Law Procedures* 22–29.
_____ '"The Lady Doth Protest Too Much" Kosovo, and the Turn to Ethics in International Law' (2002) 65(2) *The Modern Law Review* 159–75.
_____ *The Gentle Civilizer of Nations: The Rise and Fall of International Law 1870–1960* (Cambridge University Press, 2004).
_____ *From Apology to Utopia: The Structure of International Legal Argument* (Cambridge University Press, 2006).

_____ 'Conclusion: Vocabularies of Sovereignty – Power of a Paradox' in H Kalmo and Q Skinner (eds), *Sovereignty in Fragments: The Past, Present and Future of a Contested Concept* (Cambridge University Press, 2010) 222–42.

_____ 'Human Rights Mainstreaming as a Strategy for Institutional Power' (2010) 1(1) *Humanity: An International Journal of Human Rights, Humanitarianism, and Development* 47–58.

Koskenniemi, M and Leino, P, 'Fragmentation of International Law? Postmodern Anxieties' (2002) 15(3) *Leiden Journal of International Law* 553–79.

Koutroulis, V, 'The Fight against the Islamic State and Jus in Bello' (2016) 29(3) *Leiden Journal of International Law* 827–52.

Krasner, SD, 'Compromising Westphalia' (1995) 20(3) *International Security* 115–51.

_____ *Sovereignty: Organized Hypocrisy* (Princeton University Press, 1999).

Kreß, C, 'Some Reflections on the International Legal Framework Governing Transnational Armed Conflicts' (2010) 15(2) *Journal of Conflict and Security Law* 245–74.

_____ 'Major Post-Westphalian Shifts and Some Important Neo-Westphalian Hesitations in the State Practice on the International Law on The Use of Force' (2014) 1(1) *Journal on the Use of Force and International Law* 11–54.

_____ 'The International Court of Justice and the "Principle of Non-Use of Force"' in M Weller (ed), *The Oxford Handbook of the Use of Force in International Law* (Oxford University Press, 2015) 561–604.

Kreß, C and Nußberger, B, 'Pro-democratic intervention in current international law: the case of The Gambia in January 2017' (2017) 4(2) *Journal on the Use of Force and International Law* 239–52.

Kuijt, EE, *Humanitarian Assistance and State Sovereignty in International Law: Towards a Comprehensive Framework* (Intersentia, 2015).

Kunig, P, 'Intervention, Prohibition of' in *Max Planck Encyclopedia of Public International Law* (Oxford University Press, 2008).

Kunz, JL, 'Individual and Collective Self-Defense in Article 51 of the Charter of the United Nations' (1947) 41(4) *The American Journal of International Law* 872–79.

Kuwali, D, 'Protect Responsibly: the African Union's Implementation of Article 4(H) Intervention' (2010) 11(2008) *Yearbook of International Humanitarian Law* 51–108.

Landheer, B, 'The Legal Status of the Netherlands' (1943) 41(4) *Michigan Law Review* 644–64.

Lanovoy, V, 'Complicity in an Internationally Wrongful Act' (2014) (38) *SHARES Research Paper Series*.

_____ 'Self-determination in International Law: A Democratic Phenomenon or an Abuse of Right?' (2015) 4(2) *Cambridge Journal of International and Comparative Law* 388–404.

_____ *Complicity and its Limits in the Law of International Responsibility* (Hart Publishing, 2017).

Lattanzi, F, 'Humanitarian Assistance' in A Clapham, P Gaeta and M Sassòli (eds), *The 1949 Geneva Conventions: A Commentary* (Oxford University Press, 2015) 231–56.

Lauterpacht, E, 'Sovereignty – Myth or Reality?' (1997) 73(1) *International Affairs* 137–50.

Lauterpacht, H, *Recognition in International Law* (Cambridge University Press, 1947).

Le Mon, CJ, 'Unilateral Intervention by Invitation in Civil Wars: The Effective Control Test Tested' (2003) 35(3) *New York University Journal of International Law and Politics* 741–94.

Lederman, M, 'Why the strikes against Syria probably violate the U.N. Charter and (therefore) the U.S. Constitution' (2017) *Just Security* 1–7.

Lehmann, LM, 'All Necessary Means to Protect Civilians: What the Intervention in Libya Says About the Relationship Between the Jus in Bello and the Jus ad Bellum' (2012) 17(1) *Journal of Conflict and Security Law* 117–46.

Lesaffer, R, 'Too Much History: From War as Sanction to the Sanctioning of War' in M Weller (ed), *The Oxford Handbook of the Use of Force in International Law* (Oxford University Press, 2015) 35–55.

Levitt, BS, 'A Desultory Defense of Democracy: OAS Resolution 1080 and the Inter- American Democratic Charter' (2006) 48(3) *Latin American Politics and Society* 93–123.

Levitt, J, 'Humanitarian Intervention by Regional Actors in Internal Conflicts The Cases of ECOWAS in Liberia and Sierra Leone' (1998) 12(2) *Temple International and Comparative Law Journal* 333–76.

Lichtermann, S, '"(Control) Tests," the Nature of Conflict and Attribution of Responsibility for Mass Crimes and Genocide in Criminal and Civil Liability Cases: "Overall" v. "Effective" Control Test' (2012) 1(1) *Sarajevo International and Comparative Law Review* 1–17.

Lieblich, E, 'Intervention and Consent: Consensual Forcible Interventions in Internal Armed Conflicts as International Agreements' (2011) 29(2) *Boston University International Law Journal* 337–82.

_____ *International Law and Civil Wars: Intervention and Consent* (Routledge, 2013).

_____ 'Internal Jus ad bellum' (2016) 67 *Hastings Law Journal* 1–68.

Linderfalk, U, 'The Effect of Jus Cogens Norms: Whoever Opened Pandora's Box, Did You Ever Think about the Consequences?' (2007) 18(5) *European Journal of International Law* 853–71.

Livy, *Ab Urbe Condita* (Mondadori, 2007).

Locke, J, 'The Second Treatise on Civil Government' in T Laslet, (ed), *Two Treatises on Government* (Cambridge University Press, 1988).

Lowe, V, 'The Principle of Non-intervention: Use of Force' in V Lowe and C Warbrick (eds), *The United Nations and the Principles of International Law: Essays in Memory of Michael Akehurst*, 1994) 66–84.

_____ 'Responsibility for the Conduct of Other States' (2002) 101 *Japanese Journal of International Law* 1–15.

Lowe, V and Tzanakopoulos, A, 'Humanitarian Intervention' in *Max Planck Encyclopedia of Public International Law* (Oxford University Press, 2011).

Luban, D, 'Just War and Human Rights' (1980) 9(2) *Philosophy & Public Affairs* 160–81.

Lubell, N, *Extraterritorial Use of Force against Non-State Actors* (Oxford University Press, 2010).

Lyons, GM and Mastanduno, M (eds), *Beyond Westphalia? National Sovereignty and International Intervention* (John Hopkins University Press, 1995).

Mačák, K, *Internationalized Armed Conflicts in International Law* (Oxford University Press, 2018).

MacDonald, E, and Alston, P, 'Sovereignty, Human Rights, Security: Armed Intervention and the Foundational Problems of International Law' in P Alston and E MacDonald (eds), *Human Rights, Intervention, and the Use of Force* (Oxford University Press, 2008) 1–32.

MacFarlane, SN, *Superpower Rivalry & Third World Radicalism: The Idea of National Liberation* (Johns Hopkins University Press, 1985).

Macklem, P, *The Sovereignty of Human Rights* (Oxford University Press, 2015).

Malmvig, H, *State Sovereignty and Intervention: A Discourse Analysis of Interventionary and Non-Interventionary Practices in Kosovo and Algeria* (Routledge, 2006).

Marks, S, 'International Law, Democracy and the End of History' in GH Fox and BR Roth (eds), *Democratic Governance and International Law* (Cambridge University Press, 2000) 532–66.

_____ *The Riddle of All Constitutions: International Law, Democracy, and the Critique of Ideology* (Oxford University Press, 2003).

_____ 'What has Become of the Emerging Right to Democratic Governance?' (2011) 22(2) *European Journal of International Law* 507–24.

Marsavelski, A, 'The Crime of Terrorism and the Right to Revolution' (2013) 28(2) *Connecticut Journal of International Law* 241–95.

Matheson, MJ, 'Just War and Humanitarian Intervention: Comment on the Grotius Lecture by Professor Jean Bethke Elshtain' (2001) 17(1) *American University International Law Review* 27–33.

McCauliff, CMA, 'The Right to Resist the Government: Tyranny, Usurpation, and Regicide in Shakespeare's Plays' (2007) 14(1) *ILSA Journal of International & Comparative Law* 9–44.

McCorquodale, R, *International Law beyond the State: Essays on Sovereignty, Non-state Actors and Human Rights* (Cameron May, 2011).

McCoubrey, H, 'The Qualification Framework of International Humanitarian Law: Too Rigid to Accommodate Contemporary Conflicts?' (2011) 34(1) *Suffolk Transnational Law Review* 145–82.

Mcmahan, J, 'Intervention and Collective Self-Determination' (1996) 10 *Ethics and International Affairs* 1–24.
McNulty, M, 'From Intervened to Intervenor: Rwanda and Military Intervention in Zaire/DRC' in O Furley and R May (eds), *African Interventionist States* (Ashgate, 2001) 173–89.
McQueen, N, 'Angola: Exporting Civil War' in O Furley and R May (eds), *African Interventionist States* (Ashgate, 2001) 93–117.
Mégret, F, 'Le Droit International Peut-il Etre un Droit de Résistance? Dix Conditions pour un Renouveau de l'Ambition Normative Internationale' (2008) 39(1) *Revue Études Internationales* 39–62.
_____ 'Beyond the "Salvation" Paradigm: Responsibility To Protect (Others) vs the Power of Protecting Oneself' (2009) 40(6) *Security Dialogue* 575–95.
_____ 'The Apology of Utopia: Some Thoughts on Koskenniemian Themes, With Particular Emphasis on Massively Institutionalized International Human Rights Law' (2013) 27(2) *Temple International and Comparative Law Journal* 455–97.
Meron, T, 'Classification of Armed Conflict in the Former Yugoslavia: Nicaragua's Fallout' (1998) 92(2) *The American Journal of International Law* 236–42.
_____ 'The Humanization of Humanitarian Law' (2000) 94(2) *The American Journal of International Law* 239–78.
_____ *The Humanization of International Law* (Martinus Nijhoff, 2006).
Merriam, CE, *History of the Theory of Sovereignty since Rousseau* (Columbia University Press, 1900).
Milanović, M, 'State Responsibility for Genocide: A Follow-up' (2007) 18(4) *European Journal of International Law* 669–94.
_____ 'The Applicability of the Conventions to "Transnational" and "Mixed" Conflicts' in A Clapham, P Gaeta and M Sassòli (ed.), *The 1949 Geneva Conventions: A Commentary* (Oxford University Press, 2015) 27–50.
Milanovic, M and Hadzi-vidanovic, V, 'A Taxonomy of Armed Conflict' in N White and C Henderson (eds), *Research Handbook on International Conflict and Security Law: "jus ad bellum, jus in bello," and "jus post bellum"* (Edward Elgar, 2012) 256–314.
Mill, JS, 'A Few Words on Non-Intervention' (1859) 8 *Foreign Policy Perspectives* 1–6.
Miller, DM, 'Non-International Armed Conflicts' (1982) 31 *American University Law Review* 897–933.
Miller, R, 'Self-Determination in International Law and the Demise of Democracy?' (2003) 41(3) *Columbia Journal of Transnational Law* 601–48.
Moir, L, *The Law of Internal Armed Conflict* (Cambridge University Press, 2002).
_____ 'The Concept of Non-International Armed Conflict' in A Clapham, P Gaeta and M Sassòli (eds), *The 1949 Geneva Conventions: A Commentary* (Oxford University Press, 2015) 391–414.
Möller, A, *International Law in Peace and War, Part II* (Levin & Munksgaard, 1935).
Molodcov, SV, 'The Principle that States should Refrain from the Threat or Use of Force in International Relations' in *WFUNA Seminar* (1965).
Moore, JN, 'Introduction' in JN Moore (ed), *Law and Civil War in the Modern World* (Johns Hopkins University Press, 1974) i–xiii.
Morsink, J, *The Universal Declaration of Human Rights: Origins, Drafting, and Intent* (University of Pennsylvania Press. 1999).
Moynihan, H, 'Aiding and Assisting: Challenges in Armed Conflict and Counterterrorism' Chatham House Research Paper, November 2016.
Müllerson, R, 'Jus Ad Bellum: Plus Ça Change (Le Monde) Plus C'Est La Même Chose (Le Droit)?' (2002) 7(2) *Journal of Conflict and Security Law* 149–89.
Murphy, SD, 'Democratic Legitimacy and the Recognition of States and Governments' in GH Fox and BR Roth (eds), *Democratic Governance and International Law* (Cambridge University Press, 2000) 123–54.
_____ 'The International Legality of U.S. Military Cross-Border Operations from Afghanistan into Pakistan' (2009) 84 *International Law Studies* 109–39.

Murphy, S, 'Unique in International Human Rights Law: Article 20(2) and the Right to Resist in the African Charter on Human and Peoples' Rights' (2011) 11(2) *African Human Rights Journal* 465–94.

Nahlawi, Y, 'The legality of NATO's pursuit of regime change in Libya' (2018) 5(2) *Journal on the Use of Force and International Law* 295–323.

Neff, SC, *War and the Law of Nations: A General History* (Cambridge University Press, 2005).

Neuberger, B, *National Self-Determination in Postcolonial Africa* (Rienner, 1986).

Nolte, G, *Eingreifen auf Einladung: zur völkerrechtlichen Zulässigkeit des Einsatzes fremder Truppen im internen Konflikt auf Einladung der Regierung* (Springer, 1999).

_____ 'Intervention by Invitation' in *Max Planck Encyclopedia of Public International Law* (Oxford University Press, 2010).

Nolte, G and Aust, HP, 'Equivocal Helpers – Complicit States, Mixed Messages and International Law' (2009) 58(1) *International and Comparative Law Quarterly* 1–30.

Nolte, G and Randelzhofer, A, 'Action with Respect to Threats to the Peace, Breaches of the Peace, and Acts of Aggression, Article 51' in B Simma, DE Khan, G Nolte, A Paulus and N Wessendorf (eds), *The Charter of the United Nations: A Commentary* II (Oxford University Press, 2012) 1397–1428.

Nowak, C, *The changing law of non-intervention in civil wars – assessing the production of legality in state practice after 2011* 5(1) (Taylor & Francis, 2018).

Nowrot, K and Schebacker, EW, 'The Use of Force to Restore Democracy: International Legal Implications of the ECOWAS Intervention in Sierra Leone' (1998) 14 *American University of International Law Review* 321–412.

Nußberger, B, *Military strikes in Yemen in 2015: intervention by invitation and self-defence in the course of Yemen's 'model transitional process'* 4(1) (Taylor & Francis, 2017).

Nyamuya, J and Coleman, A, 'Changing the Guard – The Price of Democracy: Lessons from the Arab Spring on Constitutionalism' in G Wilson and C Panara (eds), *The 'Arab Spring': New Patterns for Democracy and International Law* (Martinus Nijhoff, 2013) 1–28.

O'Connell, ME, 'Defining Armed Conflict' (2008) 13(3) *Journal of Conflict and Security Law* 393–400.

_____ *International Law and the Use of Force* (Foundation Press, 2009).

_____ 'Saving Lives through a Definition of International Armed Conflict' (2010) 40 *Proceedings of the Bruges Colloquium, Armed Conflicts and Parties to Armed Conflicts under IHL: Confronting Legal Categories to Contemporary Realities* 19–27.

_____ 'The Prohibition of the Use of Force' in D Nigel and C Henderson (eds), *Research Handbook on International Conflict and Security Law: "Jus ad Bellum, Jus in Bello," and "Jus post Bellum"* (Edward Elgar, 2013) 89–119.

O'Connor, L, 'Legality of the use of force in Syria against Islamic State and the Khorasan Group' (2016) 3(1) *Journal on the Use of Force and International Law* 70–96.

O'Rurke, VA, 'Recognition of Belligerency and the Spanish Civil War' (1937) 31(3) *American Journal of International Law* 398–413.

Obse, K, 'The Arab Spring and the Question of Legality of Democratic Revolution in Theory and Practice: A Perspective Based on the African Union Normative Framework' (2014) 27(4) *Leiden Journal of International Law* 817–38.

Oglesby, RR, *Internal War and the Search for Normative Order* (Martinus Nijhoff, 1971).

Ohlin, JD, *The Assault on International Law* (Oxford University Press, 2015).

_____ 'The Doctrine of Legitimate Defense' (2015) 91 *International Law Studies* 119–54.

Omorogbe, EY, 'A Club of Incumbents? The African Union and Coups d'Etat' (2011) 44(1) *Vanderbilt Journal of Transnational Law* 123–54.

Onuf, NG, 'The Principle of Non-intervention, the United Nations, and the International System' (1971) 25(2) *International Organization* 209–27.

Oppenheim, L, *International Law: A Treatise. Volume 2: Disputes, war and neutrality* (Longmans, 1952).

_____ *International Law: A Treatise* (Longmans Green, 1963).

—— *Oppenheim's International Law* (Oxford University Press, 2008).
Orakhelashvili, A, 'Legal Stability and Claims of Change: The International Court's Treatment of Jus ad Bellum and Jus in Bello' (2006) 75(3) *Nordic Journal of International Law* 371–407.
—— *Peremptory Norms in International Law* (Oxford University Press, 2008).
—— 'The Impact of Human Rights on General International Law' (2010) 17(3) *International Journal on Minority and Group Rights* 491–99.
—— 'Undesired, yet Omnipresent: Jus ad Bellum in Its Relation to Other Areas of International Law' (2015) 2(2) *Journal on the Use of Force and International Law* 238–56.
—— 'Changing Jus Cogens Through State Practice: The Case of the Prohibition of the Use of Force and its Exceptions' in M Weller (ed), *The Oxford Handbook of the Use of Force in International Law* (Oxford University Press, 2015) 157–75.
Orford, A, *Reading Humanitarian Intervention. Human Rights and the Use of Force in International Law* (Cambridge University Press, 2003).
—— *International Authority and the Responsibility to Protect* (Cambridge University Press, 2011).
Osiander, A, 'Before Sovereignty: Society and Politics in Ancien Régime Europe' (2001) 27(05) *Review of International Studies* 119–45.
—— 'Sovereignty, International Relations, and the Westphalian Myth' (2001) 55(2) *International Organization* 251–87.
Padelford, NJ, 'The International Non-Intervention Agreement and the Spanish Civil War' (1937) 31(4) *American Journal of International Law* 578–603.
—— 'Foreign Shipping During the Spanish Civil War' (1938) 32(2) *The American Journal of International Law* 264–79.
Palwankar, U, 'Mesures auxquelles peuvent recourir les Etats pour remplir leur obligation de faire respecter le droit international humanitaire' (1994) 76(805) *International Review of the Red Cross* 11–28.
Paulus, AL, 'Human Right to Participate in Armed Revolution and Related Forms of Social Violence: Testing the Limits of Permissibility' (1983) 32(2) *Emory Law Journal* 545–82.
—— 'Jus Cogens in a Time of Hegemony and Fragmentation' (2005) 74(3) *Nordic Journal of International Law* 297–333.
—— 'International Law, Dignity, Democracy, and the Arab Spring' (2013) 46(1) *Cornell International Law Journal* 1–19.
Perkins, JA, 'The Right to Counter-Intervention' (1987) 17(2) *Georgia Journal of International and Comparative Law* 171–227.
Peters, A, 'Le Droit d'Ingérence et le Devoir d'Ingérence – Vers une Responsabilité de Protéger' (2002) 79(3) *Revue de droit international et de droit comparé* 290–308.
—— 'Dual Democracy' in J Klabbers, A Peters and G Ulfstein (eds), *The Constitutionalization of International Law* (Oxford University Press, 2009) 263–341.
—— 'Humanity as the Alfa and Omega of Sovereignty' (2009) 20(3) *European Journal of International Law* 513–44.
Peterson, MJ, *Recognition of Governments: Legal Doctrine and State Practice 1815–1995* (Palgrave MacMillan, 1997).
Petrasek, D, *Ends and Means: Human Rights Approaches to Armed Groups*, International Council on Human Rights Policy, Geneva, 2000.
Phillips, A, *Engendering Democracy* (Polity Press, 1991).
Phillipson, C, *The International Law and Custom of Ancient Greece and Rome* (Macmillan, 1911).
Pictet, JS, *Geneva Convention for the Amelioration of the Condition of the Wounded and Sick in Armed Forces in the Field: Commentary* (International Committee of the Red Cross, 1952).
—— *Commentary on the Third Geneva Convention: Convention (III) relative to the Treatment of Prisoners of War. Geneva 12 August 1949* (International Committee of the Red Cross, 1952).
Piirimäe, P, 'The Westphalian Myth and the Idea of External Sovereignty' in H Kalmo and Q Skinner (eds), *Sovereignty in Fragments: The Past, Present and Future of a Contested Concept* (Cambridge University Press, 2010) 64–80.

Pinto, R, 'Les Règles du Droit International Concernant la Guerre Civile' (1965) *Collected Courses of the Hague Academy of International Law* 451–582.

Pitts, J, 'Boundaries of Victorian International Law' in *Victorian Visions of Global Order: Empire and International Relations in Nineteenth-Century Political Thought* (Cambridge University Press, 2007) 67–88.

Prost, M, *The Concept of Unity in Public International Law* (Hart Publishing, 2012).

Pufendorf, S, *Le Devoir de l'Homme et du Citoyen selon la Loi Naturelle* (Presses universitaires de Caen, 1998).

Quane, H, 'The United Nations and the Evolving Right to Self-Determination' (1998) 47(3) *International & Comparative Law Quarterly* 537–72.

Raaflaub, KA, 'Politics and Interstate Relations in the World of Early Greek Poleis: Homer and Beyond' (1997) 31 *Antichthon* 1–27.

—— 'Introduction: Searching for Peace in the Ancient World' in KA Raaflaub (ed), *War, Peace and International Law in Ancient Greece* (Blackwell Publishing, 2007) 1–33.

Raič, D, *Statehood and the Law of Self-Determination* (Martinus Nijhoff, 2002).

Randelzhofer, A and Dörr, O, 'Article 2(4)' in B.Simma, DE Khan, G Nolte, A Paulus and N Wessendorf (eds), *The Charter of the United Nations: A Commentary* (Oxford University Press, 2002) 200–34.

Rauert, T, 'Early Modern Perspectives on Western Just War Though' in HM Hensel (ed), *The Prism of Just War: Asian and Western Perspectives on the Legitimate Use of Military Force* (Ashgate, 2010) 87–114.

Raymond, GA, 'The Greco-Roman Roots of the Western Just War Tradition' in HM Hensel (ed), *The Prism of Just War: Asian and Western Perspectives on the Legitimate Use of Military Force* (Ashgate, 2010) 7–28.

Redaelli, C and Casey-Maslen, S, 'Protecting Civilians in Populated Areas during the Conduct of Hostilities after the Gotovina Case' in S Casey-Maslen (ed), *The War Report: Armed Conflict in 2013* (Oxford University Press, 2014) 454–74.

Regan, PM, 'Choosing to Intervene: Outside Interventions into Internal Conflicts as a Policy Choice' (1998) 60(3) *Journal of Politics* 754–79.

Reichberg, GM, 'Jus ad Bellum' in L May (ed), *War: Essays in Political Philosophy* (Cambridge University Press, 2008) 11–29.

Reisman, WM, 'Coercion and Self-Determination: Construing Charter Article 2(4)' (1984) 78(3) *The American Journal of International Law* 642–45.

—— 'Allocating Competences to Use Coercion in the Post–Cold War World: Practices, Conditions, and Prospects' in L Fisler Damrosch and DJ Scheffer (eds), *Law and Force in the New International Order* (Westview Press, 1991) 26.

—— 'Governments-in-Exile: Notes Toward a Theory of Formation and Operation' in Y Shain (ed), *Governments-in-Exile in Contemporary World Politics* (Routledge, 1991) 238–48.

—— 'Why Regime Change is (Almost Always) a Bad Idea' (2004) 98(3) *American Journal of International Law* 516–25.

—— 'Sovereignty and Human Rights in Contemporary International Law' (2017) 84(4) *The American Journal of International Law* 866–76.

Reus-Smit, C, 'Human Rights and the Social Construction of Sovereignty' (2001) 27(04) *Review of International Studies* 519–38.

—— 'The concept of intervention' (2013) 39(5) *Review of International Studies* 1057–76.

Rodley, N, 'Can Armed Opposition Groups Violate Human Rights?' in KH Mahoney and P Mahoney (eds), *Human Rights in the Twenty-First Century: A Global Challenge* (Martinus Nijhoff, 1993) 297–318.

—— 'Humanitarian Intervention' in *The Oxford Handbook of the Use of Force in International Law* (Oxford University Press, 2015) 775–96.

Rodogno, D, *Against Massacre: Humanitarian Interventions in the Ottoman Empire 1815–1914* (Princeton University Press, 2012).

Rogers, WD and others, 'The Brezhnev Doctrine and the Reagan Doctrine: Apples and Oranges?' (1987) 81 *Proceedings of the Annual Meeting (American Society of International Law)* 561–78.
Röling, BVA, 'The Ban of the Use of Force and the U.N. Charter' in A Cassese (ed), *The Current Regulation of the Use of Force* (Martinus Nijhoff, 1986) 3–8.
Ronzitti, N, 'Resort to Force in Wars of National Liberation' in A Cassese (ed), *Current Problems of International Law* (Giuffré, 1975) 319–53.
—— *Rescuing Nationals Abroad through Military Coercion and Intervention on Grounds of Humanity* (Martinus Nijhoff, 1985).
—— 'Use of Force, Jus Cogens and State Consent' in A Cassese (ed), *The Current Legal Regulation of the Use of Force* (Martinus Nijhoff, 1986) 147–66.
—— 'The Expanding Law of Self-Defence' (2006) 11(3) *Journal of Conflict and Security Law* 343–59.
—— *Diritto dei Conflitti Armati* (Giappichelli, 2011).
Roscini, M, 'Threats of Armed Force and Contemporary International Law' (2007) 54(2) *Netherlands International Law Review* 229–77.
—— 'Neighbourhood Watch? The African Great Lakes Pact and Jus ad Bellum' (2009) 69(3) *Heidelberg Journal of International Law* 931–59.
Rosenau, JN, 'Intervention as a Scientific Concept' (1969) 13(2) *Journal of Conflict Resolution* 149–71.
Rosenstein, N, 'War and Peace, Fear and Reconciliation at Rome' in KA Raaflaub (ed), *War and Peace in the Ancient World* (Blackwell Publishing, 2007) 226–44.
Rosenstock, R, 'The Declaration of Principles of International Law Concerning Friendly Relations: A Survey' (1971) 65(5) *The American Journal of International Law* 713–35.
Roth, BR, 'Governmental Illegitimacy Revisited: Pro-Democratic Armed Intervention in the Post-Bipolar World' (1993) 3(2) *Transnational Law & Contemporary Problems* 481–515.
—— *Governmental Illegitimacy in International Law* (Clarendon Press, 1999).
—— 'The Enduring Significance of State Sovereignty' (2004) 56 *Florida Law Review* 1017–50.
—— 'Secessions, Coups and the International Rule of Law: Assessing the Decline of the Effective Control Doctrine' (2010) 11(2) *Melbourne Journal of International Law* 393–940.
—— *Sovereign Equality and Moral Disagreement: Premises of a Pluralist International Legal Order* (Oxford University Press, 2011).
Ruffert, M, 'Reprisals' *Max Planck Encyclopedia of Public International Law* (Oxford University Press, 2015).
Ruys, T, *'Armed Attack' and Article 51 of the UN Charter: Evolutions in Customary Law and Practice* (Cambridge University Press, 2010).
—— 'Of Arms, Funding and "Non-Lethal Assistance" – Issues Surrounding Third State Intervention in the Syrian Civil War' (2014) 13(1) *Chinese Journal of International Law* 13–53.
—— 'The Meaning of "Force" and the Boundaries of the Jus Ad Bellum – Are "Minimal" Uses of Force Excluded from UN Charter Article 2(4)?' (2014) 108(2) *American Journal of International Law* 159–210.
—— 'The quest for an internal Jus ad Bellum: international law's missing link, mere distraction or Pandora's Box?' in C Kreβ and R Lawless (eds), *Necessity and Proportionality in International Peace and Security Law* (Oxford University Press, 2019).
Ruys, T, and Ferro, L, 'Divergent Views on the Content and Relevance of the Jus Ad Bellum in Europe and the United States? The Case of the U.S.-Led Military Coalition Against "Islamic State"' in C Giorgetti and G Verdirame (eds), *Concepts on International Law in Europe and the United States* (Cambridge University Press, 2016) 1–32.
—— 'Weathering the Storm: Legality and Legal Implications of the Saudi-led Military Intervention in Yemen' (2016) 65(1) *International and Comparative Law Quarterly* 61–98.
Samuels, K, 'Jus Ad Bellum and Civil Conflicts: A Case Study of the International Community's Approach to Violence in the Conflict in Sierra Leone' (2003) 8(2) *Journal of Conflict & Security Law* 315–38.

Sapienza, R, *La guerra civile nell'evoluzione del diritto internazionale* (Editpress, 2010).
Saranti, V, 'Pro-Democratic Intervention, Invitation, or "Responsibility to Protect"? Challenges to International Law from the "Arab Spring"' in C Panara and G Wilson (eds), *The Arab Spring: New Patterns for Democracy and International Law* (Martinus Nijhoff, 2013) 169–201.
Sassòli, M, 'The Legal Qualification of the Conflict in the Former Yugoslavia: Double Standards or New Horizons for International Humanitarian Law?' in S Yee and T Wang (eds), *International Law in the Post-Cold War World: Essays in Memory of Li Haopei* (Routledge, 2001) 307–33.
—— 'State Responsibility for Violations of International Humanitarian Law' (2002) 84(846) *International Review of the Red Cross* 401–34.
Sassòli, M, Bouvier, AA and Quintin, A, *How Does Law Protect in War?* (International Committee of the Red Cross, 2011).
Sassòli, M and Olson, LM, 'The Judgment of the ICTY Appeals Chamber on the Merits in the Tadic case' (2000) 82(839) *International Review of the Red Cross* 733–69.
Saul, B, 'Defending "Terrorism": Justifications and Excuses for Terrorism in International Criminal Law' (2006) 25 *Australian Yearbook of International Law* 177–226.
Schachter, O, 'The Legality of Pro-Democratic Invasion' (1984) 78(3) *The American Journal of International Law* 645–50.
—— 'The Right of States to Use Armed Force' (1984) 82(5) *Michigan Law Review* 1620–46.
—— *International Law in Theory and Practice: General Course in Public International Law* (Martinus Nijhoff, 1985).
—— 'In Defense of International Rules on the Use of Force' (1986) 53(1) *The University of Chicago Law Review* 113–46.
Schindler, D, 'Le Principe de Non-intervention dans les Guerres Civiles' (1975) 56 *Annuaire de l'Institut de Droit International* 411–74.
Schmitt, MN, 'Wings over Libya: The No-Fly Zone in Legal Perspective' (2011) 36 *Yale Journal of International Law Online* 45–58.
—— 'Legitimacy versus Legality Redux: Arming the Syrian Rebels' (2014) 7 *Journal of National Security Law & Policy* 139–59.
—— 'The Use of Cyber Force and International Law' in M Weller (ed), *The Oxford Handbook of The Use of Force in International Law* (Oxford University Press, 2015) 1110–30.
Schrijver, N, 'The Changing Nature of State Sovereignty' (2000) 70(1) *The British Yearbook of International Law* 65–98.
Schroeder, PW, *The Transformation of European Politics 1763–1848* (Oxford University Press, 1994).
Schütte, R, *Civilian Protection in Armed Conflicts: Evolution, Challenges and Implementation* (Springer, 2015).
Schweizer, B, 'Moral dilemmas for humanitarianism in the era of "humanitarian" military interventions' (2004) 86(855) *International Review of the Red Cross* 547–64.
Schwendimann, F, 'The Legal Framework of Humanitarian Access in Armed Conflict' (2011) 93(884) *International Review of the Red Cross* 993–1008.
Serralvo, J, 'Government Recognition and International Humanitarian Law Applicability in Post-Gaddafi Libya' (2015) 18 *Yearbook of International Humanitarian Law* 3–41.
Sevastik, P, 'Some Aspects on the Effects of Human Rights Law and its Implications on International Law' in P Sevastik (ed), *Aspects of Sovereignty: Sino-Swedish Reflections* (Martinus Nijhoff, 2013) 33–61.
Sewall, S, Raymond, D and Chin, S, *Mass Atrocity Response Operations (MARO): A Military Planning Handbook*. (Center for Human Rights Policy, Harvard Kennedy School, and the US Army Peacekeeping and Stability Operations Institute, 2010).
Shaw, MN, 'Peoples, Territorialism and Boundaries' (1997) 8(3) *European Journal of International Law* 478–507.
Shelton, D, 'Sherlock Holmes and the Mystery of Jus Cogens' in M den Heijer and H van der Wilt (eds), *Netherlands Yearbook of International Law 2015: Jus Cogens: Quo Vadis?* (Springer, 2015) 23–50.

Simms, B, '"A False Principle in the Law of Nations": Burke, State Sovereignty, [German] Liberty, and Intervention in the Age of Westphalia' in B Simms and DJB Trim (eds), *Humanitarian Intervention: A History* (Cambridge University Press, 2011) 89–110.

Simpson, G, 'The Guises of Sovereignty' in C Sampford and R Thakur (eds), *Re-envisioning Sovereignty: The End of Westphalia?* (Ashgate, 2008) 51–72.

Siotis, J, *Le Droit de la Guerre et les Conflits Armés d'un Caractère Non-international* (Librairie Générale de Droit et de Jurisprudence, 1958).

Sivakumaran, S, 'Application of the Convention on the Prevention and Punishment of the Crime of Genocide (Bosnia and Herzegovina v. Yugoslavia (Serbia and Montenegro))' (2007) 56(3) *International and Comparative Law Quarterly* 695–708.

—— *The Law of Non-International Armed Conflict* (Oxford University Press, 2012).

Skinner, Q, *The Foundations of Modern Political Thought, Volume One: The Renaissance* (Cambridge University Press, 1978).

Slaughter, AM, 'International Law in a World of Liberal States' (1995) 6(4) *European Journal of International Law* 503–38.

Solis, GD, *The Law of Armed Conflict: International Humanitarian Law in War* (Cambridge University Press, 2010).

Southall, R and Fox, R, 'Lesotho's General Election of 1998: Rigged or De Rigeur?' (1999) 37(4) *The Journal of Modern African Studies* 669–96.

Sperduti, G, 'Governi in Esilio e Comitati Nazionali all'Estero' (1952) 7 *La Comunità Internazionale* 404–13.

Spieker, H, 'Humanitarian Assistance, Access in Armed Conflict and Occupation' in *Max Planck Encyclopedia of Public International Law* (June) (Oxford University Press, 2015).

Spinedi, M, 'On the non-attribution of the Bosnian Serbs' conduct to Serbia' (2007) 5(4) *Journal of International Criminal Justice* 829–38.

Stahn, C, 'Terrorist Acts as "Armed Attack": The Right to Self-Defense, Article 51 (1/2) of the UN Charter, and International Terrorism' (2003) 27(2) *The Fletcher Forum of World Affairs* 35–54.

—— 'Responsibility to Protect: Political Rhetoric or Emerging Legal Norm?' (2007) 201(1) *American Journal of International Law* 99–120.

—— 'Between Law-breaking and Law-making: Syria, Humanitarian Intervention and "What the Law Ought to Be"' (2013) 19(1) *Journal of Conflict and Security Law* 1–24.

—— 'Syria and the Semantics of intervention, aggression and punishment: On "red lines" and "blurred lines"' (2013) 11(5) *Journal of International Criminal Justice* 955–77.

Stapleton, AG, *Intervention and Non-intervention; or, The Foreign Policy of Great Britain from 1790 to 1865* (J Murray, 1866).

Starski, P, 'Silence within the process of normative change and evolution of the prohibition on the use of force: normative volatility and legislative responsibility' (2017) 4(1) *Journal on the Use of Force and International Law* 14–65.

Steiger, H, 'From the International Law of Christianity to the International Law of the World Citizen – Reflections on the Formation of the Epochs of the History of International Law' (2001) 3(2) *Journal of the History of International Law* 180–94.

Stein, E, 'International Integration and Democracy: No Love at First Sight' (2001) 95(3) *American Journal of International Law* 489–534.

Stone, J, *Legal Controls of International Conflict: A Treatise on the Dynamics of Disputes and War Law* (Stevens & Sons, 1959).

Stromseth, J, Wippman, D and Brooks, R, *Can Might Make Rights? Building the Rule of Law after Military Interventions* (Cambridge University Press, 2006).

Suárez, F, *Selections from three works of Francisco Suárez, S.J.: De legibus, ac Deo legislatore 1612, Defensio fidei catholicae, et apostolicae adversus anglicanae sectae errores 1613, De triplici virtute theologica, fide, spe, et charitate 1621* (Clarendon Press, 1944).

Sullivan, BR, 'Involvement Fascist Italy's Military in the Spanish Civil War' (1995) 59(4) *The Journal of Military History* 697–727.

Sylvan, D and Majeski, S, *US Foreign Policy in Perspective. Clients, Enemies and Empire* (Routledge, 2009).

Talentino, AK, *Military Intervention after the Cold War: The Evolution of Theory and Practice* (Ohio University Press, 2005).

Talmon, S, 'Who is a Legitimate Government in Exile? Towards Normative Criteria for Governmental Legitimacy in International Law' in G Goodwin-Gill and S Talmon (eds), *The Reality of International Law. Essays in Honour of Ian Brownlie* (Oxford University Press, 1999) 499–537.

—— *Recognition of Governments in International Law: With Particular Reference to Governments in Exile* (Oxford University Press, 2001).

—— 'A Plurality of Responsible Actors? International Responsibility for Acts of the Coalition Provisional Authority in Iraq' in P Shiner and A Williams (eds), *The Iraq War and International Law* (Hart Publishing, 2008) 185–230.

—— 'Recognition of the Libyan National Transitional Council' (2011) 15(16) *ASIL insights*.

—— 'The Difference between Rhetoric and Reality: Why an Illegitimate Regime May Still be a Government in the Eyes of International Law' (2011) *EJIL, Analysis* 1–2.

—— 'Recognition of Opposition Groups as the Legitimate Representative of a People' (2013) 12(2) *Chinese Journal of International Law* 219–53.

Tams, CJ, 'The "International Community" as a Legal Concept' in J D'Aspremont and S Singh (eds), *Fundamental Concepts of International Law* 6 (Edward Elgar, 2005) 1–22.

Tanca, A, *Foreign Armed Intervention in Internal Conflict* (Martinus Nijhoff, 1993).

Tancredi, A, *La Secessione nel Diritto Internazionale* (CEDAM, 2001).

—— 'A Normative "Due Process" in the Creation of States rough Secession' in MG Kohen (ed), *Secession: International Law Perspectives* (Cambridge University Press, 2006) 171–207.

Tasioulas, J, 'Human Rights, Legitimacy, and International Law' (2013) 58(1) *The American Journal of Jurisprudence* 1–25.

Tesón, FR, 'The Kantian Theory of International Law' (1992) 92(1) *Columbia Law Review* 53–102.

—— *A Philosophy of International Law* (Westview Press, 1998).

Thielbörger, P, 'The Status and Future of International Law after the Libya Intervention' (2012) 4(1) *Goettingen Journal of International Law* 11–48.

Thomas, A and Thomas, AJ, *Non-intervention: The Law and Its Import in the Americas* (Southern Methodist University Press, 1956).

Thomas, CA, 'The uses and abuses of legitimacy in international law' (2014) 34(4) *Oxford Journal of Legal Studies* 729–58.

Thürer, D, 'Failing States' in *Max Planck Encyclopedia of Public International Law* (Oxford University Press, 2009).

Thürer, D and Burri, T, 'Self-determination' in *Max Planck Encyclopedia of Public International Law* (Oxford University Press, 2008).

Tigerstrom, B, *Human Security and International Law: Prospects and Problems* (Hart Publishing, 2007).

Tiroch, K, 'Governments in Exile' in *Max Planck Encyclopedia of Public International Law* (Oxford University Press, 2011).

Tomasevski, K, 'The Right to Peace' (1982) 5(1) *Current Research on Peace and Violence* 42–69.

Tomuschat, C, 'Obligations Arising for States without or against Their Will' (1993) 241 *Collected courses of The Hague Academy of International Law* 195–374.

—— 'The Applicability of Human Rights Law to Insurgent Movements' in H Fischer and others (eds), *Krisensicherung und humanitärer Schutz: Festschrift fur Dieter Fleck* (Berliner Wissenschafts-Verlag, 2004) 573–91.

Tourinho, M, Stuenkel, O and Brockmeier, S, 'Responsibility while Protecting: Reforming R2P Implementation' (2016) 30(1) *Global Society* 134–50.

Trachtenberg, M, 'Intervention in Historical Perspective' in C Kaysen and L Reed (eds), *Emerging Norms of Justified Intervention* (American Academy of Arts and Science, 1993) 15–36.

Trahan, J, 'Defining the "grey area" where humanitarian intervention may not be fully legal, but is not the crime of aggression' (2015) 2(1) *Journal on the Use of Force and International Law* 42–80.

Trapp, KN, 'Unauthorized Military Interventions for the Public Good: A response to Harold Koh' (2017) 111 *AJIL Unbound* 292–96.

Treves, T, 'Customary International Law' in *Max Planck Encyclopedia of Public International Law* (Oxford University Press, 2006).

Tritle, LA, '"Laughing for Joy": War and Peace Among the Greeks' in KA Raaflaub (ed), *War and Peace in the Ancient World* (Blackwell Publishing, 2007) 172–90.

Tuck, R, 'Grotius, Hobbes and Pufendorf on Humanitarian Intervention' in S Recchia and J Welsh (eds), *Just and Unjust Military Intervention: European Thinkers from Vitoria to Mill* (Cambridge University Press, 2013) 96–112.

Van Alebeek, R, 'The Judicial Dialogue between the ICJ and the International Criminal Courts on the Question of Immunity' in LJ Van den Herik and C Stahn (eds), *The Diversification and Fragmentation of International Criminal Law* (Martinus Nijhoff, 2012) 93–116.

Van den Driest, S, '"Pro-Democratic" Intervention and the Right to Political Self-Determination: the Case of Operation Iraqi Freedom' (2010) 57(01) *Netherlands International Law Review* 29–72.

—— *Remedial Secession: A Right to External Self-Determination as a Remedy to Serious Injustices?* (Cambridge University Press, 2013).

Van den Hole, L, 'Towards a Test of the International Character of an Armed Conflict: Nicaragua and Tadic' (2005) 32(2) *Journal of International Law and Commerce* 269–87.

Van der Vleuten, A and Ribeiro Hoffmann, A, 'Explaining the Enforcement of Democracy by Regional Organizations: Comparing EU, Mercosur and SADC' (2010) 48(3) *Journal of Common Market Studies* 737–58.

Van Hessen, J, 'De Facto Regimes in International Law' (2012) 28(74) *Utrecht Journal of International and European Law* 31–49.

Van Steenberghe, R, 'L'emploi de la Force en Libye: Question de Droit International et de Droit Belge' (2011) 26(6444) *Journal des Tribunaux* 529–37.

Vandewoude, C, 'The Rise of Self-Determination Versus the Rise of Democracy' (2010) 2 *Goettingen Journal of International Law* 981–96.

Vattel, E, *The Law of Nations: Principles of the Law of Nature, Applied to the Conduct and Affairs of Nations and Sovereign* (Clarendon Press, 1758).

Ventura, MJ, 'Two Controversies in the Lubanga Trial Judgment of the International Criminal Court: The Nature of Co-perpetration's Common Plan and the Classification of the Armed Conflict' in S Casey-Maslen (ed), *The War Report 2012* (Oxford University Press, 2013) 473–91.

Verdebout, A, 'The Contemporary Discourse on the Use of Force in the Nineteenth Century: A Diachronic and Critical Analysis' (2014) 1(2) *Journal on the Use of Force and International Law* 223–46.

Verosta, S, 'The unlawfulness of wars of aggression before 1914' in EG Bello and BA Ajibola (eds), *Essays in Honour of Judge Taslim Olawale Elias. Volume 1: Contemporary International Law and Human Rights* (Martinus Nijhoff, 1992) 117–24.

Vidmar, J, 'Remedial Secession in International Law: Theory and (Lack of) Practice' (2010) 6(1) *St Antony's International Review* 37–56.

—— 'Judicial Interpretations of Democracy in Human Rights Treaties' (2014) 3(2) *Cambridge Journal of International and Comparative Law* 532–55.

—— 'The Use of Force as a Plea of Necessity' (2017) 111 *AJIL Unbound* 302–06.

Visser, L, 'May the Force Be with You: The Legal Classification of Intervention by Invitation' (2019) 66(1) *Netherlands International Law Review* 21–45.

Vité, S, 'Typology of Armed Conflicts in International Humanitarian Law: Legal Concepts and Actual Situations' (2009) 91(873) *International Review of the Red Cross* 69–94.

Von Elbe, J, 'The Evolution of the Concept of the Just War in International Law' (1939) 33(4) *The American Journal of International Law* 665–88.

Waldock, CHM, The Regulation of the Use of Force by Individual States in International Law (1952) 81 *Collected Courses of the Hague Academy of International Law* 455–514.

Walzer, M, 'The Moral Standing of States: A Response to Four Critics' (1980) 9(3) *Philosophy and Public Affairs* 209–29.

—— 'War and Peace in the Jewish Tradition' in T Nardin (ed), *The Ethics of War and Peace: Religious and Secular Perspectives* (Princeton University Press, 1996) 95–114.
—— *Just and Unjust Wars. A Moral Argument with Historical Illustrations* (Basic Books, 2006).
Wedgwood, R, 'The Use of Force in Civil Disputes' (1996) 26 *Israel Yearbook on Human Rights* 239–52.
Wehberg H and Zeydel, EH, *The Outlawry of War: A Series of Lectures Delivered before the Academy of International Law at The Hague and in the Institut Universitaire de Hautes Etudes Internationales at Geneva* (Carnegie Endowment for International Peace, 1931).
Weisburd, AM, 'The Emptiness of the Concept of Jus Cogens, as Illustrated by the War in Bosnia-Herzegovina' (1995) 17(1) *Michigan Journal of International Law* 1–52.
Weiss, TG, 'RtoP Alive and Well after Libya' (2011) 25(3) *Ethics & International Affairs* 287–92.
Welsh, JM, 'The Security Council and Humanitarian Intervention' in V Lowe, A Roberts, JM Welsh and D Zaum (eds), *The United Nations Security Council and War: The Evolution of Thought and Practice since 1945* (Oxford University Press, 2008) 535–62.
Westlake, J, *Chapters on the Principles of International Law* (Cambridge University Press, 1894).
Wheaton, H, *Elements of International Law* (Sampson Low, Son & Co, 1866).
Wilmshurst, E, 'Principles of International Law on the Use of Force by States in Self-Defence' (2005) Chatham House Research Paper, October 2005.
Wilson, GG, 'Insurgency and International Maritime Law' (1907) 1(1) *The American Journal of International Law* 46–60.
Wilson, HA, *International Law and the Use of Force by National Liberation Movements* (Clarendon Press, 1988).
Wilson RA and Brown, RD, 'Humanitarianism and Suffering: The Mobilization of Empathy Introduction' in RA Wilson and RD Brown (eds), *Humanitarianism and Suffering: The Mobilization of Empathy* (Cambridge University Press, 2008) 1–28.
Wilson, RR, 'Recognition of Insurgency and Belligerency' (1937) 31 *Proceedings of the American Society of International Law at Its Annual Meeting (1921–1969)* 136–44.
Wippman, D, 'Treaty-Based Intervention: Who Can Say No?' (1995) 62(2) *University of Chicago Law Review* 607–87.
—— 'Change and Continuity in Legal Justifications for Military Intervention in Internal Conflict' (1996) 27(3) *Columbia Human Rights Law Review* 435–86.
—— 'Military Intervention, Regional Organizations, and Host State Consent' (1996) 7(1) *Duke Journal of Comparative and International Law* 209–39.
—— 'Pro-Democratic Intervention by Invitation' in GH Fox and BR Roth (eds), *Democratic Governance and International Law* (Cambridge University Press, 2000) 293–327.
—— 'The Nine Lives of Article 2(4)' (2007) 2 *Minnesota Journal of International Law* 387–406.
—— 'Pro-Democratic Intervention' in M Weller (ed), *The Oxford Handbook of the Use of Force in International Law* (Oxford University Press, 2015) 797–815.
Wolff, C, *Jus Gentium Methodo Scientifica Pertractatum* (Clarendon Press, 1934).
Wolfrum, R, 'Legitimacy in International Law' in *Max Planck Encyclopedia of Public International Law* (Oxford University Press, 2011).
Wood, M, 'The Principle of Non-Intervention in Contemporary International Law: Non-Interference in a State's Internal Affairs Used to be a Rule of International Law: Is it Still?' (2007) *Chatham House International Law discussion group meeting.*
Wright, Q, 'Changes in the Conception of War' (1924) 18(4) *American Journal of International Law* 755–67.
—— 'The Present Status of Neutrality' (1940) 34(3) *The American Journal of International Law* 391–415.
—— 'Intervention 1956' (1957) 51(2) *American Journal of International Law* 257–76.
—— 'United States Intervention in the Lebanon' (1959) 53(1) *American Journal of International Law* 112–25.
—— *The Role of International Law in the Elimination of War* (Manchester University Press, 1961).

—— 'Subversive Intervention' (1960) 54(3) *The American Journal of International Law* 521–35.
—— 'The GOA Incident' (1962) 56 *American Journal of International Law* 617–32.
Wright, R, 'How the Arab Spring Became the Arab Cataclysm' *The New Yorker*, 15 December 2015.
Xenophon, *Anabasis* (Rizzoli, 1978).
Youssef, MAE, 'Security Council Resolution 1973: A New Interpretation of the Notion of Protection of Civilians?' in C Panara and G Wilson (eds), *The Arab Spring: New Patterns for Democracy and International Law* (Martinus Nijhoff, 2013) 145–67.
Sandoz et al, Y, *Commentary on the Additional Protocols of 8 June 1977 to the Geneva Conventions of 12 August 1949* (Martinus Nijhoff, 1987).
Zacharias, D, 'Holy Alliance (1815)' *Max Planck Encyclopedia of Public International Law* (Oxford University Press, 2007).
Ziegler, KS, 'Domaine Réservé' *Max Planck Encyclopedia of Public International Law* (Oxford University Press, 2013).
Zimmern, A, *The League of Nations and the rule of law 1918–1935* (Macmillan, 1939).

Index

www.ingramcontent.com/pod-product-compliance
Lightning Source LLC
Chambersburg PA
CBHW071303180926
51613CB00001B/116
9781509940547